Applied Communication Research Methods

A hands-on guide for applying research methods to common problems, issues, projects, and questions that communication practitioners deal with on a regular basis, this text demonstrates the relevance of research in professional roles and communication and media careers.

The second edition features updated material that covers major communication research methods including surveys, experiments, focus groups, and observation research while also providing key background information on ethics, validity, reliability, concept explication, statistical analysis, and other current topics. It continues to foster student engagement with research through its numerous features and practical activities, including:

- *Research in Depth*—examples of methods as applied in scholarly research
- *Reflect & React*—problems and issues that promote reflection and discussion
- *Voices from Industry*—Q&As with professionals working in communication industries
- *End-of-Unit Activities*—exercises that reinforce concepts and content.

The text is ideally suited to both undergraduate and graduate courses in mass communication research methods.

Online resources, including sample syllabi, PowerPoint slides, and test banks are available on the companion website: www.routledge.com/cw/boyle.

Michael P. Boyle is a Professor in the Department of Communication and Media at West Chester University, USA.

Mike Schmierbach is an Associate Professor in the Donald P. Bellisario College of Communications at The Pennsylvania State University, USA.

Applied Communication Research Methods

Getting Started as a Researcher

Second Edition

Michael P. Boyle and Mike Schmierbach

Routledge
Taylor & Francis Group

NEW YORK AND LONDON

Second edition published 2020
by Routledge
52 Vanderbilt Avenue, New York, NY 10017

and by Routledge
2 Park Square, Milton Park, Abingdon, Oxon, OX14 4RN

Routledge is an imprint of the Taylor & Francis Group, an informa business

First edition published by Routledge 2015

Library of Congress Cataloging-in-Publication Data

Names: Boyle, Michael P., 1975– author. | Schmierbach, Mike, 1976– author.
Title: Applied communication research methods : getting started as a researcher / Michael P Boyle, Mike Schmierbach.
Description: Second edition. | New York : Routledge, 2020. | Includes bibliographical references and index.
Identifiers: LCCN 2019040222 (print) | LCCN 2019040223 (ebook) | ISBN 9780367178710 (hardback) | ISBN 9780367178727 (paperback) | ISBN 9780429296444 (ebook)
Subjects: LCSH: Communication—Research. | Communication—Methodology.
Classification: LCC P91.3 .B69 2020 (print) | LCC P91.3 (ebook) | DDC 302.2072/1—dc23
LC record available at https://lccn.loc.gov/2019040222
LC ebook record available at https://lccn.loc.gov/2019040223

ISBN: 978-0-367-17871-0 (hbk)
ISBN: 978-0-367-17872-7 (pbk)
ISBN: 978-0-429-29644-4 (ebk)

Typeset in Sabon
by Apex CoVantage, LLC

Visit the companion website: www.routledge.com/cw/boyle.

Printed in the United Kingdom
by Henry Ling Limited

Unit Overview

Contents

Preface

Welcome to the 2nd edition of *Applied Communication Research Methods*. We appreciate your interest in our book.

Let's get this out of the way early: a research methods course can be challenging both for the student and for the instructor. There are a lot of terms to know. Many of them sound similar—should you be calculating the mean, the median, or the mode if you want to find the midpoint of your data? Others are more unfamiliar and complex—what is heteroscedasticity, and why does it sound like a new electronica band? It is a subject area that often sends fear down the spines of communication majors. For example, you may have heard—or even said—some of the following: "I became a communication major so I wouldn't have to deal with numbers!" "I just want to make ads, not do research." "Reading journal articles is hard, and they are boring." "I just want to know what the terms mean and how to use them." "This is too complex!" This is only a short list of the many concerns that students express about research methods.

But here's another thing to get out of the way early—you are already doing research! It's true. If you've asked around for opinions on a class to take, a car to buy, a movie to see, or a restaurant to eat at, then you have done research. If you've read reviews about television shows or books, inquired about professors before taking their classes, or consulted an expert for advice on what outfit to wear, then you have done research. Just to get by and make decisions in modern society, you are already doing research. Of course, the type of research that you are already doing is not as formalized, structured, and scientific as the research that will be discussed in this book. But getting from one to the other is simply a matter of taking the kinds of research you are already doing and figuring out how to improve those approaches so that you can be confident in the information your research yields. Good research leads to good information. Good information leads to good decisions. Good decisions lead to all kinds of good things—money, promotions, success, praise, life satisfaction, even fancy cars or great dinners. You name it, and understanding how to do research well can help you accomplish it.

In all seriousness, we know that mastering research methods alone won't turn you into a titan of industry. But people who are successful in the many professional areas that fall within the field of communication understand the value that having a depth of knowledge about research methods can bring to someone pursuing a career in communication. Throughout this book, you will have the opportunity to hear directly from people who are successful communication practitioners, from political strategists and consultants to media executives and market researchers. They all agree that the best decisions—whether it be deciding which version of an ad to use, which logo to select, how to best start a speech, or how to respond to a corporate crisis—are rooted in good research. Those of us who teach and do research also know something else: research methods do not have to be difficult, scary, or boring. In fact, research can even be engaging, straightforward, and fun! We figure that if we make material accessible and transparent, use varied and detailed examples, and provide opportunities for application, then your experience, learning, and retention will all be enhanced.

For many of you, the course you are currently taking and this textbook are your first forays into research methods. Although you are just beginning, the knowledge and skills that you will develop in this course will lay the groundwork for the rest of your career. Others may be returning to research methods for more advanced training and skill building. In either case, to help strengthen that foundation, what we have sought to do with this textbook is to create a resource that is clear and direct in its presentation of information, is rife with examples, and presents a range of activities, thought-provoking questions, and other opportunities for critical thinking and, most importantly, application of research methods. As we indicate in Unit 1 of the book, the best way to learn research methods is to think about research, talk about research, and do research. Therefore, we have designed the book to allow you to use the information and activities provided in a way that will help you build your basic research skills and tailor what you are learning to your career goals and interests. Clear definitions give you the basic knowledge. Terms listed in the margin alongside entries are important related concepts that can be found elsewhere in the book, within the unit listed. Multiple examples provide insight into the many areas that research in the field of communication can explore. Activities and prompts—within and at the end of each unit—provide many opportunities to talk about, think about, and do research, giving you an opportunity to apply the knowledge you have gained.

One of the unique aspects of this textbook is that it is designed as an enhanced glossary. Because of this, we have taken care to offer clear and concise definitions of important concepts at the beginning of each entry. We want you to be able to find out what a term means quickly, whether you are reading straight through the book or looking up an unfamiliar term you encountered in class or in an assignment. We have also grouped related ideas under umbrella terms that provide greater context and insights into how all of these different concepts fit together in the broader research process. Although this approach may be different from what you are used to seeing in typical textbooks, we think it's a great way to explore research methods. There is no one right order to learning all of this material, and you should expect to go back and forth between ideas as you realize that understanding new ideas will require reviewing older ones. We've tried to make that as easy as possible.

A second unique aspect is the use of in-unit activities that provide you with numerous opportunities to apply what you have been learning. In some cases, these may be assigned by your instructor; however, they are also designed so that you can use these activities on your own, whether for studying, skill building, or working through your own research project. These activities give you a chance to practice talking about and conducting research. Even if you aren't required to complete them, they are a great way to review your understanding of the material. These in-unit activities include *Steps to Success* that provide checklists covering aspects of the research process, *Research in Depth* segments that give examples of how a concept is used in scholarly research, and *Reflect & React* activities that give you a thought-provoking problem or issue to think about. These activities, in addition to fully developed end-of-unit activities, are useful for helping make sure you understand a concept and for helping you retain that understanding.

Finally, we have included even more *Voices from Industry* entries, which provide the perspectives of communication professionals and practitioners throughout the book. These Q&As with professionals in communication and media industries provide an opportunity for people who are working in the areas many of you will be employed in a few years from now the opportunity to talk firsthand about the value of communication research methods to their particular job and to the industry overall. You will see that the ways in which research can be applied vary just as widely as the career options in the communication industry. At the core, though, the basic skills needed to use these methods are the same: understanding terminology, knowing how to apply those approaches to different situations, and being willing to think like a scientist by being creative, open to what the data tell you, and thoughtful, organized, and formal in your approach to solving problems.

We hope that your experience with this book is a positive one and that you begin to see the research process the way we do: as engaging, straightforward, fun, and incredibly important step to effective decision making and success in the many communication industries and professions that you will encounter throughout your career. Remember: good research leads to good information; good information leads to good decisions; and good decisions lead to success.

unit 1

basic principles of research and a guide to using this book

Principles of Research

Research methodology can be a complex topic, but it is also one of the most rewarding subjects you can study. To understand why, it's important to answer two critical questions: what is "research," and why would you want to study it?

The short answer to both questions is that research is the process through which *science* is conducted. The approach to research described throughout this textbook is rooted in the scientific method—perhaps the greatest human accomplishment of the last millennium. Amazing things have been created through chemistry, technology, and industry. Remarkable wonders of the universe have been seen by astronomers and described by physicists. Medicine and agriculture have extended human lives and reduced the suffering of billions. But at the heart of these accomplishments and myriad more is the fundamental principle that understanding any phenomenon requires following a clear process whose core practices are shared by all scientists, including those who engage in communication research.

You may not think that the kind of research conducted by most communication scholars is the same as that carried out by biologists, chemists, or even psychologists. It is true that because communication research involves human behavior and not natural laws, the findings we obtain are less certain and absolute. But the logic at the heart of communication research is the same as that behind the establishment of the theory of relativity, the unraveling of the human genome, or the discovery of continental drift. All true research meets four important standards: it is (1) **empirical**, (2) **systematic**, (3) **intersubjective**, and (4) **cyclical and self-correcting**. Communication research is no exception. By following these four standards, *any* research produces superior answers to whatever questions you might ask, whether about the "laws" of the universe, the effects of playing violent video games, or the power of advertisements to influence behavior.

To understand why, we need to briefly explain each of these four standards. The remainder of this book explains a diversity of key terms in research, and everything stems from these basic principles. At the end of this section, we will return to the question of why this helps ensure that research provides optimal answers and, in turn, why understanding research makes you better equipped for the challenges of the modern world.

Empirical

Research is a way to understand the real world. As such, it must draw upon observations or measurements of that world. Researchers want to learn directly about the things they are studying. If we want to understand how moviegoers will react to a film, we should watch them while they watch the movie. If we want to know whether customers will frequent a business following an ad campaign, we should monitor sales. In short, we need to measure behaviors, attitudes, communication patterns, media content, and anything else that matters to our research question. As much as possible, these measures should be direct and unfiltered. Empirical inquiry requires minimizing, if not eliminating, the number of "filters" between what we're studying and our descriptions of those things. The less we rely on someone else to observe or describe a phenomenon, and the more we directly watch or ask about it, the better. By getting rid of those filters, we cut down on the chances that personal biases will affect our results, whether those biases are held by researchers or by those who package and pass on information about the topics we want to understand.

In the following pages, we will talk about the best ways to directly measure a variety of individual attitudes and behaviors as well as to categorize the forms of communication that people use every day, whether it be watching television, posting on Facebook, conversing face-to-face with friends, or giving a speech in public. A major portion of research methods is focused on improving our measurement, but at the core we believe that you must get as close as possible to the thing you want to measure. Inventing hypothetical or ideal examples is never as good as collecting real data.

Systematic

research questions
→ Unit 3

bias
→ Unit 3

Research is about more than observing and measuring. It takes a systematic approach to gathering and analyzing data, which means that researchers follow a set of rules, set by the standards of science and by the researchers themselves, to ensure that they can make sense of empirical data. In short, systematic research is organized, involves planning, and follows procedures to avoid mistakes. For example, scholars who are interested in studying the effects of violent movies on children would not simply throw groups of children in front of a television and hope that a violent movie comes on. They would develop a plan for how to select the children, what kinds of content to show them, and how to measure the children's responses. This would give them a set of data from which the researchers could seek patterns. Research is systematic because it follows a plan; researchers develop and employ logical guidelines to shape and limit their data gathering. The terminology of research methods presented throughout this textbook will help you construct an effective plan for answering questions and explain your plans to others so they can understand your findings.

Intersubjective

results section
→ Unit 3

replication
→ Unit 3

Research is a collective process. Knowledge is built gradually, one study at a time. Therefore, no single study stands on its own. When you investigate a question, you will look to see what others did before you to approach similar questions. When you write your results, you will do so in a way that is easy to comprehend and that helps the reader understand how your results fit into the bigger picture that you are trying to understand. Many of the ideas we study in communication are not natural laws, with absolute meaning and objective definitions. But as a research community, we need to be able to compare our findings. To do this, we must define each idea we study in a clear fashion, so that our "subjective" meaning can be shared with others. By explaining the context of our study, the meaning of our terms, and the assumptions under which we operated, we allow others to test our results. Instead of a subjective definition that has a meaning just for us, we create an "intersubjective" definition—the meaning is shared between researchers across studies. ("Inter" means "between" in Latin.)

It's important not to assume that other people would approach questions the same way we do; we must explain what we did and why. In doing so, we make it possible for people to replicate our findings. The idea of replication, and the terminology we use to share our findings in a reproducible manner, is considered in later units.

Cyclical and Self-Correcting

Allowing other scholars to check our work is a core aspect of science. Individual studies can be wrong. Even very smart people make mistakes, based on the limited data available to them. Isaac Newton and Albert Einstein were two of the smartest physicists ever, and yet their models of the universe are at odds— and it's probably the case that neither is entirely correct. The collective process of research offers a way to identify these mistakes and develop more effective approaches to understanding the world around us. Because we can replicate prior research, we can decide whether the results of one study apply to a larger context or are attributable to chance. If you follow the practices described in this text, you too will contribute to this cumulative development of knowledge.

Maybe you heard about a theory in your intro class that seemed wrong to you? Maybe you read a study for a research paper and felt it was poorly done? By learning about research, you can revisit those ideas, test them further, and help us understand what's really going on. Remember, research is empirical. We observe the real world. No idea about communication is valid if it doesn't match what really happens, and we can only find out what really happens by continually measuring and testing our ideas.

Cumulatively, then, research involves following basic rules to find information about the real world. Abstract, idealized descriptions or theories are only as good as the real observations that support them, and no single study can stand on its own. This does not mean that every research article you read or every study you carry out will be perfect. The strength of science lies not in a single trial but in the entire process. Science is sometimes wrong, but the reason we know this is thanks to the further efforts of science. Consider that there was a time in history when the Earth was "known" to be the center of

| theory |
| → Unit 2 |
| empirical |
| → Unit 1 |
| authority |
| → Unit 3 |
| qualitative versus quantitative |
| → Unit 3 |
| quantitative |
| → Unit 2 |

the universe. All theories about the seasons, night and day, and our place in the universe were dictated by this core belief. Yet too many scientific observations didn't make sense based on this belief, and so our understanding changed as better measures and approaches were developed to confirm that the Earth rotates around the sun and not the other way around. Some political figures slowed the transition, but it was science that made sure the better understanding won out, and long before anyone set sail to find the long way to India.

This example also illustrates how people who base their beliefs on something other than research may sometimes be right. There may have been ancient people who had a hunch about the solar system before scientists agreed on the sun-centric model. Science doubters may be right when single research studies are wrong, or even when a series of studies were done poorly. But ultimately, we don't have any way to know that they are right without science. Without future research, we cannot sort the good ideas from the bad. No other way of answering questions can claim this. You might want to trust an authority, but those experts are only as right as the source of their expertise. If they are drawing on prior research, it's better to learn to understand and critique that research yourself. Only the scientific process provides a clear way to decide whether to accept our existing beliefs or to embrace new ones. People have believed incorrect things in the past and will do so in the future, but carefully following the ideas in this book will help us fight those false beliefs and know that when we change our views, we do so for good reason.

This is the best answer for why you should study research methods. The choices we make are only as good as the tools we use to make them. In the long run, research conducted through the scientific method is the best set of tools we have. If you want to make smart decisions—whether those decisions are for your family, for a company, or for society—you need to know how to gather information and evaluate the information gathered by others.

As a more practical matter, understanding research methods will help you make sense of the ideas you encounter in your classes and in your life. Communication phenomena are everywhere at all times. Ours is a communication-driven species, constantly sharing ideas through ever more complex technologies. Future leaders need to know how to connect with the public. Companies need ways to reach their customers. Citizens need to be able to see through deceptive messages and understand what's really going on. Couples need effective tools to help them deal with conflict. Communication directors need effective strategies to speak to large groups or the press. All these situations, and many more, require the best information we have about how communication works. If you understand research methods, then you will have access to that best information.

You can evaluate studies done by others and carry out studies of your own. You can understand findings, whether from descriptive, qualitative studies or from the increasingly common quantitative data sets that describe every aspect of modern society. You can explain these studies to an employer, a family member, or yourself and your employees. You can make smart choices about how to communicate interpersonally or within organizations, how to use media and how to make your way through an increasingly media-shaped future—provided you have a good understanding of communication research.

Using This Book

Understanding why research is valuable and what unites it is the first step. As you move through this book, you will discover many important ideas, techniques, and resources to help your learning and to help you realize how much you already know about research and why it matters. A central premise of this text is that research is an everyday experience. That is, people use research in many situations—from the mundane to the serious—to help make decisions. Just as an advertising agency might use formal focus groups to test which advertising slogan they should use, you might consult friends and family members when deciding which book to read next, where to go to college, or what to write in an e-mail to your professor. Often, what separates the kind of research we do on an everyday basis from what we might do in a more professional

focus groups
→ Unit 12

empirical
→ Unit 1

theory
→ Unit 2

validity
→ Unit 6

concept explication
→ Unit 5

surveys
→ Unit 10

experiments
→ Unit 9

Steps to Success: The Research Process

As you work through your research projects, you will complete the following steps. Check them off as you complete them.

_____ Identify the research problem.
_____ Determine guiding research questions.
_____ Consult relevant theory and literature.
_____ Ask specific research questions and/or state hypotheses.
_____ Specify and define your concepts.
_____ Determine the research method or methods.
_____ Develop effective measures of key variables.
_____ Identify the population you wish to study.
_____ Choose your sample.
_____ Collect data.
_____ Enter and clean data.
_____ Analyze data.
_____ Write research report.
_____ Draw conclusions and identify limitations.
_____ Repeat the process!

setting (or scientific approach) is the amount of preparation, the use of theory to guide our understanding, and the formality of the process. Making good decisions can be the difference between the success and failure of your company or your country. Gathering information through well-thought-out research makes it much more likely that you will both collect quality information and make good decisions.

As we discuss the distinction between everyday research and more scientific research, we will consider key concepts such as validity (the accuracy of our measures and findings), concept explication (the process of deciding how to define and measure the things we are studying), surveys, experiments, and many others. In each case, we will provide clear definitions of what those terms mean and how they relate to other terms listed in the text. We'll also give examples of the terms in research situations. This will allow you to see how the terms apply not only to everyday situations—and how you might already be doing what you are reading about—but also to more scientific research that is used to guide decisions in the professional world.

Each unit starts with a research situation to spur critical thinking about the topic of that unit and to provide examples of research problems you might face in your career as a communication professional. Following that, the first entry in each unit is the master term. We not only define this term but also use the definition as an opportunity to show how all the terms in that same unit are interconnected. This helps reinforce the integrative nature of the research process and clarify the specific concepts you should understand for the broader topic covered in that unit.

Throughout each unit, we provide additional information to help you learn more about the topic. This additional information fits into one of four categories: (1) *Reflect & React*, (2) *Research in Depth*, (3) *Steps to Success*, and (4) *Voices from Industry*. These elements are designed to provide greater depth to the topics discussed in the textbook. They also provide an opportunity for you to learn more about the topic at hand and push you to consider the everyday application of the terms.

Specifically, the *Reflect & React* material gives you a prompt to think about, drawing upon your personal experience and everyday observations to see the logic of research in action. The *Research in Depth* sections give additional information about actual research, taken from published studies, organization reports, and more. These can help you learn more about topics mentioned in the text and point you to resources and examples to explore further. The *Steps to Success* entries provide checklists and overviews of key steps at pivotal points in the research process, helping you make sure your own studies are on track. Finally, the *Voices from Industry* entries provide clear examples of the important role that research plays in a variety of communication industries. We asked professionals from a range of areas, including strategic communication, social media, marketing, news gathering, and political communication, to tell us not only how they use research but also what kinds of research they use. You will hear directly from these professionals about the value of research in their success as communication professionals, and they will give you advice on how to use research more effectively as you prepare for your own career as a communication professional.

At the end of each unit, we provide detailed *Activities* and *Suggested Readings for Further Exploration*. The *Activities* are designed to promote deeper and more integrative thinking about the content from the textbook. The goal is to see the real ways that you already use research to inform your life and to think critically about the research you are already conducting. By seeing the definition of a term, its application to everyday life, and then its application to more scientific research, it is much easier to understand not only what the term means but also how to use it. *Suggested Readings for Further Exploration* provides opportunities for you to extend your learning—and reading—outside this book through magazine articles, books, and journal articles. Many of the suggested readings include *examples* of the methods and procedures discussed in this book. Other suggested readings present opportunities for *advanced discussion*, exploring these topics in greater depth and at a more advanced level. They are by no means required reading, but if a topic piques your interest, these suggestions will give you good places to continue exploring the many topics presented in this text.

Taking the time to complete the activities that are included in this book will help you better understand and remember the meaning of the terms. You'll find yourself doing better on exams and building skills you'll need in future classes and the professional world. The more you can connect what you read about in this book and learn in your class to everyday life, the better off you will be. Even if these activities are not directly assigned by your instructor, they are beneficial as you study the course material. Besides, they can also be fun!

Terms provided in each unit (and listed at the opening of each unit) provide the basic tools to carry out the activities and assignments you will encounter throughout this course—or in your own research projects. As we see it, the best way to learn how to do research is to think about research, talk about research, and do research. Doing the reading and then doing the activities will help you see how aspects of the research process are connected. The glossary-style presentation of the terms, and the activities provided throughout, work together to give you the basic tools and terminology of communication research and to provide mechanisms through which those tools can be applied in real-world research situations. The integrative and applied nature of this text make it a valuable tool for you in not only understanding what key research terms mean but also knowing how to use the defined ideas once you get into the "real world" and need to do research as part of your job.

Voices From Industry

Jessica and Ziggy Zubric— Customer Experience Consultants

Jessica and Ziggy Zubric have been conducting research together for more than 15 years. After running their own business, they joined the team at White Clay—a consulting firm focused on information solutions, customer assessment, and management consulting— where they spend their days improving their clients' customer experience through a variety of research and training techniques.

A Multi-Method, Multi-Application Approach

Achieving success in corporate research is much easier for those with a flexible, multi-method approach to their endeavors. Throughout our careers, we have come to realize that there is no best research method, as every method has its strengths and weaknesses and is effective at answering some questions but not others.

As you read this textbook and conduct your own research, pay particular attention to the benefits and blind spots of every method. As a researcher, your ability to deeply understand and clearly communicate these trade-offs can set you apart from others and help you make better and more informed decisions for your company or client.

"When your only tool is a hammer, every problem becomes a nail." Locking yourself into one research approach limits your ability to effectively answer questions.

For instance, if you focus solely on survey research, what happens when your company needs to you acquire a deep, rich understanding of how customers feel about a new product line? Sure, you could try to field a telephone survey with 25 open-ended questions (we've seen crazier things), but think about the drawbacks. Your completion rate will suffer as fatigue sets in and respondents hang up. The respondents will be less thorough and thoughtful over the phone than they would be in person. And conducting the interviews in isolation negates the opportunity for respondents to engage with each other and build off of each other's comments. This just isn't a problem that quantitative work can solve. And if you concentrate only on qualitative research, what do you do when your company asks you to answer three quick questions on a tight budget with an even tighter timeline? Focus groups would take far too long, break the budget, and have no hope of being representative of the larger population.

Ultimately, the best method is the one that maximally aligns your objectives, budget, and timeline.

Finally, always remember to integrate your findings into larger contexts. Make your research as useful to your employer as possible. In politics, this is so easy that no one ever gets it wrong. . . . Clearly, the end goal of political research is to get a certain candidate elected or help a particular ballot initiative succeed.

But such connections are easily overlooked in the corporate world. Too often, the research team is assigned a specific problem, they collect data to solve that problem, and then they analyze their data and report back. And that's great.

But so often there are ideas in that data that could transform an entire organization if only someone were proactive enough, curious enough, and had a broad enough perspective to look. So we encourage you to always elevate your thinking to consider all of the implications of your research, not just how the results apply to the problem at hand.

For instance, do the results of your ethnographic research give insights into product development? How about customer service and frontline employee training? Would the marketing department benefit as they develop the next ad campaign?

Your ability to proactively seek opportunities to use your research can set you apart in the business world. It demonstrates your ability to think at an organizational level and to maximize the return on investment of every research project.

Suggested Readings for Further Exploration of Unit 1 Topics

Examples

Benko, J. (2013, November 12). The hyper-efficient, highly scientific scheme to help the world's poor. *Wired.com*. Retrieved from www.wired.com/wiredscience/2013/11/jpal-randomized-trials/

Advanced Discussion

Barnett, G. A., Huh, C., Kim, Y., & Park, H. W. (2011). Citations among communication journals and other disciplines: A network analysis. *Scientometrics, 88*(2), 449–469. doi:10.1007/s11192-011-0381-2

Berger, C. R., Roloff, M. E., & Roskos-Ewoldsen, D. R. (2010). What is communication science? In C. R. Berger, M. E. Roloff, & D. R. Roskos-Ewoldsen (Eds.), *Handbook of communication science* (2nd ed., pp. 3–20). Los Angeles, CA: Sage Publications.

O'Keefe, D. J. (1975). Logical empiricism and the study of human communication. *Speech Monographs, 42*(3), 169–183. doi:10.1080/03637757509375892

unit 2

basic concepts
of research

Imagine you're working for a local animal shelter. The organization wants to encourage people to spay or neuter their pets, and it even offers low-cost services to help make this possible. However, the shelter's leadership suspects there are many people out there who don't know about the service or why it would be valuable. They think that targeted advertising might be useful, but they aren't sure whom to target, what media to use, or how to construct the message. A big company might try lots of different tactics and see what happens, but as a nonprofit, your organization cannot afford to spend money needlessly. How do you make sure that your campaign will be effective without wasting resources?

Communication research is designed to answer such questions and many more. If you want to know the effects of playing violent video games, the consequences of cable news for democracy, or the best strategy to promote a nonprofit, research offers a set of techniques to guide you to the most effective answers, and a vocabulary to understand the answers that others have come up with. At the heart of all research is understanding the fundamental concept of a variable, and then building from there to see how we describe and predict relationships among those variables.

Variable

A variable represents a selected quality or characteristic of individuals that has a single value for a given individual but differs among individuals. For example, when raising money for our animal shelter, we might want to focus on individual people because they are potential donors. One variable that we could measure is the amount of money a person donates in a year. This will be a single number for each person—you cannot donate a total of both $5 and $50 in a year. But not all people donate the same amount of money. Therefore, identifying and clearly defining variables is essential to successful and effective research. Much of what we will learn about the research process is focused on identifying, defining, and measuring variables. Learning to identify and focus on individual variables rather than trying directly measure or test a relationship is a critical aspect of learning to think like a researcher. The first step in this process is determining just what "individual" means—this is defined as the **unit of analysis**. For example, individual people are commonly studied as units of analysis in social science research. Consider the many possible ways that people can differ from one another, such as height, weight, income, race, happiness, sense of humor, and athleticism. In each case, the researcher must develop a clear approach to observing those individual variables. Returning to the spay-and-neuter campaign discussed in the introduction, there are a number of variables that could be of interest to us. For instance, we might be interested in knowing how many pets people have. This variable could be a useful predictor of a second variable—attitudes toward spaying and neutering.

All research involves measuring at least one variable. But in most cases, researchers also want to consider the **relationship** between variables. That is, we want to know whether the value of one variable for an individual can help us form a **prediction** about the value of another variable. Thus, most research is focused on identifying and measuring multiple variables, allowing us to consider the resulting data to look for patterns. Often, we think about these relationships in specific ways. For example, most of the time researchers have an **independent variable** and **dependent variable** in mind. They expect that one variable is the starting point or origin of the relationship, and that they can use it to predict the other. Sometimes they also consider **third variables,** or other aspects of the individual that might be important to understanding a more complete picture of the relationship. This might involve **mediation,** in which the independent variable has an influence on this third mediating variable, and then the mediating variable has an influence on the dependent variable. Or they might be interested in **moderation,** or the way that individual differences alter the relationship between the independent and dependent variables. Furthermore, not all relationships show the same pattern, and researchers distinguish between **positive and negative relationships.**

One critical goal for exploring relationships is to try to establish **causality,** showing that a change in the independent variable will lead to a change in the dependent variable. This requires more than simply showing a relationship. It also involves establishing **time order,** showing that the independent variable changed prior to the dependent variable. And it means accounting for **confounds,** or third variables that might actually have been the cause of changes in both the independent and dependent variables. Determining not only the presence of relationships but the mechanisms behind them is part of the process of developing **theories** of communication. Absent a clear theory, researchers may start by testing broader **research questions,** and use the answers to better understand the relationships between variables and gradually form a more abstract description. Through this process, researchers proceed through both **inductive and deductive reasoning** to create models that describe how and why variables relate to one another. This allows researchers to talk in general terms but also to make predictions about how the variables will be related in specific, untested contexts. These predictions are known as **hypotheses,** and much of research is designed to test them. This is because a key aspect of science is **falsification,** or the testing of predictions to see whether they are supported or rejected. Claims that cannot be falsified do not serve as effective theories and do not advance science. In addition, good theories have considerable **scope,** offering predictions across a range of contexts. But they are also **parsimonious,** keeping the complexity of the overall model low and introducing as few exceptions or additional variables as possible.

Unit of Analysis

poll
→ Unit 10
social artifact
→ Unit 11

In general, the unit of analysis in research is a description of the specific type of individual or thing that is being studied. These are the individuals who differ from one another such that they won't all have the same value for a variable, but each individual has only one value. Most often, these individuals will be people. For example, in an election poll, the unit of analysis is the individual potential voter. Because elections are won by persuading more people to vote for one candidate and not another candidate, what matters is how each individual feels.

In some cases, the unit of analysis will not be an individual person but rather a group or even an artifact—something created by people and left behind, such as a newspaper story or a tweet. For example, a public relations researcher might want to understand how corporations use Facebook pages to improve their public image. You might want to draw conclusions about how individual consumers respond to the page, in which case individual people would be your unit of analysis. But you might want to know the factors that lead a whole company to employ a specific type of page. In that case, the company would be the unit of analysis, not just one person. You might even simply want to describe the types of content found on each Facebook page. That would mean you were studying the artifact (or "text") of the Facebook page as the unit of analysis.

Sometimes you might not be able to directly observe or measure your intended unit of analysis. For example, when studying a company's Facebook strategy, you might want to know how corporate attitudes toward technology affect the use of social media. You can't ask the company or its website for answers. But you could ask several people at the company for their opinions and then combine those opinions into a single value for the company as a whole. The individual people interviewed would be the unit of observation, while the company would be the unit of analysis, as your conclusions would describe the company, not individual people. It's always important to keep these two ideas straight and to remember that sometimes you can consider something other than people, even when your study will start out by talking to individual people.

Independent Variable

In relationships between variables, the independent variable is the one that causes or influences the dependent variable—the value of the independent variable helps dictate the value of the dependent variable. Consider the example of the factors that might contribute to people knowing about and supporting a local animal shelter. The independent variables would be these factors, as they are meant to help predict or explain how much a person supports the shelter. For example, we might expect that the number of pets a person has will predict how positively they feel about the local shelter. In this case, the number of pets would be an independent variable, and people would be the unit of analysis. So each person would have a specific number of pets, and this number would vary between people. In turn, the intensity of positive feelings would be the dependent variable. Note that labeling something as the independent variable doesn't necessarily mean that it *causes* changes in the dependent variable. Whenever researchers have a reason to think of a variable as coming first or being an explanation for other variables, they consider this as an independent variable. But additional criteria must be met in order to say a causal relationship is actually present.

theory
→ Unit 2

Dependent Variable

Variables that are affected or caused by other variables are referred to as dependent variables. This is because the value of the dependent variable *depends* upon the value of the independent variable. In the example of the animal shelter, a dependent variable could be whether a person does or does not know that the shelter provides free spay and neuter services. You might expect that this is influenced by, or "depends upon," whether a person has been exposed to social media messages from the shelter. The more messages a person has consumed, the more likely you think it is that they will know about these services. Thus, while knowledge is the dependent variable in this case, and the person is the unit of analysis, the number of messages consumed would be the independent variable.

As was the case for independent variables, labeling something a dependent variable doesn't necessarily mean it was caused by the independent variable. Additional elements must be considered to test for causality. Furthermore, a variable can serve as both an independent and dependent variable in different relationships. For example, whether people know that your shelter offers free clinic services might be a dependent variable when considering the relationship with exposure to social media messages. But it might be the independent variable when considering the relationship with the amount of money a person is willing to donate, if knowing about the good an organization does makes people more willing to give. That said, certain variables can never or almost never be considered dependent variables. For example, age or gender identity cannot be altered, and so any time a variable like that is listed you can be confident that it is serving as an independent variable or as a third variable.

Third Variable

Not every variable tested in research is necessarily thought of as a dependent or independent variable. Many variables serve other roles, and thus they are generically referred to as "third" variables. Most common is the measurement of third variables that are meant to serve as *control* variables. When a variable is used as a control variable, the researcher wants to remove (or control) the influence that variable has in the relationship between the independent and dependent variable. Other types of third variables are used in evaluating mediation and moderation. In these cases, the third variable is expected to have an important influence, somehow contributing to or altering the relationship between the independent and dependent variables. Regardless of the specific role that a third variable plays, it must be carefully explicated and effectively measured, just like any other variable.

The use of control variables is especially important in evaluating the relationship between independent and dependent variables. In many cases, there are numerous variables that share relationships with one another. However, researchers are often interested in testing only specific relationships between dependent and independent variables, as dictated by hypotheses or research questions. Control variables allow researchers to increase their confidence in findings showing a relationship between the variables of interest if a relationship is found after control variables are included.

For example, numerous variables could account for why someone does or does not do well on a standardized test (e.g., ACT or SAT), such as study habits, age, educational background, family income, effort, or time of day. Perhaps researchers are specifically interested in the role that test preparation centers play in improving scores. To test this relationship, the researchers could simply measure whether the test taker used a test preparation center (the independent variable) and how he or she did on the test (the dependent variable). A more rigorous approach, however, would be to measure some of the other variables that might influence performance and include those as control variables. After all, students with a greater interest in college or wealthier parents are more likely to use test preparation services, but they would also likely do better on a standardized test even without those services because of potential structural biases in standardized tests. If the researchers are still able to observe the relationship between the use of test preparation centers and test scores *after* including those other variables as controls, then this demonstrates that test preparation centers have great value. Any multivariate statistics can be used to account for the role of control variables. Alternatively, focusing only on individuals with one specific attribute of a control variable ensures that there is no variation in the control and that patterns found are not due to that control variable. For example, in the testing center study, you could focus only on families with incomes in a specific, narrow range. If those who used testing services still performed better, you would be confident that income was not the reason.

Relationship

The focus of research is establishing and explaining the relationships between variables. A relationship describes a link between at least two variables, such that we can make a more accurate prediction about one characteristic of an individual based on information about at least one other variable describing that person. Critically, relationships describe connections between variables. If the individual values do not vary between people, then we are not able to identify a pattern to show a relationship. For example, if everyone in our study identifies as a woman, we cannot say whether gender is related to another variable, because we have no way to see if there is a way to distinguish women from men. In the case of our nonprofit work for an animal shelter, we may be interested in several relationships. For example, we may want to know whether specific types of people are more likely to know about the spay-and-neuter program. If we can identify the characteristics of those people, we can predict who *isn't* aware of the program and make sure our advertising reaches them. We may also want to know the relationship between the format of our ad and the willingness of viewers to give money to our program. If the ad shows kittens, perhaps it will work better than an ad showing grown cats. We could then predict that our money would be better spent on the ad with kittens.

Most relationships are described in terms of a connection between an independent and dependent variable. But more information about the exact pattern linking these variables can be provided, revealing different types of relationships. For example, relationships may be positive, where increasing values of one variable predict increasing values of the other variable. Or they may be negative, where high values in one variable are associated with lower values for the other. Some relationships involve additional variables, taking on forms such as mediation or moderation. Still other relationships are specifically described as causal, such that we believe that altering the independent variable would reliably lead to a predictable change in the dependent variable. Understanding causal relationships is particularly important to researchers. It helps build theory and give us a more complete understanding of human behavior and the influence of media. As such, recognizing the criteria by which potentially causal relationships are judged and the research designs that help establish those criteria is a core aspect of research methods.

Prediction

One way of defining a relationship is in terms of whether it allows for an effective prediction. That is, thanks to the knowledge about the relationship obtained from a study, the information about the value of one variable for an individual is helpful in estimating the value of another variable. Consider a situation in which you know nothing about a voter except that he or she intends to vote. Without knowing the person's party, age, gender, or any other characteristics, it would be hard to guess which candidate he or she would vote for. You might guess the person would be slightly more likely to vote for the candidate in the lead, as more voters will support that person, but otherwise you could just flip a coin.

Then consider the added insight you would have if you *did* know more about the voter. If you knew his or her political party, for example, you could probably guess they would vote for the candidate from their party. You wouldn't always be right, but you would do much better than chance. If you further knew that the person was female and had data that showed other women were more likely to support a specific candidate, your guess would be better still. This ability to improve your estimate of the value of one variable thanks to your knowledge of other variables is critical to the idea of measuring relationships, and it all starts with the logic of making an informed prediction about the outcome variable that draws upon more than just luck. Indeed, this idea of improving the accuracy of a prediction by using other information is critical to an important concept in statistics: explained variance.

Positive Versus Negative Relationship

One important distinction drawn in many hypotheses and in statistical testing is the difference between a positive and negative relationship. A *negative relationship* between two variables exists when the value of one variable decreases as the value of the other increases—that is, when the two variables move in opposite directions. For instance, consider the relationship between hours spent partying and college grade-point average (GPA). It is likely that these two variables share a negative relationship: as the number of hours spent partying increases, the student's GPA will likely decrease. Similarly, informative media use and entertainment-oriented media use likely share a negative relationship. In this case, the more time you spend seeking information (e.g., watching the news or reading the newspaper), the less time you will spend on entertainment content (e.g., watching movies). Keep in mind that words like "increase" and "decrease" here don't necessarily describe changes for an individual over time. Rather, they describe differences between individuals. Imagine you lined up all 300 students in a large class by their GPA, from 0.0 all the way up to 4.0. As you go up the line, from low grades to high, you would expect to see people saying that they party less and less. Yes, there will be some heavy partyers among the top grades, and some folks who stay at home among those with lower marks. But on average, as you identify people with increasingly high grades, you'll see the time they report partying drop.

A *positive relationship* occurs when the values of two variables move in the same direction—as the value of one variable goes up (or down), so does the other. For instance, whereas hours spent partying shares a negative relationship with GPA, hours spent studying is likely to have a positive relationship with GPA, such that as the number of hours spent studying increases, the student's

| variable |
| → Unit 2 |
| **independent variable** |
| → Unit 2 |
| **dependent variable** |
| → Unit 2 |
| **bivariate statistics** |
| → Unit 15 |

19

GPA will also likely increase. Similarly, informative media use is likely to share a positive relationship with political participation.

Mediation

When one or more variables are influenced by the independent variable and, in turn, influence the dependent variable, this is called *mediation*. That is, mediation occurs when one variable falls in the "middle," providing a key link between an independent variable and the ultimate outcome. Hypothesizing and testing for mediation can be helpful in developing theory. Most good theories do more than simply list basic relationships; they explain why variables are related. By establishing the intermediate steps between changing an initial variable and the final outcome, tests of mediation help provide this explanation.

When scholars talk about mediation, they use the shorthand of referring to the independent variable as X, the dependent variable as Y, and the mediating variable as Z. For example, suppose you found that students who worked on a group project using an online message board rated their peers more positively than those who worked face-to-face. In this case, the dependent variable (Y) is peer ratings, and the independent variable (X) is online versus face-to-face communication. Possible mediating variables might include the productivity of the group or the number of arguments the team had—both of these could be designated Z. Or maybe you think that exposure to social media messages about a local animal shelter will increase positive feelings about the shelter, and that in turn positive feelings will increase willingness to give money. The amount of exposure is the IV (X), the amount of positive feelings is the mediator (Z) and the willingness to give money is the DV (Y).

Testing mediation statistically involves specific statistical techniques that quantify the exact indirect relationships. But the basic logic is straightforward. The IV must cause a change in the mediator, and the mediator must in turn cause a change in the DV. So there should be an overall relationship between X and Y, a relationship between X and Z, and a relationship between Z and Y. And the causal direction of this relationship must proceed from X, to Z, and then to Y. If these requirements are not met, mediation is not present. For example, if the people in the online group didn't rate their peers any higher, then there is no relationship to explain. If online activity doesn't affect productivity, then it can't be true that people rated their peers more highly in that condition because they were more productive. Similarly, if being productive doesn't lead to higher peer ratings, then no influence on productivity will explain the higher evaluations. Note that these relationships don't have to be positive. If working online causes fewer arguments, this is a negative relationship between X and Z. But if fewer arguments in turn cause more positive ratings, this is also a negative relationship. These two negatives "cancel out" to generate a positive, indirect effect.

An additional requirement is that the initial relationship between X and Y should be weaker once the influence of Z is considered. Fully understanding this requires learning about control variables, but the basic premise is straight-forward. Suppose connections with peers mediates the effect of online interaction evaluations. Specifically, suppose those who interacted online rated their peers 20 percent higher than those who interacted offline. The reason for this should be, at least in part, that they also said they were more connected with their peers, which caused them to give higher evaluations. If you were to focus only on those people who felt highly connected with their peers, the difference between the online and offline groups should be much smaller. Those who interacted online but didn't connect should not be particularly nice in their evaluations, whereas those who interacted offline but managed to connect should be nice. They would be the exception rather than the rule, but they would show that connection was the critical factor linking online interaction to evaluations for the majority of students.

Figure 2.1 Relationship between group mode and peer evaluations before mediating variable considered

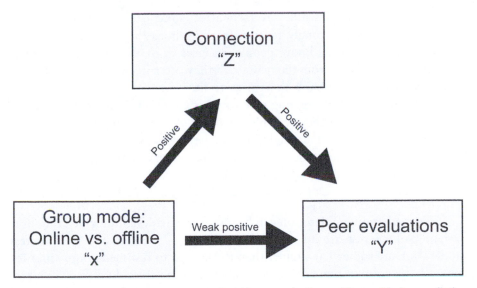

Figure 2.2 Relationship between group mode and peer evaluations while considering mediating variable of "connection" between group members

Moderation

Like mediation, moderation involves the influence of one or more third variables (*Z*) on the relationship between an independent variable (*X*) and a dependent variable (*Y*). Specifically, moderation occurs when the relationship between *X* and *Y* is not constant but depends upon the value of *Z*. For example, if we're examining what makes people give money to an animal shelter, we might consider income as a moderating variable. Previously we speculated that exposure to social media messages about the shelter (the IV, X) might cause an increase in the amount of money a person would be willing to give (the DV, Y). However, the power of such messages might depend upon income. For someone with low income, the effect of reading messages might be very small. No matter how persuasive the message, they simply don't have enough money to give freely. But for someone with a higher income, the relationship between X and Y might be strong. Because giving money is relatively painless, exposure to even a few messages could easily trigger a large donation.

Reflect & React: Moderation

Many students wonder why the findings reported in research on communication don't seem to apply to them or to people they know. In some cases, it might be that the relationships described are not universal; instead, key moderating variables determine which kinds of people are affected.

Think about your own experience with media. Representations of violence, sexually explicit content, and unrealistic images of attractiveness have all been shown to adversely affect some people. Certain types of people respond strongly to cues from authority or are reluctant to speak out when they know people disagree with them. People learn about current issues from the news, and they often decide that the issues covered more are probably more important.

Do these descriptions ring true to you? Can you think of people or situations for which they weren't accurate? Are there any general patterns you can identify that might indicate key moderating variables—factors that explain why some people are more influenced by media or more likely to show these responses than others?

Like mediation, moderation can be tested in any design in which the three variables of interest are all measured or known. The statistics used to test moderation are somewhat simpler than those used to test mediation, and they generally focus on testing an interaction between variables. Exploring moderation helps clarify and develop theory. If only some individuals respond to a message, this suggests that some characteristic or quality of those individuals is necessary for the message to have an effect. Studying moderation also has practical value: an organization or company that finds a moderating variable can identify the audience worth focusing on in further efforts.

Causality

Demonstrating a relationship between variables is important, but just because you've labeled one variable the independent variable and one the dependent variable, that doesn't necessarily reveal the whole story. When researchers are trying to fully develop theory and explain relationships, they try to determine whether the connection between variables is *causal*. In a causal relationship, a shift in one variable (the independent variable) alters the value of another variable (the dependent variable). For example, if we think that using news media causes people to increase their political knowledge, we expect more than just finding that more knowledgeable people watch more news. We must show that if you take a less knowledgeable person and show them news, their knowledge will increase.

Three main criteria are necessary to determine causality: establishing a relationship, confirming time order, and eliminating confounds or alternative explanations. The second and third elements are important enough to have their own entries, but establishing a relationship between the variables is a critical first step. After all, the basic definition of a relationship is that we can predict changes in one variable based on changes in the other. And the definition of causality is that changes in one variable directly influence the values of the other variable. If causality is occurring, we would necessarily observe that the value of the independent variable has some correspondence with the dependent variable. Any research design that measures both the independent and dependent variables can be used to show the existence of a relationship. Another approach to showing a relationship is found in experimental research, where we manipulate the value of the independent variable and then observe or measure what happens to the dependent variable. Here again, we know the value of each variable, either because we controlled it or simply observed it.

Demonstrating relationships, of course, is the main purpose of research. Remember, though, that any test of a relationship requires having a clear, distinct indicator of the value of that variable, by itself. We cannot "measure" causality or a causal relationship. We measure the independent variable with questions or observations. And we also measure the dependent variable. And then we look to see if the value a person has for one variable helps predict the value of the other. Researchers are often interested in knowing whether an independent variable shares a causal relationship with a dependent variable because this can allow for more effective predictions. For instance, if you know that studying shares a causal relationship with GPA but wearing new shoes does not, then you know to focus on studying and to ignore other activities (such as buying new shoes) that may share a spurious relationship with performance.

relationship → Unit 2
variable → Unit 2
independent variable → Unit 2
dependent variable → Unit 2
explanation → Unit 3
application → Unit 3
experiment → Unit 9

Consider an instance in which an advertising agency knows that a particular advertising approach shares a causal relationship with sales of a particular type of product (e.g., ads featuring sex appeal increase sales of perfume). In this case, this knowledge would be incredibly beneficial—and lucrative—for the agency because it would help it produce successful advertisements.

Time Order

The second main requirement for showing that a relationship is causal is determining the time order of the variables. Any change in the independent variable must occur *before* any change in the dependent variable, an idea sometimes termed *temporal precedence*. In the case of news use, we might find that we can accurately predict that news viewers know more about current events. But showing that doesn't demonstrate time order. Our IV is the amount of news a person uses, and our DV is the level of knowledge they have—how many facts they can correctly give about current events and politics. Time order would require that first a person watches the news, and then after watching the news their knowledge increases. But the opposite pattern could emerge. Maybe people who already know about current events are more inclined to follow them further. In this case making someone watch the news wouldn't increase their knowledge, and the relationship wouldn't be causal. We have to show that the change in news viewing comes first.

Addressing time order is a difficult and critical aspect of many studies. Some basic designs struggle to show what comes first. For example, a cross-sectional survey (like an opinion poll or a customer satisfaction form) measures both the independent variable and the dependent variable at the same time. This makes it hard to know whether one came first. Other designs are better at establishing time order. In an experiment, for example, we measure the dependent variable after exposure to the independent variable, which allows us to definitively know which variable came first. Additionally, we use random assignment to help ensure there weren't existing differences in the dependent variable that might have caused variation in the independent variable. In panel surveys, we can measure variables more than once, and see whether information about a variable at time 1 helps us predict the other variable (or even changes in the variable) at time 2.

Confounds

A confound is a type of third variable that creates the impression of a causal relationship between an independent and dependent variable, but is actually the variable that influences both, creating the spurious impression of a relationship. If you were to look only at people with a single value for the confound, you would no longer see any pattern linking the independent and dependent

24

variable. Consider again the IV of time watching news and the DV of political knowledge. If better-educated people tend to both watch news and know about current events, and if this is the sole reason for the relationship, then no amount of increased news use will make the less educated more knowledgeable. This requirement for causality is one of the primary reasons control variables are often included in research studies. By measuring the alternative explanation, we can be sure it isn't driving the pattern we find. However, no study can measure every possible third variable. In experiments, we use random assignment to place people in conditions, which should balance all potential third variables equally across all values of the independent variable. But in general, we want to measure and account for any alternative explanations if showing causality is important.

An example outside of communication research that you may have experienced in your college life can illustrate this further. Suppose that every Friday, you make the 2-hour drive home for the weekend, and at the end of that drive, you are very happy and excited. At first glance, you might conclude that driving for 2 hours makes you happy. This conclusion meets the first criterion for causality in that there is an observed relationship: each Friday you drive for 2 hours, and you are happier at the end of that drive than when you started the drive. It also meets the second criterion, time order. The driving precedes the increase in happiness—your happiness was low when you started the car and high 2 hours later—so we can also safely conclude, at least, that being happy does not cause you to drive.

You probably can sense that this relationship does not meet the third criterion, as a third variable likely accounts for your happiness. In this case, unless you really love driving, it is likely that being home (the third variable) causes your increase in happiness, and the relationship between driving and happiness is merely spurious. This example underscores why researchers should not be quick to conclude that a causal relationship exists and must consider third variables that could explain what is truly happening.

Theory

One of the main goals of scholarly research is to develop and test theories. A theory is a model or description of a set of variables that reflects how they relate, has a basis in empirical evidence, and allows researchers to make predictions about relationships in future research. The best theories don't simply describe relationships; they explain the mechanisms that cause variables to be related.

A well-known example of theory in mass communication is *agenda setting*. According to this theory, the more a particular issue is covered by the news, the more important people think that issue is. Like all true theories, this idea encompasses multiple variables: the amount of news coverage and the

independent variable
→ Unit 2

dependent variable
→ Unit 2

third variable
→ Unit 2

experiment
→ Unit 9

spuriousness
→ Unit 16

random assignment
→ Unit 9

relationship
→ Unit 2

variable
→ Unit 2

third variable
→ Unit 2

prediction
→ Unit 2

empirical
→ Unit 1

level of importance expressed by the public, in this case. Because these concepts are quite broad, we are able to use them to make predictions across many different contexts, an idea known as scope. For example, consider our efforts on behalf of the local animal shelter. We might think that the number of online news stories initially written or shared is important to explain how important people consider animal welfare. If our unit of analysis is an individual person, we would think about this in terms of two variables: the number of stories a person is exposed to through news and social media, and how important the person considers the issue of animal welfare. While our basic theory was broad, it has allowed us to make a much more specific prediction for our study. This prediction is known as a hypothesis, and forming and testing hypotheses is a central element of most academic research.

Thus, the bare minimum criteria for something to be a theory is that it is based in evidence, describes relationships between variables, and allows the formation of falsifiable hypotheses. Additionally, the best theories have broad scope; they cover many different contexts. And they are relatively parsimonious; they involve relatively few variables and don't require numerous exceptions and adjustments for different contexts.

The process of developing theory involves both deductive and inductive reasoning. Initially theories are built inductively, starting from existing observations to identify larger patterns. Then, as the theory is established, it allows deductive tests of the general rules of the theory in specific hypothesized contexts. This means that even when researchers are simply exploring or describing human behavior, the knowledge created still helps form theories. But not all researchers are equally focused on theory. Many applied studies are primarily interested in solving a specific contextual problem. In this case, the existence of theory related to the topic might be helpful, but the main goal is not to add to or test that theory.

Inductive Versus Deductive Reasoning

theory
→ Unit 2

hypotheses
→ Unit 2

scope
→ Unit 2

empirical
→ Unit 1

An important distinction in theory development is the broad difference between deductive and inductive reasoning. Although both kinds of reasoning contribute to the development of knowledge, the logic of *deductive reasoning* is particularly important to the process of theory development through hypothesis testing. The core notion of deductive reasoning is that a theory provides us with the framework to develop a set of expectations that result in hypotheses. We then test those hypotheses as a way of building knowledge. Note that in more formal logic, the ideas of both deductive and inductive reasoning are linked to the creation of logical rules, but in a research context the connections between variables are not stated in strict logical terms or expected to hold absolutely true. Rather they are statements based on probability, with a deductively supported theory showing a general pattern and not perfect infallibility.

For example, your reading in interpersonal communication might suggest that friendly greetings are more likely to generate positive outcomes than unfriendly ones. To test this idea, you could keep track of what happens after you use a positive greeting (e.g., cheerfully saying "Hello, how are you?"), as well as what happens after you use less cheerful greetings (e.g., grumbling "Hey"). If your expectations (i.e., hypotheses) are supported, then this provides evidence that the theory works and is useful to researchers and practitioners in making predictions and explaining communication phenomena. Further research will continue to test the theory in a range of contexts to better understand the scope of phenomena it can explain. However, if the hypotheses are not supported, this suggests that the theory needs to be adjusted. Researchers should go back to the drawing board to consider other mechanisms to "fix" the theory or consider abandoning the theory if little or no empirical evidence can be found to support it.

In contrast, *inductive reasoning* is not intended to test theory or hypotheses but rather starts with observations that are used to develop a theory. Consider a situation in which you notice low rates of communication between professors and students in some of your classes. You could develop more formal observation procedures and take better notes on this phenomenon in the hope of gathering enough empirical evidence to draw conclusions about why this is happening. Using inductive reasoning, you would look more closely at the observations to find patterns that help explain why in some classes the professor and students communicate well and in others they do not. For instance, you might notice that communication levels are highest in afternoon classes and in upper-division courses yet lowest in night classes and in larger classes. The patterns you identify would form the basis of a theory that could then be used to make future predictions about when student-to-professor communication will be high (or low). At that point, you would use deductive reasoning to test that theory.

Although formal hypothesis testing is a primary focus of research, both types of reasoning play an important role in the development of knowledge. Consider again our research question focusing on how to use social media to promote a nonprofit organization. Ultimately, we would like to draw upon theory and prior research to express and test formal hypotheses. Because this involves making predictions first, then testing those predictions, this is deductive reasoning. But before appropriate theories could ever emerge, scholars had to observe what happened when different types of campaigns and messages were used, using inductive reasoning to identify potential patterns that could be measured and developed in further research.

Reflect & React: Developing and Testing Theories

Consider the following situation: Since you have gone away to college, your parents seem to call you all the time. They have been calling so frequently that you decide to keep a log of how often they call, including the day, time, length of call, and topic of the call. In what ways could you use inductive reasoning to explain what is happening? What specific relationships and patterns would you look for in your observations? Finally, consider the ways that you could use deductive reasoning to understand why your parents are calling so often.

prediction
→ Unit 2

hypotheses
→ Unit 2

variable
→ Unit 2

operational
definition
→ Unit 5

relationship
→ Unit 2

knowledge
→ Unit 3

Falsification

One defining element of a theory is that it is *falsifiable*. That is, a theory must produce predictions that can be shown to be incorrect. For example, consider again the basics of agenda setting theory. It predicts a positive relationship between the amount of news coverage of an issue and the level of importance assigned that issue. In order for this to be falsifiable, we have to think of how we could get evidence that doesn't fit this prediction. For example, we might conduct a survey in our community and see how many people rate animal welfare as important. Then we could work with the local newspaper and television stations to run a series of stories about the local shelter and other pet issues. We could also make sure those stories were shared widely on social media. Then we could do a second survey. We would expect to see an increase in the number of people saying animal welfare matters. If the two surveys return exactly the same results, then clearly all that extra coverage didn't matter. Our initial prediction was false, and something about the theory must be altered since it doesn't fit reality.

Another example can illustrate this further. One theory says that idealized images of models cause people to engage in upward comparison, where they think about how they look worse than the models. In turn, this lowers their self-esteem. The minimum evidence to support this would require showing that people who use more media with idealized body types will have lower self-esteem. Thus, the theory would be directly falsified if such evidence couldn't be obtained in a survey. But just because we found a correlation wouldn't mean the theory was true. Other tests would be needed to show if the relationship was causal, and whether it worked for many different types of media, with different images, and on people of different ages and personalities. Every test of a theory could show something about it is false, but just because something isn't falsified doesn't mean it is completely supported and true.

Now think about a "theory" that doesn't make falsifiable predictions. Maybe we think that only "vulnerable" people will feel worse about themselves after viewing thin models, and we define "vulnerable" as people who feel worse about themselves. Whenever we find people feeling more negative, our theory is supported. But whenever we find people who don't feel worse about themselves, we'll say they aren't "vulnerable" and still think our theory is right. This violates a basic principle of science—that we learn from and correct our mistakes.

More broadly, knowledge is generated by rejecting theories that fail to work and keeping those that do work so that we can test them further. It is through this testing process that researchers discover the limits of a theory and better understand its applicability to various phenomena. When a theory is not supported—meaning that hypotheses generated by the theory are not supported—the limitations of that theory are revealed. A theory is falsifiable if it makes predictions about variables that we can actually observe or measure. After all, if we cannot conduct research on a theory, we cannot show it is wrong. Furthermore, a theory must be concrete and precise in its predictions, so that we can operationalize the variables and state the expected relationship as a concrete hypothesis.

Research in Depth: Theories in Communication

Communication is an incredibly broad field that encompasses mass, interpersonal, organizational, and other forms of communication. Here are some common theories that are used in communication research to get you started in thinking about the relationship between theory and research.

Agenda setting predicts that the media does not tell people what to think but rather what they should think about. In a basic sense, the more an issue is presented in the media, the more likely it is to be on people's "agenda" and to be something they think about.

Cultivation theory says that the more people watch television, the more their views about the world will match those presented on television and the less their views will match the real world. As a result, heavy television watchers often overestimate things such as crime because it is so common on television but less common in the real world.

The *elaboration likelihood model* proposes that there are two ways in which people process messages: (1) the central route, which involves careful scrutiny, and (2) the peripheral route, which relies on mental shortcuts based on external cues. For example, someone who is not involved in an issue might agree with a speaker just because the speaker is attractive or charming. Someone who is strongly interested in the issue will overlook those superficial qualities and carefully evaluate the logic of the speaker's argument.

Uncertainty reduction theory posits that individuals will attempt to reduce uncertainty about situations they are in—such as a new job or relationship—by seeking information. For instance, when you first start dating someone, you might feel anxious about all of the details of his or her life you don't know. A way to reduce that uncertainty about the relationship is to seek more information about that person by asking questions and to share information in the hope that your partner will reciprocate and reveal more details about himself or herself.

hypotheses
→ Unit 2

scope
→ Unit 2

explanation
→ Unit 3

falsification
→ Unit 2

empirical
→ Unit 1

positive versus negative relationship
→ Unit 2

Parsimony

One criterion that helps distinguish better theories from weaker ones is *parsimony*, which refers to the simplicity of a theory. A parsimonious theory does not involve any more variables or contextual exceptions than are necessary to provide accurate predictions. It is also vital for a theory to be straightforward and simple to explain and understand. If all things are equal and two theories have equivalent predictive power and can explain the same scope of phenomena, the more parsimonious explanation is preferable.

If a theory is straightforward and easy to explain, it is more likely to lend itself to hypothesis testing and falsifiability. As a theory is tested repeatedly, the strength of evidence supporting it grows, so having a theory that is easy to examine and test is important to developing knowledge.

An example of a theory that is noted for its parsimonious explanation of media effects is cultivation theory. The premise behind cultivation theory is that the more television a person watches, the more their view of the world matches that presented on television and the less it matches the real world. For example, heavy television viewers tend to perceive more crime than those who consume lesser amounts of television content. Considerable empirical data support this theory, finding a positive relationship between television viewing and perceived amounts of crime (and other characteristics from the television world). The fact that the explanatory mechanism behind the theory is parsimonious likely played a big role in the success of the theory.

Voices from Industry

Meghan E. Kennedy—Search Engine Marketing Strategist, Tower Marketing

Why are good research skills important in your field?

As a search engine optimization specialist, it is my job to optimize websites so that they are better found by their intended audience within search engine page results. A huge part of my job includes research of all kinds (e.g., keyword research, audience segmentation research, competitor research). If I don't do research on audience's search intent, keywords, or phrases they're looking for, or how my client's competitors are performing within search engine page results, then I simply cannot do my job. I am a thinker, a strategist, and researcher of search intent or keyword terms.

What specific method or methods do you encounter most?

I utilize quantitative data that will give me more qualitative results. For example, I conduct keyword research for websites so that way we can integrate the keywords in a genuine, natural way. However, based on the research I conduct, I am then having to organize my data because I may find 100+ keywords, but I must use methods to group the keywords and assign them to pages that make the most sense. So in terms of methods, I utilize tools, export my data or analytics, organize the data, and then present the data to internal team members or even display charts or graphs for clients that outline their website traffic data, based on how I organize and group my findings.

Can you name specific instances where you have used data collected from research?

I use data from my research on a daily basis, in a variety of ways. For example, one of my clients is a local Amish farmers market. Our content team had to write a blog for Christmas time and was in need of 'popular topics' that users were searching for online that would make for a great blog post. I conducted keyword and topical research to see what users were searching for on Google to see which topics would have high search volume, low difficulty, and high organic click-through rate (meaning a user isn't clicking on an ad, but our blog post because we are matching their search intent). I used internal software programs (Google keyword explorer, MOZ, and SEMrush) to export keyword data that I found. Then I organized the data into categories (e.g., Christmas cookie ideas, holiday dinner essentials, and holiday food gifts). I presented the keyword groupings to my content team to see which topic gave the best direction for our writers.

How did research you conducted help inform your decision?

Research that I conduct for my line of work determines the strategic direction my Internet marketing team takes when handling the overall website performance and reputation for our clients. The research that I conduct for keywords, links that direct users back to our clients' websites, and other areas are implemented and integrated to the overall marketing strategies that we use for our clients.

What are one or two pieces of advice or insights you would give about research to students in a communication research methods course?

When I took this course as a sophomore at West Chester University, it opened my eyes to the line of work I wanted to get into. I have a creative mind, but I am an analytical person. Research that elicits data that helps teams or groups of people make an informed decision is the environment I live in now, as a search engine optimization specialist. Research may seem boring or dull to some, but you have to step back and look at the bigger picture that research in marketing is what sets the precedence for your strategy. I never randomly tell my team to write about 'uses for coffee beans' for our farmers market client because I 'felt like that seemed cool'. I tell my teams to write about that topic for a blog because I prove from my research that users are searching for this term at a high monthly volume, it would be a low difficulty to rank for in Google, and the organic click through rate the topic is getting is also high. Research is the foundation to marketing, plain and simple.

---

explanation → Unit 3
hypotheses → Unit 2

Scope

A second criterion used to differentiate better and weaker theories is scope, the diversity and breadth of phenomena that they can be used to explain. Theories that have broader scope (also referred to as "range") can be used to explain more phenomena and can be applied to more contexts than narrower or more limited theories. Therefore, theories that cover more diverse topics are generally considered more valuable. Scholars often talk of a "grand theory" of communication that broadly explains communication phenomena and can be applied across many contexts. While this is unlikely, there are theories that have been applied to a broad array of phenomena ranging from interpersonal communication to mass communication. For example, uncertainty reduction theory has been applied to a variety of phenomena, including romantic relationships, workplace communication behaviors, and mass media information seeking. Not every test has worked out, thereby limiting the scope of the theory, but within the set of topics that work for this theory, the results have been consistent and support the value of the theory.

Although theories with a broad scope are desirable, highly specific theories can be valuable as well—particularly if they offer especially powerful and accurate explanations and predictions. For example, prospect theory is drawn from psychology and focuses on gain and loss framing. In communication, this means that the theory has a limited scope—that is, if a persuasive or descriptive message doesn't explicitly compare equal circumstances in terms of gain versus loss, the theory may not apply. But within that narrow scope, the theory remains powerful and effective, and it shapes ideas about what media "framing" entails. Researchers are able to discover the limits to the scope of a theory by testing hypotheses generated by that theory in a variety of contexts. Through either supporting or falsifying hypotheses, researchers can come to understand the circumstances under which a theory works and the circumstances under which it does not.

Research Questions

The research process is designed to answer questions. In some cases, these questions may lead to theory development, but this does not have to be the case. In general, a *research question* is a driving point of inquiry that scholars hope to answer. For example, in the case of our interest in the link between thin model images and self-esteem, our basic research question is whether these two variables are linked. When we have a clear theory, it provides a likely answer to a research question and allows us to develop and test hypotheses. A research question is what guides the researchers in structuring their study as appropriate theories are consulted and methods are constructed to answer that central question. For instance, a researcher might be interested in understanding the role that news coverage of politics plays in political participation. In this case, the researcher would be guided by the following research question: *What role does political news play in affecting political participation?*

The term "research question" is also used in a more specific sense: in cases in which theory is not developed enough to allow a researcher to confidently state hypotheses, we instead express the relationship we want to test in terms of a research question. These specific research questions are then directly tested, and the answers are reported in the results section of a scholarly article. A more specific research question might look something like this: *Does political news use have a positive or negative relationship with voting?* In this case, the question specifies the variables more explicitly than the general, guiding question. This allows for easier testing of the question because the researcher can more effectively devise a method to measure and subsequently evaluate the relationship between the variables to provide an answer to the question.

Hypotheses

When existing theory is more developed, researchers do not need to simply pose a research question. Instead, they can offer clear predictions about the relationship between variables—that is, they can make hypotheses. Hypotheses should draw upon theory or prior observation and, at minimum, state an expectation that two variables will be related. In some cases, hypotheses state a particular direction of the relationship—positive or negative—and thus are referred to as *directional hypotheses*.

Hypotheses may further express specific characteristics of the relationship in question. A hypothesis might suggest the presence of a moderating or mediating variable, for example. For instance, men might be affected differently by representations of the thin ideal in the media than women, suggesting that gender moderates the effects of exposure to these images for some dependent variable (e.g., self-esteem).

| **relationship** → Unit 2 |
| **results section** → Unit 3 |
| **variable** → Unit 2 |

| **relationship** → Unit 2 |
| **variable** → Unit 2 |
| **positive versus relationship** → Unit 2 |
| **moderation** → Unit 2 |

33

Moreover, while a research question may reflect a broad interest in the typical or general pattern of relationships, a hypothesis should be concrete. A proper hypothesis reflects a prediction about what will take place in your specific research study, and therefore it should name the exact variables being measured and tested in that study. Consider again the potential to research the effects of thin-ideal images on those who view them. While a broad research question might simply ask about the link between images and self-esteem, a proper hypothesis would be more precise. For example, you might hypothesize that exposure to images of women who are 20 percent thinner than the average woman will result in lower self-esteem than exposure to images of women who are 20 percent heavier than the average woman.

Another example, drawn from media research, involves third-person perception. Third-person perception theory suggests that we perceive others as more likely to be affected by negative media content than ourselves. A general prediction that should emerge from this theory is that estimates of perceived effects on oneself will be *lower* than estimates of perceived effects on others. A more specific hypothesis would consider the specific design of the study. For example, a hypothesis might state: Participants will perceive other college students as more affected by violent movies than themselves. Hypotheses typically are identified by numbers (e.g., the first hypothesis is H1, the second hypothesis is H2), which makes it easy to identify them when they are discussed in the results and discussion sections. Finally, stating hypotheses has important implications for statistical tests and probability. Because of these statistical implications, it is generally not acceptable to predict a null hypothesis—that is, to expect that two variables will be unrelated. The reasons for this are considered further in the discussion of inferential statistics. When the extant theory and literature don't suggest clear patterns or relationships, researchers often pose research questions instead.

Effectively wording hypotheses is critical to developing strong studies. If a hypothesis does not clearly state its predictions in a way that identifies each relevant variable and provides a clearly testable prediction, you cannot figure out what to measure or analyze. Consider these examples of flawed hypotheses:

- People are negatively affected by thin-ideal media.
- Using thin-ideal media will cause vulnerable people to have lower self-esteem.

In each case, we cannot clearly test the hypothesis. In the first example, we are talking about being "negatively affected," without specifying the actual variables we expect to be related. Perhaps we think that these "negative effects" are changes in self-esteem. We would have a far clearer hypothesis if we stated, "Use of thin-ideal media will be negatively related to self-esteem." Now we know we must measure use of media and also self-esteem, and we know that we expect those who use thin-ideal media the most to have the lowest self-esteem.

The second example more clearly states that use of thin-ideal media and self-esteem are thought to be related. But what do we mean by "vulnerable people"? If a vulnerable person is someone who is influenced by the use of media, then this hypothesis cannot be falsified. Every person we find who uses thin-ideal media and has low self-esteem must be vulnerable, but anyone who doesn't show that pattern—even if that's nearly everyone we study—can simply be dismissed as not vulnerable. This violates the basic logic of using hypotheses to put our theories to the test.

Activities

Activity 2A: Getting Started With a Research Question or Hypothesis

See terms: variable; research question; hypothesis

Think about a topic related to communication that you would like to know more about. In doing so, identify at least one variable that is specific to communication and at least one other variable that might either cause that communication or result from that communication.

- Which variable do you see as the independent variable and which do you see as the dependent variable?
- Why is this an interesting research question to ask?
- To what audiences would the research question you are asking or hypothesis you could state be most interesting?
- Do you feel confident stating a hypothesis for what you expect to happen?
- What practical application might this research have?
- What is the next step you think you should take to move forward on trying to answer this research question?

Activity 2B: Independent and Dependent Variables

See terms: dependent variable; independent variable; third variable.

Consider each set of three concepts listed below. For each group of concepts, describe a potential relationship that would involve all three concepts, such that one concept would be an independent variable, one would be a dependent variable, and one would act as a third variable of some kind. Explain why you assigned each variable to the category you chose. Specify whether the relationship between the independent variable and dependent variable would be positive, negative, or something else.

- Set 1: Aggressive behavior, television viewing, age
- Set 2: Advertising exposure, interest in a product, willingness to purchase a product
- Set 3: Cable news viewing, political ideology, attitudes regarding global warming
- Set 4: Personality type, number of Instagram followers, level of physical activity (exercise)
- Set 5: Gender, communication style, relationship satisfaction.

Activity 2C: Causality

See terms: causality; counfounds; time order.

For each of the research studies described later, discuss why their conclusion about the specific nature of the relationship could be wrong using the basic standards for causality.

Scenario 1: Researchers were interested in understanding the role that life satisfaction plays in academic performance. To test this relationship, they conducted a series of interviews with college students. After conducting the interviews and evaluating the responses, the researchers noticed that students who reported higher levels of satisfaction with life in general also had higher GPAs and test scores. Therefore, the researchers concluded that life satisfaction causes higher levels of academic performance.

Scenario 2: A group of political scientists were curious about the role that using online news sources plays in political activity (e.g., voting or attending political events). To study this, they asked a sample of 500 people an identical set of questions about their media use habits and how frequently they engage in various political activities. The results indicate that those people who used online news sources more frequently were more likely to participate in political activities. The political scientists concluded that using online news sources causes increased political activity.

Scenario 3: An advertising agency was interested in testing the effectiveness of its latest advertising campaign that was designed to increase awareness of a new organic cleaning product. To do this, they conducted a series of group interviews in which they asked the participants about the advertising campaign, their use of the product, and their attitudes toward the product. The data show that participants had trouble remembering the advertising campaign and demonstrated low levels of awareness of the product but high levels of satisfaction when using the product. The advertising agency concluded that the campaign caused increased awareness of the product.

Scenario 4: A college sports conference was interested in determining whether giving pep talks before games improves performance during games. To assess this, the conference randomly selected half of the coaches to give pep talks before the first game and half of the coaches to skip their pep talks. They then repeated this process throughout the season. At the end of the season, the data showed that when teams were given pep talks before the game they scored an average of seven more points in the first quarter than teams who did not receive pep talks. Teams receiving pep talks also won 55 percent of the time (with teams not receiving pep talks winning 45 percent of the time).

Suggested Readings for Further Exploration of Unit 2 Topics

Examples

Berger, C. R. (1991). Communication theories and other curios. *Communication Monographs*, *58*(1), 101–113. doi:10.1080/03637759109376216

Bostrom, R. N. (2003). Theories, data, and communication research. *Communication Monographs*, *70*(4), 275–294. doi:10.1080/0363775032000179106

Eveland, W. P. (2003). A "mix of attributes" approach to the study of media effects and new communication technologies. *Journal of Communication*, *53*(3), 395–410. doi:10.1111/j.1460-2466.2003.tb02598.x

Advanced Discussion

Bryant, J., & Oliver, M. B. (2008). *Media effects: Advances in theory and research*. New York, NY: Routledge.

Craig, R. T. (1993). Why are there so many communication theories? *Journal of Communication*, *43*(3), 26–33. doi:10.1111/j.1460-2466.1993.tb01273.x

Craig, R. T. (1999). Communication theory as a field. *Communication Theory*, *9*(2), 119–161. doi:10.1111/j.1468-2885.1999.tb00355.x

O'Keefe, B. (1993). Against theory. *Journal of Communication*, *43*(3), 75–82. doi:10.1111/j.1460-2466.1993.tb01278.x

Pavitt, C. (1999). The third way: Scientific realism and communication theory. *Communication Theory*, *9*(2), 162–188. doi:10.1111/j.1468-2885.1999.tb00356.x

Potter, W. J. (2008). *Arguing for a general framework for mass media scholarship*. Thousand Oaks, CA: Sage Publications.

Shoemaker, P. J., Tankard, J. W., Jr., & Lasorsa, D. L. (2004). *How to build social science theories*. Thousand Oaks, CA: Sage Publications.

unit 3

scholarly research and the creation of knowledge

In Unit 2, we considered the challenge of effectively raising funds and awareness for your local animal shelter. If you were working for the shelter, your immediate goal would have been to get people on board with the newest promotion or to address the most recent crisis. But with continued time on the job, you might start to feel like you could think about the bigger picture. Eventually you would have a broader understanding of what kinds of campaigns worked and what sorts of messages brought in the most donors. Gradually, as we answer questions through research, we build knowledge.

In the academic community, this process occurs as well, and it's a central mission of universities and professors. Consider the example of advertisements and other media that depict thin, sexualized models. Such images are pervasive, created by a combination of carefully selected models, unrealistic photo shoots and extensive digital editing of photos. Because of this, researchers have asked whether exposure to such images might have effects on self-esteem and eating behaviors. In the previous unit, we encountered the challenges of conducting an individual study that would effectively test whether exposure actually *causes* changes in self-esteem. But research is a process that doesn't rely on single studies. Rather, it is cyclical and self-correcting. By developing theories and continuing to test them, and by publishing the results so other researchers can learn from them, scholars meet the goals of not merely describing but also explaining the effects of media, building knowledge in the process.

Knowledge

Our understanding of the relationships between variables, the larger theories that explain these relationships, and the strength of evidence regarding both constitute knowledge. That is, knowledge is what we understand to be true about the world. Critically, what we know may not always be true. Some scholars differentiate knowledge from belief—the former is what we correctly think is true, while beliefs are everything we hold to be true even if we are wrong. But in practice, we act based on our beliefs because we assume they represent knowledge. Thus, the vital question is how we create beliefs and refine them over time so that they are accurate, representing genuine knowledge of the world.

Research is one critical mechanism. Because research is empirical, we know that it is based upon how things actually work in the world. Because research is systematic, we know that we have not altered our procedures or our results to fit our personal **bias**. Because research is intersubjective, we know that other researchers could follow our procedures, engaging in **replication** of our studies and providing **triangulation** that confirms our results through other methods, and reveals when those results were false (so long as we avoid **publication bias**). We can also engage in **secondary** analysis, where we analyze data collected by other researchers. And because of all these reasons, research is cyclical and self-correcting, allowing us to improve our knowledge in ways that other ways that we obtain knowledge cannot. For example, we might rely on **authority**, trust our own **intuition**, or cling to existing beliefs due to **tenacity**. But none of these offer a mechanism for comparing completing knowledge claims and correcting ourselves when what we "know" proves to be false.

Ultimately, knowledge is the central **goal of research**. But we distinguish between more subtle goals to represent the entire process of knowledge creation. Some research, like our effort to help an animal shelter succeed, is focused primarily on **application**, or concrete and specific knowledge that helps with a practical problem. Other research strives for **exploration**, giving preliminary information about a topic where we have little knowledge. From there, we might proceed to **description**, identifying patterns and offering a sense of how broadly our new knowledge holds true. Finally, we might work at **explanation**, supplementing our knowledge of what relationships exist with clear theories about why they occur. At every stage, we may try to provide **quantitative** knowledge by counting variables or more **qualitative** descriptions that offer greater depth and detail.

Researchers do not simply hope to acquire knowledge; they work to share it. This is done primarily though academic **research articles**. Such articles contain many common elements that help other researchers quickly understand the findings, including the **abstract, literature review, method section, results section, discussion section**, consideration of **future directions**, and **reference list**. Many articles also include an **appendix, tables**, or **figures** to further convey the knowledge they contain. Some articles are not focused on providing information about original research, and don't follow this format; examples include **literature review articles** and **meta-analyses**. Increasingly, research-based knowledge is also conveyed outside of academic journal articles in formats such as **data-driven journalism**.

authority → Unit 3
validity → Unit 6

Bias

The ultimate goal of building knowledge is for that knowledge to be a true representation of reality. Bias represents anything that systematically distorts our knowledge, so that it differs from reality. That is, a source of knowledge or a technique for acquiring it is biased if it always gives an answer that differs from truth in a consistent way. Thus, the best way to answer questions and gain knowledge is a way that avoids bias. However, we don't necessarily know the "true" answer to many questions—if we did, we wouldn't have to ask them. And some questions may not have an objective truth. This is why we describe research as intersubjective. If we agree on how to define our variables, then we should reach the same conclusions about the values of those variables for a population or the relationship between those variables. Bias then describes any circumstance where even when someone is using the same definition, they claim systematically different knowledge. For example, consider trying to obtain knowledge about how much violence airs on television. If we ask 10 authorities, and nine of them roughly agree on a number but the tenth person gives a much higher estimate, we can reasonably conclude the tenth expert is biased. Not all errors represent bias; if a study of television violence included several extremely violent episodes of normally peaceful shows by chance, it would overestimate the level of violence on television. But running the same study again with a different set of shows might underestimate violence if it instead included more peaceful episodes by chance. Both of these studies contain errors, but not due to a bias in the design. However, if the people conducting the study deliberately chose only shows that aired between 9:00 p.m. and 11:00 p.m. but were trying to reach conclusions about all 24 hours of broadcast television, this method *would* bias the results because the time frame chosen contains a systematically higher amount of violence.

Two additional points about bias are critical to remember. First, bias doesn't only occur due to deliberate choices by researchers or others. Many studies suffer from bias in the results because of mistakes in the design of the study; the authors of those studies would much rather have found more accurate findings. Researchers take steps to minimize any bias by carefully evaluating the validity of their study and by selecting the right way to evaluate their findings. Second, bias isn't the same thing as having an opinion or drawing a conclusion. The truth is never biased. For example, just because some people erroneously say the Earth is flat doesn't make an astronomer biased for saying the Earth is round. All of the best available evidence for thousands of years proves the Earth is round. Pretending as though flat-earthers had equally valid claims would be biased, despite the "balance" of information this would imply.

Authority

When you want knowledge, there are many ways to obtain it. One is to rely on authority, the supposed expertise or knowledge of some respected or trusted source. For example, if you are trying to understand the effects of thin-ideal images in media, you might talk to a psychiatrist who specializes in disordered eating. Or you might get a book from the library written about someone's personal experience as a model. Authority may or may not be an effective way to answer a question or support an argument. Authorities may have put time and energy into studying a question, and their insights could be quite accurate. Perhaps the psychiatrist is versed in the latest research and has contributed her own scholarship. However, relying on authorities does not guarantee a correct answer. Perhaps the psychiatrist is instead mostly interested in getting on talk shows and selling books, and that bias leads to overstating the harms of media and ignoring systematic research. The information provided by an authority is only as good as the technique used to obtain that information.

If an authority has not directly studied a topic, his or her conclusions will be based either on other sources or on intuition. In many cases, the evidence shows that authorities do not have better intuition than anyone else. For example, research shows that fund managers—individuals charged with selecting stocks and other investments—do no better than chance would dictate. That is, some will do better than simply picking the stocks that performed best the previous year, but an equal number will do worse, and there is no reliable way to know who will succeed and who will fail. People picking stocks would be far better off picking a fund that includes all major stocks, balancing out the random strong and weak performers—by the time you factor in the fees charged by active managers, you'll come out ahead by not trusting the so-called experts.

Research in Depth: The Power of Authority

Psychological research confirms the tendency of people to obey and be persuaded by authority and expertise. In a classic example, Yale University professor Stanley Milgram (1974) carried out a series of experiments showing that a subset of people would obey a researcher in a lab coat when ordered to administer electric shocks. In the area of persuasion, evidence suggests that individuals will respond more favorably to arguments that come from experts than from nonexperts, even when those arguments are low in quality (DeBono & Harnish, 1988; Petty, Cacioppo, & Goldman, 1981). An important element of this research shows that individuals who are highly motivated, involved, or interested in a topic can overcome this tendency and focus instead on the quality of the argument. In other words, it is possible to carefully evaluate the actual quality of evidence. As you learn more about research, you will come to recognize when the argument given is valid.

This doesn't mean that relying on authority to answer a question is always a bad idea. If the expert source has collected information about the topic in a way that provides valid answers, then those insights are useful. After all, no one—not even experts—has the time to carry out a research study about every question he or she may want to answer. But there are two important points to consider before you trust authority as a source of information. First, does the authority clearly indicate his or her sources? Because the insights of an authority are only as good as the ways they were obtained, a reliable authority should clearly describe the basis for those insights. Second, does the authority rely upon appropriate types of evidence? As discussed throughout this text, research offers a superior way to answer questions. It minimizes the potential for bias to interfere with the information provided and offers a way to gradually correct mistaken beliefs. Trusting an authoritative source that lists many valid research studies as the basis for its conclusions is a smart idea; trusting someone with a fancy title or television show who won't explain his or her conclusions will often lead to mistakes.

Intuition

Intuition is another source of knowledge, in which your conclusion is based upon your instinctive understanding of the question. For example, maybe you personally read a lot of beauty and fashion content. Your feeling is that this stuff cannot have much effect—after all, it doesn't influence you, and so it just makes sense that it must not affect others. As in this example, intuition might have a basis in personal experience, or even in knowledge you gained in the past, but no further information is collected to answer this question, and no one has directly provided us an answer. Thus, intuition can often lead to flawed conclusions if your previous knowledge and experience are not relevant to the current situation or are otherwise incorrect.

One reason that research is sometimes dismissed is that in many cases, the findings may match those derived from intuition. For example, many people might dismiss some research on video games as common sense. Studies have shown that players enjoy games that have "natural" controls, where the controller feels like the real-world action. For example, a driving game with a steering wheel is more fun than one that uses a controller. But without doing the research, you cannot know when common sense will prove wrong. Even if only 1 in 10 studies deviates from intuition, there is no way to predict which ones will deviate. In contrast to the driving study, for example, another study found that a motion-controlled bowling game was less enjoyable than one that used a traditional controller, and another study came to the same conclusion for a football game. Without conducting those studies, we might have assumed that motion controls and similar innovations are always better, but clearly something else is going on. Because intuition is largely based on widely held beliefs and past experience, even if both are mostly correct, there is no way to anticipate when they will be wrong.

| bias |
| → Unit 3 |
| **tenacity** |
| → Unit 3 |
| **authority** |
| → Unit 3 |

Reflect & React: Counterintuitive Findings

Here are some examples of findings that could be considered counterintuitive: (1) Wright and Bae (2013) found that men who viewed pornography regularly became more tolerant of homosexuality. (2) Halevy, Shalvi, and Verschuere (2014) found that just 5 percent of people account for 40 percent of the lies told in a given day, and those individuals appear to have been honest about their tendency to lie based on a variety of measures. (3) Knobloch-Westerwick, Gong, Hagner, and Kerbeykian (2013) discovered that watching tragic movies and feeling sad about them made people happier about their lives.

45

Having considered these studies, think of findings in your own life that might not mesh with these particular findings. In what ways do your own experiences run counter to these findings? In what ways do your own experiences corroborate these findings? What further research would you conduct to verify the findings of these studies?

authority
→ Unit 3

intuition
→ Unit 3

Tenacity

When knowledge is based on tenacity, it is linked to some prior instruction or belief that people are unwilling to alter. These beliefs may have been taught by their family, friends, religious leaders, or community members, but ultimately the individual believes them because this is what they have "always" felt. For example, suppose your mother refused to buy any magazines that showed sexualized images when you were growing up, telling you that those magazines were immoral and the women were objectified. Having internalized that belief, you now consider it fact without reflection, and any specific question related to the effects of such images will always be answered the same way. Note that the line between tenacity and authority or intuition is not always sharp. If individuals insist that such a belief was taught to them by someone with special knowledge or expertise, this would instead be an appeal to authority. If individuals do not have a previous belief about a question but simply make a conclusion on the basis of what "feels right," this would be intuition. But ultimately both of these examples share the flaw of tenacity: If we refuse to change our minds in the face of new information, we have no way to ever correct false beliefs.

The critical aspect of tenacity is that it involves consistently applying the same understanding to similar issues, regardless of observation or confirmation. For example, consider someone who believes that television "rots the brain" or makes people less intelligent. Every time this person is asked to make a conclusion about the effect of television, he or she will offer some variation on this idea, regardless of the specific details or what others might say or have observed. The individual need not know anyone who watched a lot of television and became less smart; the individual simply has a strong and consistent belief that shapes his or her understanding.

theory
→ Unit 2

variable
→ Unit 2

sample
→ Unit 8

Replication

Research that re-creates some or all the aspects of a previous study, testing to see whether the results can be reproduced and confirmed, represents replication. This process is critical to gaining knowledge from research. Because each replication involves the collection of new empirical evidence, it means that we don't just keep relying on the same information. Instead, we build a growing pool of knowledge and have a way to identify false beliefs.

In many cases, scholars simply carry out a *partial* replication, in which some aspects of the original study are duplicated but others are changed. By carrying out a partial replication, a researcher can test whether a finding or theory applies to a broader range of contexts. For example, suppose you find that women in Ohio were persuaded by an ad for a new type of car that focused on how the car could connect you to your family, but men were not. You might want to see whether a different product could be advertised similarly; maybe it works for cars but not for vacuum cleaners. If you found this, you would start to better understand the reasons why the ad was effective in the first study. Another example of partial replication would be a study in which you tried to measure the same variable in a different way. You might test the same ad on women in Ohio but have them go shopping after they viewed the ad to see whether their behavior was changed instead of simply asking them about their plans for purchasing.

Exact replication is a more specific type of replication, in which every aspect of the original study is duplicated as carefully as possible—the only difference is that the study uses a different sample. That is, the same methods are used, but on a different group of individuals. This allows researchers to be certain that the original findings were accurate and not just attributable to chance. In some cases, even a well-designed study can produce incorrect results because the sample chosen behaved oddly or other unexpected events occurred. The replication of prior findings is important to confirm that our theories are correct and that our findings are worth acting upon. Consider the example of the Ohio car study once again. Maybe this study was based on talking to just 50 women, and the results weren't very strong. Before a company commits to spending millions of dollars on this new campaign, it would want to be sure that the result would still hold up when tested on additional women. In the academic domain, we don't want to automatically assume we have a strong understanding of communication processes until we're sure they apply to more than a handful of undergraduates in an exploratory study. Replication allows for greater confidence.

Research in Depth: Understanding the Reproducibility Crisis

Over the past two decades, a major question has dogged the social sciences, and psychology in particular: How much confidence should we have in published results? The answer, unfortunately, seems to be "less than we generally assume." This concern has come about for multiple reasons, including unethical behaviors by researchers, problematic research and statistical practices, and publication bias in favor of "significant" results. But the net effect has led to something known as the "reproducibility crisis" (or "replication crisis")—too many studies have never been subjected to a replication, and when those replications finally came the results often didn't reproduce.

Savvy researchers had been warning about this possibility for some time. In 2005, Ioannidis published an influential paper that carried the alarming title "Why Most Published Research Findings Are False." Importantly, we don't know if that dramatic sentence is true; in communication, at least, it likely is not true that the most widely tested theories are incorrect. But the core argument made was important: Because of the strong bias for publishing significant and also unexpected results, a lot of the published research probably represented the most extreme or unusual estimates for relationships that were actually likely to be much smaller or nonexistent.

In the early 2010s, a collaborative effort by dozens of research teams tried to replicate 100 prominent studies in psychology; only about one-third were "significant' in the follow-up study, according to the published results (2015). That doesn't mean that only one-third of the original studies were "correct," though. It is possible that some of the findings from the follow-up study were underestimating the relationships. It's also possible that even some results that were statistically significant twice wouldn't hold up to further testing.

All this illustrates the importance of understanding the overall research process when reading and evaluating studies. Most important, replication and triangulation are vital parts of the research process. A textbook or TED Talk that makes a big deal of a single clever, unexpected study is probably describing a false positive rather than a robust theory. Only when we have accumulated multiple tests of a core idea can we begin to have confidence in the result. And it's important that these tests include exact replications. In some of the examples of psychology findings that didn't hold up, other research had claimed to be testing the same theory but with completely different variables and experimental designs. For reasons we will consider later in this book, these "conceptual" replications didn't actually demonstrate that the theory was robust and the results reliable.

None of this means research is broken or that you cannot trust any of the information you've learned in your classes. Plenty of theories in communication have seen repeated testing that clearly replicates past findings. And good scholarship is coming along, having learned from past mistakes, to develop better tools for ensuring research is cyclical and self-correcting. You can play a role by not being swayed by a single, small study that claims to give "one simple trick" for anything from improving your mood to having the confidence to give a speech. If it sounds like a headline from a dodgy web advertisement, it probably isn't good science.

Ioannidis, J.P. (2005). Why most published research findings are false. *PLoS Medicine, 2*(8), e124. doi:10.1371/journal.pmed.0020124

Open Science Collaboration. (2015). Estimating the reproducibility of psychological science. *Science, 349*(6251), aac4716. doi:10.1126/science.aac4716.

Triangulation

Another way to ensure that results are consistent is *triangulation*. This is when researchers use two or more distinct research methods to explore a single topic or research question. Unlike replication, which uses the same approach as a previous study, in triangulation we want to see whether different techniques give the same outcomes. For example, consider a situation in which you are trying to decide which version of an advertisement to use to generate interest in your product. One approach would be to use an experiment to test which version of an ad is more effective. You could then follow that up with focus groups to gather more detail on why one version of the ad was preferred and to ask participants in the group to weigh in on which ad they prefer. By using both approaches, you get a fuller picture of not only which ad is preferred but also why the ad is preferred, gaining both depth and breadth on the topic.

Another way to think about triangulation is using flashlights to look into a dark room. If you shine just one flashlight, you will be able to see a bit of the room and learn some things about it. Yet much of the room will remain dark. However, if you add a second flashlight shining from a different direction, you will learn even more about the room. Parts where both lights are shining on the same spot will be especially bright, but other areas of the room will be exposed as well. Therefore, you will be able to see things in greater detail and also see things you didn't notice before. If we apply this idea to research, it would be the equivalent of using a survey questionnaire, for example, to learn about an issue and then following up with qualitative interviews on selected participants to get further information on the topic. The survey provides some initial insights and a sense of what is going on, but adding a second method allows for greater detail and clarification. Further, the use of the two (or more) methods allows a researcher to offset some of the weaknesses that individual methods have. Just as using one flashlight from one spot allows you to peek into a room yet leaves a lot of that room darkened, using just one method will give some valuable insights into our units of analysis but likely will miss some key elements as well. It is the process of combining different methods that allows for multiple perspectives and data points on an issue, leading us to a more comprehensive and fuller understanding of a topic.

research questions
→ Unit 2

replication
→ Unit 3

experiment
→ Unit 9

focus groups
→ Unit 12

qualitative versus quantitative
→ Unit 3

Voices from Industry

Chris Nietupski—Communication Consultant

Chris Nietupski has more than 16 years of experience in the field of communication from various perspectives—working for Fortune 20 corporations, small businesses, communication agencies, and leading nonprofit organizations. Chris is a perceptive, positive, and articulate team leader and liaison who excels at mentoring and developing others and inspiring team commitment and accomplishment. Establishing strategic alliances and partnerships, strategizing and implementing high-profile programs, and creating reciprocal exposure opportunities are highlights of his professional performance. Characterized as a strategic thinker and a problem solver, Chris routinely identifies process bottlenecks, implements quality improvements, and increases productivity and efficiency. Delegating team assignments, strategically allocating project resources, and going beyond the job description to achieve business objectives have been the consistent results.

Why are good research skills important to your field?

I can't think of a day on the job when my research skill set isn't tested and my proficiency that I began honing in higher education environments rewarded.

On the individual level, from the get-go, stepping into the interview, the more you know about the company and the industry, the better. Corporate life can be cutthroat, and while teamwork is praised, the cream rises to the top. Young professionals looking to climb the corporate ladder quickly would be wise to use research and data to develop and support each and every assertion they make in the conference room. In this way, you may very well stand out above the others.

At the company level, if you're a major player in your industry, you will be constantly scrutinized by your competition, the media, and your target clients. Utilizing prepared research that is analyzed, digested, and delivered in meaningful sound bites can help people associate positive images with your brand on their own. Consider an article published offering a tough yet fair look into your industry. Public relations pros that deliver prepared and thoughtful messages to reporters backed up by research may be spared in the article or positioned in a more positive light than competitors who shied away.

What specific method or methods do you use or encounter most?

Corporations love using quantitative data to shape their story in a positive light. As a result, corporate communication professionals are often asked to develop employee and customer surveys. You'd be surprised how many professionals fail to grasp even the most basic lessons in a research stats class regarding sampling, significance, question structure, and so forth. Bringing this skill set to the table will allow the company to unearth statistically significant research with tangible uses and will separate you from your peers as you demonstrate proficiency and help grow their bottom line.

Can you name some specific instances for which you have used data collected from research?

Absolutely. I consulted with a health care company that was implementing wellness clinics at employee call centers around the country. Nearly a year after opening a handful of clinics, noticeable declines in use were noted. Quantitative data collected by surveys showed us that employees were excited about the existence of the clinics but failed to get at the root of the issues. I was brought in to execute individual and group qualitative interviews that were recorded and then coded to uncover far deeper issues. Specifically, the clinics were still a hit, yet management wasn't allowing for proper time away to utilize them.

How did the research you conducted help inform your decision?

We were able to recommend strategies that worked with management to encourage and reward clinic use as opposed to discouraging it. As a result, clinic use rose and justified the expense of their implementation. Had we not utilized a qualitative research approach in conjunction with our quantitative surveys, it is possible the clinics would have closed and would have been inaccurately deemed a failure, costing the company millions of dollars.

What are one or two pieces of advice or insights you would give about research to students in a communication research methods course?

KEEP UP AND LEAD: When I entered the professional world, master's degrees were preferred but not required. Now they are much more commonplace and many times a prerequisite. A background in research methods at one time could give you a leg up on the competition, but now it may end up simply keeping you in the game. Not a day will go by that you will regret what you learned about the execution of research methods in the professional world.

THE ACT OF RESEARCHING: You may leave school without remembering the name of one single theory or method; however, mastering the skills needed to conduct research properly will place you ahead of the pack every day. Research takes the skills of forethought, discipline, patience, and evaluation. And even if you think you'll never use this training again—though trust me, you will—these skills are transferable to nearly endless aspects of your professional life.

Secondary Analysis

Not every study involves developing original measures and collecting new data. Many existing sources of data are available, and these can help test hypotheses and advance theory as well. The use of existing data to test additional research questions is known as secondary analysis. For example, the General Social Survey has been conducted for decades and includes basic measures of media use as well as questions about attitudes regarding a variety of issues, such as fear

representative sample
→ Unit 8

trend
→ Unit 10

longitudinal design
→ Unit 10

51

of crime and tolerance of homosexuality. Scholars have used the General Social Survey to test predictions generated from cultivation theory, among others.

Secondary analysis offers several advantages. Often, the data are drawn from a large, high-quality representative sample. Collecting those data yourself would be prohibitively difficult and expensive, but many secondary data sets are publicly available or can be purchased for a small fee. Additionally, because the data are widely available, you can compare your findings to those of other studies, both to ensure that your work is novel and to see how it relates to other research. Finally, many publicly available data sets have been collected regularly, providing an opportunity for trend studies. Even if you wanted to develop your own study spanning decades, you would have to wait for that time to pass before you could evaluate your findings. Because secondary analysis can look back in time across many prior studies, you can immediately carry out elaborate longitudinal analysis.

However, secondary analysis also presents some disadvantages. A study designed by other researchers is unlikely to include every variable of interest to your study. Moreover, the measures used may be too simplistic or have shortcomings in validity. Often, large data collections prioritize consistency across time and broad appeal rather than careful measurement of a few important concepts. Thus, secondary analysis is most often used as a way to replicate and expand findings from more focused studies rather than as the primary source of insight.

Publication Bias

Replication and triangulation are important processes to help address bias as well as minimize the effects of random error. But these processes can only improve our knowledge if they are shared. Unfortunately, publication bias is a common problem where both researchers and journals often favor studies that produce certain results. Most often, this means that studies that have statistical significance are more likely to be submitted to journals, more likely to be published in those journals, and more likely to be noticed when they are published. That is, a study that finds larger differences will get more attention than one with smaller differences. Other sources of publication bias can be from the tenacity of researchers who are convinced they already know the answer to key questions based on prior findings or even their own beliefs and superstitions.

Publication bias is a critical flaw in the scientific process. Research is cyclical and self-correcting, but only when the strongest studies with the most robust results are all available. If worse studies are published only because they had unexpected or unusually large findings, it undermines the self-correcting nature of science. Fortunately, the research community in many fields is increasingly aware of this problem, but it will take time and effort to overcome many years of bad habits. You can help in many ways. Learn to tell good research from bad and to focus on the quality of the methods rather than the drama of the findings. Resist believing news stories, speakers, and even textbooks that insist a single study provides conclusive knowledge. But also remember that being wrong is part of the research process, and the only way we can eventually overcome false knowledge is by continuing to do research rather than reverting to intuition or tenacity.

Goals of Research

While all research provides information about relationships, not all research has the same purpose. When an area of study is new or little is known, researchers often engage in exploration and seek merely to identify the important variables. In some cases, researchers try to develop a basic understanding of the world and simply describe key variables, thereby painting a picture of the universe they are trying to understand. In other instances, the goal is to explain why things are happening. Of course, researchers also want to make good decisions and be able to predict future behavior—such as whether the advertisement they have designed will work or not. It is important to note, however, that the progression through these goals is not always linear. Researchers are constantly learning new things, and therefore at times they may be exploring and explaining at the same time, or they may be able to explain and predict some things while exploring or describing others. This illustrates the cyclical nature of the research process.

Steps to Success: Goals of Research

Following this checklist can help you decide what the primary goal of your research project is going to be. Be sure to search the literature for relevant studies and theoretical perspectives on your research topic. Check yes or no for each of the following statements.

If you answer yes to any of the following statements, then one of the goals of your research is exploration:

There are few conclusive research studies on my topic: Yes ___ No ___
There is no clear sense of the key variables for this topic: Yes ___ No ___
Relevant theories are speculative and not clearly tested: Yes ___ No ___

If you answer yes to any of the following statements, then one of the goals of your research is description:

Key variables have been identified, but not much is known about them:
Yes ___ No ___
Previous research has only considered a few populations: Yes ___ No ___

If you answer yes to any of the following statements, then one of the goals of your research is explanation:

The topic of study is well documented, but it is unclear which variables are independent and which are dependent: Yes ___ No ___
Understanding of causal relationships for key variables is unclear: Yes ___ No ___
It is clear something is happening, but researchers aren't sure why: Yes ___ No ___
Findings in this area have yet to be confirmed or replicated: Yes ___ No ___

If you answer yes to any of the following statements, then one of the goals of your research is application:

Many studies have been conducted, but few have explored what happens in "real-world" contexts: Yes ___ No ___
The theory behind the research seems sound, but it isn't clear how the findings can be used by industry professionals: Yes ___ No ___
You have specific practical goals and want to be sure they can be met through a planned communication process: Yes ___ No ___

cyclical → Unit 1 **theory** → Unit 2 **description** → Unit 3 **exploration** → Unit 3 **explanation** → Unit 3	

Application

As students, a lot of the research you encounter is conducted by scholars who are focused on developing a theory and more fully understanding communication. But that is only a small slice of all the research that is done. Much of it is applied, meaning that it focuses on answering concrete questions that allow for practical responses to naturally occurring situations. In this case, the purpose of the research is to address those specific issues, not to expand theory. Such research can offer description, exploration, or explanation, just like theory-driven research, so long as it also fulfills a practical goal. If you are advertising a product, you might not care as much about the larger theory of how thin-ideal models affect consumers. But you might have a practical concern about whether your specific advertisement is ethical or likely to cause a backlash. Understanding the specific effects of the images you choose for that ad will be important, and answering that question demonstrates applied research. As another example, a political campaign will poll potential voters to see which issues they think are most important, and it will use that information to suggest topics for the candidate to focus on in future speeches. Similarly, an advertising agency might want to test the effectiveness of a campaign by showing consumers examples of their new ads and then asking for responses. In such cases, the goal is not to reach general conclusions about how all voters feel or all consumers behave but to determine the best course of action in this situation and to be able to act on that information. This research still tries to find relationships. The link between the issue presented and voter attitudes, or the connection between seeing a particular ad and having specific feelings about a product, are types of relationships. However, the focus is finding patterns that can have practical use.

Even though applied research is sometimes contrasted with theory-driven research, the two can work together. Many scholars will include a discussion of practical applications even when their research tests theories. A study of video games might explain the reasons players enjoy a game in terms of broad psychological processes—games work best when players feel they have the freedom to make powerful choices. But that study also has implications for people who develop games, and the authors may discuss how better educational games could be made by providing certain options. On the other hand, game developers might simply want to find out how players respond to different options in a game, but they could still draw upon the theoretical literature to help generate ideas for the design.

Exploration

A first step for many researchers when considering a topic that has received little research is to design a study for exploration. This research looks for potential relationships among variables and provides basic insights about topics not yet considered by researchers. For example, research on the effects of thin-ideal models might have started by interviewing women to see what kinds of feelings and behaviors they report in response to such images, or with a content analysis of pictures in magazines to identify common tropes. In an exploratory study, scholars tend to consider variables whose connections have not yet been tested. They might also test whether findings from different types of content might apply in a new context. For example, an exploratory study might set out to learn whether Internet users have the same motivations as consumers of television and newspapers, without having any firm expectations. Unlike descriptive studies, exploratory studies may include many variables not already known to be related, and they are not meant to offer firm measures of those relationships. Unlike explanatory studies, exploratory studies make no attempt to provide a clear test of how and why variables are related, seeking only to see whether a correlation can be found.

In general, exploration is the first step of research. It provides empirical evidence to show a relationship but doesn't go beyond that. Future studies that

variable → Unit 2
description → Unit 3
explanation → Unit 3
correlation → Unit 15
empirical → Unit 1
replication → Unit 3
prediction → Unit 2

replicate exploratory findings might try to make more sense of the results and quantify them more precisely. Exploratory studies are a great starting point if you can't find any relevant research on a topic. For example, you might want to know how exposure to video game streaming affects views of the games played. A literature search might reveal several interesting studies about other kinds of game advertising and even some preliminary studies of why people like streamers, but nothing that directly reflects how they feel about the games. You could start looking into this topic with an exploratory study that simply asked many questions of those who watch video game streams, looking for examples of opinions about the games and factors that predict those opinions, without any clear sense of which factors are likely to emerge as important. Once you evaluate these exploratory data, you might form some clearer expectations that could be more precisely described or even make predictions about how and why variables are related that could be tested with explanatory research.

variable
→ Unit 2

causality
→ Unit 2

theory
→ Unit 2

application
→ Unit 3

survey
→ Unit 10

Description

Some research focuses on providing a description of relationships without necessarily explaining those relationships. That is, this *descriptive* research identifies patterns that link variables, often in a way that confirms existing patterns established in other studies. But it doesn't try to identify the reasons why those relationships exist or show clear causality between variables. If you are studying the relationship between thin-ideal media and self-esteem, you might conduct a representative survey to confirm the average self-esteem among consumers of such media, and the strength of any correlation. Descriptive research plays an important role in the larger process of theory development. It also provides clear benefits for applied research. Descriptive research helps establish under what conditions specific relationships occur and how strong those relationships are. Showing the degree to which two variables are related can help with application by determining whether a specific variable is important enough to consider.

For example, consider a company that wants to know how to increase employee morale. The company may call in a research consultant to determine how much employees value several different techniques to boost morale, such as providing additional benefits, changing the appearance of the workplace, and using different communication techniques to talk with employees. By conducting a survey, the consultant could describe exactly how much each technique was valued. This research would not be explanatory; the exact reasons why employees valued one approach more than another would not be measured. But the research is also not merely exploratory, as the study would start from a list of possible ways to make employees happy.

More generally, description is contrasted with exploratory and explanatory research. It falls in between these two goals. Descriptive research tries to establish the exact relationship among variables already known to be important, but it does not try to show why those variables are related. In some cases, a study might have to settle for describing relationships because proposed explanatory mechanisms could not be fully established.

Explanation

The goal of much academic research is not merely to explore or describe relationships but to explain them. Explanatory research tries not only to clearly measure relationships but also to understand the reasons why variables are related. In trying to understand the relationship between thin-ideal media and self-esteem, you would ultimately want to know why exposure to one could reduce the other. One explanation could be social comparison theory, which states that people tend to contrast themselves with others. Thin-ideal media present an opportunity for upward comparison, when people think they compare poorly with others and feel bad as a result. Research to test this could design a careful experience that manipulated media exposure and also encouraged or discouraged social comparison. If people only reacted poorly to the thin-ideal content when they were prompted to engage in social comparison, then we would have a better sense of what was happening. Furthermore, we could actually use this to help people who experience lower self-esteem and other harms as a result of exposure. By training them to avoid social comparison and providing media literacy to help them understand that images of models are not a realistic basis for such comparison, we can help them resist these messages. Research that offers explanations is critical to developing and testing theories. To provide a meaningful explanation, research must do at least one of two things: establish a causal relationship or identify intermediate mechanisms that account for relationships.

Both of these ideas can be illustrated by thinking about the relationship between watching entertainment news shows such as *The Daily Show* and voting. A descriptive study could show that these two things are correlated: People who watch *The Daily Show* are more likely to vote. But there are many possible reasons for that relationship. People who already vote might be drawn to *The Daily Show* because the humor appeals to them or because they are interested in politics and want to learn about the campaign. An explanatory study could help establish whether watching *The Daily Show* actually *causes* people to vote more. Beyond that, a study might also show what connects these two behaviors. For example, watching *The Daily Show* might cause people to also consume mainstream news about politics, and this, in turn, could prompt voting. Or, watching *The Daily Show* might lead people to talk about politics with their friends, which might make them more interested in voting. In summary, explanation involves making sense of the relationship between two or more variables by establishing which variable causes which and what mediating variables help create these connections.

variable
→ Unit 2

exploration
→ Unit 3

theory
→ Unit 2

causality
→ Unit 2

mediation
→ Unit 2

Qualitative Versus Quantitative

Research doesn't just vary in the kinds of questions it seeks to answer. It also varies in the kinds of evidence it produces. One key distinction in research is between qualitative and quantitative approaches—that is, between approaches that focus on detailed description and those that focus on numbers. Often, students assume that research requires statistics and counting. While quantitative research involving numbers can be very useful, it is not the only type of data used in research. Qualitative research involves providing a nuanced description of individuals without counting or otherwise assigning numbers for each variable. Qualitative analysis looks for patterns or interesting details in these descriptions without trying to employ statistics or provide firm numerical estimates.

Many concepts can be measured both quantitatively and qualitatively. Our example of studying thin-ideal media can illustrate this. You could easily talk with people who had just viewed such images, asking them to describe their feelings. Or you could come up with a list of questions that measure self-esteem, using a 7-point scale, and have them pick the number representing their response to each to compute a single number that reflects their current self-esteem. Another example comes from research on the theory of agenda setting—the public's issue agenda. This can be quantified by having people rank a set of issues from first to last. The highest-ranked issue is assigned a 1, and so on, down to the last issue. In this way, it is easy to average the rank of each issue and assign them numbers. However, important details might be missed. A qualitative approach could simply let individuals name the issues they thought were important and discuss how important they found each one (as well as the reasons for this). This would allow you to find out about issues you might not have thought to include and to better understand why specific individuals were highlighted.

Each type of research has its advantages. When relationships are relatively small, using statistics can help you be confident the pattern you're seeing is real and not just a reflection of your personal biases or expectations. Qualitative research won't allow for such precise measurement. Quantitative research is also useful when exact numbers are important for the population. For example, political polls give the exact percentage of respondents who indicate they will vote for each candidate. Elections are decided based on numbers, so being able to estimate those numbers is very important. Finally, quantitative research tends to be more intersubjective than qualitative work. Because the researcher has to decide whether a pattern is clear and which responses reflect similar concepts, there is a greater tendency toward subjectivity in qualitative studies. However, qualitative research can be much more detailed and is less likely to miss important ideas simply because they don't fit an established numerical measurement. This is especially true when focused on exploratory research. Because scholars don't know much about the topic in advance, any quantitative scale they come up with is likely to miss important factors, and since all the researchers have is a set of numbers, those gaps won't be obvious. A qualitative approach would allow participants to identify the topics that matter to them, revealing material that otherwise would have been missed.

Parts of a Research Article

A critical aspect of developing knowledge through research is being able to access and understand prior research findings. Most scholarly research is presented in a standard article format, which will include an abstract, literature review, method section, results section, discussion, and other common elements. Such articles appear in peer-reviewed journals. In the peer-review process, other experts in the field carefully read and evaluate submitted articles. Only those articles that receive approval from reviewers are published in the journal. These journals present research so that other scholars can draw upon, evaluate, and potentially replicate the insights gleaned from the original study.

Because the development and dissemination of knowledge is an important part of academic life, researchers face considerable pressure to carry out and publish such scholarship. Publication is therefore a competitive process, and the peer-review system helps ensure that the theory, method, and results of a study all make sense and meet the standard of intersubjectivity. Peer review does not ensure that only flawless research is published, as even the results from flawed studies can offer important insights; all research papers include a discussion of future directions, listing potential shortcomings and ideas about how additional research could take the findings further. But peer review does help winnow out particularly weak or flawed studies and ensure that results are presented in a valid way. To help ease this process and the dissemination of research, scholars have developed a standard format for presenting findings. Learning the elements of this format can help you read and understand scholarly research more easily and find the most important information for your purposes.

Steps to Success: Effectively Reading a Research Article

Reading a research article can seem like a daunting task at times. Following a systematic approach can help you get the most out of the articles you read. Here are some steps and guiding questions to use as you read an article:

1. Start by reading the abstract and understanding the broad goals and method of the research article.

2. As you read through the literature review, note the different theories that are discussed and the expected relationships between concepts that are presented. Before moving on from the literature review, ask yourself the following questions: Do I understand why the researchers predicted the hypotheses? What is known and not known about this area of study?

3. In reading the method section, note details about the sample size as well as how the units of analysis were selected. Also look critically at how variables were measured. Before moving on from the methods section, ask yourself the following questions: Are the measurement strategies for key variables valid? How might I improve them or change them? Is the method appropriate for the topic of study and the hypotheses proposed?

4. In reading the results section, look for clarity of data presentation. Look closely at figures and tables and develop a clear understanding of the central findings of the paper. Take note of which hypotheses were supported by the data and which were not. Before moving on from the results section, ask yourself the following questions: Are figures and tables clear and effective in presenting data? Are the results clearly stated such that it is evident which hypotheses were supported and which were not?

5. In reading the discussion section, take note of the key findings of the study. You should also note limitations and suggestions for future directions. Compare the discussion to the results to see whether the authors are accurately describing their findings and to the literature review to see whether they actually answered their core research questions. Before finishing your reading of the discussion section, ask yourself the following questions: Do the conclusions drawn by the researchers match their data? Do the researchers clearly acknowledge any limitations of their methods or measures?

---

sample
→ Unit 8

Abstract

The abstract is a brief description of a research article that appears at the beginning of the article (after the title and author information but before the introduction or literature review). The purpose of the abstract is to give the reader a sense of what the article is about and whether the article is worth further reading. A good abstract should include the following information: theoretical focus, sample characteristics and size, key findings, and implications of the findings. In some cases, authors will mention key limitations faced by the study. A typical abstract ranges from 75 to 120 words, although the length varies based on the specific journal and discipline. In any case, the reader should come away with a clear sense of the purpose of the article based on reading the abstract. Here is a sample abstract:

Information-seeking behavior in audiences is vital to news users and producers. While it seems intuitive that photos contribute to audience interest, little research has explicitly tested their role in generating information seeking. We assess the influence of photographs on information seeking about study abroad using one of three experimental conditions—(1) story with no photo, (2) story with classroom photo, or (3) story with class photo in an outdoor setting—using a sample of 327 undergraduate students from a mid-size Midwestern university. Findings indicate support for the visual framing perspective, such that the classroom photo suppresses information seeking and interest. Implications for information seeking and news production are discussed.

Literature Review

The literature review is one of the main sections of a research report or journal article. The purpose is to review the relevant and notable literature in a given area and present a clear argument based on that literature. Any previous research publications or other sources that are mentioned in the literature review should be fully cited in the reference list. The literature review allows the reader to understand the broader context for the study the researchers are conducting and what is known and not known in that area. In doing so, the literature review should begin the concept explication process by presenting and defining key concepts used in the study. Perhaps most important, the literature review allows researchers to provide the theoretical framework that is being tested. In some cases, multiple theories are presented and discussed, particularly if there are competing explanations of a phenomenon or if a phenomenon is sufficiently complex as to require two or more theories to explain.

Hypotheses and research questions are typically stated in the literature review, after the researchers present their discussion of relevant theories and previous research. The reader should never be confused by the hypotheses stated at the end of the literature review. In a good literature review, the hypotheses should emerge clearly and make sense to the reader. The reader should also fully understand the context of the study and the history of the phenomenon under study. By adequately addressing what is known and not known, researchers provide a firm foundation for their own research, allowing the reader to understand the unique contribution that a study makes to the field.

Method Section

The method section should provide all the necessary detail that would allow other researchers to replicate the study being described. First, researchers should make clear the specific method that is being employed (e.g., experiment, survey, or focus group) in the study and provide any necessary justification for that approach. Second, researchers should clearly describe the sample—including the number of participants, their basic demographics, and other relevant characteristics—as well as the sampling approach used to recruit participants. Any incentives provided to participants should be presented in the method section.

reference list
→ Unit 3

concept explication
→ Unit 5

hypotheses
→ Unit 2

research questions
→ Unit 2

replication
→ Unit 3

experiment
→ Unit 9

survey
→ Unit 10

focus group
→ Unit 12

sample
→ Unit 8

incentive
→ Unit 8

variable
→ Unit 2

indicators
→ Unit 5

descriptive statistics
→ Unit 14

61

Finally, clear details should be provided for all variables measured as part of the study. Often, researchers will organize this section by separating the independent, dependent, and control variables, but this is not always necessary. In any case, for each variable, it should be clear how many indicators were used to measure it, what the basic descriptive statistics are for the variable (e.g., range, standard deviation, or mean) any appropriate reliability measures (if needed), as well as what the response options were (e.g., on a 5-point scale, where 1 denotes "disagree completely" and 5 denotes "agree completely"). Because space is limited, full question wording for each item is often included in an appendix, but researchers should provide a basic sense of the individual indicators used. If measures were derived from previously published scales, those should be clearly cited.

Results Section

The results section is one of the most important sections of a research report or journal article. It directly follows the method section and precedes the discussion section in a typical quantitative research report. The answers to any research questions or outcomes of any hypothesis testing are presented in the results section. A good results section will clearly and directly test all hypotheses and answer all research questions in a succinct and clear manner. Further, in the case of quantitative analytical methods, the researcher should indicate any statistical tests that were used while also including the following: relevant coefficients, p-values, degrees of freedom (df) when necessary, and any appropriate measures of power or effect size. For example, we might encounter the following in a results section dealing with the third-person perception:

> H1 stated that participants would perceive other college students as more affected by violent movies than themselves. This hypothesis was tested using a t-test, which revealed that estimates of effects on self ($M = 3.6$; $SD = 1.4$) were smaller than estimates of effects on others ($M = 4.5$; $SD = 1.4$)—t ($df = 180$) $= 3.14$; $p = .04$. As such, H1 was supported.

Note that the hypothesis is restated, the statistical test used to evaluate it is clearly stated, and the outcome of the test is made clear as well.

The results section should be straightforward. The place for expanding on the meaning of findings and relating things back to theory is the discussion section. The objective of the results section is to simply present the results of the observations, tests, and other analytical procedures that were conducted in a concise way. In quantitative research, results sections can be quite "numbers heavy," so it is important to develop some familiarity with basic statistical concepts such as p-values, coefficients, and inferential statistical tests. This will improve your ability to comprehend results sections and allow you to better critique the discussion section, where researchers talk about what their results mean.

Discussion Section

The discussion section of a research article provides the reader with a sense of the implications of the findings presented in the results section. The discussion section is an opportunity for the authors to elaborate on what the results suggest and to provide a sense of what those findings mean for the theories presented in the literature review. The discussion should also indicate why the findings are important to relevant fields or subfields (e.g., political communication scholars, small-group scholars), as well as to professionals and practitioners in those relevant fields. For instance, a research study that shows the valuable role that interpersonal communication can play in generating higher rates of political participation would be useful broadly to communication scholars but also specifically to political communication scholars, interpersonal communication scholars, political strategists, nonprofit executives, and political activists, among others.

Beyond discussing both the general and specific implications of the research, the discussion section should also clarify any limitations of the research study and provide suggestions for future directions. It is essential to discuss the limitations of any research project because this gives the reader context for how confident they should be in the findings and provides an opportunity for the authors of the study to indicate areas they would like to improve. Every research study has at least some limitations. Common ones include issues with question wording, less-than-ideal samples, and variables or concepts that were omitted because of lack of space or time. Because of this, the limitations portion of a discussion section often leads to fruitful ideas for future research. Therefore, it is good practice as you read research articles throughout this course to pay close attention to the limitations the authors discuss. Consider whether some limitations are discussed more frequently than others and whether you saw a limitation but it was not mentioned by the authors.

| literature review |
| → Unit 3 |
| **future directions** |
| → Unit 3 |
| **sample** |
| → Unit 8 |
| **concept explication** |
| → Unit 5 |

Future Directions

After discussing what their findings mean, it is important for researchers to make suggestions for additional research on a given topic to guide future study in an area. These suggestions for future research are typically provided near the end of the discussion section, after the limitations of the study have been addressed. Often these suggestions involve ideas for improving measurement and question wording, suggestions for using different samples (e.g., would a nonstudent population respond differently to this study?), and suggestions for considering different contexts or topics for the theory tested in the current study. Researchers also show that they are aware of the limitations of their own study by offering suggestions for how future studies could improve upon the work that they have done. Further, such suggestions often lead to valuable follow-up research that

| population |
| → Unit 8 |
| **theory** |
| → Unit 2 |
| **scope** |
| → Unit 2 |

63

allows researchers to improve and expand on knowledge in a given area but also understand the limitations and scope of any theory or method.

Reference List

This list should provide the road map for locating any sources that are discussed in the research article. While there are numerous citation styles available, two of the most common in the field of communication are APA (American Psychological Association) style and Chicago style (outlined in the *Chicago Manual of Style*). Although there are some differences between these styles, the primary information included in each is similar. Typically, each entry in a reference list should include the following: author name(s), year of publication, title of article (or chapter in a book), source title (including journals, books, or other edited volumes), page numbers, and sometimes the volume number for journal articles. Book entries will also include the name and city of the publishing company, as well as the names of any editors for edited volumes. It is important to note that each journal will have its own specifications; researchers must also note that style rules are periodically updated and change over time. Therefore, whenever authors submit their research articles for consideration in journals, they must consider the specific needs of the journal and consult the website or handbook for the style being used.

- Information on APA style can be found at www.apastyle.org
- Information on Chicago style can be found at www.chicagomanualofstyle.org.

Appendix (or Appendices)

Researchers often have limited space in writing research reports, book chapters, or journal articles, so they need to focus on crafting a strong literature review, giving clear methodological detail, writing up results, and drawing conclusions. Further, certain types of information—such as a survey questionnaire—would not work well included in the main body of an article. However, at times this additional information on experimental stimuli, question wording, or other contextual information is necessary to include so that readers can clearly interpret and potentially replicate a study. Such information is often included in an appendix, which appears after the main body of the article (typically after the discussion section but before the reference list).

If a researcher uses an appendix to provide more information, he or she should refer to that appendix by its appropriate letter designation in the body of the article. For example, "For a complete list of the items used in this study, please see Appendix A." The reader knows that the passage in the body of the article refers to a specific appendix and can consult that appendix for

literature review
→ Unit 3

questionnaire
→ Unit 7

stimulus
→ Unit 9

replication
→ Unit 3

more information. With the growth of electronic distribution of articles, some appendices are only published online, allowing the journal to save space and printing costs while making more detailed information available for scholars who may need it in their own research.

Tables

Researchers are often looking for compact ways to present data and the results of statistical tests to readers. Two ways this challenge is sometimes met are tables and figures. Tables are probably the more common of the two, representing a simple grid within which important statistics or other information can be presented. Tables should be clearly labeled and designed so that they stand alone from the research report. Before preparing tables, it is important to consult the appropriate style guidelines for the journal you are submitting the manuscript to, as there are often differences in labeling and overall presentation from one journal to another. Generally speaking, the columns and rows of a table should be clearly labeled, and any necessary notes needed to improve understanding and readability of the table should be included directly below the table. For example, common notations include clarification of measurement question wording (e.g., higher scores = more support), groups for sorting variables (e.g., male = 1 and female = 0), and p-values (* $p < .05$) for coefficients.

An important point about tables (and figures) is that the table itself (see Table 3.1) does not constitute evidence, and the inclusion of data in a table does not mean the actual study is any stronger. Space and format restrictions

figures
→ Unit 3

statistics
→ Unit 14

***p*-value**
→ Unit 15

Table 3.1 ANCOVA for media news information seeking, discussion information seeking, sharing information, and interest by photo condition controlling for story length

	No photo	Outside photo	Classroom photo	*F*-value	*p*-value
Information seeking through news media	3.80A (.156)	3.79A (.152)	3.24B (.157)	4.173	.016
Information seeking through discussion	3.88AB (.191)	4.19A (.186)	3.45B (.193)	3.844	.023
Information sharing via expression	3.31A (.128)	3.14AB (.125)	2.74B (.130)	5.048	.007
Interest in study abroad	4.06A (.169)	3.84AB (.164)	3.48B (.171)	2.964	.053

Source: Boyle & Schmierbach (2008).

Notes: Standard errors are in parentheses; Means with different superscripts are statistically different at the $p < .05$ level using Scheffe's post hoc tests.

may preclude including some results in tables, but the results are still important and subject to peer review. Conversely, just because data are presented in a table, that doesn't mean those data were gathered in a valid and appropriate manner. Remember when reading articles that tables are a way to clarify and concisely explain the results, but the results themselves are what matter.

Figures

Figures are visual ways that scholars can present research to their audience. Figures are typically found either in the body of the article near the finding that is illustrated or included in the appendix. The goal is for the figure to effectively convey information to the audience. As such, a few tips should be followed. First, good figures should have a clear title that allows the figure to stand alone if it were to be viewed without the context of the journal article. Second, high contrast and clear labeling should be used as well, so that a quick look at the figure will reveal the core finding and meaning demonstrated by it. Common figures are bar graphs and line graphs. Figures can be used effectively to show differences in scores across treatment conditions of an experiment, to visually demonstrate a statistical interaction, or to compare scores across a range of sorting variables (e.g., demographics), among other uses.

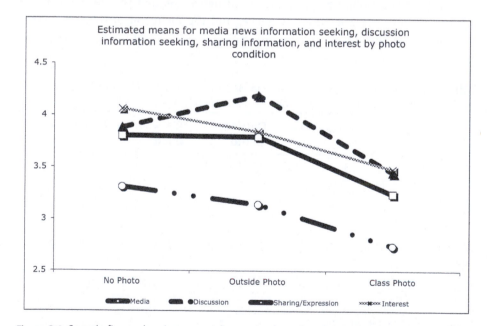

Figure 3.1 Sample figure showing correct formatting based on APA style, 6th edition
Source: Boyle and Schmierbach (2008).

Steps to Success: Identifying Research Articles

Understanding the elements of a research article is only one part of the process of building upon previous knowledge. You also want to be sure that you can find good articles to review in the first place. Not every study that describes itself as research or contains numbers is a peer-reviewed publication. Here are some tips to help find articles and make sure what you've found fits the criteria for high-quality research.

1. Know where to search. An ordinary Google search is not a good way to find research. Use a specialized search engine. Most university libraries will have options for conducting a search and ways to specify that you're looking for peer-reviewed work and for a journal article. Alternatively, Google does offer their Google Scholar tool, which can be useful. If your school allows it, there are even ways to specify within Scholar what library you're searching from, so you can find links to any articles that are available electronically or on the shelf.
2. Pay attention to the source. Depending on the search engine, not everything you find will be a research article from a trustworthy journal. Sometimes magazines and even newspapers will report on research and come up in a search, but these do not publish original research. If an author is writing about their work, it can help guide your search, but a column in a magazine is not a place where original research is presented.
3. When in doubt, check the publication's website. If you aren't sure whether something is a scholarly, peer-reviewed source, you can go to their website and look for details. A scholarly outlet will include information for contributors and details about the peer-review process. It will have an editor and editorial board primarily made up of notable faculty at reputable universities from throughout the country or world.
4. Watch out for low-quality and scam journals. Unfortunately, there is a lot of money to be made in publishing articles, and where there is money there are people willing to commit fraud. A growing number of bogus "predatory" journals claim to provide peer review and to be selective outlets for publication, but they charge high fees to print articles and actually do little other than cash the check. A librarian named Jeffrey Beall used to maintain a list of suspect journals at publishers, but he has stopped maintaining that list. It is archived online and still remains a useful resource (http://beallslist.weebly.com). That same page provides other helpful links, including guidelines for how to spot a predatory journal. In communication, it is extremely rare for journals to charge publication fees, so one sign that you should avoid a journal is if it prominently indicates the cost of publishing. Other signs include journal websites that emphasize the speed and ease of publication; journals that seem absurdly broad in scope, covering everything from psychiatry to computer science, for example; and websites and articles that seem poorly formatted and edited, indicating that the journal isn't actually providing even minimal pagination and proofreading. Many reputable journals in communication are associated with one of the major organizations in

67

the field, including the International Communication Association, the National Communication Association, the Association for Education in Journalism and Mass Communication, the American Academy of Advertising, and the American Psychological Association.

5. Know the difference between theses, dissertations, conference presentations, and journal articles. Graduate students (and even some undergraduates) write theses and dissertations as part of their degrees. These can be excellent works of scholarship and great resources for finding references, but they have not undergone the same review process as published work. They will be clearly labeled as a thesis or dissertation, and instead of a journal as the source it will most often list a university. Conferences are gatherings of scholars where research papers are presented, sometimes as completed work and other times based on abstracts, outlines, or proposals. On occasion, these papers are compiled in a proceedings journal. But otherwise, they are not considered published, and they may not be as carefully reviewed and edited as a journal article. Watch for citations that indicate the paper was "presented at" a specific conference or event, giving a location and date.

6. Exercise your own judgment. Compare the format and content of the article to the description of common features of research articles in this text. Read the explanation of the method employed to see if it makes sense and is described in detail. Look at the references to see if the authors seem aware of the literature and are citing appropriate work. And remember that just because something is published—even in a top-tier journal—it isn't necessarily a good study. Research is cyclical and self-correcting. Sometimes flawed or incomplete studies are published, and as scholars we work together to sift out that work and correct it with better research.

Other Types of Articles

Although most of the work published in peer-reviewed journals follows the typical format of a research article described earlier, not every publication in a peer-reviewed journal presents original research, and not all original research appears in peer-reviewed journals. It's important to understand the other types of articles and features that might appear in a journal. If a professor asks you to locate an original research article or you are trying to replicate previous studies, you want to be sure you recognize the difference between these types. Just because a publication includes numbers or talks about data doesn't make it peer-reviewed research, although many of these formats can be helpful to developing research in their own ways. two other important types of work are also common: literature review articles and meta-analyses.

A peer-reviewed journal should clearly identify itself as such on its website, and explain the submission and review process. University libraries often provide search tools that can help focus only on peer-reviewed sources, and Google Scholar provides a similar resource. Librarians can also help distinguish more trustworthy and reliable sources from less credible ones. But even finding such a source is only part of making sure that a given article fits the criteria for a typical research piece. In addition to reviews of the literature and meta-analyses, many journals also include reviews of books, essays on theoretical topics or introducing issues, and correspondence and debates over published work. All of these have an important role in documenting research, but they are not models of how to write your own research paper or appropriate sources when asked to find published research.

At the same time, plenty of research appears in outlets other than peer-reviewed sources. Some academic books compile many different research studies, or present a longer and more detailed discussion of a single study. These can be great sources, but make sure they actually meet all four criteria for research; not every nonfiction book is actually presenting original, empirical research in a systematic way. Many companies and organizations conduct applied research for professional purposes. While this is often proprietary and not widely available to the public, some executive summaries and reports are shared broadly. These can also be useful sources of evidence, but keep in mind that many organizations have an incentive to share facts that fit their particular goals, and may not fully meet the standards of intersubjectivity and transparency necessary for their work to be replicable. Finally, a growing amount of research appears in journalistic settings, a trend known as data-driven journalism.

Reflect & React: Effective Tables and Figures

Remember, a good figure or table should be able to stand alone. In looking at the sample figure, how would you evaluate its effectiveness? What would you change? Take some time to locate a research article that has a figure in it. What do you like or dislike about the figure? How would you improve the figure, if necessary? Does it effectively and clearly present the message of the data?

Literature Review Article

A literature review article focuses entirely on previous research. The authors do not present original findings, so there are no method or results sections. However, this does not mean that a literature review article does not attempt to advance

method section
→ Unit 3

results section
→ Unit 3

theory
→ Unit 2

theory. Instead, a central goal of many literature review pieces is to make comparisons and connections across prior studies to give a broader picture of the evidence supporting a theory. Even though individual studies will include a review of prior research, scholars may miss relevant studies that use different labels or come from different disciplines. In addition, because the literature review in a typical research article focuses on justifying the specific study, research dealing with the theory that doesn't address certain variables may be left out. A good literature review article will give a more complete picture of prior scholarship. It also allows scholars to suggest why a theory may work in some circumstances and not others, as well as to offer more detailed suggestions for future research than can fit in a single research article. Because such pieces are valuable, there are journals that primarily or exclusively publish review articles or theory pieces.

Consider the question posted at the start of this unit: What is the effect of images of thin models? Many studies have been published on this topic, not only in media and communication journals but also in medical and psychology journals, as well as other outlets. Sorting through all this information to decide which theories are relevant to your study would be challenging. A good review article would summarize many important findings, let you know about relevant theories and particularly important studies, and help you identify unanswered questions that still need to be researched. Starting by reading one or more articles of this type would position you to more effectively research the topic.

Meta-analysis

relationship
→ Unit 2

variable
→ Unit 2

statistics
→ Unit 14

random error
→ Unit 6

statistical significance
→ Unit 15

experiment
→ Unit 9

moderation
→ Unit 2

population
→ Unit 8

Like a literature review article, a meta-analysis also attempts to summarize prior research. Unlike a literature review article, though, a meta-analysis presents new statistical analyses to help with this process. A good meta-analysis will include a literature review that summarizes prior research, but it also draws upon the data found in earlier studies. An effective meta-analysis requires two critical steps. First, scholars will collect statistical information from prior studies conducted on the topic. For example, if a meta-analysis was exploring the connection between images of thin models and effects on self-esteem and eating behavior, the authors would search the published literature to find any results that tested this relationship. In addition, scholars try to find unpublished but valid studies to include in the analysis as well. This is meant to offset publication bias, or the "file drawer problem."

Having identified all relevant studies, scholars then find a way to numerically standardize the various ways that results are reported. There are many different statistics that can be used to describe and test relationships. In a meta-analysis, the goal is to combine these into a single set of data that can be "averaged" and further analyzed. Once the results converted to comparable statistics, the authors can find the average effect found across all the identified studies. This gives a better estimate of the real relationship between variables, as individual studies may have included atypical results and contain more random error. This "average" finding is then evaluated for statistical significance, taking advantage of the additional power provided by the larger number of individuals obtained from combining multiple studies. For example, a single experiment on the effects of thin images might include just 50 college students. Those students may show only a slight reaction to the stimulus, and the authors may be unable to conclude from such a small result that the effect is meaningful. However, if many experiments all report a similar number, we could be much more confident that the effect is real and that it describes how people in general react to thin images.

Another benefit of meta-analyses is the ability to consider differences between studies as potential moderating variables. Suppose you found 20 studies that considered college students and 20 that considered children under age 18. If the studies on college students consistently showed weaker effects than those on children, it could be that thin images have a bigger effect when people are younger. A single study on just one of these populations couldn't reach such a conclusion, but by combining multiple studies and looking for patterns, a meta-analysis could identify this difference.

Data-Driven Journalism

A growing number of outlets publish content based upon original data or analyses of existing data that broadly meets the standards for research, but that doesn't appear in peer-reviewed outlets. One label for such materials is data-driven journalism. For example, the *New York Times* formerly published Nate Silver's Fivethirtyeight blog, and later a special section known as The Upshot, both of which specialized in analyzing data and presenting the findings to a general audience. Organizations such as the Pew Research Center specialize in collecting data that are shared with media outlets but also directly reported in detailed reports available through their website. These publications often include topics such as political attitudes and behaviors, technology use, scientific knowledge, and even sports and entertainment. For example, a boom in advanced statistics for evaluating player performance emerged from independent sources like Baseball Prospectus and data compilers like Bill James.

There is no uniform definition of what constitutes data-driven journalism. Some examples reflect truly original research, where reporters collected information about variables through traditional research methods such as surveys and content analysis. Other examples involve secondary analysis, using data that are already available from sources such as Pew and the federal government, but conducting original analyses and presenting the findings. Still others are collaborations between journalists and researchers, with journalists helping visualize and contextualize results also reported in more traditional academic formats. Critically, though, all of these formats involve original

| variables |
| → Unit 2 |
| **secondary analysis** |
| → Unit 3 |
| **qualitative versus quantitative** |
| → Unit 3 |

contributions from the content creators, not simply summaries of already published work. A news story that simply reworks a press release on a recent journal article would not qualify as data-driven journalism, and such stories often distort rather than contribute to science. Furthermore, data-driven journalism pieces work to present the results in a way that is both scientifically robust but also accessible, helping a broader audience understand issues through research rather than mere anecdotes and the claims of experts. Because of this, many examples use interactive visualization tools and otherwise take advantage of the growth of online resources available to make quantitative information more accessible and engaging.

However, data-driven journalism is not a substitute for academic publications. The goals of journalists are to inform but also entertain. Some examples of data-driven journalism are driven by advocacy in a way that may generate bias. Stories are not as heavily anchored in timely news hooks as other types of journalism, but they still go through a far shorter process than typical scholarly research. Peer review is not a component of the process, and flawed conclusions and incorrectly interpreted data are more likely as a result. Of course, journal articles can also contain flaws. Any research should be reviewed carefully, paying attention to the many threats to validity described in this book.

Activities

Activity 3A: Reviewing the Theoretical Literature

See term: research question; theory.

Think of a research question that you are interested in asking. If you previously completed activity 2A consider using the research question you developed as part of that activity. If not, think about a topic related to communication that you would like to know more about. Be sure to identify at least one variable that is specific to communication and at least one other variable that might either cause that communication or result from that communication. Once you have identified a guiding research question, work through the following prompts:

- Conduct a brief literature search to identify 2–3 scholarly articles that address the topic you are interested in studying.
- Identify a specific theory based on the literature that might predict an answer to this research question. To help with this step, consider the different theories mentioned in the literature reviews of the article you have found—which ones stand out as particularly useful to what you are doing?
- Once you have selected a theory, describe the theory and why it is relevant to your research question.

Activity 3B: Triangulation in Everyday Life

See term: triangulation.

We often use research in our everyday lives to learn about the world we live in and to make informed decisions. Further, we often use multiple methods so that we are more confident in the answers we find.

Consider making a decision to see a movie. You are down to your last $15 and have just enough for one ticket and a small soda. Therefore, you need to make the right decision. One way to learn about a movie is to watch the preview. In this case, you learn what the creators of the film would like you to know about it. This is certainly biased, so you decide to also read a review from your favorite movie critic (a second method). Finally, you decide to ask a friend (a third method) whether he or she enjoyed the movie. If all three of these approaches point toward the movie being good, you are likely to feel confident in deciding to see it.

For this activity, you are to consider the different ways that you use research to learn about the world you inhabit and to specifically consider multiple approaches to one topic. For the following list of questions, indicate at least two different techniques you might use to find an answer. To further enhance the activity, share your ideas with your peers and see what options they would choose to answer the questions.

1. How do you decide what courses to pick—and which ones not to take—for a given semester?
2. You came into some money and would like to buy a new car. You want to choose one you have never driven before. How would you decide which car to buy?
3. If you own a pizza shop, how would you learn how your customers feel about the service?
4. You have an interview scheduled for a job you are excited about—how would you find out more about the company?

Activity 3C: Comparing Qualitative and Quantitative Research

See terms: qualitative; quantitative; variable.

For the first part of this activity, read each description given below and decide whether you think it is describing qualitative or quantitative research. Explain your answer.

- Researchers have recruited four participants for in-depth interviews. Each interview will take about 45 minutes. Interview participants were recruited through contacts with local community activist groups. The researchers are interested in the relationship between news use and political participation among activists.
- A study on attitudes toward same-sex marriage included 1,200 participants from across the continental United States. Participants were selected through the use of random-digit dialing and asked to answer a series of yes/no questions and to provide some basic demographic information. The typical time it took to complete the questionnaire was 5 minutes.
- An advertising firm is trying to decide which version of an advertisement to use. It has produced three versions of the ad, but the client only wants to pay for one ad to air. To make the final decision, the ad agency has decided to bring in three different focus groups to evaluate and discuss each version of the ad. Each group will consist of 8–10 people and the sessions will last about 60 minutes. A moderator will lead the discussion.

For the second part of this activity, consider the list of variables given next. For each, develop both a qualitative and a quantitative way of measuring the variable and describe that approach. In doing so, consider the inherent strengths and weaknesses of each approach.

- Happiness
- Television news watching
- Relationship satisfaction
- Public speaking ability.

Activity 3D: Knowledge Gaining

See terms: authority; intuition; observation; tenacity.

For each of the following statements, indicate which knowledge-gaining approach is being described—authority, intuition, observation, or tenacity—and explain your answer.

- Your research methods book tells you that qualitative methods use detailed and individual descriptions to evaluate variables.
- In looking for colleges to attend, you visit a few to see what they are like in person. You decide which one to go to, having noted how well you rated the schools on each of five criteria.
- In deciding which version of an advertisement to air, the director of the agency decides to pick one because it "feels right."
- A television news commentator warns that the president's latest budget proposal will cost taxpayers $1,000, and you accept this view.
- As a kid, you always had posters from a certain university hanging on your wall and always knew you would go there. You decide to apply only to that school because you are sure it is the right one for you.
- You are in charge of selecting a new snack for your company's cafeteria. You send a questionnaire to all of the employees asking them which three snacks they like best and use that information to make your decision.
- You are considering five colleges, so you watch a football game from each school on television. While watching the games, one of the schools just feels like the right place, so you decide to go there.

For the second part of this activity, determine what you would do to gather the knowledge needed for the two situations provided next and describe how you would you use each of the four approaches to knowledge gaining (authority, intuition, observation, and tenacity).

- You have an interview lined up for a potential internship, but you are not sure what the appropriate attire would be. How would you decide what to wear?
- You and your roommate do not seem to be communicating very well. How could you determine some effective strategies for resolving this uncomfortable situation?

Activity 3E: Evaluating Research Applications

See terms: application.

Locate a research report or journal article. Read the entire article, but focus on how the authors talk about the practical applications of their research. Once you have read the article, write a description of the article that includes the following:

- Author, title, and source information (please use the appropriate style as indicated by your instructor).
- In what ways do the researchers make the case for how this research can be applied to real-world situations?
- What groups of people (e.g., students, parents, or different professionals) would find this research most valuable?
- Is this research qualitative or quantitative? How can you tell?
- How would using another approach or method strengthen this research?
- How much attention does the article pay to practical application compared with theoretical development? Do you feel that this is a good balance?

References

Boyle, M.P., & Schmierbach, M. (2008). Do pictures matter?: Effects of photographs on information seeking and issue involvement. Paper presented at the *Association for Education in Journalism and Mass Communication* annual conference: Chicago, IL.

DeBono, K.G., & Harnish, R.J. (1988). Source expertise, source attractiveness, and the processing of persuasive information: A functional approach. *Journal of Personality and Social Psychology*, *55*(4), 541–546. doi:http://dx.doi.org.ezaccess.libraries.psu.edu/10.1037/0022-3514.55.4.541

Halevy, R., Shalvi, S., & Verschuere, B. (2014). Being honest about dishonesty: Correlating self-reports and actual lying. *Human Communication Research*, *40*(1), 54–72. doi:10.1111/hcre.12019

Knobloch-Westerwick, S., Gong, Y., Hagner, H., & Kerbeykian, L. (2013). Tragedy viewers count their blessings: Feeling low on fiction leads to feeling high on life. *Communication Research*, *40*(6), 747–766. doi:10.1177/0093650212437758

Milgram, S. (1974). *Obedience to authority: An experimental view*. New York, NY: Harper & Row.

Petty, R.E., Cacioppo, J.T., & Goldman, R. (1981). Personal involvement as a determinant of argument-based persuasion. *Journal of Personality and Social Psychology*, *41*(5), 847–855. doi:10.1037/0022–3514.41.5.847

Wright, P.J., & Bae, S. (2013). Pornography consumption and attitudes toward homosexuality: A national longitudinal study. *Human Communication Research*, *39*(4), 492–513. doi:10.1111/hcre.12009

Suggested Readings for Further Exploration of Unit 3 Topics

Examples

Levitt, S.D., & Dubner, S.J. (2005). *Freakonomics: A rogue economist explores the hidden side of everything*. New York, NY: HarperCollins.

Milliken, F.J., Morrison, E.W., & Hewlin, P.F. (2003). An exploratory study of employee silence: Issues that employees don't communicate upward and why. *Journal of Management Studies*, *40*(6), 1453–1476. doi:10.1111/1467-6486.00387

Van de Venter, G., & Michayluk, D. (2008). An insight into overconfidence in the forecasting abilities of financial advisors. *Australian Journal of Management*, *32*(3), 545–557. doi:10.1177/031289620803200309

Advanced Discussion

Berger, M., & Cirasella, J. (2015). Beyond Beall's List: Better understanding predatory publishers. *College & Research Libraries News, 76*(3), 132–135.

Keyton, J., Bisel, R.S., & Ozley, R. (2009). Recasting the link between applied and theory research: Using applied findings to advance communication theory development. *Communication Theory, 19*(2), 146–160. doi:10.1111/j.1468-2885.2009.01339.x

Roloff, M.E. (2002). The state of the art of interpersonal communication research: Are we addressing socially significant issues? In M. Allen, R.W. Preiss, B.M. Gayle, & N. Burrell (Eds.), *Interpersonal communication research: Advances through meta-analysis* (pp. 423–445). Mahwah, NJ: Lawrence Erlbaum Associates.

Solomon, D., & Theiss, J. (2013). *Interpersonal communication: Putting theory into practice*. New York, NY: Routledge.

unit 4

ethical research

Often, we focus so much on how to collect data efficiently that we forget the larger purpose of research, which is to answer questions for the benefit of society (or our client). There is little value in research that is efficient if, in the process, we harm those we are meant to be helping. When research is conducted in an unethical fashion, it hurts both the people being studied and the larger enterprise of scholarship, ultimately harming the people conducting the research as well. When research is done on behalf of a client, such as your employer, unethical research can also undermine the reputation of that client, far outweighing any insights that might be gained.

Unfortunately, the history of social science and research in general is marked by a number of questionable studies. For that reason, careful protocols have been developed to help ensure that modern research is conducted in an ethical way. These principles and procedures are important to making sure that research is done the right way, but ultimately, the researchers themselves are the most important check on research practices. Always ask yourself whether your behavior is just and honest, and never carry out a study that does not meet the core ethical principles, no matter the perceived benefit. In the past, researchers have not always lived up to that standard. Many of the examples given here are taken from actual studies rather than hypothetical situations.

Principles of Ethical Research

Although scholars often focus on how to test relationships most effectively, whether to develop theories or answer applied questions, they must balance this with the need for ethical practices. Ethical research requires that all individuals involved in a research project are treated in a just manner that does not risk undue **harm** or infringe upon their personal rights.

In recent decades, scholars have increasingly stressed the importance of following ethical standards, and organizations that oversee research have taken steps to monitor research and ensure that it is carried out in an ethical manner. These organizations engage in **institutional review** to be sure that someone other than the researcher monitors study practices. The review process is simply a check to confirm that researchers are following the ethical standards they should hold themselves to. These standards include providing potential research participants with a clear description of the research process and likely outcomes, so that they can give **informed consent,** by which they express their willingness to engage in **voluntary participation**. No participant should ever be coerced into taking part in a study, whether through undue pressure or dishonesty on the part of the researcher.

Furthermore, information about study participants should be protected as much as possible to allow for some degree of **privacy**. At a minimum, most research studies provide **confidentiality,** ensuring that those outside the study

81

are unable to identify individual participants' responses. In some cases, they even offer **anonymity**, such that even the researchers are unaware of participants' identities.

Certain types of research questions are difficult to answer while providing participants with a complete description of the study prior to participation. For example, some studies include **confederates** who act as study participants but actually are familiar with the study design and act in a predetermined manner. In cases such as this, which involve **deception**, the study may still be ethical provided that a proper **debriefing** procedure is followed. As a rule, though, researchers are expected to be as honest as possible with participants, providing answers to any questions. Moreover, the expectation of **honesty** extends to all aspects of the research process. Researchers who fabricate data or engage in **plagiarism** seriously harm the scientific process, and institutions strive to monitor and punish such actions as well.

Avoid Harm

If researchers are operating ethically, they take time to consider the possible harm that could affect participants in their research. Although physical harm is often the first type of harm that many people consider, it is only one of many ways that research participants can be negatively affected. Other types of harm include psychological or emotional harm (e.g., depression or self-esteem loss) and social harm (e.g., participants being ostracized or bullying). In some cases, multiple types of harm may be present, or certain types of harm can lead to other harms, such as psychological harm (e.g., depression) leading to eventual physical harm.

Perhaps the best example in American history of harm resulting from research is the Tuskegee study on the long-term effects of syphilis (a sexually transmitted infection that is curable but if untreated can be fatal). In this study, the researchers knowingly withheld treatment for syphilis from the study participants in order to better understand the long-term effects of the disease. To do so, they engaged in deception by telling participants that they were being treated for the disease even though they were not. Further, the researchers took steps to make it difficult for participants to leave the study once effective treatments for the disease became readily available, violating the voluntary participation tenet of research ethics. The time frame of this study extended for a number of decades. As such, it is highly likely that the harm caused to these participants extended well beyond the scope of those participating in the study, as many of the men in the study unknowingly spread the disease to their partners at home.

Beyond these specific concerns, the study also highlighted a tremendous imbalance in power, as the study participants were African American males from a low-income community during a time when African Americans were struggling for equal rights in the United States (the study began in the early 1900s,

voluntary
participation
→ Unit 4

**institutional
review**
→ Unit 4

population
→ Unit 8

well before the civil rights movement had any impact on the rights of African Americans and other minority groups).

As a result of this study, new codes of ethics were developed to ensure that greater care is taken when researchers study people. Further, many universities and research institutions have instituted training protocols that require researchers to develop a better understanding of the numerous ethical concerns researchers face. These training protocols also allow researchers to read up on famous ethical violations such as the Tuskegee study and others.

When researchers want to conduct a study on a university campus, they must first pass this training protocol and then must submit a research proposal for consideration by an institutional review board (IRB), whose role it is to ensure that the rights of participants are fully considered and protected. Research on populations such as children, prisoners, and other vulnerable groups is given a greater level of scrutiny to prevent researchers from taking advantage of their situation (e.g., some groups may feel less comfortable saying no to a study because of fear of reprisal). You can read further on the Tuskegee study and its impact on research involving human participants on the Centers for Disease Control and Prevention's website (www.cdc.gov/tuskegee/index.html).

Informed Consent

In most cases, reviewing agencies expect research participants to be provided with enough information to make an informed decision as to whether they want to participate in a research study. The process typically begins with a recruiting letter (or e-mail) that directs people to the study. From there, participants should first encounter a consent form. An effective consent form should be clearly written in language that is accessible to a wide array of participants. Specifically, a good consent form should clearly state the following items: (1) any potential risks or harms, (2) the length of the study, (3) any potential benefits of participation, (4) the procedure for withdrawal from the study and clarification that this can be done without penalty, (5) contact information for the lead investigator and the IRB, and (6) any special circumstances or procedures associated with the study. In short, participants should know what they are getting into.

After reading the consent form, participants can then make a decision about whether to participate in the study. If they agree to participate, they can either sign the form (if printed) or click on the "agree to participate" (or similarly worded) button on an online form. If participants do not agree to participate, they should be free to exit the study without penalty or concern for reprisal or punishment of any kind. Typically, consent forms are limited to one page. However, each university or research institution has different procedures, so it is best to check with the IRB at your university. Further, when researchers from different universities work together, the specific needs for proper consent forms of each of the universities must be met before the research study can proceed.

harm
→ Unit 4

institutional review
→ Unit 4

participant observation
→ Unit 10

debriefing
→ Unit 4

Although informed consent is often used in research, there are times when it is not desirable from the researcher's perspective. For instance, consider conducting participant observation, where your goal might be to observe the natural communication patterns that exist in social groups. You could study this by joining some campus organizations and observing their communication patterns. Yet telling everyone that you are studying them could alter their behavior, and the situation then becomes much less natural and the inherent advantages of naturalistic observational research begin to go away. In such a case, it may be more effective for you to conduct your observations and then thoroughly debrief the participants afterward. In any case, you should work with your IRB before proceeding with such a study. Any time that research is conducted without informed consent or voluntary participation, the researcher must make a compelling case for doing so.

Voluntary Participation

population
→ Unit 8

informed consent
→ Unit 4

validity
→ Unit 6

incentive
→ Unit 8

A guiding principle of ethical research is that participants willingly choose to participate in research of their own volition. They cannot be forced to participate and can choose to leave a study at any time, for any reason, without fear of punishment of any kind. However, some classes of individuals are not seen as participating voluntarily without further oversight, including children and prisoners. Because of this, many universities require special procedures to conduct research using those populations. Central to the premise of voluntary participation is that the researcher provides a clear consent form so that participants can willingly agree to participate in research with informed consent.

This ethical consideration is rooted partly in the medical atrocities of concentration camps during World War II. During this time, people in concentration camps were unwillingly used as participants in medical research and were subjected to a wide array of horrific procedures. Instances such as these led researchers to more thoughtfully consider the costs and benefits of research and to take into consideration the rights of study participants. As a result, all universities and most research institutions have clear procedures in place to make sure that participants fully understand their rights, particularly when it comes to voluntary participation.

Although the use of voluntary participants is now a requirement, it also makes good research sense. Good research rests on the validity of the data. How confident can a researcher be in the validity of a participant's responses if that participant has been forced or otherwise coerced (such as with an overly strong incentive or fear of punishment) to participate in the study? As a result, because of the critical importance of quality data, researchers would rather have participants who willingly agree to participate in a study than those who do not want to be part of the study.

For instance, consider a situation in which you have to take a test for a class you don't care about if you know the test will have minimal impact on your grade. It might be that you are likely to put in minimal effort simply because you don't care. There is no guarantee of this—perhaps you try as hard as you can in all classes, regardless of the circumstances—but it easily raises the potential that the answers you provide are a direct result of your feelings toward the situation and not a true (i.e., valid) test of what you actually know.

Steps to Success: Creating an Effective Consent Form

Use the following steps as a starting point for putting together a consent form. Specific requirements may vary from one institution to another, so always check with your local IRB before submitting research for review.

1. Identify any potential risks or harms that might come to study participants through involvement in your study, including physical, emotional, and psychological harm.
2. Use pre-testing to get an accurate estimate of how long the study will take.
3. Determine what benefits the participants might receive from this research, such as knowledge gained or access to medications.
4. Determine what procedures you will use to safeguard participants' data and identities. This could entail storing personal information in a separate location from the data used in the study, changing identifying information in the reporting of data, or detailing where and for how long you will store data files and copies of questionnaires.
5. Determine an alternative activity that participants who refuse consent can complete to receive the incentive offered to study participants. Please note that the alternative activity should be equivalent in time and complexity to participating in the study.
6. Identify contact people for your Institutional Review Board and cross-check your consent form with examples provided by your IRB.
7. Determine whether there are any special or at-risk populations needed to complete the study (e.g., prisoners and minors), as special procedures may be required in such cases.
8. Determine whether any deception, use of confederates, or other similar procedures will be involved in the study, as special training or permissions may be needed in such cases.
9. Make sure there is a space for the participant to sign the consent form as well as for the researcher (or designee) to sign as a witness. If using an online form, the consent box or button should be clearly marked and easy for the participant to find.

Privacy

Researchers should take steps to protect the privacy of participants in their research. In a way, the researcher and the study participants enter into a contract whereby the participant provides the researcher with information under the expectation that the information will be used ethically. One aspect of that ethical use is not revealing private or identifying information about participants without their explicit consent.

Protecting privacy is important for two reasons. First, it can protect participants from any harm that might result from their identities being revealed. Potential harms could include being ostracized, feeling guilty, or even being physically harmed as a result of information revealed. This concern is particularly important when dealing with vulnerable populations such as minors, victims of abuse, or prisoners. Second, ensuring that the participants' privacy is protected can make it more likely that they will feel comfortable answering questions honestly. If participants know that their identities will remain anonymous or that the researcher will at least maintain confidentiality, the decision to answer highly personal or revealing questions likely becomes easier. The researcher should clearly indicate in the consent form what procedures are in place to protect privacy.

There is a clear difference in the ease of maintaining privacy when comparing qualitative and quantitative research. Because qualitative research typically looks in great detail at a small number of cases, it is much easier to connect a person's responses to his or her identity. For that reason, in reporting qualitative data, the researcher should take extra steps to protect individual participants' privacy by altering certain personal details (e.g., name, city of origin, or employment) to obscure their true identities. Although quantitative researchers should still prioritize participants' privacy, the concern is somewhat different given the nature of this type of research. Specifically, quantitative data analysis usually involves large numbers of participants and, from an analysis standpoint, tends to look at patterns across large samples and large numbers of variables. This makes it difficult to identify any particular participant in the study. Even so, the quantitative researcher should still take clear steps to protect the privacy of participants and make sure that access to any data is limited to the primary researcher and trusted research partners.

At times, large-scale quantitative data sets are made available to other researchers for use in secondary analysis. In these cases, it is good practice to remove any identifying characteristics of individual participants (e.g., phone number, Social Security number, address) in order to protect their privacy and to prevent specific responses they have given from being connected to their personal information. For example, perhaps a questionnaire might include items about drug use and other potentially illegal activities. If these answers were given in confidence that the researcher would maintain and protect the participant's privacy, it would be a clear ethical violation if the data set were released with the personal information intact. However, whenever you have questions about these kinds of issues and are unsure how to proceed, you should check with your IRB office.

Anonymity

The most stringent way to protect participant privacy is to ensure anonymity. For participation to be anonymous, the researcher must in no way be able to connect responses to any particular study participant. This can be accomplished in a variety of ways depending on the format of the study. For an online study, researchers will often direct any personal details to an alternative database that is separate from the main questionnaire items. For a pencil-and-paper study, the researcher can provide a tear-off sheet to collect personal information and then have the participant drop the completed forms into different boxes. If this is done correctly, the researcher doesn't handle any specific questionnaires until all are collected and can in no way attach personal details to responses given on the main questionnaire. This process allows the researcher to keep track of participants so as to provide them with incentives or administer follow-up procedures, but their name, address, or other personal information cannot be connected with any of their answers.

There are a number of reasons why researchers strive to protect the privacy of their participants. Specific to anonymity, it is likely that participants will feel more comfortable answering highly personal questions when they know their identities are completely protected. Further, anonymity can help protect against researcher biases because the researcher does not know who provided particular answers and who was assigned to various experimental conditions. In many cases, anonymity is difficult to preserve (e.g., depth interviews), so researchers pledge to protect privacy by maintaining confidentiality.

privacy
→ Unit 4

incentive
→ Unit 8

researcher bias
→ Unit 9

treatment groups
→ Unit 9

Reflect & React: Ethical Concerns in Applied Research

Think about how these kinds of concerns about privacy would apply in an industry setting. For example, you may be asked to perform an annual review for a coworker or fill out an evaluation form for your boss or manager. In such cases, there could be concerns about retribution if you give someone a negative review. What kinds of safeguards could you put in place to avoid such situations? How could you assure employees that their information will be kept anonymous and their identities protected?

Confidentiality

The other way to ensure privacy is to maintain the confidentiality of participant responses. This involves ensuring that no one outside the research team is aware of the identities of participants or able to link responses to individuals. Unlike anonymity, where the researcher simply cannot connect the participants to their responses, confidentiality applies when the researcher adjusts how data are reported and discussed.

qualitative data analysis
→ Unit 13

harm
→ Unit 4

qualitative versus quantitative
→ Unit 3

informed consent
→ Unit 4

For instance, in qualitative data reporting, the researcher could use alternative names (or simply the first letter of a participant's name) or adjust personal details (e.g., age, race, marital status) to protect the identities of participants. At the same time, in-depth reports such as those constructed in qualitative research may require the inclusion of some personal details because they are relevant to the study. This creates a tension between preserving privacy and reporting results, but researchers should always be mindful of the importance of privacy. If responses are highly sensitive or could result in some harm to study participants if their identities are revealed (such as in studies of abused spouses, drug or alcohol use, or other sensitive topics), the need to maintain privacy is especially important. In all cases, researchers are obligated to fulfill their stated promises to protect participants.

Quantitative studies tend to report general patterns or averages. As such, statistical analyses of quantitative data are much less likely to reveal details about one particular participant. Nevertheless, when sharing the data, researchers need to be sure they maintain their promises of privacy, as discussed in the context of anonymity. Any steps used to provide confidentiality (or anonymity) should be clarified in the informed consent process so that study participants can evaluate whether their privacy will be adequately protected.

In some cases, data that are collected end up being shared with other researchers. When researchers do this, they should check with their institutional review board for any specific institutional policies regarding data sharing. Whether using data collected on their own or from another source, researchers should strive to be careful and proactively find ways to protect participant's information.

Techniques and Procedures

Certain types of research tend to create a greater likelihood of unethical behavior. For example, the use of confederates or other forms of deception may violate the principle of informed consent. For that reason, specific procedures have been developed to help offset the potential harm of such techniques, as well as to oversee the research process. Most notable of these is the implementation of an institutional review process, which was a direct response to some of the unethical historical behavior described earlier.

experiment
→ Unit 9

debriefing
→ Unit 4

harm
→ Unit 4

Confederates

At times, researchers will employ people who pretend to be participants in the research but who are actually working with the researchers and may be following a specific script as part of the study design. Confederates are frequently used to help carry out experimental manipulations.

One of the most famous uses of confederates is the so-called Milgram experiment, in which participants were instructed to give electric "shocks" to their partner if he or she provided the wrong answer to a question. In this case, the partner was actually a confederate and was not being shocked at all—the confederate was simply acting as if he or she had received a shock. The premise of the study was to determine the degree to which people would follow orders from an authority figure, even if doing so meant causing harm to another person.

To enable this possibility, Milgram brought in participants and assigned them to a partner who was supposed to have memorized a list of word pairs. The participant would read a word, and then the partner would then answer with the appropriate response. Any time the partner provided the wrong response, the participant was instructed to tell the partner that he or she was wrong, indicate the voltage of the shock (the intensity of the shock increased with every wrong answer), and then administer the shock. The confederate was used to help provide some realism to the scenario; the confederate would act upset and continue to protest being shocked as the study progressed. This allowed Milgram to assess how far people would continue to shock their partners, even after some of the partners complained about chest pain and even stopped complaining (presumably having passed out from being shocked at high-voltage levels). The study provided valuable insights into the nature of authority and the premise that individuals engage in undesirable behavior because they are "following orders."

Milgram's approach was made possible by the use of confederates. However, the study raises some ethical concerns because of the use of confederates to deceive the study participants, as well as the potential psychological harm that might be done to participants, who now may see themselves as the kind of person who would continue to shock a person who is in pain simply because an authority figure (in this case the researcher) told them to continue. Any time that confederates are used, researchers should pay special attention to debriefing participants at the conclusion of the study. That said, debriefing does not excuse otherwise unethical behavior; in the case of the Milgram study, many people have suggested that the psychological harms outweighed the insights gained, and the debriefing process did too little to address those harms.

Deception

The use of confederates fits within a broader practice of using deception in research—that is, obscuring or altering information presented to study participants to hide the true purpose of a study or simply to enable the researcher to carry out the study procedures effectively. Consider the Milgram experiment, which led participants to believe they were actually shocking and causing harm to another participant. The researchers used deception as a means to carry out the central part of the study. It is likely that the researchers thought the deception used in this case would be less harmful than actually having the participants shock other study participants.

debriefing
→ Unit 4

experiment
→ Unit 9

institutional review
→ Unit 4

validity
→ Unit 6

informed consent
→ Unit 4

It is true that researchers should work to minimize harm and also to minimize deception, but the medical and Milgram examples highlight the fact that, in some cases, the use of deception or exposure to potential harms is necessary to ensure the validity of the study. Deceptive practices, including the use of confederates, are allowed in research, but they are the focus of particular scrutiny from IRBs and are especially at risk of violating basic principles of ethical research. Specific steps must be taken to ensure that the use of deception does not create undue risk and to allow participants to address the lack of complete informed consent. These include the use of debriefing procedures.

Reflect & React: Critically Analyzing Research

In some cases, opinions about the ethical nature of research evolve over time as critics and scholars re-evaluate research from the past. The Stanford Prison Experiment is a good example of research that has cause considerable critical reaction. It is a landmark and highly influential study in psychology but has not been without its critics, particularly regarding some of the ethical principles discussed in this unit. As you visit the website for the study (http://prisonexp.org), consider which of the ethical principles you would bring up as concerns in evaluating this research. To what extent do the researchers address these ethical principles? Do you see these potential ethical violations as necessary for the research? What are some alternative approaches you might use to study this topic that would allow you to avoid some of these potential ethical concerns?

deception
→ Unit 4

confederates
→ Unit 4

harm
→ Unit 4

field research
→ Unit 12

rapport
→ Unit 10

Debriefing

In situations in which deception is used, researchers may not be able to completely describe the true purpose of the study or the nature of specific measures without invalidating the method employed. After the study has concluded, however, the participants can learn more about the study without affecting the results. Debriefing is an opportunity for the researcher to reveal the true purpose of the study to the participants.

In debriefing, a complete and accurate description of the study is provided, with particular reference to any features previously concealed from the participants. Part of this debriefing will include the description of any use of confederates or other forms of deception, the reason for such practices, and the reality of the situation in which deception was employed. The general idea behind the debriefing process is that the researcher should attempt to return participants to the emotional, physical, or psychological state they were in before they participated in the study (this falls under the "no harm" aspect of ethical concerns). Because of this, the debriefing process must be more detailed and involved in cases of heavy deception or potential for harm. For instance, consider the Milgram study: in this case, it was essential for the researchers to make clear that no one was really shocked, to identify who the confederates were, and to work with the participants to help them understand both the objectives of the research study and the reasons why they might have "shocked" someone even when they didn't really want to harm them.

In some cases, researchers can use the debriefing process as an opportunity to leave the door open for follow-up research. For instance, in a field study, the researcher should exit the field on good terms with the people under study (if possible) and leave the door open for follow-up research in the future. In this case, a successful debriefing process can be essential to the success of any future research as it helps maintain positive rapport and trust.

Institutional Review

Beyond specific techniques that may create or alleviate ethical concerns, many nations, including the United States, have established broader oversight of the research process, at least for funded institutions. For example, anyone carrying out research who is employed by a university must submit human subjects research for review, even if the specific study is not receiving any kind of federal funding. This evaluation of the ethics in research is often carried out by an Institutional Review Board, which is also referred to as a Human Subjects Committee on some university campuses. Typically, these boards consist of researchers who come from a diverse array of backgrounds and provide varied perspectives on ethical considerations in research. Because of this, a proposal that you prepare for research on communication patterns in the workplace might be reviewed by a chemist, a biologist, and an anthropologist. Therefore, proposals to an IRB must be clearly written and explain processes and procedures in detail using language that is not reliant on field-specific jargon.

The primary goals of these boards are to ensure that researchers consider the rights of participants in carrying out research and that proper procedures are followed, such as ensuring privacy and guaranteeing informed consent. In many cases, an IRB will require researchers to pass a training course (these usually take a few hours) before a proposal can be submitted. These training programs help remind researchers of the principles of ethical research and also demonstrate proper procedures for conducting research (procedures may vary from one campus to another).

It is important to initiate the IRB review process well before you plan to collect data so that you have time to address any concerns. For instance, it could be that the sample (e.g., minors or prisoners) you wish to use requires additional

privacy
→ Unit 4

informed consent
→ Unit 4

sample
→ Unit 8

91

approval or a special exemption or a particular procedure you wish to employ (e.g., DNA collection) requires additional certification. These extra steps could either be prohibitive to your study or simply take extra time. It is better to know this early in the process so you have time to make any adjustments.

Honesty

Beyond specific procedures and potential pitfalls, a guiding principle for researchers to follow when reporting data and interacting with participants is that they should strive for honesty and clarity in conducting and reporting on research. While the other aspects of ethical research primarily focus on the process of collecting data and interacting with participants, this consideration relates to every stage of the research process. For the process of inquiry and knowledge building to work, it is essential for researchers to honestly and openly discuss their research.

Researchers can follow a number of basic guidelines for honesty in their work. First, the researcher should provide all of the details of the procedure for the study so that others can replicate it and identify potential weaknesses or limitations. Second, researchers should clearly present their findings even when they do not reach statistical significance or run counter to hypothesized expectations. There is often great pressure on researchers to produce results and to have statistically significant findings, and many times statistically significant results are perceived as more interesting or important than when researchers fail to find statistical support for their hypotheses. However, if we accept that falsification is central to theory development and hypothesis testing, then we should recognize that nonsignificant findings tell us something useful as well. Therefore, results from data analysis should be reported accurately, honestly, and thoroughly.

Third, researchers should identify and describe any limitations or special concerns they observed in the course of their study. For instance, this could involve some unique event that occurred on a college campus during the course of data collection or some glitch in software designed to assign participants to various experimental conditions. In any of these cases, it is important for those reading the study to be aware of all of these issues so that the reader can make an effective judgment as to the quality of the study. It is important for all researchers to recognize that any study will have weaknesses and things that need to be improved—there is no perfect study—and it is through open and honest dialogue that researchers can develop a better understanding of what they are studying.

Fourth, it is essential for researchers to give credit where it is due and not plagiarize ideas from others. There is nothing wrong with building on the knowledge that others have provided, but it is wrong to take credit for the work of others. Any time a researcher presents ideas, information, methods, or language that come from other sources, those sources should be clearly cited.

Fifth, researchers should strive for honesty in their interactions with participants. Although some degree of deception is sometimes required to obtain valid results, it is important for researchers to be open about any potential harms that may come to the participant, how long the study will take, how the data will be used, the general topics that will be considered, how the participant can go about leaving the study, and how the participant can find out more about the study if interested. The informed consent process is the ideal place to begin developing an honest relationship with research participants.

Finally, researchers should indicate the presence of any conflict of interest and disclose any funding sources for their research. In some cases, researchers serve on corporate boards, have financial investments, or are otherwise affiliated with an industry that they research. In these cases, it is important for the researcher to share these affiliations so that the audience has important contextual information. Similarly, when researchers receive financial support—whether through grants or other funding agencies—they should provide information on these funding sources so that the audience understands who is supporting the research and they can then draw their own conclusions about the research. Ultimately, it is important for researchers to be clear with information both in terms of how research was methodologically and analytically conducted but also be clear about themselves and whoever is supporting their research.

Plagiarism

A specific aspect of honesty that has emerged as an ever-greater concern is the issue of plagiarism. Any use of language or ideas taken from other sources without proper credit constitutes plagiarism. In an academic setting, students are often taught the basic concept and warned about the implications for their grades, but plagiarism is also an issue for researchers that can lead to negative repercussions as well, such as loss of employment, social stigma, and retracted or discredited research. From an ethical standpoint, it is important that researchers acknowledge the contributions of others to the process of knowledge building. This not only allows others to understand the process of how an idea or theory has developed but also allows readers of research articles to track down that prior research and look directly at the original source.

Research is a collaborative process, in that multiple researchers often work together on specific projects and the broader process of knowledge building is collaborative and dependent upon the contributions of research across many areas of study. For instance, in looking at the study of news treatment of protest groups, it is clear that researchers from communication studies, political science, and sociology, among other fields, have all made key contributions to the broader understanding of how and why protest groups are treated the way that they are. Therefore, when developing a literature review and building toward a particular theoretical perspective it is necessary—and appropriate—to give

literature review
→ Unit 3

reference list
→ Unit 3

theory
→ Unit 2

cyclical and
self-correcting
→ Unit 1

93

credit where it is due. This premise holds at any level, whether you are writing a report for a class or a researcher is submitting work for consideration by a journal. It is simply a good habit to get into to take clear notes and always provide the appropriate citation information.

Beyond concerns about copying the work of others, researchers need to also avoid self-plagiarism. In many cases, research projects develop out of previous work by the researcher. In these cases, it is important for the new work to be meaningfully unique and to avoid direct copying of previous language. The former concern is sometimes described as "salami-slicing" to illustrate the premise of making small adjustments from one study to the next. For instance, a researcher may have a large data set with a number of different variables and run a series of small analytical models predicting the dependent variable only using a few of the independent variables at a time. This allows the researcher to produce more publications but not produce meaningfully distinct work and does little to expand knowledge within the field.

Research in Depth: Fabrication of Data

Although most research is conducted by trustworthy individuals, dishonesty continues to be a problem for some scholars. The website RetractionWatch. com monitors retractions from academic journals, and it has reported many alarming examples. Retractions occur when a published paper is determined to not meet the standards of ethical research and publication practices. In many of the cases, RetractionWatch.com reports involve plagiarism, including "self-plagiarism." This occurs when authors reuse findings or even language from prior papers—a serious ethical lapse. Self-plagiarism can distort the literature, creating the impression of stronger evidence in favor of certain conclusions and making it harder to accurately evaluate what we know about an issue.

Some of the most serious cases of ethical violations involve the actual fabrication of data. One notorious example is Dutch psychologist Diederik Stapel (Bhattacharjee, 2013). Stapel was found to have completely invented the data reported in more than 50 papers. His dishonesty seriously compromised the foundation of many ideas in social psychology. Not only did it lead to his dismissal and the loss of his reputation, but also it harmed many of his peers. Individuals who attempted to replicate his fraudulent findings or who based studies on his insights wasted time and energy. Those who authored papers with him found their own reputations and work questioned, even though, in most cases, there was no evidence that they had known of the fraud. The fabrication of data is one of the most serious and damaging ethical violations possible in research.

Activities

Activity 4A: Develop a Consent Form for Your Study

See terms: informed consent; harm; privacy.

For this activity, you should begin the process of preparing materials to submit for review to the Institutional Review Board or Human Subjects Committee on your campus or at your workplace. Follow these steps as you work through the process of creating a consent form.

1. Visit the website or office of the IRB on your campus and obtain any forms or specific instructions for creating a consent form. Each campus could have unique requirements, so it is best to go right to the source.
2. Use the forms you obtained from your IRB and the definitions from the glossary in this unit to construct a list of items that must be included in your consent form.
3. Identify a specific research study from the literature that sounds interesting to you. It is typically useful to find research that uses a similar methodology, as it will share some of the procedures as well as problems that you might face with your own research interests. Based on the description of this activity found in the method section of that article, create a consent form that would meet the requirements you identified in Steps 1 and 2.

Activity 4B: Ethical Principles and Alternative Approaches

See terms: ethical research; harm; informed consent; voluntary participation; privacy.

Read through the following research scenarios and identify any ethical violations that you notice. After identifying any ethical problems, describe an alternative approach that you would take that eliminates that ethical concern.

1. A research team is interested in determining what kinds of bosses achieve the highest levels of worker productivity. The team designs an experiment in which workers will be randomly assigned to one of three "boss types." Each boss will require the workers to perform a set task, and the quality of the outcomes will be compared on a predetermined scale. Keen to find participants, the team approaches a large local company that is interested in the results and mandates that its workers spend one Tuesday participating in the study. When they arrive on that day, workers are told about the purpose and nature of the study, assigned to a group, and set to work.

2. Researchers are interested in the effects of viewing violent movie scenes; they speculate that exposure to violence desensitizes viewers. Because of concerns over participants knowing the true purpose of the study and contaminating results, they determine that study participants should not know the topic in advance. Thus, participants are told only that they will be viewing scenes from a new movie. Participants are recruited from crowds at a local cinema; they are asked to participate in a preview of a new movie. Those assigned to the nonviolent condition are shown 30 minutes of various nonviolent movie scenes. Those assigned the violent condition are shown 30 minutes of graphic violence from recent R-rated films. After each group fills out a questionnaire, the participants are told that the study dealt with the effects of media, thanked, and sent on their way.

3. A professor is studying student performance and instructor techniques. She suspects that certain techniques, such as discussion groups and hands-on practice, are more effective in engaging student interest. To explore this, she carries out a series of in-depth interviews with students at her university, many of whom deliver scathing assessments of their instructors. The professor publishes a paper on the project, describing the university, the courses in which students were enrolled, their performance and grade at the point of the interviews, and the general teaching approach of the instructor. She is careful to use pseudonyms for each interview participant.

4. As part of an initiative to study the effects of alcohol on interpersonal communication, a group of researchers decide to create a study testing the effects of alcohol consumption on teamwork using a group obstacle course. Specifically, they plan to measure performance on the obstacle course as well as the quality of interpersonal communication throughout the exercise. The treatment group will be asked to consume two alcoholic beverages before completing the group obstacle course. The performance of the alcohol consumption group on the group obstacle course will be compared with a control group that has not consumed alcohol. The comparison will enable researchers to determine whether alcohol affects interpersonal communication quality and whether that then influences performance on the group task.

Activity 4C: Consent Form Evaluation

See terms: ethical research; harm; deception; informed consent; privacy.

Participate in a study and keep the consent form (or use a consent form provided by your instructor). Evaluate this form based on the following criteria:

- How well does this consent form meet each requirement for an ethical consent form?
- Be sure to address all relevant criteria.
- Is there any information omitted from this form or any misleading information that might create ethical problems?
- Is there any information included that does not need to be present or that does not contribute to ethical research practices?
- What changes or improvements would you make to this consent form? Be as concrete and detailed as possible.

References

Bhattacharjee, Y. (2013, April 26). Diederik Stapel's audacious academic fraud. *New York Times*. Retrieved from www.nytimes.com/2013/04/28/magazine/diederik-stapels-audacious-academic-fraud.html

Suggested Readings for Further Exploration of Unit 4 Topics

Examples

Milgram, S. (1974). *Obedience to authority: An experimental view*. New York, NY: Harper & Row.

Reverby, S. M. (2009). *Examining Tuskegee: The infamous syphilis study and its legacy*. Chapel Hill, NC: University of North Carolina Press.

Advanced Discussion

Allen, C. (1996). What's wrong with the "golden rule"? Conundrums of conducting ethical research in cyberspace. *The Information Society*, *12*(2), 175–188. doi:10.1080/713856146

Birnbaum, M. H. (2004). Methodological and ethical issues in conducting social psychology research via the internet. In C. Sansone, C. C. Morf, & A. T. Panter (Eds.), *Handbook of methods in social psychology* (pp. 359–382). Thousand Oaks, CA: Sage Publications.

Borgatti, S. P., & Molina, J.-L. (2005). Toward ethical guidelines for network research in organizations. *Social Networks*, *27*(2), 107–117. doi:10.1016/j.socnet.2005.01.004

Capurro, R., & Pingel, C. (2002). Ethical issues of online communication research. *Ethics and Information Technology*, *4*(3), 189–194. doi:10.1023/A:1021372527024

Zimbardo, P. (2007). *The Lucifer effect: Understanding how good people turn evil*. New York, NY: Random House.

unit 5

concept explication and measurement

What is media use? How do you know it when you see it? How do you measure it? There are many possible ways to determine how much and what kinds of media a person consumes. Consider having such a conversation with friends about who uses media the most in your social circle. Maybe you want to figure out who the biggest television watcher is. In such a case, a person who spends more hours in front of the television would be considered a "heavy" media user, whereas someone who rarely watches television would a "light" user. Another way of determining a person's media use is to compare the number of media devices that people have. Under this approach, you would conclude that those who have more media devices (e.g., televisions, radios, MP3 players, smartphones, DVD players) would be heavier media users than those who have fewer devices. A third approach might consider what people are doing when they use media. Perhaps you assess this by asking everyone to keep a media diary for a week in which they indicate all of their media activities throughout the course of the day. Using such an approach would allow you to assess how frequently various devices are used, as well as what people are doing with their devices. You might then decide that the people who multitask (i.e., use multiple media at the same time) most frequently are the heaviest or most sophisticated media users.

The various possibilities for measuring media use illustrate that decisions about how concepts are defined and measured can significantly alter the conclusions you reach through research. Because many topics in communication research cannot be objectively defined, we have to make choices about what we mean to study in our own research questions and evaluations of how others have measured those ideas to ensure intersubjectivity. Ultimately, we commit to a particular definition and develop the best measures we can based on that understanding. This unit will deal directly with such issues and highlight the process of concept explication, through which we create the best possible measures for key ideas in our study.

Concept Explication

Concept explication is the process of deciding how to define and then measure concepts. A **concept** is anything that we are trying to study, and it can range from abstract and complicated—such as personality or communicative ability—to more straightforward—such as height, age, or income. The first step in the concept explication process is to develop a **conceptual definition** that clarifies what you mean by the term, drawing upon prior literature and distinguishing the elements that fit your concept from those that are distinct and should not be included in a valid measure. Consider again the concept of media use. By turning to prior research, you would be able to find out how this concept has been measured and perhaps identify a narrower and more focused term that better fits your intentions. This will make the development of a measurement strategy much easier.

variable
→ Unit 2

statistics
→ Unit 14

Of course, the more abstract and complex a concept is, the more **dimensions** or subsets the concept will have. For instance, a concept such as media use might have a number of dimensions because, as indicated in the introduction to this unit, there are many possible ways to consume media. Use might be divided by different media or by different goals or styles of use. A good conceptual definition will clarify possible dimensions.

Following the conceptual definition, the process continues until you figure out how to measure the concept and thereby develop an **operational definition**, which clarifies the exact **indicators** (note: the term "item" is also used to refer to individual measures or questions) used to measure the presence or absence of the concept. This lets us specify the exact variables we need to measure in a study and the possible **attributes** of those variables that each individual might possess. That is, we know what we need to learn about people in order to decide exactly what value of a variable they have. For example, if our variable involves news use, we know that people can indicate their news use by listing all of the shows they watch, all of the publications they read, and all of the websites they visit. Then, we can say whether someone has the attribute of consuming no news, some news, or a great deal of news. Having identified these dimensions, scholars will later evaluate the actual data through techniques such as **factor analysis** to see whether the empirical results match that expectation.

The other important outcome of concept explication is that it can help us identify the right **level of measurement** for evaluating our variables. These variations in level of measurement result in four specific types of variables: **nominal, ordinal, interval,** and **ratio**. In general, the level of measurement tells us about the way the specific attributes relate to one another. Are they just discrete categories with no logical ordering? Or are they specific numbers that give an exact count? Identifying the level of measurement helps develop good questions and carry out the right statistical analysis, and it is an important aspect of explication.

attribute
→ Unit 5

indicators
→ Unit 5

dimensions
→ Unit 5

conceptual definition
→ Unit 5

theory
→ Unit 2

Concept

Two of the most important decisions researchers must make involve *who* they will study and *what* characteristics of those individuals they need to measure. Concepts are the "what" part of that process. Concepts start out as abstract ideas; they must be clarified and focused through the process of concept explication in order to be usable in research studies. Our understanding of a concept must go from abstract and broad to more concrete, specific, and observable. Concepts can be just about anything, but common ones for communication researchers include things such as media use, political attitudes, relationship satisfaction, age, socioeconomic status, race, personality, and attitudes toward an array of social issues, among others. This is a tiny segment of the many different topics that communication researchers consider, but even this segment reveals that concepts can range greatly in terms of complexity. More complex concepts tend to require more complex measurement, drawing upon a greater number of indicators and potentially slicing the concept up into dimensions.

The first step in dealing with concepts is to form a clear conceptual definition. Without being clear about what we mean by a given concept in the abstract, we cannot develop an effective, intersubjective approach to measuring that concept. Researchers start working with concepts at the theory level, and concepts are part of the research questions that they use to guide their work.

For example, researchers might be interested in the following question: *What is the relationship between political attitudes and media use?* In this case, the research question specifies two concepts: (1) political attitudes and (2) media use. The researcher must then work with each of these concepts to get to the point of being able to observe or otherwise measure them as variables. At the start, the concepts are both abstract and "fuzzy"—either one could be taken in any number of directions, depending on the researchers' interests or methodology. For instance, political attitudes could be measured by asking how liberal or conservative people are, or you might ask people about their support for or opposition to specific issues. Thus, not every instance of a concept will be defined in the same way. Abstract labels such as "political attitudes" may be used to refer to a range of actual ideas, and part of the concept explication process is to narrow those ideas to more precise and focused terms.

research question
→ Unit 2

variable
→ Unit 2

Reflect & React: The Many Ways to Measure One Thing

Concepts can vary widely in terms of how abstract or concrete they are at the start of a research project. Consider a situation in which you are assessing presidential State of the Union speeches. One concept that you might want to measure is the length of the different addresses. Length could be a key control variable or even an independent variable. Length is a fairly straightforward concept that could be measured easily without dimensions. One approach would be to simply total the number of words. Another approach would be to time the address in minutes and seconds. Notice how this particular concept is fairly concrete and thus does not have any additional dimensions—we can simply proceed to directly measuring the concept without considering any subsets of the concept.

Of course, you might also be interested in a second concept—how optimistic the addresses are. The level of optimism of a State of the Union address could be a key dependent variable, and it might be something that is affected by external conditions such as the economy or foreign affairs, as well as the personality of the president giving the address. However, optimism is a more complicated concept than the length of the address. For instance, levels of optimism about the present might be different than levels of optimism about the future, suggesting possible dimensions of optimism (both present optimism and future optimism). How might you assess how optimistic a State of the Union address is? Are there different types (i.e., dimensions) of optimism? What are specific things that you would look for in the address to let you know whether it is high or low in optimism?

Conceptual Definition

A conceptual definition presents an abstract description of the meaning of the concept, offering clarity about the intention of the researchers and the boundaries of what the concept does and does not entail. A conceptual definition should be easily understood without reference to particular operational measures, and it should reflect the intersubjective understanding of the term as used in the selected theory. The conceptual definition is the first step in allowing the researcher to move a concept from being abstract to being specific enough to observe. As such, the conceptual definition allows the research to move forward more easily with the concept explication process as the definition offers focus and precludes many possible operational approaches.

For example, in studying media use, researchers might use the following definition: *Media use consists of how frequently people watch television, read the newspaper, and visit web pages.* This definition specifies that the concept is explicitly about three particular types of media—television, newspapers, and websites. It also implicitly indicates that this concept is not about the particular shows people are watching, their attitudes toward particular shows, or how many televisions they own. Researchers should continually return to the conceptual definition they are using as they work through the process of developing dimensions and indicators for their concepts.

It is important to note that conceptual definitions for similar concepts used across a variety of studies may vary somewhat from one study to another. Often, when concepts are new, researchers are trying different approaches to defining and measuring a concept. These differences typically get worked out by the research process through replication and triangulation as researchers adjust and refine concepts. Ultimately, the success of conceptual and operational definitions should rest on whether they reflect an intersubjective understanding, lend themselves to theory development, and result in clear and valid operational definitions.

Dimension

In the concept explication process, concepts often need to be broken up into smaller pieces—also called dimensions—in order to move the concept from its conceptual definition to its observable form. A way to approach this is to think of dimensions as subsets or smaller parts of a concept. The more abstract or complicated a concept is the more dimensions it will likely have. For instance, consider the concept of height, which we could define as "how tall someone is from the bottom of their feet to the top of their head." This is a fairly concrete concept without any smaller parts to it. It really is just one thing—the distance from the bottom of someone's feet to the top of their head. There aren't any dimensions to a concept like this. Now let's consider a more abstract concept—media use, which could be defined as "how frequently people watch television, read the newspaper, and visit websites." In this case, three dimensions of media use are specified: (1) frequency of use of television, (2) frequency of use of newspapers, and (3) frequency of use of websites. From here, the researcher should provide a clear definition for each of these dimensions and then develop appropriate indicators for each dimension. Note how these dimensions fit under the broader concept of "media use." They are distinct parts of this concept but related in the sense that they fit under the concept. For example, how much a person watches television is distinct from how much they read the newspaper, but they are both speaking to the person's media use. This means that by measuring one dimension, we learn something about a concept. By measuring all of the relevant dimensions of a concept, we learn even more about that concept.

relationship → Unit 2
variable → Unit 2
concept → Unit 5
conceptual definition → Unit 5
indicators → Unit 5
theory → Unit 2

Steps to Success: Effective Concept Development

Don't reinvent the wheel—find one that works or improve an existing one! It is almost always a good idea to start by looking at how others have measured a concept before you. Use what previous researchers have done as a starting point, but work to improve upon their measures. Perhaps some indicators were missing or questions were not worded correctly in those previous studies. In other cases, you need to make adjustments because of differences in the topic you are studying versus the original research you are using as your starting point. You can make the necessary adjustments for your research and produce a better, more valid measure. Pre-testing is a good idea as well. Just as you want to test-drive a car to make sure it works and feels good to drive, it also makes sense to try out the measures you have developed on a smaller scale before investing the time and money needed to complete a full-blown study. Use this checklist to develop good conceptual and operational definitions:

1. Identify the concept you wish to explicate.

2. Develop a clear conceptual definition (consult literature for ideas on where to start).
3. Identify and define any needed dimensions (again, consult the literature for ideas).
4. Check your dimensions against your conceptual definition to make sure that they fit.
5. Develop indicators for each of your dimensions.
6. Check your indicators against your conceptual definition to make sure that they fit.
7. Pre-test your indicators to identify any missing dimensions or indicators and other problems that could occur.
8. Conduct your observations and analyze data.
9. Assess the quality of your measurement and make any needed adjustments for future studies.

Whether researchers use dimensions and how many they end up using depends on the particular concept and its conceptual definition. Here we specified three dimensions, yet such a concept could be defined in many ways. For instance, consider if we defined media use as "how frequently people consume different types of content." In this case, the relevant dimensions could be informational-focused content such as news and entertainment-focused content such as dramas or comedies.

The decision about whether and how to divide a concept should be based upon several factors. Most important, the theory or other basis for the study should give some sense of whether the concept needs to be divided. If you have a theory that assumes the specific features of a medium are important, for example, it makes sense to separately evaluate use of newspapers, television, and the Internet. But if you want to measure media use as an outcome of personality or gratifications sought, a different dimensional structure would work better. Additionally, previous research can help establish whether there are logical divisions within a concept. If a prior study showed that two dimensions of media use had distinct relationships with another variable, you should keep that in mind when explicating the concept for your own study. Finally, the empirical results of your own study, based upon the answers participants give and statistical analysis as applicable, can also help clarify the dimensions of a concept.

relationship
→ Unit 2

variable
→ Unit 2

Factor Analysis

Factor analysis is a statistical procedure that allows researchers to look at all of the indicators they have used for a concept or dimension and determine whether they work together effectively or not. Researchers use two approaches in factor analysis: (1) confirmatory and (2) exploratory.

In confirmatory factor analysis, researchers can simultaneously evaluate each of the indicators for a concept to be sure that they measure the intended dimension and don't measure another dimension as effectively. This is an important step in concept explication because it will either provide confirmation that the researcher has effectively explicated the concept or show that further work is needed to improve the measurement approach.

Alternatively, exploratory factor analysis is used when the researcher has a less clear understanding of whether indicators will work and which indicators will fit under which dimensions. For instance, it could be that media use items fit together by the type of media (e.g., traditional media or social media), or it could be that media use items fits together by how they are used (e.g., entertainment or information seeking). Exploratory factor analysis would help address issues such as these. This process is typically used in researching a new area or when researchers are testing a new approach to measuring something. Numerous statistical programs can be used to conduct factor analysis, but the core underlying principle considers the shared relationships between each of the items under consideration. The details of such statistical approaches are beyond the scope of this text, but they are covered in many more specialized volumes.

indicators
→ Unit 5

concept
→ Unit 5

dimension
→ Unit 5

Operational Definition

Whereas the conceptual definition specifies a concept's abstract meaning and scope, the operational definition indicates how that concept and its dimensions will be measured by specifying the indicators that will be used. That is, the operational definition provides the framework for how the researcher will observe the concept in question. Operational definitions are unique to the specific method that the researcher is using. This means that there is an important connection between an operational definition and the specific measurement that is used for a concept or dimension. For example, in survey research, the operational definition of a concept typically includes a series of particular questions that will be asked of participants. These operational measures will be defined in terms of quantifiable outcomes or response options if the study is quantitative in nature. As such, the measurement part would be the implementation of the questions and the responses given to them. The operational definition is used to guide how the concept or dimension is measured. In methods involving interviewing (such as depth interviews or focus groups), on the other hand, the operational definition might consist of one open-ended interview question that generates in-depth discussion about the customer's experience.

Because quality of measurement is so important to the success of any research project and to the quality of the data, the process of determining how to measure concepts and dimensions can be time-consuming and take a lot of trial and error. Researchers typically use previous research as a starting point and then lots of pre-testing and good sense to help them develop effective

conceptual definition
→ Unit 5

concept
→ Unit 5

dimensions
→ Unit 5

indicators
→ Unit 5

survey
→ Unit 10

experiment
→ Unit 9

treatment groups
→ Unit 9

qualitative versus quantitative
→ Unit 3

depth interviews
→ Unit 12

open-ended
→ Unit 7

conceptual
definition
→ Unit 5

operational definitions. The development of an operational definition should clearly emerge from the conceptual definition, so the researchers are confident that the specific measures they are employing will actually measure what they hope to measure. That is, any dimensions specified by the conceptual definition should be clearly measured, just as the concept as a whole should be.

concept
→ Unit 5

operational
definition
→ Unit 5

dimension
→ Unit 5

variable
→ Unit 2

research question
→ Unit 2

hypotheses
→ Unit 2

content validity
→ Unit 6

Indicator

Through the process of concept explication, a concept is moved from an abstract and theoretical idea to something that is concrete and observable. As part of that process, indicators are the exact pieces of information specified by the operational definition that the researcher uses to observe the presence or absence of the concept (or dimension). When these indicators are measured with individual questions or precise observations, we refer to them as *items*. Each item will reflect a specific indicator, and the sum of these indicators captures the variable as a whole. Once the researcher has decided what specific questions, items, or processes will be used to indicate a concept, it then becomes a variable and is now something the researcher can observe and use to answer research questions or test hypotheses.

The more abstract and complicated concepts and dimensions are, the more indicators will be needed to adequately measure them. For instance, the concept of height can be simply defined as the distance in inches from the bottom of the feet to the top of the head while standing upright with your back against the wall. As such, height can be measured with one indicator—a tape measure or similar device. It is not an abstract concept, even though there might be multiple ways to observe height. On the other hand, complex concepts such as personality and intelligence are often measured using tests with dozens or even 100 or more indicators. These concepts often have multiple dimensions (e.g., openness, conscientiousness, and agreeableness are all identified as important personality traits), and may also be abstract and complicated to understand. As researchers develop the particular indicators they plan to use, it is necessary to consider both face validity and content validity to ensure that the necessary indicators are included to appropriately measure the concept.

For media use, the indicators would likely be more complex, but there would also be more of them. For instance, we would likely want to cover television use, newspaper reading, and Internet use. Further, given the many different purposes for which people can use those media, we likely need a few indicators of each. For instance, we might assess how frequently they use each for entertainment purposes, for information seeking, and for relationship maintenance. This results in three indicators for each of the three dimensions, for a total of nine indicators. In many cases, the number can be even higher, but it should always be dependent on what you *need* to measure as a researcher.

Attribute

Another important feature of variables is the potential attributes they encompass. For a given variable, each individual case (here, the "individual" is the unit of analysis) will have one specific attribute. Thus, we generally talk about the attributes of an individual, but the possible values for these attributes are determined by the variable being measured.

The number and nature of these categories depends on the level of measurement. That is, the kind of variable you are creating and the way you are able to evaluate it numerically (if at all) are directly tied to the attributes specified. For instance, in considering the nominal-level measure of your favorite communication technology, in which there are no numbers and each answer is simply a descriptive term, the possible technology choices are the attributes, and each individual, in listing one favorite, will possess that specific attribute. In this case, they might include texting, e-mail, Facebook, and Twitter, among others. Similarly, for the measure of temperature, the attributes are the individual degrees (e.g., 0 degrees, 32 degrees, 100 degrees)—as we will discuss, temperature is an interval-level variable, and these attributes reflect that property. A specific object or day being measured will have the attribute of a specific temperature, while the set of all objects will vary in terms of temperature because of the range of possible attributes. Individual attributes should typically be mutually exclusive in that the categories are explicitly distinct. For example, if researchers are categorizing people based on hair color, they would need to make explicit how the hair colors are different (e.g., blonde, gray, or brown) and eliminate categories that overlap (e.g., brown and auburn or dirty blonde and light brown).

Further, the full set of attributes for a given variable should be exhaustive in that all possible responses should be included. For instance, if researchers want to know how many days a week people watch *The Daily Show*, then the response options should range from 0 to 4 days (new episodes air Monday through Thursday). Excluding any of those options would mean that the list of attributes is not complete, and the validity of the variable becomes compromised. What if the researchers forgot to include 0 as a possible response—how would those who never watch the show answer the question? They would either have to leave the question blank (if answering honestly) or make up an answer. Neither possibility is good for the researcher.

Levels of Measurement

All measures or variables have a specific level of measurement, which defines the mathematical properties of how the possible values for each individual relate to one another. By default, any variable, even if it is qualitative, must be able to be expressed as at least a nominal-level measure. Subsequent levels of measurement retain the qualities of the "lower" level of measurement while adding additional

variable
→ Unit 2

unit of analysis
→ Unit 2

level of measurement
→ Unit 5

nominal
→ Unit 5

range
→ Unit 14

mutually exclusive
→ Unit 7

exhaustive
→ Unit 7

validity
→ Unit 6

quantitative versus qualitative
→ Unit 3

variance
→ Unit 14

range
→ Unit 14

random error
→ Unit 6

traits. The next level of measurement, ordinal, adds a logical order to the values. Interval-level measures have meaningful intervals between values—that is, the gap between two scores on a variable is equivalent to the value of the smaller score subtracted from the larger score, regardless of the specific values. Finally, ratio-level measures have all of the previous traits and also possess a true 0, such that an individual with a score of 0 has none of whatever is being measured. The higher the level of measurement, the more detail is captured.

Consider two possible approaches to measuring use of a product, such as frozen meatballs. The first, a nominal-level measure, would simply ask individuals whether they use the product or not (i.e., do they prepare or eat frozen meatballs or not). Because all individuals fall into one of the two categories, there is little variance, and there is a wide range of amounts of use compressed into the "user" category. A ratio-level measure might ask individuals how many meatballs they eat each month. This would provide far more variance, distinguishing individuals who ate only a few meatballs from those who ate hundreds each month.

The level of measurement also determines which statistical tests can be used, with more sophisticated tests often requiring higher levels of measurement. However, higher levels of measurement also assume more about the answers provided, and those assumptions may not always be met if participants or observers don't carefully follow directions or cannot answer with the expected level of detail. People simply may not remember how many meatballs they ate, and if they are just guessing, this could create a large amount of random error that would offset any value to using a more nuanced level of measurement.

Because the level of measurement of a variable has implications for the types of statistical tests that can be used to evaluate it, it is useful for researchers to anticipate the types of tests they expect to run so that they have a good idea of how to effectively measure the variables they will need. In general, it is a good idea to use the highest level of measurement possible. This is because a ratio variable can be converted to an interval variable, an interval variable can be converted to an ordinal measure, and an ordinal measure can be converted to a nominal-level measure. However, you cannot construct variables going the other way. For instance, a nominal variable cannot be converted to an ordinal, interval, or ratio variable. In this case, you would be stuck with the nominal measure and therefore limited in how you can use that variable in statistical analyses.

Steps to Success: Determining Level of Measurement

Figuring out the level of measurement for a variable can be challenging, but it is critical to identifying the right statistics to use, the correct way to word hypotheses, and many more steps in the research process. When you are explicating your variables, you may be able to choose the level of measurement for a given variable. However, some variables necessarily fit into a particular level of measurement. In addition, if you are dealing with existing data, you will want to know the level of measurement for variables. Because each level of measurement adds a new requirement beyond the previous level, an effective way to determine the level of measurement is to approach each variable with the following questions:

First, make sure it is a variable. That is, ask yourself who (or what) the unit of analysis is for the variable—that is, the individual or social artifact being described. Then, ask whether each of those individuals necessarily has one and only one value for this variable. Finally, ask whether there are differences among individuals—do some people have a different value, or attribute, than others? If the answers to all of these questions are yes, you know that you have a variable.

Next, determine whether the variable has some logical ordering. Can you say that a person with one value is necessarily "higher" on the scale than a person with another value? Don't just assume that because people are given numbers, these numbers have any meaning. Ask yourself whether you could logically sort all of the different individuals in your study from "least" to "most." If so, then you know you have at least an ordinal-level measure. If not, your variable must be nominal, and you can stop asking questions here.

The level after ordinal is interval. For this, ask yourself whether the numbers tell you something more than just the order of individuals. Consider someone who answers 1, someone else who answers 2, and a third person who answers 3. Do you feel reasonably confident that the person who said 2 is just as different from the person who said 1 as the person who said 3? Sometimes, this means that each person filled out a scale where each answer was numbered and equally spaced, and you can logically think about those spaces. So long as you feel reasonably confident in this spacing, you have at least an interval-level measure. However, if you answer no to the question about spacing, you have an ordinal-level measure and can stop here.

Finally, you should figure out whether your variable is ratio level. That is, does it make sense to talk about someone having a value, or attribute, of 0? Even if no one actually falls into the 0 value in the data, it might still be logical to have a value of 0. Most variables for which we actually count things, using numbers like those you learned on Sesame Street, are ratio-level measures. If you are confident that a logical 0 exists, then you have a ratio-level variable. Otherwise, because you answered yes at all of the earlier stages, you have an interval-level measure.

Nominal-Level Measure

The most basic level of measurement is nominal. In order to be a variable, any measurement must meet two standards. First, it must be mutually exclusive—that is, each individual must fall into only one value for the measure. Second, it must be exhaustive—that is, every individual must fall into some value of

level of measurement
→ Unit 5

variable
→ Unit 2

111

the measure. Basically, each person must have one and only one value for the variable.

For example, if a study of social networks asks you which technology is most important to you for keeping in touch with your friends, a measure of this would have to do two things. First, it would have to be worded and designed such that each person would pick only one technology, such as social networking sites, e-mail, voice conversations, texting, and so on. Because the question asks which is *most* important, only one answer would be valid. You might use other technologies, but only one can be the most important. Second, it would have to include all possible technologies, even if this means offering an "other" category.

Nominal-level measures are sometimes described as qualitative because, although they describe the specific value of a variable for each individual, they don't count that variable in any way, as a quantitative measure would. This doesn't mean that nominal-level measures cannot be used in quantitative analysis with statistics. Several tests of relationships can compare individuals who fall into different groups, as captured by a nominal-level measure. However, relying on nominal-level measures does limit the amount of information captured by a measure. When possible, it is helpful to use a higher level of measurement.

Ordinal-Level Measure

The ordinal level of measurement meets all of the requirements for a nominal-level measure—each individual fits into one and only one value—and additionally has a logical order to the values. That is, the values can be sorted from lowest to highest or vice versa. This is often done by assigning numbers to the values. For example, the lowest value might be 1, the highest 7, and the values in between set between 2 and 6. However, these numbers don't have a true quantitative meaning; you could just as easily assign values of A through G to indicate the logical order.

For example, consider a study in which you want to understand media preferences. You might ask people to rank their three favorite comic book characters of all time. One participant might rate Batman first, Squirrel Girl second, and Wolverine third. But this doesn't mean that the respondent feels that Batman is better than Squirrel Girl by as much as Squirrel Girl is better than Wolverine. Maybe she thinks that Batman and Squirrel Girl are almost equally good and then chooses Wolverine from a long list of "so-so" heroes. Suppose you are comparing the effects of advertisements featuring each hero. With an ordinal-level measure, you would expect that an ad with Batman would perform best for this person, and an ad with Wolverine would do worst (of the three). But you wouldn't assume that the ad with Batman would increase sales over the Squirrel Girl ad by exactly the same amount as the

Squirrel Girl ad would over the Wolverine ad. The difference between values is not constant or meaningful.

In general, ordinal-level measures are more nuanced than nominal-level measures, but there are many statistical approaches that don't work for these measures. For example, you cannot calculate the mean for an ordinal-level measure. In many cases, scholars attempt to construct ordinal-level measures to resemble interval-level measures as much as possible. For example, a scale that measures how much people agree or disagree with a statement, ranging from "strongly disagree" to "strongly agree," could be considered an ordinal-level measure. But by providing a larger numerical range for these answers, deleting labels between the two extreme anchors, and representing the remaining answers on an equally spaced numerical scale (e.g., 1–7 scale), researchers can approximate an interval-level measure. This "interval-like" approach is often used in communication research, while ordinal-level measures are relatively rare.

Interval-Level Measure

Variables measured at the interval level have all of the qualities of nominal- and ordinal-level measures, along with the additional trait of possessing equal intervals between consecutively numbered values. That is, the difference between individuals scoring a 3 and a 4 on the chosen scale should be the same as the difference between those individuals scoring a 4 and a 5. The measure must also have a logical ordering of values, and each individual should fall into one and only one value. However, interval-level measures do not have a true 0, unlike ratio-level measures.

An excellent example of an interval-level measure is temperature. No matter how cold or warm it is, increasing the heat by 10 degrees always means the same thing and reflects the same amount of heat. If you turn up the thermostat 10 degrees, you will soon feel 10 degrees warmer, whether that takes the temperature from 40 to 50 or from 80 to 90. As a consequence, it's possible to use addition and subtraction when thinking about interval-level measures. For example, suppose you know that the average temperature in your town is 75 degrees Fahrenheit. If today's temperature is 65, you can subtract that from 75 and say that it is 10 degrees below normal. If tomorrow the temperature is 10 degrees above normal, you would add 10 to 75 and determine that tomorrow's temperature is 85. This ability is important in computing many statistics, such as the mean and standard deviation. Because these values are, in turn, important to many other statistical techniques, scholars strive for at least interval-level measures whenever possible.

In communication research, however, it can be difficult to have truly interval-level measures. For example, many studies of politics ask individuals to place political figures on a "thermometer scale" ranging between 0 and 100.

nominal-level measure
→ Unit 5

ordinal-level measure
→ Unit 5

ratio-level measure
→ Unit 5

statistics
→ Unit 14

mean
→ Unit 14

standard deviation
→ Unit 14

113

The "warmer" the score, the more favorable the opinions. Similar scales are used for measuring attitudes toward companies and brands. Even though this scale sounds like a temperature scale, it may not be a perfect interval-level measure. People may not see the gap between 10 and a 20 (both highly negative scores) and 45 and 55 (moving from negative to positive) as equivalent. The latter may be a perceptually bigger difference.

Despite this, scales that have many values, presented numerically and sometimes visually in a way that implies equal intervals, are often called "interval-like" and usually can be treated as interval-level measures for analysis. An example of this is the use of Likert-type items, which are often measured using a 7-point scale with "strongly disagree" to "strongly agree" as anchor points. In many cases researchers use multiple Likert-type items as indicators, which they combine into more measures that more closely approximate characteristics of interval-level measures than they do of ordinal level measures. Because of this, it is easy to find examples of researchers using those types of measures in statistical procedures that require as least interval-level measures. Note, though, how these types of measures still meet the primary interval characteristic of not having a true zero point. Consider how much you might agree or disagree with a statement such as "I enjoy going to the park." There is no true zero amount of attitude; you either agree or disagree with that statement to some degree. The closest approximation to zero would be the midpoint, which often represents more neutral feelings toward a Likert-type item. Although some researchers will assign that a value of 0 and have a scale that ranges from −3 to 3, that "zero" doesn't represent the absence of feelings, just more tepid feelings toward something.

Ratio-Level Measure

The ratio level of measurement meets all of the requirements for an interval-level measure: each individual should fall into one and only one value, the values are logically ordered, and the numbers assigned to each value accurately reflect the gap between values. In addition, a ratio-level measure also has a true zero—that is, for individuals who are assigned a value of 0 for the scale, they truly have none of whatever is being measured.

For example, suppose you are measuring exposure to advertisements. Individuals who report having seen no ads will be assigned a value of 0, and this number indicates they have seen no ads. In contrast, you might also measure how people feel about the advertisements and ask them to indicate their feelings on a scale from −3 (very negative) to 3 (positive), which we would treat as an interval measure. Here, a 0 would imply neutral feelings, but it does not mean the respondent has *no* feelings about the ad. In general, ratio-level measures can be analyzed with the same statistics as interval-level measures.

level of measurement
→ Unit 5

interval-level measure
→ Unit 5

statistics
→ Unit 14

linear
→ Unit 15

An additional benefit of ratio-level measures is the ability to use multiplication and division when analyzing and transforming scores on the measure. If you are measuring the number of ads a person viewed, for example, you would expect that a person viewing 4 ads would be twice as influenced as someone viewing 2 ads (assuming a linear effect). By extension, you would expect someone viewing 8 ads to be twice as influenced as someone viewing 4. Moreover, because you could also use addition and subtraction, you would also expect that the increase between viewing 4 and 8 ads (4) would be twice that of the increase between viewing 2 and 4 ads (2).

Research in Depth

Measures of media use vary widely, ranging from very broad to highly specific. These variations are often a function of needs that the researcher has based on specific research questions and hypotheses. Here are a few examples:

Dalisay (2012) measured print media and radio use using a 5-point Likert scale. The attributes ranged from 1 to 5 and included the corresponding options of never, less than once a week, once a week, a few times a week, and every day. Television use was measured by having respondents indicate the numbers of hours per week it was used. The study explored the relationship between media use and acculturation for new immigrants to the United States.

Instead of directly measuring media use, Skoric and Poor (2013) measured attention paid to specific aspects of the media, including such items as "attention paid to international politics" and "attention paid to international news other than politics," among others. Items used a scale that ranged from 1, meaning "little attention," to 7, meaning "very close attention." The study explored the role that both traditional and social media can play in online as well as traditional participation.

In a study of the relationship between television use and fear of crime, Custers and Van den Bulck (2011) took a two-pronged approach to measuring television use. Specifically, they assessed both frequency of viewing, which asked respondents how many days per week they watched television, and viewing volume, which asked participants to estimate how many hours per day they viewed television. These two indicators were used to create a total viewing measure by multiplying the frequency and volume items.

Activities

Activity 5A: Explicating Concepts

See terms: concept; concept explication; conceptual definition; dimension; operational definition.

The goal of this activity is to practice explicating concepts to familiarize yourself with how the process works. For this activity, select two communication concepts that are of interest to you (or use concepts provided by your instructor). Follow the steps given next for each concept to work through the explication process.

- Start by exploring relevant research literature to develop a clear conceptual definition for your concept.
- Based on the conceptual definition, determine what dimensions (if any) will be part of the concept. If you have identified dimensions, use the literature to develop clear definitions of those dimensions.
- Use the literature you have read to develop an operational definition for at least one of the dimensions.
- Critically assess the operational definition you have developed. What is missing? How could the measure be improved? What difficulties might you face in measuring this concept?

Activity 5B: Matching Conceptual and Operational Definitions

See terms: conceptual definition; operational definition.

The left-hand column lists a series of conceptual definitions. In the right-hand column, a series of possible indicators are listed that are part of an operational definition for one of the concepts from the left-hand column. For this activity, match each conceptual definition with the most appropriate operational definition. Explain your choice.

Table 5.1 Matching Conceptual and Operational Definitions

Conceptual definition	Operational definition
News consumption: "How frequently a person obtains news from print, broadcast, or online sources"	• How many protest marches have you attended in the past month? • How many rallies or sit-ins have you attended in the past month?
Television consumption: "How often a person watches various types of television content"	• I am typically able to get my friends to agree with my opinions. • My friends tend to listen to me for advice on life decisions.
Peer pressure: "The extent to which others influence a person's decision making"	• I seek out opportunities to join rallies and other similar events. • Marching for a cause I support is interesting to me.
Social influence: "The extent to which a person influences other people's decision making"	• How often do you read about politics in your local newspaper? • How often do you check online news sources for news about your community?
Protest participation: "How often a person participates in protest activities including marches, rallies, and sit-ins"	• I often find ways for my friends to give input before making a major purchase. • I will sometimes do things I don't want to do to make my friends happy.
Protesting interest: "A person's interest and willingness to engage in protest behaviors"	• How often do you watch reality television shows? • How often do you watch professional sports on network television?

Activity 5C: Defining and Measuring Everyday Concepts

See terms: concept; concept explication; conceptual definition; operational definition.

Next is a list of some concepts that are common to the workplace that we could explore in helping to understand how our employees are doing. For each of these concepts, follow the steps described later to develop conceptual and operational definitions and consider what challenges you might face in measuring these concepts.

- Job satisfaction
- Hours worked
- Quality of relationship with boss/manager
- Workplace communication style
- Loyalty to the company.

For each of the concepts, follow these steps:

- Develop a clear conceptual definition for your concept.
- Based on the conceptual definition, determine what dimensions (if any) will be part of the concept. If you have identified dimensions, use the literature to develop clear definitions of those dimensions.
- Develop an operational definition for at least one of the dimensions.
- What challenges might you face in measuring this concept in the workplace?

Activity 5D: Evaluating the Explication Process in Scholarly Research

See terms: conceptual definition; literature review; operational definition.

Start by finding a scholarly research article on a topic of interest to you. Next, evaluate the explication process for two of the concepts used in that article. To do so, use the following questions to guide your analysis of the explication process for each concept:

- How do the authors conceptually define the concept? Is the definition clearly presented? How well do they develop and support this definition using the literature?
- What steps do they provide along the way? (dimensions, indicators, etc.)
- Do the operational measures match the conceptual definition?
- What could the authors have done more effectively in explicating this concept?

References

Custers, K., & Van den Bulck, J. (2011). The relationship of dispositional and situational fear of crime with television viewing and direct experience with crime. *Mass Communication and Society*, *14*(5), 600–619. doi:10.1080/15205436.2010.530382

Dalisay, F. (2012). Media use and acculturation of new immigrants in the United States. *Communication Research Reports*, *29*(2), 148–160. doi:10.1080/08824096.2012.667774

Skoric, M. M., & Poor, N. (2013). Youth engagement in Singapore: The interplay of social and traditional media. *Journal of Broadcasting & Electronic Media*, *57*(2), 187–204. doi :10.1080/08838151.2013.787076

Suggested Readings for Further Exploration of Unit 5 Topics

Examples

Hecht, M. L. (1978). The conceptualization and measurement of interpersonal communication satisfaction. *Health Communication Research*, *4*(3), 253–264. doi:10.1111/j.1468-2958.1978.tb00614.x

Kiousis, S. (2002). Interactivity: A concept explication. *New Media & Society*, *4*(3), 355–383. doi:10.1177/146144480200400303

Lombard, M., & Ditton, T. (1997). At the heart of it all: The concept of presence. *Journal of Computer-Mediated Communication*, *3*(2). doi:10.1111/j.1083-6101.1997.tb00072.x

Marchionni, D. M. (2013). Journalism-as-a-conversation: A concept explication. *Communication Theory*, *23*(2), 131–147. doi:10.1111/comt.12007

Park, S. Y. (2012). Mediated intergroup contact: Concept explication, synthesis, and application. *Mass Communication and Society*, *15*(1), 136–159. doi:10.1080/15205436 .2011.558804

Stephen, T. (2001). Concept analysis of the communication literature on marriage and family. *Journal of Family Communication*, *1*(2), 91–110. doi:10.1207/S15327698JFC0102_01

Advanced Discussion

Chaffee, S. H. (1991). *Explication* (Vol. 1). Newbury Park, CA: Sage Publications.

McLeod, J. M., & Pan, Z. (2005). Concept explication and theory construction. In S. Dunwoody, L. B. Becker, D. M. McLeod, & G. M. Kosicki (Eds.), *The evolution of key mass communication concepts: Honoring Jack M. McLeod* (pp. 13–76). Cresskill, NJ: Hampton Press.

unit 6

---

reliability and validity

The task of moving furniture is something that many of us have experienced. You may be able to relate to the experience of trying to figure out whether a couch will fit through the doorway, up the stairs, and into the next room. Because most of us don't carry a tape measure with us—or we are simply too lazy to use it—we end up using other means to measure the couch. For instance, we might put our hands on either end of the couch to see how wide it is (think "the couch is *this* big!") and then hold them in place as we move over to the doorway to see whether the space between our outstretched arms is less than the width of the doorway. This is, of course, a terrible way to measure distance. The main problem is that our hands likely will move out of position as we walk across the room. The couch might be 4 feet wide, but our hands might be 3 feet apart by the time we get to the doorway. We would conclude that the couch will fit and then waste time and energy moving it over to a doorway it can't possibly fit through.

A better way to measure the length, width, or height of the couch would be to use a tape measure. We could measure the length, width, and height of the couch, write those values down, and then compare them to the measurements of the doorway. We would characterize using the tape measure as a *good* way of measuring length and using our hands as a *bad* way of measuring length.

This example illustrates the issue of measurement quality. A measure that is high quality should work consistently and be accurate. The same principles hold true for things that we measure in communication research. For example, suppose we are measuring audience interest in a film after watching a trailer. We could do so by assessing how actively people discuss it on Twitter, but we would want to be certain that our measure is a good one. That is, our method of counting tweets about the film should match the actual number of tweets sent, and we should be just as accurate every time. Moreover, counting tweets should actually tell us something about interest. It should be related to how many people actually see the movie, for example, and not just tell us that people who like to tweet were more likely to see the trailer.

In research terms, consistency and accuracy refer to reliability and validity, respectively, and they are essential to consider in producing high-quality measures. This unit will detail different ways to assess reliability and validity and provide key building blocks for producing effective measures that you can use in your own research.

Measurement Error

Effective concept explication will define the intended meaning of a variable, but actually following through on our operational definition will inevitably result in some error. Measurement error represents the difference between the observed or recorded value for a variable and the *true* value of that variable as it is conceptually defined. For example, consider a situation in which you are interested

concept
explication
→ Unit 5

variable
→ Unit 2

in tracking Twitter activity over time, and you want to know how often people tweet. One approach to this research would be to ask a sample of your peers to report how many times they tweet on a typical day. The goal of the research would be to accurately measure the *true* number of tweets that people are sending on a typical day. Any deviation from that true number would be the result of measurement error.

There are several reasons why you might not accurately measure the number of tweets in a day. Maybe your participants incorrectly reported their Twitter use, either because they misunderstood the question or simply forgot about a tweet sent late at night when they got home from the bar, for example. More broadly, all research will involve some measurement error, but the goal of concept explication and effective research design is to make that error as small as possible.

These errors can be divided into two types: random and systematic. **Random error** represents unpredictable variations between the measured and true value of a variable, while systematic error reflects bias in measurement that causes the recorded value of a variable to be consistently different from the true value. For example, suppose you are interviewing customers about whether they saw an ad for your product. Random error would result if customers had poor memories and frequently forgot whether they saw the ad. Some who said they saw it actually didn't, and some who said they didn't actually did—and unfortunately, we cannot tell which individuals were wrong. On the other hand, **systematic error** would occur if there was some reason for people to be more likely to say that they saw the ad. Maybe everyone who saw the ad remembered it, but many of those who didn't see the ad wanted to tell us what we wanted to hear. This would create a systematic error, leading us to overestimate how many people saw the ad and how much it affected them.

These general categories of errors are important in a number of contexts, but they describe any sources of error, not just problems with measurement. Researchers have more specific terms to talk about error that occurs in measurement and design: reliability and validity. **Reliable** measures are consistent and precise, minimizing random error. **Valid** measures are accurate, producing a true picture of the underlying variable. It is possible for a measure to be reliable without being valid—that is, the result is consistently inaccurate. However, it is not possible for a measure to be valid without being reliable, as a measure that isn't consistent cannot be said to regularly match the true value.

Both aspects of measurement quality are important enough that researchers have developed specific considerations and ways to test reliability and validity. When considering reliability, researchers may consider **item-total reliability, parallel-forms reliability, split-halves reliability,** and **test-retest reliability.** Another aspect of reliability, intercoder reliability, is specifically important to content analysis and addressed in that unit. Reliability is frequently considered when scholars are forming **indexes**, which are variables that are formed by combining individual items or scores. In this case, testing reliability often involves computing a statistic known as **Cronbach's alpha**. Validity is also evaluated in several ways, including **construct**, **content**, **criterion**, and **internal**. Like reliability, there are also aspects of validity such as **external validity** that matter to the overall quality of a study but aren't specifically evaluated as part of measurement construction.

Random Error

All measurement error can be categorized as either random or systematic error. Random error occurs when the measured value of a variable does not match the true value, and the differences cannot be predicted. Random error fluctuates between individuals. Consider the research project in which you are measuring the number of tweets people make per day, based on individuals' self-reported use of Twitter. Some people may have forgotten a few tweets or chosen to round down, or they simply may have used Twitter less that day and thus underestimated their average use. Others may have had an exceptionally busy day or rounded up, or they may have been thinking of tweets from others that they read but didn't retweet.

In a large enough sample, these errors would cancel one another out. While individual scores would deviate from the real value, the mean number of tweets reported would be approximately equal to the mean number actually sent. However, we would not be able to predict for any given participant whether their report was too high, too low, or just right. We might be able to predict which types of people are more likely to make an error—those who are in a hurry, or have difficulty reading, or aren't invested in the study probably make more mistakes. But we still couldn't say whether they will overestimate or underestimate their Twitter habits. Only if we were given access to their account could we compare their self-report to a better measure of the true value and know just how much error our measurement created.

Over time, researchers have found ways to address random error, by helping increase the reliability of measures and testing that reliability. The idea of reliability is closely linked to random error. Random measurement error is problematic because the goal of research is to predict the relationship between variables. Doing this involves being able to explain that different people have different values for a variable. For example, we might want to know whether women tweet more often than men. By measuring the number of tweets sent, we could see whether there is a difference in tweeting for men and women. And we could see whether the difference between men and women is meaningful, or just a tiny amount compared to the differences among people that aren't predicted by gender. If some of those individual differences are attributable

validity
→ Unit 6

systematic error
→ Unit 6

variable
→ Unit 2

sample
→ Unit 8

mean
→ Unit 14

reliability
→ Unit 6

prediction
→ Unit 2

relationship
→ Unit 2

variance
→ Unit 14

to unreliable measurements, and not to true differences, we will never be able to predict that error. People will seem more different than they actually are, and we'll always wonder where those differences came from. This problem, in which our ability to explain variance is reduced as a result of random error, is known as *attenuation*.

Systematic Error

Like random error, systematic error is one of the two types of measurement error. Systematic measurement error occurs when measured values deviate from the true value in a way that can be predicted and is consistent across individuals. Note that not *all* individuals need to give consistently incorrect (i.e., biased) responses, as long as there is a pattern to those who do give incorrect responses. That is, if half of people gave an accurate answer and the other half all gave a number that was too high, the average result would be too high and this pattern would mean we still have systematic error.

Systematic measurement error is best understood by direct comparison with random error. For example, we used the example of measuring the number of tweets to show potential sources of random error. This approach might also create systematic error. Suppose that younger individuals overestimated their Twitter use because they felt that doing so would make them seem more popular. Even though not all participants would be prone to such bias, the tendency among young individuals would lead to that group consistently scoring too high (and, importantly, scoring higher than the true number of tweets). This pattern reflects a systematic measurement error. If we estimated how many tweets people actually sent, on average, our guess would be too high. Unlike random error, though, this tendency could be predicted. If we checked the Twitter accounts of our participants to get a better estimate of the true value, we would discover that the average reported number of tweets was too high for those under age 30. We could then accurately predict that young people tend to overstate their tweets. Even if this is not true for every young person, it's still a pattern, and thus we still see a relationship.

Because issues with systematic error involve measurements that are incorrect but consistent, we tend to talk about aspects of measurement validity when thinking about ways to assess whether we have created systematic error. Unfortunately, systematic error can be difficult to measure. If we have no other way of knowing the true value for our variable, we might assume that because the measure is consistent and related to other variables in a predictable way, it is valid. We would then reach incorrect conclusions when stating relationships and making estimates about the population.

Reflect & React: Validity of Everyday Items

We often take the accuracy of products designed to measure things for granted. For example, consider the tape measure you might use to measure your couch before you move it. Typically, we buy the tape measure at a store, bring it home, and use it without questioning whether it is accurately measuring things. Is 1 inch on the tape measure truly measuring 1 inch? If we don't consider that question, then we are disregarding the potential for measurement error. In particular, if the tape measure was incorrectly designed, any measures we take using that tape measure would be rife with systematic measurement error.

What are some things you could do to validate that the tape measure you have purchased is doing its job and measuring things accurately? What are some factors that might make a tape measure produce less valid results?

Reliability

The *consistency* of a measurement is described as its reliability. A reliable measure will produce the same result each time. This is also referred to as *precision*. Reliability is an important feature of effective measures; if a variable is not measured reliably, it is impossible for the scores for that measure to be valid. After all, if a measure gives different scores every time it's used, then it can't be said to match a single, specific true value. However, just because a measure is reliable, that does not ensure it is valid.

Consider a study of aggression. One way to measure aggression would be to ask study participants to evaluate the person who administered the study. If the evaluations are harsh and might hurt the career prospects of the researcher, scholars argue, then this could be an indication of aggression. Evaluation scores are likely to be consistent; a participant who says that a researcher wasn't helpful is also likely to say that he or she was rude. But that doesn't prove that evaluation scores necessarily reflect aggression. It could be that feelings of aggression have no influence on these scores and that other factors are more important. Maybe some people are evaluated differently because of how they look. Maybe some evaluators just prefer giving lower numbers. In this case, the measure is reliable, but it is not valid in measuring aggression. That is because it is not actually measuring aggression but something else.

item-total reliability
→ Unit 6

parallel-forms reliability
→ Unit 6

split-halves reliability
→ Unit 6

test-retest reliability
→ Unit 6

descriptive statistics
→ Unit 14

Cronbach's alpha
→ Unit 6

concept
→ Unit 5

Reliability can be tested in several ways; for many measures, there are multiple elements of the approach that must be consistent. Broadly, tests of reliability focus on how well the overall measure produces the same result over time, how consistent individual items are with one another, and how well different measures or observers match up. Not all of these are considered in this unit. Aspects of reliability that are directly addressed here include item-total reliability, parallel-forms reliability, split-halves reliability, and test-retest reliability. Some of these aspects can be quantified, as with Cronbach's alpha, which measures item-total reliability. Each aspect is tested a different way, but all tests are focused on the same core idea. If a measurement is reliable, then every part of that measure should give the same result as the other parts and as the whole measure, every time, no matter who is doing the research.

Item-Total Reliability

The item-total approach to measuring reliability involves comparing scores on individual items, such as single questions, to the total score for all items used to construct the measure. (Remember, an *item* is a single piece of information, often in the form of a number taken from a quantitative question or observation.) This is particularly relevant when forming indexes, in which several questions that reflect the same concept are combined to create a single quantitative variable. In your own life, you've probably encountered the idea of item-total reliability many times without realizing it. Think about an exam that has 20 short-answer questions, each graded on a 0–5 scale. The total possible exam score is 100; this represents the "total" aspect of this approach to reliability, or the overall index score. Each test question is an item, just as a series of Likert questions on a survey could be individual measures of a broader concept. The goal of the exam is to measure how well you understand the material from the class. If "understanding" is something that has just one dimension, then someone who understands the material well should be likely to do well on any question, and someone with poor understanding should show a tendency to do poorly across all the questions.

We can use this idea to illustrate how tests of item-total reliability work. Suppose you are the professor looking over students' grades on this exam. You might wonder how well scores on each question match the overall exam scores. If each question is consistent and reflects the same concept, then, on average, people who did well on the exam as a whole should score better on each question. Now suppose that one of the questions doesn't show this pattern. Instead, students who scored 4 or 5 on this question tended to earn a D or F on the exam, whereas those who scored 1 or 2 otherwise did very well and received an A on the exam. Something is clearly wrong with that question: it might be a good measure of something, but it isn't consistent with what the other exam questions measured. Thus, you would reject this question on the basis of item-total reliability.

reliability
→ Unit 6

index
→ Unit 6

concept
→ Unit 5

variable
→ Unit 2

dimension
→ Unit 5

indicators
→ Unit 5

relationship
→ Unit 2

reliability
→ Unit 6

This same process can be applied any time multiple questions are used with the idea that they can be combined into a single score to measure a concept, a common practice in social science research. When you evaluate item-total reliability you are determining whether the items in question should be grouped together or if an item or two should be removed from the list. As the previous example illustrates, if an item (or question) stands out and doesn't match the pattern of the overall measure, it likely should be removed from the group of items you intend to use.

Parallel-Forms Reliability

The parallel-forms approach to reliability involves matching scores from different ways of measuring the same concept to see whether they are consistent. For example, consider an exam in which the instructor includes both short-answer and multiple-choice questions. If the intention of the exam is to test overall understanding of the course, and the same material is addressed in both sections, then the scores on each section should be similar.

Consider what it would suggest if this were not true. For example, what would an instructor conclude if the people who did well on the multiple-choice questions didn't score any better on the short-answer section than those who failed the multiple-choice section? Several things could be true. The multiple-choice scores may reflect a good set of questions, but the short-answer questions could be flawed. Or the multiple-choice questions may just reflect random guessing, while the short-answer questions are good indicators of the true concept. It could also be that *neither* set of questions is effective, and the reason some people did better than others on either section has to do with chance and not meaningful knowledge.

Parallel-forms reliability does not necessarily indicate which form is reliable and which is not. It simply shows that the two forms are not consistent, and this could reflect some sort of random error. However, in some situations, it is possible to be a little more certain. Scholars have developed certain scales that are known to work well, and they have published papers that provide evidence showing these scales are both reliable and valid. In some cases, though, these measures are ineffective for other reasons. They might be extremely long or difficult to use with specific groups of people. For example, we might know that you can measure someone's personality using a 200-question scale, but inserting that scale into a study might just take too much time and space. If a scholar can compare a new measure to this existing measure and show that the answers are consistent, this confirms that the new measure is reliable. For our personality measure, maybe we have a 20-question scale we think also works. With a small group of people we could ask for the 20-question and 200-question scales and look for consistency, letting us be confident that the 20-question scale will be reliable even when we use it by itself. This process is related to the

| concept |
| → Unit 5 |
| **reliable** |
| → Unit 6 |
| **validity** |
| → Unit 6 |
| **criterion validity** |
| → Unit 6 |
| **reliability** |
| → Unit 6 |

idea of criterion validity. Therefore, sometimes the comparison between measures used to evaluate reliability can also demonstrate that the new measure matches an existing, valid measure.

Reflect & React: Reliability Assessments in Everyday Life

There are both challenges and benefits to assessing parallel-forms reliability. The biggest challenge is ensuring that the different measures are similar enough to one another without being either too close or too far apart. Often, standardized tests such as the SAT, ACT, or GRE employ parallel forms as a way of reducing cheating. This means that multiple versions of a test are published, so that the likelihood that two people sitting next to one another will have the same test is very small, as is the likelihood that a person who repeats the test will take the same exact version again. Of course, the challenge to designers of these tests is making sure the various versions of the test are equivalent in their level of difficulty.

As way of exploring this concept, take a look at a recent test you have taken. Consider what you would do if asked to create an alternative version of the test that does not use the same questions or exact format but is roughly equivalent in difficulty. How would you go about determining whether your alternative exam is parallel to the original version?

---

concept
→ Unit 5

random error
→ Unit 6

item-total
reliability
→ Unit 6

variable
→ Unit 2

parallel-forms
reliability
→ Unit 6

Split-Halves Reliability

Split-halves reliability involves dividing all of the items used to measure a concept into two (or more) groups and seeing whether the average for each group of items is consistent with the averages for the other groups. Consider the example of a multiple-choice exam with 100 questions. An instructor might randomly choose 50 questions from the entire exam and calculate the total score for each student on those questions. Then, for comparison, the instructor would calculate the total for the other 50 items. If the overall exam is reliable, these two scores should be closely related. People scoring well above average on the first half should also score well above average on the second half. If not, then the reason people did well on some questions and not others probably has more to do with luck (a form of random error) than with knowledge of the material.

Split-halves reliability is similar to item-total reliability in that it requires a variable that combines many individual items to measure the concept, and it provides a test of whether these items are consistent with one another. It can be faster and easier to determine than item-total reliability because only one comparison between the two randomly created halves is needed, as opposed to a comparison between each item and the total. However, split-halves reliability cannot indicate which questions are creating the lack of reliability; it can only show that *some* random error must be present. Split-halves reliability is also similar to parallel-forms reliability because it involves comparing scores for the same person between two separate scales. However, with split-halves reliability, these scales are randomly created subsets of the intended final scale, whereas parallel-forms reliability involves comparisons between two distinct scales not designed to be administered together.

Test-Retest Reliability

The test-retest approach to reliability compares individuals' scores on the same question or set of questions as measured at two different points in time. If the measure is reliable, the scores from one time should be consistent with the scores at a later point. If the scores don't match, something is flawed with the measures. Perhaps there were many answers influenced by mistakes in how the questions were answered or the observations recorded. Perhaps the questions were hard to answer, and individuals just made up or guessed at their responses; after time passed, they made up new answers.

However, test-retest reliability cannot always be used to assess measurement reliability. First, some scores will naturally change over time. If we ask people about their current mood, they might report being sad; tomorrow, they could say they are happy. This doesn't mean the scale is unreliable; it simply could be that the person felt better the next day. Second, some scores will be affected by learning about the questions the first time through. Think about an exam: after you take the exam, you might talk about the answers with your friends, review your notes, or simply reflect upon the answers until you remember the right choice. If you could sit down and take the exam again, you would do better. This doesn't mean the exam wasn't reliable the first time you took it. It just means that the second time, it was measuring the effect of that further studying, as well as your additional understanding.

Finally, test-retest approaches can be too difficult or time-consuming. For example, if you were carrying out a telephone survey, it would be challenging and expensive to contact all the participants again to ask them exactly the same questions. In addition, they might be more likely to refuse to participate if they are going to be given all the same questions again; it could feel like a waste of time.

reliability
→ Unit 6

telephone survey
→ Unit 10

Validity

A measure is valid if it provides an accurate reflection of the true value of the underlying concept with minimal systematic error. More broadly, the results of a study are valid if they reflect the real values and relationships for variables in

concept
→ Unit 5

systematic error
→ Unit 6

the population of interest. When individual scores on a measure don't reflect their real value but instead are influenced by systematic error, then the variable lacks measurement validity. There are several elements to consider when establishing the validity of a measure, including content, construct, and criterion validity. Not all sources categorize the types of measurement validity in the same way, but collectively scholars agree on the different elements a measure should demonstrate to be valid. These are not the only aspects of validity that researchers must consider. Internal validity reflects the validity of the overall conclusions of a study and whether the reported patterns and relationships are, in fact, found within the population being studied. External validity reflects whether the reported results for a given sample might reasonably be expected to occur within a larger population.

Furthermore, reliability is a necessary condition for validity. That is, if a measure does not produce reliable results, it is not appropriate to consider validity. After all, if the same measure gives different scores for a person each time it is employed, the fact that on occasion that score happens to be the true value doesn't show that the measure is actually giving the true score in a way the researcher can depend upon.

Consider the use of exams in evaluating a student's performance in a class. A good exam should give an accurate indication of how well the student knows the course material. If the exam is doing what it is supposed to do (measure course knowledge), then students who are knowledgeable about the course material should do well on the exam, and students who do not know the material well should do poorly. However, if the students who know the material best do not perform well on the exam, then this suggests a problem with the validity of the exam. It is not measuring what it is supposed to measure. For this reason, teachers often include a variety of measures within any course to get a true assessment of how much students actually know about the course material—that's why exams have many questions and are supplemented with quizzes, activities, essays, and more. The terms that follow detail some of the specific ways that researchers can assess the validity of the concepts they are measuring.

Construct Validity (Convergent and Discriminant)

Construct validity focuses on whether a measured variable is logically related to and distinct from other variables. Some sources define this narrowly, focusing on construct validity only in terms of the relationship between the variable being measured and *other variables*. To keep things simple, in this text we follow this approach. If your test of validity involves a measure of a variable of interest alongside a measure of something else, it reflects construct validity. If you are measuring the same thing two different ways, it would be criterion validity. However, it's not always easy to draw the line between two measures of the same variable and two measures of distinct variables. As such, there are sources that treat criterion validity as one type of construct validity. These distinctions are less important than the basic idea. If you want to know whether a variable is measured in a valid way, you can examine the scores for that variable alongside other questions or observations and see if the patterns you find made sense and fit the conceptual definition from your explication process. Testing construct validity requires working through the concept explication process, employing the measure to be tested, and assessing related concepts by using measures believed to be valid. Then, two relevant comparisons can be made.

concept
→ Unit 5

relationship
→ Unit 2

positive versus negative relationship
→ Unit 2

correlation (Pearson's r)
→ Unit 15

factor analysis
→ Unit 5

Reflect & React: But Is the Test Fair?

Tests are a good way of looking at the concept of validity and how it can be applied in everyday life. Consider the driver's examination. Most states in the United States have some variation of a driving test in which a prospective driver has to exhibit certain skills in order to receive a driver's license. In theory, these tests allow each state to determine who is fit to drive and who is not. If the driving tests are working properly, then only people who are considered good drivers should be able to pass the test and receive a driver's license. Those who are not yet good enough drivers should not be able to pass the test if it is a valid test of driving ability.

Take a closer look at the driving test that is used in your home state. Is the test a valid indicator of driving ability? Could a poor driver who is unfit for the road pass this test? What would you change about the test? Now think about the last time you took an exam at school or for a job. Did you think the test was fair? Assessing the fairness of a test is one way of getting at the question of validity. A test that is not fair would not be as valid as one that is determined to be fair. Of course, fairness can be highly subjective. Therefore, think more deeply about the test and consider what you would change about the test to improve not only its validity overall but also its external validity and its applicability to assessing "real-world" knowledge.

First, *convergent validity* focuses on whether the measurement in question shows a relationship with other variables to which it should be related. For example, suppose you want to measure how much people support a nonprofit organization that helps adopt out unwanted animals. You expect that people who support such an organization like animals in general. You probably think that people who have volunteered for other animal welfare organizations would also support this one. On the other hand, you might think that

133

people who believe that too much money is spent on pets rather than people would not have a favorable view of the organization. If you measure each of these variables (volunteering for other animal organizations and negative attitudes toward spending money on animals), you could test whether these scores are correlated with the scores for feelings toward the animal welfare organization.

These relationships can be positive or negative. A negative relationship still shows a meaningful pattern, and it can still help validate a variable. For example, if you are studying how people feel about the Democratic candidate in an election, a good way to validate the scale would be to compare feelings toward the Republican candidate. If the two are negatively related, that would be a good sign that your measures work. Correlations do not need to be extremely strong in order to provide construct validity. The idea is that you are comparing two variables that should, on average, be related.

The other key indicator of construct validity is *discriminant validity*. While convergent validity is about showing that related things have some relationship, discriminant validity shows that two variables that measure distinct concepts cannot be treated as equivalent. That is, while the measure of one variable might be related to another variable, there should be some way to tell them apart. Maybe the correlation is only moderate, or there are differences in the factor loadings between the two sets of questions. Or maybe one variable predicts an outcome while the other does not. Consider two measures that are commonly used in advertising research: purchase intention and purchase behavior. We expect that people who plan to buy a product are more likely to actually buy that product. But that doesn't mean that every person who plans to buy something actually will, and if intention and behavior are different variables we shouldn't always get the same number no matter which variable we are measuring. A person can legitimately intend to buy a product, but then outside factors can intervene, keeping him or her from making the purchase. Therefore, intention and behavior are conceptualized as related but distinct.

Consistent with the idea of convergent validity, we would expect measures of intention and behavior to be correlated. But we would also expect that a factor analysis or similar test would show that there are differences between the two variables. Some individuals might be more likely to show a link between intention and behavior, while others might fail to follow through quite often. By showing these differences, scholars can demonstrate that a particular variable is being measured in a valid way and that it isn't simply another way to test some other, already well-measured concept. In some cases, we might even expect two variables to be completely unrelated, with essentially no correlation between them.

Content Validity

Evaluating content validity requires assessing the selected items intended to measure a variable and determining whether they reflect the full range of the conceptual definition of that variable. That is, content validity is about whether the measures being used match what we intend to measure. Unlike construct and criterion validity, it does not involve collecting data or making statistical comparisons. Because many of the judgments involved in content validity reflect looking at whether individual questions appear valid "on face," aspects of content validity are sometimes known as "face validity."

The process of assessing content validity involves both subjective reflection on the items based upon the explication process and careful consideration of the literature. As part of concept explication, it's important to think about each element of the variable of interest. For example, you might want to measure verbal aggression. This could be defined as including words meant to insult others, provoke or express anger, or evoke a threat. You might develop a way to gauge this by recording spoken exchanges in an online video game. This coding scheme would need to include measures addressing each of these elements. One approach would be to have coders simply mark whether *any* of these types of language occurred. However, it is often more effective to measure each operationally defined indicator of a concept separately. This can allow for index development and reliability testing, as well as clarify measurement. In this example, you might list a series of phrases or terms that reflect each element of the definition. Perhaps you would list many insults that could occur and many phrases that would be intended to make opponents angry or feel threatened. In establishing content validity, you might realize that you aren't coding for expressions of anger from the players; you would want to add a measure or measures to specifically capture that aspect of the concept. As this example shows, content validity requires both being clear about the best indicators for a concept, and being certain that your measurement approach will give you information about all of those indicators.

To develop this further, consider the example of a final exam. For an exam to be a good test of course material, it should cover the material that the book and/or instructor presented to the students. If key topics are not covered on the exam, we might conclude that the exam lacks content validity because it is not measuring knowledge of all the content. However, this illustrates a challenge faced by researchers and test writers alike—a test cannot possibly cover *everything*. Some things must be omitted when designing a test or writing questions for a questionnaire. In such cases, the most important and central items should be maintained. This is typically the reason tests focus on key concepts that teachers discuss frequently in class and ignore less common items and

variable
→ Unit 2

conceptual definition
→ Unit 5

concept explication
→ Unit 5

coding
→ Unit 11

indicator
→ Unit 5

concept
→ Unit 5

index
→ Unit 5

reliability
→ Unit 6

questionnaire design
→ Unit 7

validity
→ Unit 6

small details. When assessing content validity, we keep this balance in mind. We cannot possibly ask every last question, so we make judgments about how to capture the most important or central indicators, and think about questions that give us as much clear information as possible.

Criterion Validity (Concurrent and Predictive)

Criterion validity focuses on whether a measurement approach to a variable meets a specific criterion, or rule, that any valid measure of a concept would have to fulfill. Most often, this involves *concurrent validity*, which tests whether two measures of the same variable produce equivalent results. Optimally, one of these measures is an established, validated approach or a form of measurement that necessarily produces valid results. Thus, if your new measure obtains the same score as this valid approach, your measure meets the rule that it *must* give a score that matches the known valid approach.

For example, you might want to measure which television programs a person watches. One approach would be to provide people with a diary in which they record whether they watched television during any given half-hour block and, if so, which program they were viewing. This is basically the approach used during sweeps period by the Nielsen ratings company. The problem with such diaries is that people may not accurately recall their television viewing, or they may deliberately deceive researchers. To test whether diaries have concurrent validity, researchers can also directly observe or record the programs viewed by a set of participants. In this case we actually see people watch a program, we know they viewed it, so this is a valid approach. If the diaries and observations match for these individuals, this suggests that the diary approach is valid, and even when only the diaries are used, researchers can still be confident in their results.

Another, less common approach to criterion validity involves *predictive validity*. In this case, researchers test whether a measurement of a variable effectively predicts some future value or outcome that should necessarily be linked to the variable based on the conceptual definition of the variable. That is, the basic definition of our concept is, in part, that it leads to or predicts some outcome, so by rule if our measure is valid then it will predict that outcome accurately. For example, presidential polling can be tested through predictive validity. Polling asks people whom they intend to vote for. Early in the election cycle, this might change, and it's difficult to know whether answers are valid. But as the election grows close, few people will change their minds. The purpose of polling is to accurately predict how voters will behave. When the polls are being conducted, there is no easy way to test the criterion validity of those polls, as no clear, valid alternative measurement is available. But after the election, we can compare the percentage of people who voted for each candidate to the percentages predicted by each poll. A valid poll should predict the actual percentage of voters voting for each candidate.

variable
→ Unit 2

conceptual
definition
→ Unit 5

poll
→ Unit 10

parallel-forms
reliability
→ Unit 6

construct validity
→ Unit 6

prediction
→ Unit 2

relationship
→ Unit 2

One important note about both predictive and concurrent validity is that they should not be confused with parallel-forms reliability. In the latter, the purpose is simply to establish that a given measure does not include any more *random error* than another measure. The distribution of scores should be similar, and one score should predict the other. But neither form necessarily must be shown to be valid. For concurrent validity, one of the comparisons must be a valid measure of the variable or the relevant outcome. Because of this, testing concurrent validity for certain difficult-to-measure variables can be complex or even impossible. Scholars must rely on other tests of construct validity to make the best possible case for their measure.

Overall, a measure that has good criterion validity should allow us to make predictions about scores for other variables. For instance, if, as previously discussed, a final exam is a good indicator of knowledge of the course material, it should share relationships with other items that are also indicators of knowledge of the course material. This means that scores on the exam should share a positive relationship with papers written for the course and any quizzes taken during the semester. This illustrates concurrent validity—measures that occur at or near the time of the primary measure (in this case, the exam) should share a relationship. If those who do well on the test also do well on quizzes and papers, this helps to confirm that the test is accurately measuring performance in the course. Further, if the test is a good measure of course knowledge, it should allow us to predict performance on other measures as well. For instance, if the test is for a public speaking course, we would expect those who do well on the test to also perform well on speeches they give in the future after the class has ended (demonstrating predictive validity).

concept
→ Unit 5

operational
definition
→ Unit 5

construct validity
→ Unit 6

Internal Validity

An effective study needs to do more than simply measure a single variable effectively; it must also show that the relationships established between variables are accurately described within the study. This is described as the *internal validity* of a study's results. Many threats exist that can affect internal validity, such as mortality, researcher bias, and demand characteristics. Some of these also influence external validity—the degree to which the results of one study hold true for a larger population of interest. Establishing internal validity starts at the measurement stage. First, each variable being considered must be measured in a valid fashion. If some variables are measured in a way that creates random error, our conclusions about the strength of relationships will necessarily underestimate the size of that relationship. Because internal validity involves our conclusion about *how* variables are related and not just *whether* they are related, that would compromise internal validity. Conversely, if variables are measured in a way that creates systematic error for a subset of all individuals, this could create the illusion of a relationship where none is present.

variable
→ Unit 2

relationship
→ Unit 2

mortality
→ Unit 9

researcher bias
→ Unit 9

external validity
→ Unit 6

population
→ Unit 8

Jake Weigler—Political Strategist

An accomplished political strategist, Jake Weigler has managed numerous election campaigns and worked for several national political organizations. Jake has worked in communications for several statewide officials, including a governor, attorney general, and state superintendent of public instruction. Jake grew up in Portland, Oregon, where he lives with his wife and two daughters.

Why are good research skills important to your field?

Research is critical both for helping understand public opinion and understanding how to frame and articulate an argument. There are many ways you can approach a public discussion about an issue or candidate. Research informs how you can frame that discussion to ensure it best resonates with your audience.

What specific method or methods do you use or encounter most?

Most typically, I am working with quantitative survey work and qualitative focus groups. I also encounter a fairly broad range of social science research and analysis of public data. It is important to understand statistical analysis so arguments can be parsed and compared.

Can you name some specific instances for which you have used data collected from research?

I do a considerable amount of work in gun violence prevention, an area where federal research has been systemically underfunded for decades. There are numerous causalities that bring people to commit gun violence on themselves and others. Accordingly, data and statistical analysis helps inform which policy changes can have the biggest impact in reducing gun violence.

How did the research you conducted help inform your decision?

Comparisons of the rates of gun violence in different states can help inform which gun policies can have the biggest impact. Similarly, assessing public attitudes, including those of gun owners, informs which policies will be most readily implemented and lead to change in behavior.

What are one or two pieces of advice or insights you would give about research to students in a communication research methods course?

Research is a skill that will provide value for the rest of your life. Being able to understand statistics, survey data, and other research methods will give you the ability to critically evaluate information provided to you, rather than just taking it at face value.

For example, if men tend to overstate their number of sexual partners but women do not, this would suggest a relationship between gender and sexual frequency—even though this is impossible among heterosexuals. That said, not all systematic errors necessarily affect the internal validity of conclusions about relationships. For example, if *all* individuals overstate the number of sexual partners they have, then we could still accurately test whether viewing sexually explicit content is related to sexual frequency. Suppose there is a relationship—those who did not view sexually explicit content might report an average of 5 partners, and those who did might report an average of 10. If the true values were 2 and 7, as a result of systematic error, our finding of a relationship would still have internal validity.

In many cases, researchers must make a choice between emphasizing internal validity and external validity. For example, for a study to make an internally valid evaluation of causality, several specific requirements must be met. Because these requirements may involve very deliberate manipulation and control of specific variables, this can undercut the realism of the study. Whereas measurement validity can always be further improved, internal validity may sometimes be sacrificed in favor of external validity. This is one reason why triangulation is important. By employing study designs that emphasize internal validity and other designs that focus on external validity, researchers can better establish whether a relationship holds up to both standards.

random error → Unit 6
systematic error → Unit 6
external validity → Unit 6
causality → Unit 2
validity → Unit 6
triangulation → Unit 3

External Validity/Generalizability

The degree to which the results of a given study are true for the larger population being studied reflects the external validity of the study. This is also referred to as the ability to *generalize* from the study to a population. Many factors can threaten the *external validity* of the study. If the design lacks ecological validity, meaning that the experience does not mirror a natural setting, this will reduce the applicability of the results for the population. If the study's sample is not representative, then it could be that the results would not hold for more typical members of the population, or they may be limited to a certain subset of individuals who are over-represented in the sample.

Some threats to the internal validity of a study can also undermine external validity by creating unrealistic situations or introducing unintended variables that don't occur naturally. Researchers take steps to increase the external validity as much as possible, relying on diverse samples and natural settings. However, in experiments, the primary focus is on ensuring internal validity, as experiments are especially good for establishing causality. This focus can mean a trade-off in which external validity is sacrificed to increase internal validity. For example, consider a study meant to test what individuals learn from news. Obtaining a large, diverse sample and showing participants an entire newscast as the stimulus would increase external validity, but at the cost of control over

population → Unit 8
ecological validity → Unit 9
sample → Unit 8
internal validity → Unit 6
external validity → Unit 6
variable → Unit 2
natural settings → Unit 12
experiment → Unit 9
causality → Unit 2

reliable
→ Unit 6

valid
→ Unit 6

the design. By using a narrower sample, researchers can pick content they know is relevant to participants. And by showing a briefer clip, the researchers can be sure participants will be relatively attentive to the content meant to produce knowledge.

External validity is important for researchers to consider because it deals directly with the extent to which the findings of a study apply to the real world. For example, if a new weight-loss drug works incredibly well in laboratory settings but does not produce results in the "real world," it would lack external validity, meaning that the results are not valid outside of the study. Ultimately, the goal of a good research study is to use reliable and valid measures to produce findings that are usable in the context they are designed to be used in. Returning to the example of measuring Twitter use, our goal is not simply to accurately count the number of tweets. More broadly, we want to understand how Twitter use relates to other factors. We could have people use a form of Twitter-like software in a laboratory setting to see whether manipulating features of the software or their networks affects the number of tweets they send. We would be able to obtain a highly reliable and accurate count of tweets because we created the software. And we could say with confidence that this number is linked to the specific features we developed. But we would be hesitant to say that these participants would show the same outcome when using Twitter itself, as their long-established social connections and other behaviors might interfere with our "pristine" set of findings.

Steps to Success: Ensuring Measurement Validity

Although there is no perfect formula to ensure measurement validity, following these steps can help produce more valid measures of your key concepts:

1. Carefully explicate your concepts. Unless you have a clear conceptual definition for what you're trying to measure, you won't be able to effectively evaluate whether your operational approach actually matches up.
2. Review the literature. In many cases, existing measures are available for common concepts. Even if no previously validated measure is out there, simply knowing how similar concepts have been measured can help generate ideas. The literature can also provide measures of related concepts for use in testing convergent validity. If an existing measure is out there but seems cumbersome for use in your study, consider including it in a pilot test to establish concurrent validity.
3. Establish a clear list of all of the important aspects of your concept. This may draw upon the existing literature, your explication process, qualitative interviewing, or suggestions from experts.
4. Develop questions that reflect all aspects of your concept, as established earlier. This helps ensure content validity.

5. Carefully review each question for clarity and focus. Have others review and respond to the questions as well, helping make sure they are clear, understandable, and related to the intended aspects of your concept. This helps ensure face validity.

6. Identify concepts that should be clearly distinct from as well as similar to your concept. Include measures of these in your data collection or pilot study, so you can evaluate construct validity, both convergent and divergent. In addition, if any existing measures of your concept exist, include the best validated as a way to establish concurrent validity.

7. Collect data. Ideally, if the concept is important and you have multiple other measures, such as concepts to be used for evaluating construct or concurrent validity, obtain these data through a preliminary, small-scale pilot study before using the concept in your primary design.

8. Evaluate data for evidence of construct validity. Ensure that your measure is correlated with other variables that the literature suggests should be related and that it is not strongly related to items that should be distinct. Factor analysis can help establish that your measure represents a distinct concept from other scales included in the data.

9. Compare your measure to any criterion measures, whether concurrent or predictive.

10. Evaluate reliability (see Steps to Success: Using Cronbach's Alpha to Improve Measurement).

11. If these steps were part of a pilot study, make any logical adjustments and then carry out primary data collection.

Index

An index combines information from multiple questions, observations, or other measures to form a single variable that better captures the underlying concept that researchers hope to measure. Think about an index in a book. In that index, information is pulled together from the entire book and turned into a single list. The details of that information are not found within the index, but a new resource emerges that combines many elements in a condensed form. Similarly, when forming an index in research, we put aside the precise details of how individuals answered each question. Instead, we have a broader reflection of the concept as a whole.

Forming an index offers several advantages. First, instead of having to deal with many individual items, we can instead evaluate a single, broader measure of our concept. This makes it easier to test hypotheses and reduces the ambiguity of our results. Consider a situation in which you want to know whether the amount of reality television a person views is related to how narcissistic they are. (Perhaps you have hypothesized that reality show viewers have higher

variable
→ Unit 2

concept
→ Unit 5

hypotheses
→ Unit 2

operational definition
→ Unit 5

random error
→ Unit 6

validity
→ Unit 6

opinions of themselves because the people on the shows are similarly self-centered.) You could measure show viewing by asking several questions, such as how many shows they watch, how many hours they watch, and whether they consider themselves avid reality show viewers.

Testing whether each of these questions is related to narcissism, you might find mixed results, with a clearer pattern for one question than another. It would be hard to know whether your findings really supported your hypothesis. However, if you combine all the items into a single index, you have a simplified test. In addition, you also have a better measure of reality television viewing than using one item at a time because indexes *generally* do a better job of measuring a variable than a single item. After all, concepts can be complicated, and in the process of explicating them, we may recognize many important indicators that contribute to our operational definition. We cannot ask about all those indicators in a single question, but we still think they are all part of our concept. In this case, no one question gets at everything we mean by "reality show viewer," but using multiple questions brings us closer to our definition.

Indexes can also reduce random measurement error. A person might make a mistake answering a single question, giving an answer that is higher than the true value. Then, for the next question, they might give too low an answer. Because the errors are random, the more questions we ask, the more they will cancel out. Think about rolling a pair of dice. We might think of the most common value, 7, as the "true" value. But on some rolls, we will get values lower than 7, and on other rolls, we will get values higher than 7. This is just due to randomness; there is no systematic reason for dice to add up to low or high values. Because of this, using multiple measures to form an index is helpful, even when we can think of a single question that would directly reflect the concept. That one question will be more vulnerable to random error than a set of similar questions.

Consider again measuring the frequency with which a person uses Twitter. It may be that simply asking about the number of tweets posted in an average day would be an adequate measure, but because this is just one item, we would likely have issues with reliability that could not be easily assessed. We might want to employ a more nuanced approach, such as asking how often people posted on the previous day as well as on an average day, how subjectively "frequent" they would say their posting is, and whether they think of themselves as a heavy user. Even if we ultimately decided the "average day" measure was most valid, by having the other scores, we could at least consider forming an index as well as have a way to better test reliability and validity.

reliability
→ Unit 6

index
→ Unit 6

Cronbach's Alpha

One way to measure the reliability of an index is by computing a statistic called Cronbach's alpha (α). This statistic measures how well scores on the individual questions that form the index match the overall score for the index. Thus, Cronbach's alpha is a type of item-total reliability.

Consider an index formed from three items, each measured on a 7-point scale. Maybe we're asking people how much they agree that a particular website is useful, helpful, and well-designed. If a respondent who answers the first two items by saying 7 also answers the last item with a 7, this would be highly reliable and would suggest that the index is effective. On the other hand, if a respondent who answers the first two questions with a 7 then answers the third question with a 4, this might not be reliable. What if another respondent answers 1 to the first two questions? We would expect this respondent to give a lower score on the third question. If he or she also answers the third question with a 4, something is wrong. That question isn't consistent with the other items. Forming an index including that item would not help reduce random error, which is one goal of making indexes. This means the item isn't reliable. Cronbach's alpha would be low, in this case, because you're trying to form an index with just three items and one of them doesn't work well.

In general, the more items you include that are inconsistent with the overall total, the lower Cronbach's alpha will be. In rare cases in which there is a negative relationship between items, alpha can actually be negative as well. Normally, this suggests the need to reverse some of the items. (That is, we should adjust the scale so that the lowest attributes or values for that variable are assigned high numbers, and the highest are given low numbers.) More often, alpha ranges between 0 and 1. An alpha of 1 means that each item perfectly matches the others. This suggests there is no random error; nothing is causing small variations in how people answer each question.

However, a high alpha does not guarantee that your measurement is valid. If each question has the same amount of systematic measurement error, then the reliability is strong, but the measure is still invalid. Think about a study that asks people how many tweets they send, how many days a week they tweet, and whether they agree that they are a "frequent user" of Twitter. Someone would be expected to answer each question in a similar way, and alpha would be high. But some people might not want to admit they use Twitter regularly (a case of social desirability). They would answer each question dishonestly, stating too low a number. Alpha would still be high, but the questions could still be flawed. Thus, while Cronbach's alpha is one important tool for evaluating the effectiveness of an index, it's not the only factor to consider.

Most of the time, alpha will not be exactly 1.0, but it is generally acceptable even if the value is .9, .8, or sometimes even lower. There is no absolute rule on how low a score is allowable. In cases in which you are relying on a small number of questions and there are reasons to expect some variation between items, scores below .7 might even be acceptable. In other cases in which many questions all meant to reflect precisely the same concept are used, such a low score would be problematic. Just remember this—the lower the alpha, the more random measurement error. Because random error can never be predicted, a low score for alpha means you will be less able to effectively predict relationships by explaining variance. Additionally, alpha takes into account the number of

item-total reliability
→ Unit 6

random error
→ Unit 6

positive versus negative relationship
→ Unit 2

variable
→ Unit 2

systematic error
→ Unit 6

social desirability
→ Unit 7

concept
→ Unit 5

prediction
→ Unit 2

variance explained
→ Unit 15

143

Table 6.1 Cronbach's alpha scores for five items assessing public speaking delivery

Alpha value = .83	Alpha if item deleted
Pace	.82
Tone	.88
Volume	.83
Pronunciation	.65
Clarity	.61

items as well as the item-total reliability. This makes sense. An index with 10 items is less affected by random error in one of the questions, and the overall number of items will better cancel out individual random errors. But it also means that in situations in which few questions were available, you might need to be more tolerant of somewhat lower alphas.

Output from statistical analysis that measures Cronbach's alpha not only includes the alpha value (ranging from .0 to 1.0) but also typically indicates the overall alpha for the index if an item is removed. (This is typically labeled the "alpha if item deleted.") This way you can tell which items will either lower or raise the alpha value. For example, consider the five items used to assess delivery noted in Table 6.1.

Note that the overall alpha is .83. This is regarded as an acceptable value for scale reliability. If pace, tone, or volume were removed, there would be very limited impact on the alpha value. For instance, removing pace from the newly created delivery measure would only drop the alpha from .83 to .82. However, removing pronunciation or clarity would have a much greater impact. For instance, removing clarity from the list of items and only using the remaining four would drop the alpha value to .61. This indicates that the measure is much more consistent and precise when clarity and pronunciation are included.

Steps to Success: Using Cronbach's Alpha to Improve Measurement

Cronbach's alpha measure of scale reliability can be a valuable tool to help us improve measurement of key concepts. However, effective use of it requires planning and forethought. Follow these steps to guide you through the process of using Cronbach's alpha to assess scale reliability:

1. Consult with previous research and relevant theories before designing your questions—taking your time and doing things right in the concept explication

process can save you a lot of time and energy when you get to analyzing your data.

2. After you have collected your data, look at the correlations between the indicators and dimensions you expect to be related—each should share reasonably strong positive relationships.

3. Analyze your data using a statistical analysis program that can compute Cronbach's alpha.

4. Look at the output to determine whether the overall alpha level meets acceptable standards.

5. Look at individual items to see the listed value for "alpha if item deleted."

6. At this point, you should consider removing items only if they will meaningfully raise the alpha level and/or they seem questionable from a face validity standpoint. However, if the overall level is acceptable and removing individual items would only have a small influence on the score, it is typically better to not remove any items.

7. If you remove an item, re-run your analysis after removing the item in question. Proceed slowly and only remove one item at a time. As a note, your decisions should always be thoughtfully guided and should not be based only on statistical output. Use theory and previous research as well as sound logic to help guide your construction of multi-item measures so that your measures maintain good face and content validity.

Activities

Activity 6A: Validating Communication Research Concepts

See terms: construct validity; content validity; criterion validity.

The goal of this activity is to develop approaches to validating existing communication research concepts. To do so, locate a research article on a topic of interest to you and select two of the concepts used in the study. Follow the prompts given next to continue this activity:

- Assess the content validity for each of the concepts by considering whether the indicators used make sense and whether all needed indicators are present. Would you characterize the content validity as good or bad? Why?
- To what extent do the authors assess construct validity? What additional concepts might you consider measuring to assess construct validity?

Activity 6B: Cronbach's Alpha

See terms: Cronbach's alpha; reliability.

Three scenarios are provided later. For each scenario, you should make two decisions: (1) Does the index meet acceptable levels of reliability? (2) Do any items need to be removed to help the index reach acceptable levels of reliability? Finally, in your assessment, be sure to explain your decisions.

Table 6.2 Scenario 1: Measuring happiness

Alpha value = .57	Alpha if item deleted
Home life satisfaction	.51
Work life satisfaction	.57
Relationship satisfaction	.42
Salary	.72

Table 6.3 Scenario 2: Measuring information-seeking media use

Alpha value = .77	Alpha if item deleted
Newspaper reading	.65
Listening to NPR	.61
Watching the local news	.72
Reading news blogs	.82

Table 6.4 Scenario 3: Measuring interpersonal communication skill

Alpha value = .54	Alpha if item deleted
Nonverbal skill—sending messages	.51
Verbal skill—sending messages	.57
Nonverbal skill—receiving messages	.42
Verbal skill—receiving messages	.40

Activity 6C: Validity Critique

See terms: content validity; validity.

For this activity, find a scholarly research article that focuses on developing or validating a concept or measure and evaluate how well the article addresses the various types of validity. Use the following prompts to guide your work:

- Record the author, title, and source information (please use the appropriate style as indicated by your instructor).
- Identify the key concept or concepts and indicate the conceptual definitions provided by the authors.
- What specifics are provided about how the concepts are measured?
- What specific types of validity do the authors address in discussing the measurement of these concepts?
- What limitations to the measurement of this concept do the authors discuss?
- What improvements would you suggest the authors could make in the measurement of this concept?

Activity 6D: Applying Validity in Everyday Life

See terms: criterion validity; triangulation; validity.

For this activity, imagine that you are in a corporate setting working for an advertising agency. The agency has just released a large-scale media campaign with mostly 30-second television spots for a client (an organic soap company looking to generate greater product awareness and increase sales). Your agency has been asked by the client to measure how effective the campaign is.

Use the following prompts to complete this activity:

- Explain how you would measure the effectiveness of the campaign. Specifically, discuss the following:
    - ☐ The concepts you would measure (hint: remember what the ad is intending to do)
    - ☐ The dimensions and/or indicators you would use in your operational definitions
- Explain how you would validate the effectiveness of these measures so you know they are good ones.

Suggested Readings for Further Exploration of Unit 6 Topics

Examples

Dallimore, E. J. (2000). A feminist response to issues of validity in research. *Women's Studies in Communication, 23*(2), 157–181. doi:10.1080/07491409.2000.10162567

Eveland, W. P., Jr., Hutchens, M. J., & Shen, F. (2009). Exposure, attention, or "use" of news? Assessing aspects of the reliability and validity of a central concept in political communication research. *Communication Methods and Measures, 3*(4), 223–244. doi:10.1080/19312450903378925

Hayes, A. F., Glynn, C. J., & Shanahan, J. (2005). Validating the willingness to self-censor scale: Individual differences in the effect of the climate of opinion on opinion expression. *International Journal of Public Opinion Research, 17*(4), 443–455. doi:10.1093/ijpor/edh072

Kohring, M., & Matthes, J. (2007). Trust in news media development and validation of a multidimensional scale. *Communication Research, 34*(2), 231–252. doi:10.1177/0093650206298071

Lee, C., Hornick, R., & Hennessy, M. (2008). The reliability and stability of general media exposure measures. *Communication Methods and Measures, 2*(1–2), 6–22. doi:10.1080/19312450802063024

Mazer, J. P. (2012). Development and validation of the student interest and engagement scales. *Communication Methods and Measures, 6*(2), 99–125. doi:10.1080/19312458.2012.679244

McCroskey, J. C., Beatty, M. J., Kearney, P., & Plax, T. G. (1985). The content validity of the PRCA-24 as a measure of communication apprehension across communication contexts. *Communication Quarterly, 33*(3), 165–173. doi:10.1080/01463378509369595

Niederdeppe, J. (2014). Conceptual, empirical, and practical issues in developing valid measures of public communication campaign exposure. *Communication Methods and Measures, 8*(2), 138–161. doi:10.1080/19312458.2014.903391

Rubin, R. B. (1985). The validity of the communication competency assessment instrument. *Communication Monographs, 52*(2), 173–185. doi:10.1080/03637758509376103

Schemer, C., Matthes, J., & Wirth, W. (2008). Toward improving the validity and reliability of media information processing measures in surveys. *Communication Methods and Measures, 2*(3), 193–225. doi:10.1080/19312450802310474

Advanced Discussion

Adcock, R., & Collier, D. (2001). Measurement validity: A shared standard for qualitative and quantitative research. *American Political Science Review, 95*(3), 529–546. doi:10.1017/S0003055401003100

Levine, T. R. (2005). Confirmatory factor analysis and scale validation in communication research. *Communication Research Reports, 22*(4), 335–338. doi:10.1080/00036810500317730

unit 7

effective measurement

Imagine that you are working for the human resources department of a large corporation. You have been charged with determining employee satisfaction with communication from management and devising new strategies to improve the efficiency of that communication. Management would like to make sure they are effectively communicating with their employees and determine what, if anything, needs to be fixed in the process. Gathering valid data—and therefore knowing how the employees truly feel about communication from management—will be important to making good decisions about whether to institute new policies or simply maintain current procedures. It is important to make good decisions rooted in high-quality data because any changes you recommend could cost the company money or even cost some workers their jobs.

There are, of course, many options for how you could go about addressing this issue. A common approach would be to devise a questionnaire. Often, questionnaires are used in these situations because they are fairly simple to develop and easy to distribute to large groups, whether through e-mail or hard copy. However, although the act of sending out an e-mail with a questionnaire might be simple, developing an effective measurement approach for a questionnaire takes great care and time. For instance, a disorganized or poorly worded questionnaire can leave respondents confused and produce results that lack validity. An overly long questionnaire can leave respondents frustrated and result in incomplete questionnaires. In short, there are many potential issues that can occur if time and care are not taken to develop effective measures. While this example illustrates measurement issues specific to questionnaires, this unit will also consider broader issues that affect measurement quality, including errors in observation, questionnaire development, and scale development.

Effective Measurement

Effective measurement of a variable can help minimize the effects of measurement error and improve the validity of the variable being measured. Poorly worded questions, inconsistent observations, and lack of proper use of **filter questions** to provide flow to the **questionnaire** can create serious problems for researchers and negatively affect their ability to draw meaningful conclusions from the data they collect. Researchers also have to be on the lookout for **order effects**—that is, when the order in which the questions are presented influences responses to them. In many cases, such problems can be avoided by effectively preparing an observation strategy or thoughtfully constructing a questionnaire.

In many cases, scholars will use **self-report** data collection techniques that often involve participants filling out a questionnaire, whether self-administered or delivered as part of an interview. A variation on this is **others' reports**, where a similar approach is used but someone other than the unit of analysis is questioned to obtain data about the individual in question.

validity
→ Unit 6

variable
→ Unit 2

measurement error
→ Unit 6

validity
→ Unit 6

self-administered survey
→ Unit 10

interview-style survey
→ Unit 10

Good question wording is essential to creating an effective measurement tool. Scholars must decide between using **closed-ended questions** that provide participants with a limited set of responses or **open-ended questions** that may provide more information and allow the participant to answer the question as they see fit. When using closed-ended questions, it is important that the responses be **exhaustive**, meaning that all possible choices are offered. To avoid confusion, the response categories must also be **mutually exclusive**, such that an answer will only fit into one of the categories.

In terms of writing style, questions should strive for **clarity**, be accessible to a broad range of participants, not be biased in any way (e.g., **leading questions** that push people to respond in a particular way), play upon **social desirability**, and focus on a single item at a time. When more than one item is included in a question at a time, this is referred to as a **double-barreled question**, and it can create confusion for the participant as well as the researcher attempting to interpret the data.

In many cases, these items are grouped together to form indexes, particularly when a concept or variable is complex. Most often, indexes are formed from items measured on a standard scale. One of the most common approaches is to use **Likert-type** items that ask study participants to indicate how much they agree or disagree with a series of statements. These scales typically involve a 5-point response that includes categories such as "strongly disagree," "disagree some," "neutral," "agree some," and "strongly agree." Another common alternative is **semantic differential** items, in which participants are presented with 5- or 7-point items with opposite words as the anchor points of the scale.

In addition to asking questions, measurement of variables can occur either through **direct observation**—where the researcher sees the phenomenon as it occurs—or **indirect observation**—where the researcher sees the results of the phenomenon being studied. For instance, researchers could study the effects of various types of political advertisements and conceptualize effectiveness based on watching people's behavior while viewing an ad, noting which ones generate the most laughter, excitement, or angry comments. Alternatively, using indirect observation, those same researchers might track which candidates receive the most campaign donations and declare the advertisement that generated the most donations the most effective. Beyond studying people directly, researchers can also study the messages and communication that people produce and leave behind. These social artifacts include all kinds of things, such as movies, diaries, books, and newspapers.

Such approaches to studying people can differ in the extent to which measures are **reactive**, which can result in the participants changing their behavior because they are aware they are being observed. Scholars opting for less interference with the people they are studying will choose less reactive measures and develop indirect means of observation. Regardless of the approach, researchers should try to avoid **observation errors**.

Observation

The act of experiencing the world around us firsthand is known as observation. Unit 3 presented a number of ways of knowing, including authority, intuition, and tenacity. Each of these is a way of learning about the world around us through some means other than seeing—or sensing—it for ourselves. For instance, intuition would suggest following our gut and making a decision based on "feel" as opposed to observing the data for ourselves. This might lead us to look at a stack of job applications and pick one to hire because we have a good feeling about that person. However, using observation would lead us to look more closely at the applications before we draw any conclusions.

How we conduct those observations can vary in a number of ways. We might experience phenomena using either direct or indirect observation. Direct observation would involve looking at the act itself, such as a conversation two people have at their workplace. Indirect observation would involve looking at the outcomes of the act to draw conclusions about it. For instance, is one person happier than the other after the conversation ends? Does one person have greater or lesser understanding of the issue discussed than the other? Further, observations can vary in the extent to which they are reactive. More reactive measures have a greater chance of influencing the people being observed than less reactive measures do. Finally, not all phenomena can be easily or effectively observed, in the sense that we can actually see them, such as attitudes or strength of opinion. In these cases, we often rely on self-report measures to capture these kinds of information.

knowledge
→ Unit 3

authority
→ Unit 3

intuition
→ Unit 3

tenacity
→ Unit 3

direct and indirect observation
→ Unit 7

reactive measures
→ Unit 7

self-report
→ Unit 7

Direct and Indirect Observation

Sensing and experiencing the world around us allows us to better understand what we are trying to study. We can do so in both direct and indirect ways. *Direct* observation involves actually observing the specific behavior that we are intending to study. *Indirect* observation, on the other hand, involves looking at evidence that is left behind that indicates the presence of the behavior (or other phenomena) we are trying to study.

For example, consider researchers interested in finding out whether playing violent video games leads to aggressive behavior in children. Using direct observation, the researchers could have elementary school children play violent games and then observe them interacting with others on the playground. In this case, the researchers could directly see any violent or aggressive behavior the children might engage in after playing the video games.

The researchers could also rely on indirect observation to study this question. One approach would be to keep track of game play and then look for evidence that indicates violent and aggressive behavior, such as bruises, black eyes, and reports of fights at school. If violent video games cause aggressive behavior, the researchers would expect to find that those who play more violent video games are more likely to have bruises and black eyes and more likely to get into fights at school.

The challenges facing a human resources director described earlier present another example of direct and indirect observation as tools for research. If you are charged with evaluating employees, you would want to use both approaches. Your direct observations might include actually watching employees carrying out the duties of their job, such as making presentations or working with customers. Indirect observation could involve looking at the work produced by employees or checking e-mail logs to see whether employees engaged in non-work-related communication using their work accounts. As this illustrates, researchers can effectively combine both forms of observation, linking either to self-report data such as interviews with the employees, which would allow them to describe their contributions to the firm.

Reflect & React: The Uses of Indirect Measures

Indirect measures can take many different forms and can be a valuable way for researchers to look at a topic from different perspectives. For example, consider the many ways that you could assess employee satisfaction with the workplace. One way would be to evaluate internal communications such as e-mails and memos, looking for indicators that the employees find their place of work enjoyable. A second approach would be to evaluate each person's office. You might conclude that workplaces where office spaces are nicely decorated with plants, posters, and pictures of family members suggest a greater level of satisfaction than office spaces that are sparsely decorated and not personalized.

There are, of course, many other ways to study this topic. As you think about places you have worked, consider what indirect measures you would use to assess your colleagues' satisfaction with the workplace. What particular aspects of your work would you focus on? What items would best work as indirect measures? Which ones would be best assessed using direct measures that could potentially be reactive? Would you expect differences when using direct versus indirect measures?

variable
→ Unit 2

social desirability
→ Unit 7

Self-Report

While observation can be a useful tool, the most common approach to measurement involves asking questions. Measures that rely on study participants to provide answers are typically referred to as *self-report* measures. For example, researchers might be interested in how frequently people use different types of social media, and therefore they would ask them to indicate how many minutes a day they spend using Facebook, LinkedIn, and Twitter. Similarly, a human resources representative might want to know about these behaviors as well but, specifically, when they take place at work. In this case, the researchers are relying on the participants to both recall and honestly answer how often they use each of these different social media.

Self-report measures are common in communication research because many of the variables being tracked are otherwise difficult to observe. For example, consider measuring how often people watch various television programs. One approach would be to install a device on each study participant's television or cable box that transmits to the researchers what shows are being watched. However, this would be quite expensive for a large-scale study and require considerable resources that many researchers do not have access to. As a result, the researchers might decide to use television viewing diaries as a type of self-report measure, asking the study participants to keep track of everything they watch in the diary and then submit completed diaries once a week to the researchers. The television viewing diaries require considerably fewer resources than the transmitting devices. However, a common critique of self-report measures is that they can be of questionable accuracy, in light of the possible influence of memory effects and social desirability. Therefore, observation of a behavior is ideal when possible.

Others' Reports

As an alternative to self-reports, you might ask questions of people other than the ones you are studying. For example, having supervisors describe the behaviors of their employees is a report from another (the supervisor) about a selected unit of analysis (the employee). Considering the challenge of measuring television viewing noted earlier, one way to reduce the possibility of dishonest, socially desirable answers is to ask someone other than the person who is the focus of the study about viewing patterns. This approach is particularly common when studying children. Parents can often provide detailed information about what their children watch. Obviously, though, parents do not always perfectly monitor their child's behavior, and they may also be prone to socially desirable responses—few parents want to admit their children watch many hours of television each day. Similarly, they may commit the same errors of memory as children do, honestly misremembering the amount of viewing. Moreover, others cannot always accurately report on an individual. Parents may be able to say what their children watch, but they may not know how much children enjoy the program or what they remember from it.

self-reports
→ Unit 7

unit of analysis
→ Unit 2

hypotheses
→ Unit 2

theory
→ Unit 2

research questions
→ Unit 2

prediction
→ Unit 2

Observation Errors

While self-report data are obviously prone to error as a result of social desirability, flawed questions, invalid measures, and other factors, observational data

self-report
→ Unit 7

social desirability
→ Unit 7

are not immune to error. In particular, poor preparation, hasty conclusions, and research bias can all generate error. For direct observation, the reactivity of measurement can also generate errors.

One of the basic errors in observation is a lack of preparation. Consider being a witness to a hit-and-run accident. Unexpectedly, one car hits another and then quickly drives away. In such a case, you would have little time to make sense of what happened and keep track of key details. The longer it takes for the police to get there, the more likely it is that you will forget or confuse the details of what you witnessed. However, if you had been prepared to make this observation, you might have had your camera ready to take a photo and also had your pen and notebook ready to record key details and take notes. Most researchers don't go looking for car accidents, but they must be similarly prepared for unexpected occurrences as well as expected ones when planning observations. This includes ways to record and keep track of information so that future analysis does not rely solely on memory and is therefore more likely to be valid.

A second common error in observation results from researchers being too quick to draw conclusions about what they are seeing. That is, when researchers fail to be systematic about the research process, they can fall into the trap of making broad conclusions based on a small set of observations. Consider your first few days at a new place of employment. The first few people you meet might be exceptionally friendly, leading you to conclude after your first or second day that you're lucky to be at such a friendly and inviting workplace. However, in a workplace with dozens or perhaps hundreds of employees, those few people might be the exception to the rule. As you meet more and more people over the first few weeks, you might realize that your new place of employment isn't the happy place you first thought it was. This shows the value in being systematic about your approach and not being too quick to settle on an opinion. It is better to observe further and draw more reasoned conclusions based on additional data. For example, if after meeting 25 of your new coworkers and concluding that 23 of them are really nice (and the other two are just kind of nice), the evidence would be quite strong to conclude that your new place of employment is filled with nice people. However, that conclusion is less certain after meeting only three people and observing that two of those three people are really nice.

A third and final common error in observation is that researcher biases can lead to selective observations. This error is—to a degree—related to the previous error and stems from a lack of systematic processes. However, it also emerges when we let our natural tendency to be subjective drive the observations we make. Consider the new workplace with the friendly colleagues. If the first few colleagues you meet are especially friendly, you might conclude that everyone there is friendly. As a result, you are much more likely to notice the friendly things that other colleagues do and ignore evidence suggesting that your colleagues are unfriendly. This occurs because you let your bias about what you are expecting guide your observations. It is essential for researchers to strive to be as objective as possible and to refrain from drawing conclusions until all of the evidence is gathered. The more formal and systematic we can be in our research process, the more confident we can be in the quality of the data we have collected.

Reflect & React: Context Matters

We should not always be so quick to accept the notion that "seeing is believing." Although empirical observation is the best bet for scientific study, it takes hard work and preparation to work the way it should and produce valid measures. Because of this, it is important to maintain a critical eye when reading research reports and to consider what errors in observation may have affected the quality of the data—and therefore the conclusions drawn—in the report you are reading.

Think about a television program you like. Observe that program and note all the things you find enjoyable. Now, ask yourself how many of those observations would hold if you had never seen the show before— how much of your enjoyment depends upon information not immediately observable? For comparison, watch a long-running, complicated show that you have never seen before. Was this less enjoyable? What things required more observation than this one show to understand, and how might you have misinterpreted the show because of your limited exposure?

Reactive Measures

Measurement approaches can vary in the extent to which they interfere with or cause a change in the people being studied. As such, the reactivity of a measure refers to the extent to which the measure (or observation) used has the potential to influence the person (or people) being studied. As a note, in some instances you may see the terms "obtrusive" or "unobtrusive" used to describe measures. These refer to the same general idea such that obtrusive measures imply some degree of interference with the people you are studying and unobtrusive measures imply minimal likelihood that you are interfering with the people you are study. Regardless of the specific terminology used by different people, it is useful to consider the extent to which the measures you are deciding to use could cause some change in the people you are observing.

To help clarify what is meant by reactive measures, consider observing activity at a local shopping mall. One approach would be to watch shoppers

validity
→ Unit 6

informed consent
→ Unit 4

content analysis
→ Unit 11

159

from a secluded location where you could see them but they could not see you—perhaps a balcony or by using cameras in the surveillance system. In this case, your approach to studying people would have no effect on them at all and would be considered nonreactive. On the other hand, you could also study people at the mall by talking with them about their shopping experience, giving them a brief questionnaire, or even accompanying someone as they travel from store to store. In each of these cases, the measures are reactive because carrying out the observations has the potential to change the participants in some way. That is, they could react to being observed and therefore act differently. Perhaps the person you follow buys more than usual and spends a longer amount of time shopping because he wants to impress you. The opposite could also happen as well—the shopper may be shy or reserved about his behavior and do *less* shopping because he knows he is being observed.

Even among potentially reactive measures, the degree to which observation or measurement affects behavior can vary. Administering a brief questionnaire is much less likely to have a strong influence on the participants' behavior than going shopping with them. However, note that a method such as content analysis (discussed in Unit 11) would be nonreactive because you are in no way affecting any individual when conducting that kind of research. Research using social artifacts tends to be nonreactive. In any case, regardless of the specific approach, researchers strive to minimize their influence on the people they study in order to produce valid data. That said, note that nonreactive measures can sometimes create ethical considerations because you cannot obtain informed consent from someone without revealing that he or she is being observed. Some behaviors cannot be observed in a nonreactive way because of this.

survey research
→ Unit 10

experiments
→ Unit 9

variable
→ Unit 2

closed-ended
→ Unit 7

Likert-type
→ Unit 7

rapport
→ Unit 10

Questionnaire Structure

All survey research involves presenting participants with a standard list of questions, known as a *questionnaire* or *survey instrument*. Surveys are not the only type of research to use questionnaires—many experiments also evaluate important variables using questionnaires. But questionnaires have a particular importance in survey research, as they represent the sole measurement strategy in nearly every case. Thus, understanding the elements of a questionnaire and the common features that many survey questionnaires include is critical to creating an effective study, particularly when surveys are used.

Depending on the type of study, researchers may rely on more easily answered questions, such as closed-ended questions that simply ask for yes or no answers or replies to Likert-type scales. But surveys can also use open-ended questions, although these are best kept to a minimum or used only when interviewers administer the questionnaire, allowing them to build rapport.

Regardless of the details, the overall questionnaire collects all the items used in the study in one *standardized* format. Standardization is important—if specific questions are asked of specific individuals, the rules for this must be specified in advance of the study. The use of contingency questions can help give participants appropriate questions from a longer list of possible items. But if the researcher has to adjust the questions on a case-by-case basis, adapting to the specific answers supplied and probing for greater details, this moves from a survey to a more qualitative interviewing approach.

Questionnaires can be administered either through an interview—by telephone or face-to-face—or self-administered through a mail or Internet survey. Regardless of the delivery mechanism, effective questionnaires share some specific traits. First, they provide clear directions. These directions might be for the participant or for the person administering the questionnaire. For example, suppose you are measuring how many people viewed a specific television program. If you are doing this as Nielsen does, you will be using a self-administered mail questionnaire, known as a diary. It's important to the validity of the findings that the questionnaire explain exactly what it means to have "watched" a show, how long the viewing period must be to record it, and whether specific types of viewing (such as online streaming or watching on a DVR) count as viewing. Because it's a printed questionnaire, it's important that these directions be clear and understandable without special training or clarification. Interviewers may be more trained, but they still need clear directions. Often, those conducting the interviews are hired and not part of the research team. But even when they are members of the team, interviewers must be sure they follow the same guidelines as every other interviewer to avoid potential bias.

Second, questionnaires need to make it easy for participants to record their answers. Television viewing diaries are often arranged as grids, like a calendar, allowing people to fill in the exact day and hour they watched a program in a way that is familiar to anyone who has filled out a daily planner or used a calendar application. When questionnaires are administered by interviewers, they are formatted so that responses can be recorded quickly without breaking rapport—the comfortable interaction between interviewers and participants. Often, interviewers read questions from a computer and enter answers as the participant responds, allowing quick, efficient, and accurate recording.

Third, questionnaires should flow effectively and use transitions, just like normal writing. These transitions show that the questionnaire is moving forward and help reinforce rapport. They also provide an opportunity to reinforce the scale being used for closed-ended questions and clarify directions as needed. Finally, they offer a brief break for participants, letting them pause to reflect upon their answers to that point.

Fourth, related to questionnaire flow, researchers should think carefully about the questionnaire organization because question order can also have an effect: participants may answer in different ways depending on which items

filter and contingency questions
→ Unit 7

qualitative versus quantitative research
→ Unit 3

telephone
→ Unit 10

face-to-face survey
→ Unit 10

self-administered survey
→ Unit 10

mail survey
→ Unit 10

Internet survey
→ Unit 10

validity
→ Unit 6

bias
→ Unit 3

response set
→ Unit 7

principles of ethical research
→ Unit 4

informed consent
→ Unit 4

debriefing
→ Unit 4

are presented first. An effective way to address these concerns is to randomize the order in which individual questions or specific blocks of questions are presented. This helps to minimize any possible question order effects by reducing the number of occurrences of any one specific question effect. This is a common practice in polling—especially political polling—where the names of candidates are randomized such that respondents are not always asked about Candidate A before Candidate B. Finally, questionnaire designers should consider creating enough variation in the wording and format of questions to avoid the problem of participants falling into a response set, in which individuals stop paying attention to the specific question wording and simply give the same answer repeatedly.

Lastly, every effective questionnaire includes not only the actual measures but also an effective introduction and conclusion. The introduction should reiterate the rights of participants based on the principles of ethical research. That also means adequate information about the study for informed consent, if such information was not already provided—this can include details about the types of questions and the length of the study. In surveys, it is common for these elements to be the first points raised after participants are initially recruited, as many formats do not allow for a formal, signed consent form. The introduction should also help convey the importance of the study and the participants' responses, to increase rapport. The conclusion should reiterate the value of the responses, address any ethical considerations such as debriefing, and leave participants feeling that their involvement was valued. These elements should be present in self-administered questionnaires as well. Indeed, in this format, the introduction also tends to serve as the needed information for informed consent, with participants "signing" an initial page before moving forward.

Questionnaire Design

How a questionnaire is designed and organized can have implications both for the quality of the data as well as for the likelihood of completion. When someone is completing a questionnaire, he or she is investing time to help the researcher. Therefore, we should minimize the time that participants have to invest and make the questionnaire straightforward for them to complete. All questionnaires should give clear and detailed instructions so that participants know how to answer the question in a way that will provide the answer they are trying to give. For example, if you are using a 5-point scale where 1 equals "not at all" and 5 equals "very much," your instructions should indicate that. You might also want respondents to think of a particular example or period of time—such as how often they have watched a particular television show over the past 3 months. Never assume that the respondents understand what you want them to do *unless you clearly tell them.*

Voices from Industry

Michelle Rawl—Owner of Rawl Research, Inc.

Michelle is a certified librarian with over 20 years' experience and has been in business for herself since 2010.

My clients need research on two different occasions—when they are going after new business and when they are trying to gather the media coverage from a pitch or in many cases, a medical conference.

PR firms can glean a lot of information about what was done in the past by the previous agency by reviewing the media coverage over a certain period of time. They can determine if the other agency gave the client mostly press releases and the feeling is that a more balanced approach might work better—some press releases, some trades and some consumer publications. This then goes into their pitch about how they could position the client better, with more exposure. I will also compare the coverage of the company that they are targeting with six or more companies in the same industry competitors to the company they are pitching. This gives a good sense of where the company is in terms of the industry—do they have the least amount of press coverage over that period of time? Then my client can say they could increase that exposure by doing X, Y and Z.

When a campaign is launched or a medical meeting is covered with data being presented, I use media data to help PR firms confirm to their client that their media dollars were well spent. We track what outlets picked up the news about their announcement, if certain things were in the article that the company specifically wanted communicated, what the article sentiment was, what type of publication it was, who was the reporter, who was quoted and then what is the approximate reach of those publications. All that data can then be sliced and diced to pull into a report to the client telling them how far their news has travelled.

Sometimes my clients use Google to search for current news. This can work if you stay on top of it and don't get behind on the massive number of articles. If there is very little news, this method may work and also if you have a very obscure drug name. The problem comes in when you have a lot of junk to wade through—repeated articles, articles that don't match what the title was when you clicked on it. I typically will use a news aggregator database so I don't have to wade through things that are irrelevant. This is especially true if you want to go back months or years and you have a topic like oncology. There is almost no way to be able to evaluate that on Google—you need a news aggregator, because even then, a big company like Merck could have tons of results in the oncology publications. With a news aggregator, you can adjust the search until it is just right and has the amount of articles that are manageable for the task at hand.

In terms of research, you have to be good at seeing patterns and able to review large amounts of data in order to pull out important facts. Clients don't want a data dump; they want meaningful nuggets that they can work with right out of the box. My clients are leaning more toward chart and graphs in PowerPoint with the large data set sent to them separately. They want the data as backup, but they want the meaningful stuff so they don't have to sort through and find the important parts or trends.

If I had advice for someone, it would be to broaden your horizons from Google. Find other ways to research—what does the public library subscribe to? What publications does the local college have? But if you can't do that, at least learn what is credible out there online. I know it's cliché, but not everything you read on the Internet is true. Double source it—if you find it somewhere else, chances are it could be true. What is the source of the information? Is it credible? *New York Times, Wall Street Journal* . . . know what you are reading and where it is from. Look up the author—what other things have they written?

Beyond these broader organizational issues, an effective tool to streamline the design of a questionnaire is the use of filter questions. These types of questions prevent someone from having to answer questions that are irrelevant to them. Including irrelevant questions can add to the length of time it takes to complete the questionnaire and result in poor data quality if those irrelevant questions are answered. Finally, researchers need to consider question order effects, whereby the answers to later questions are affected by the types of questions asked earlier in the questionnaire.

Research in Depth: Assessing the Questionnaire

The following is an example from a questionnaire designed to measure media use and political attitudes. Note the organization of the questionnaire as well as the use of notes within the questionnaire to guide the interviewer in asking questions and knowing when to skip certain questions if a particular type of media is not used by the respondent.

Box 7.1 Political Information-Seeking Survey—2016 U.S. Presidential
          Election
Thank you for agreeing to participate in our survey.

To start, we'd like to know a little bit about your typical media use. First, about how many days each week do you read the newspaper, including newspaper content posted to the Internet?

[0–7, if 0 go to TV]

Next, over the last month, **how much attention have you paid to newspaper stories** about the following topics, where 1 is very little attention and 7 is a great deal of attention?

International news
National government and politics
State and local government and politics

About how many days each week do you watch some form of television news?

Filter: [*0–7, if 0 go to Internet*]

Over the last month, **how much attention have you paid to television news** stories about the following topics, where 1 is very little attention and 7 is a great deal of attention?

International news
National government and politics
State and local government and politics

Finally, how often do you use the following additional news sources to learn about politics and the election, where 1 is rarely and 7 is often? If you never use a source, please tell us that. [*0 = never, 1–7*]

Internet news sites associated with print or broadcast news outlets
Internet news sites not connected with print or broadcast news outlets
National Public Radio
Talk radio
News magazines
Alternative newspapers
Newsletters from an activist group
Conversations with friends and family

Next, we'd like to hear what you know so far about the two main candidates for president of the United States.

First, can you tell me the name of the Republican candidate running for president?
[0 = **wrong**, 1 = **correct** (*answer = Donald J. Trump*)]

Can you tell me the name of the Democratic candidate running?
[0 = **wrong**, 1 = **correct** (*answer = Hillary Rodham Clinton*)]

These next questions involve some particular issues that the presidential candidates have discussed during the lead up to the election. First, we're going to ask about the issue of health care. For each statement, please let us know how much you agree or disagree, where 1 is strongly disagree and 7 is strongly agree.

This issue is important.

I support government-funded universal health care.
I support Hillary Clinton's stance on health care.
I support Donald Trump's stance on health care.
I understand what's happening with health care in the United States.
I am knowledgeable about health care.
I know a lot about Hillary Clinton's stance on health care.
I know a lot about Donald Trump's stance on health care.
I wish I better understood the health care issue.
I should try to understand health care more than I do.

Steps to Success: Creating an Effective Questionnaire

Use these steps to review your questionnaire before using it to collect data.

1. *Clear directions*: Check each section for clear instructions and make sure that the anchor points of scales are clearly labeled. Any time a new set of items is used or the responses change, new directions should be provided.
2. *Start strong*: Make sure the introduction is clearly worded, contact information for the researcher is included, and any information needed to complete the questionnaire is included.
3. *Avoid response set*: Any time long sets of items are used in a row, make sure to reverse some of the items to avoid response set. Also, it is often a good idea to restate the directions when starting a new page, even if it is in the middle of a list of items.
4. *Leave space*: Be sure to leave adequate room for any open-ended questions. Also make sure there is enough space between response choices for closed-ended questions so that you can be certain which response the person intended to select.
5. *Pre-test*: Always test your questionnaire at least once on a sample that is similar to the one you will use. It is helpful to ask for feedback about the design of the questionnaire.

6. *Proofread*: In addition to regular proofreading, when you look for grammar mistakes and typos, you should also be sure that response choices are exhaustive and mutually exclusive and that you have not used any double-barreled, biased, or leading questions.

7. *Streamline and organize*: Have you used filter questions when needed? Did pretesting reveal any questions some people couldn't (or shouldn't) answer? If so, be sure to include appropriate filter questions. Also, be thoughtful about the order of the questions. Have you programmed question (or question block) randomization into your design if using questionnaire design software? Pre-testing is an important way to check for any issues here.

8. *End strong*: Be sure to thank respondents for their time and close with any instructions needed to complete the questionnaire appropriately. This might mean mailing instructions for returning the questionnaire for a pencil-and-paper questionnaire or a reminder to close their browser for an online questionnaire.

Filter and Contingency Questions

Often, a survey questionnaire will include items that only certain participants should answer. In such cases, *filter questions* are used to direct participants to answer only those questions that are relevant to them. The filtering process can be based on many different types of characteristics. For instance, if researchers are studying individuals' use of social media, they might ask a series of questions about how much and in what ways people use various social media platforms, such as Facebook, Twitter, and LinkedIn. However, not every participant will use every possible platform. To prevent people from having to answer questions about a type of social media they don't use, potentially harming rapport or generating meaningless data, the researchers could use a simple filter question before the group of questions for each type of social media. Just asking "Do you use Facebook?" would allow the researchers to identify who should answer subsequent questions about the platform. In a self-administered questionnaire, the directions should clearly indicate to participants whether they should continue or skip a block of questions. For online surveys, these types of questions often work to automatically filter people into different paths of the questionnaire.

In some cases, researchers will use filter questions early in a study to determine whether a participant should be included in the study. For instance, researchers might be interested in how social media is used by unemployed workers seeking jobs. In this case, the researchers don't need to include those who are currently employed. A filter question used early in the questionnaire asking whether the person is currently employed would filter unemployed people out of the study.

While the question used to determine whether an individual should answer subsequent items is a filter question, the subsequent questions that are

rapport
→ Unit 10

self-administered survey
→ Unit 10

validity
→ Unit 6

variable
→ Unit 2

167

answered by only a portion of the participants are called *contingency questions*. Contingency questions and filter questions are useful to researchers in keeping the length of survey questionnaires short and making sure that respondents don't answer questions that will generate meaningless results. For example, if we are studying the audience for a radio station, we would likely have some questions that only apply to listeners. A filter question identifying those listeners, followed by contingency questions directed at listeners, would be appropriate. Otherwise, we would get opinions from people with no basis for them, amounting to random noise. Ask someone whether the United States should intervene in a fictional country, and many people will express support or opposition. Using contingency questions can help avoid such a problem—most people will admit they don't know about a topic but will still try to answer questions about that topic if denied the chance to avoid it.

<table>
<tr><td>

validity
→ Unit 6

variable
→ Unit 2

</td></tr>
</table>

Response Set

In some cases, participants may become *too* familiar with the format of a questionnaire, automatically answering in a consistent fashion regardless of their actual attitude. This tendency to give the same answer to multiple questions regardless of content is known as *response set*. This tendency threatens the validity of the questionnaire data—reliance on the pattern and not careful reflection on the question accounts for the answers given, meaning that those responses don't accurately reflect a true value for the variable.

Response set tendencies typically occur when there are long lists of items in a row that all have the same anchors—that is, the high and low values consistently have the same labels and meanings. For example, you could use a series of items to assess individuals' conversation styles. One approach would be to ask respondents to indicate how much they agree or disagree with the following statements: "It is okay to interrupt others while they are talking"; "I sometimes talk over people I disagree with to get my point across"; "Sometimes it is necessary to be louder than others to get my point across"; "It is important for me to get my point across"; and "I do not shy away from offering my opinion in conversations with others." In each case, answering "agree" to these items would represent the same type of person—someone who is assertive in his or her conversational style.

The problem, however, is that having a long list of items that all point in the same direction makes it more likely that respondents will pay less attention as they progress through the list. For example, a person could feel that his or her point is important but also respect the bounds of others' styles and not be an interrupter or someone who talks over others. If a respondent falls into giving high or low answers early on, any nuance between such points will be lost. In such cases, it is important for the researcher to include reversed items that help ensure that respondents have to read each item carefully. For instance, the second item could be reversed in the following way: "Even if I disagree with someone, I try to avoid talking over them." An additional strategy to prevent response set is to avoid long lists of items and provide new headings and reminders of instructions between long lists.

Order Effects

In some cases, the order in which questionnaire items are presented can influence the responses generated by those items. Order effects concern researchers because they threaten the validity of the responses given. Specifically, if the response given is simply a function the order in which a question or item is posed, then it is not a true measure of the concept. For example, consider a set of poll questions asking participants to provide an assessment of the current president as well as their opinion on current issues. If the issues mentioned are current points of contention or criticism, the overall rating of the president will be lower. On the other hand, if most people—even critics—think the president is doing well on those issues, the rating will be higher.

Researchers are ultimately interested in finding the true opinion about a particular candidate or issue. However, question order effects can muddy the waters and introduce an additional variable. Research by McLendon and O'Brien (1988) on assessments of well-being revealed interesting question order effects. They found that respondent's assessments of their well-being were affected by whether specific questions—such as questions about marriage or health—about well-being were asked before the general question of their well-being. However, these question order effects were only present for married couples in their sample, adding another interesting wrinkle to concerns about questionnaire effects. Lasorsa (2003) studied the effects of question order on political interest finding that when a challenging political knowledge measure was administered before assessments of political interest and news attention the latter two measures were lower than when assessed before the knowledge measure.

Given these concerns, one remedy is to produce multiple versions of a questionnaire in which the order of the questions is rotated (this can be more easily done using online questionnaire design tools). However, this is not always practical. In cases in which the researchers cannot do this, they should be sure to take care to avoid presenting items early in a questionnaire that are likely to influence later responses. Pre-testing and using good sense can be the researchers' most important tools for eliminating order effects. Broadly speaking, it is good practice to start with general questions and then move to specific ones. Researchers can also put items that might affect one another in different sections of the questionnaire, reducing the likelihood that the influence of one question will carry over to the next. It is important to note that the particular effects of question order will not always be easy to determine, so erring on the side of caution and randomizing when possible is good practice.

questionnaire design
→ Unit 7

validity
→ Unit 6

concept
→ Unit 5

poll
→ Unit 10

pre-test
→ Unit 9

Question Creation

Beyond organizational and structural issues in questionnaire development, the choices that the researcher provides to the respondents filling out the questionnaire can also have implications for the information gathered. The most basic decision is whether to ask a closed-ended question with a defined set of choices or an open-ended question that can be answered in many different ways. The second key to question creation is to make sure that the response choices for closed-ended items are mutually exclusive—that is, each one should be distinct—and that choices are exhaustive, minimizing the likelihood that questions will be left blank. The goal in creating questions is to effectively measure the concept you are studying. By following basic guidelines, you can improve your chances of creating valid measures.

open-ended
→ Unit 7

concept
→ Unit 5

qualitative versus quantitative research
→ Unit 3

coding
→ Unit 11

mutually exclusive
→ Unit 7

Closed-Ended

The two basic question types for questionnaires are open-ended and closed-ended questions. Whereas *open-ended* questions allow the respondent to answer in any way he or she sees fit, closed-ended items provide the study participant with a finite set of choices in responding to any item. For example, to understand people's feelings about media coverage of elections, you could simply ask them to describe their feelings about news coverage of the most recent election. Or you could ask them to list the first five thoughts that come to their mind regarding news coverage of the most recent election. Each of these would be an open-ended way of measuring this concept. In order to use these data in a quantitative analysis, you would need to apply a coding scheme to systematically assess the responses.

To use closed-ended responses, you might employ a series of three agree/disagree items: (1) "news coverage of the 2016 presidential election was fair"; (2) "news coverage of the 2016 presidential election was in-depth"; and (3) "news coverage of the 2016 presidential election was valuable to me in making a voting decision." Each of these items taps into a different aspect of feelings about how the participant feels about news coverage of the election. Closed-ended items are typically easier and quicker to respond to, and they are easier to evaluate, as no additional coding or evaluation of the responses is necessary. Because closed-ended responses of any form generate, at minimum, nominal-level measures, they must be both exhaustive and mutually exclusive.

Let's return to the example of working for the human resources department, supposing that we are now charged with assessing employee satisfaction. Using only closed-ended questions, we might ask respondents to indicate their satisfaction with various aspects of the company on a 5-point scale, where 1 denotes "not at all satisfied" and 5 means "very satisfied." We might include items that assess satisfaction with the following: management, health benefits, retirement, and salary. In this case, we have determined the particular issues we want the respondents to assess. Further, we have defined how they can respond. Of course, it is possible that we could be missing something that is important to the employees, and we would have no way of knowing that. However, the advantage of this approach is that analyzing the responses is fairly straightforward, and we won't need to work hard to convert those responses into a quantitative form.

Open-Ended

In contrast to closed-ended questions, which present respondents with a limited set of choices in responding to each item, *open-ended* questions have no such limitations and allow for greater variety in the responses given. For example, researchers might be interested in understanding participants' feelings toward different types of television shows. Using closed-ended items, the researchers could pose a series of questions asking the respondents to indicate on a 5-point scale how much they like or dislike different types of content, including reality television, sports, news, and dramatic shows. However, it could be that researchers are interested in gathering more information or better understanding the context for responses. Therefore, they might ask the following open-ended questions: "Describe your feelings toward each of the following types of content: reality television, sports, news, and dramatic shows." In this case, the respondents are able to elaborate on their feelings toward each of these types of content and go beyond highly specific quantitative responses. Of course, such items might produce very detailed and wordy responses. The researchers must then code the responses in order to use them in quantitative analysis, or at least they must carefully evaluate them for patterns if conducting qualitative research.

The strength of open-ended questions is that they offer the opportunity for detailed responses and also allow for responses that the researchers may not have considered. As such, they can be useful in exploratory and descriptive research when researchers are trying to understand new concepts. However, the challenge with open-ended items is that responses could be lengthy, confusing, and potentially difficult to analyze in a reliable or valid way. Further, open-ended items can take much longer to complete; if the researchers are aiming for a more concise study that requires a small amount of time from participants, they may shy away from open-ended items.

Let's again consider the situation in which you are working for the human resources department and have to assess employee satisfaction. Instead of using closed-ended questions, let's consider using open-ended questions. In this case, you could use two open-ended questions in which you ask respondents to list all of the things that they like about their current job and then, separately, list all of the things they dislike about their current job. You will likely get a wide array of responses to these two open-ended questions. In some

closed-ended
→ Unit 7

qualitative versus quantitative research
→ Unit 3

coding
→ Unit 11

exploration
→ Unit 3

descriptive statistics
→ Unit 14

concept
→ Unit 5

reliability
→ Unit 6

validity
→ Unit 6

range
→ Unit 14

coding
→ Unit 14

cases, respondents will write a lot of information, but in others, respondents might list only one or two things (if anything). This range of responses occurs because you are leaving it up to the respondent to answer the question as he or she sees fit.

It is also likely that you will have to do some coding or interpreting of responses. For instance, one person might respond by saying, "other people; benefits." Another might write, "my coworkers are great and I really appreciate the health care offered by the company." In both cases, it appears that the responses are referring to two distinct things: benefits and coworkers. However, they do so in distinct ways—as the researcher, you will have to decide whether these responses should be treated equivalently. For example, you might decide that one response is stronger than another and therefore add a measure that indicates the respondent's strength of feeling.

Reflect & React: Critical Thoughts on Customer Satisfaction Questionnaires

Brief questionnaires are a common way for restaurants and other places of business to assess customer satisfaction. Often, these questionnaires include items such as satisfaction with food, service, price, and selection. Additionally, they often include an open-ended item at the end asking for "any additional comments." The next time you receive one of these comment cards, assess the quality of the questions. Is there anything missing? Are the options for the closed-ended items mutually exclusive and exhaustive? Consider any changes you might make to the questionnaire, as well as what steps you would take to ensure that more are filled out and returned as opposed to being tossed in the recycling bin.

---

pre-test
→ Unit 9

Exhaustive

A questionnaire item is *exhaustive* if the response choices include all possible answers or options for a given item. This concern applies directly to closed-ended questions, as open-ended questions do not provide choices. If a person can give any possible answer to an open-ended question, then it must be exhaustive. For closed-ended questions, listing every possible answer may not be practical, so including the option of "other" can ensure that all possible answers are covered in some way.

For example, if you are interested in knowing someone's favorite social media platform, you might provide a list of choices, such as Facebook, Twitter, Snapchat, Instagram, and Myspace. However, there could conceivably be other options not listed that would make this list incomplete. Maybe the respondent is a big fan of the Chinese website Weibo or sticks exclusively to a 10-year-old Friendster account. Because very few participants in the United States would be expected to choose those answers, it would make sense to include them under the category of "other" and add that as a choice to the list.

It is important, though, that when "other" is used as an option to make a list exhaustive, this category should not make up too large a percentage of the responses. Otherwise, the data are not as useful. For instance, if on the same list you offered the choices Twitter, Snapchat, Myspace, and "other," it is likely that a high percentage of people would select the last option. It could be that many of them are Facebook or Instagram users, but you cannot be certain that they are. To be safe, it is better to include choices if you have any reason to suspect they would be frequently mentioned or otherwise want to differentiate those choices from others. If a certain category receives only a few responses, you can always combine that with other categories to form a broader "other" or some different combined category.

Of course, in some cases, you cannot be certain what the possible answers will be. This is why using a pre-test is so valuable to the research process. One approach would be to use an open-ended question in the pre-test so that you can identify the main responses to the question. From there, you can decide which responses to include as choices in your open-ended question. If you are a human resources professional looking at reasons employees value their current job, you might have a list of potential reasons, including benefits, pay, quality supervisors, and flexible work hours. An open-ended pre-test might reveal that people consistently listed their coworkers as a reason for liking their job. If this were collapsed into the "other" category, you might miss important information. By pre-testing with the open-ended questionnaire, you could better identify important items to include.

Mutually Exclusive

Beyond being exhaustive, the list of responses for questionnaire items should also ensure that each item is unique and that there is no overlap between two or more items. For example, if researchers want to know how many days a week a person watches sports on television, they could either leave it open ended or provide a list of numbers from 0 to 7. In this case, the list of possible responses is *mutually exclusive* (and exhaustive) because each of the choices is distinct. However, consider this list of options: 0–1 days, 1–2 days, 3–4 days, 4–5 days, or 6–7 days. In this case, some choices overlap with others. Specifically, 0–1 and 1–2 overlap, as do 3–4 and 4–5. The data become difficult to interpret, if not useless, because the researcher can no longer be sure what is meant by the response given for some of the choices.

Sometimes researchers will ask participants to select "all that apply," suggesting that more than one response could be selected. While this allows

exhaustive
→ Unit 7

participants to give more than one response, each response should still have a distinct meaning. If the participant were to mark two or more responses, we would be uncertain whether that was because the two distinct options were both meaningful or because just one idea happened to be captured by the wording of each response option.

Consider again measuring employee satisfaction. Suppose we ask participants to select the aspect of their job with which they are most satisfied: coworkers, benefits, retirement package, salary, and management. From this list, there is potential for overlap between "benefits" and "retirement package" and possibly some overlap between "coworkers" and "management." Therefore, it would be beneficial to include clarifying language to distinguish the options. A new version of the list might include these options: nonmanagement coworkers, health benefit plan, retirement package, salary (not including benefits), people in management positions (defined as those who have the power to hire, fire, or determine rewards/punishments for workers). This new list is somewhat longer, but it does a better job of distinguishing the choices and makes the list mutually exclusive, unlike the previous version. This list also works in the case of asking participants to select only one or to select all that apply because each item is distinct. In such a case, we can be certain that each item is selected because the words themselves represent distinct concepts. For instance, "health benefit plan" and "salary" are distinct enough items that a person could select both without referring to the same idea, as "salary" and "pay" might suggest.

Question Wording Problems

Few things can ruin data collection more than realizing that a question was poorly worded or leading. Problems with question wording lead to problems with the validity of the resulting data gathered from those questions. Responses might prompt or lead participants to answer in a particular way, play upon social desirability, produce unintended error because of problems with clarity, or be impossible to completely answer because they reflect multiple concepts in a single answer (known as a double-barreled question). Because of this, it is essential that researchers assess questions for common question wording problems before the data collection process begins.

researcher bias
→ Unit 9

validity
→ Unit 6

Leading Questions

In some cases, questionnaire items are phrased in a way that *leads* study participants to respond in a particular way—that is, one answer or type of answer appears to be intended or more ideal than others. When this occurs, the researcher has inserted researcher bias into the items—whether accidentally or on purpose—and the subsequent responses will be of questionable validity.

For example, consider the following item from a survey questionnaire: "Do you support or oppose the new health care legislation that will hurt middle-class families and destroy jobs?" Note how the second half of the sentence adds details to the item that will "push" participants to respond in a particular way. Who wants to support legislation that will hurt middle-class families and destroy jobs? It is likely that many people will indicate that they oppose such legislation, but the answers are biased because of the question wording. A different way of phrasing the question that is not leading would be to ask, "Do you support or oppose the new health care legislation?" If the researchers wanted to understand the reasoning behind the respondent's opinion, then they could ask follow-up question, such as, "Indicate how much you agree or disagree with the following statement: 'The proposed health care legislation will harm middle-class families.'"

Sometimes, *push polling* is used by individuals or groups to create a false sense of opinion on a particular topic. For instance, an interest group that is opposed to health care reform might commission a poll that includes a biased question. Although rare, these types of polls do occur, so it is important that any time you participate in or read research you know who the researchers are and whether they are a trusted source. These polls are considered unethical and can distort opinion in two ways. First, the wording of the question may actually change the opinions of those being polled, making the actual results less important than the persuasive power they hold. Second, if the results are reported, they can create the impression that public opinion is one sided in a way that doesn't reflect reality. In most cases, though, bias in question wording is not purposeful. Often, it results from attempting to provide contextual information so that respondents understand the focus of the question. Pre-testing can help identify such issues.

Social Desirability

One reason that questions can lead people to specific response is the power of social desirability. In some cases, research participants feel pressure to answer items in a particular way based on perceptions about how their answers will reflect on them—this is social desirability. For instance, some participants may feel pressure to under-report how frequently they engage in undesirable behaviors such as smoking, drug use, or arguing with their romantic partner. On the other hand, they might simultaneously inflate self-reports of behaviors that are seen as more desirable, such as the number of hours spent volunteering, time spent reading books, or satisfaction with their current romantic relationship. When this occurs, an additional variable—social desirability—is exerting some influence on the data, threatening the validity of the findings. This is because the answer that the person is giving is not the true answer but one that is influenced by social desirability.

survey
→ Unit 10

bias
→ Unit 3

polls
→ Unit 10

validity
→ Unit 6

questionnaire design
→ Unit 7

statistical control
→ Unit 16

variable
→ Unit 2

In some cases, researchers will account for the influence of social desirability by including a series of items in their questionnaire that measure how much the participant is influenced by social desirability. In measuring topics for which social desirability is likely to be a factor, researchers can then use this additional measure as a control variable in data analysis and thereby control—or remove—the influence of social desirability on responses to various items. More broadly, researchers try to avoid questions where there is a clear socially desirable response. This occurs most often with leading questions, but even objectively worded questions can be affected by social desirability where there are strong cultural norms. Adjusting the question to be less direct can help solve this issue.

Clarity

concept
→ Unit 5

conceptual definition
→ Unit 5

variable
→ Unit 2

indicator
→ Unit 5

Even though research is a formal and careful process, it is still a form of communication. The connection between the researcher and the participant matters, and confusion on the part of either can create a breakdown in the conversation. Therefore, researchers should create clear and direct questions. When creating questionnaire items, avoid overly complex items, jargon, highly technical language, vague descriptions, and very long questions. For example, if you are trying to find out how often people communicate interpersonally with the other people in their lives, you might consider asking them, "How often do you communicate interpersonally?" Such a question would be quite difficult to answer, however, because it is unclear whom the conversational partner is, what time frame the research is considering, and even what constitutes "interpersonal" communication, as some people may not be familiar with this term or may understand it differently from the researcher. To improve the clarity of measurement for this concept, it would be useful to include several items that more precisely state the communication partner and to better explain what "interpersonal" communication with those partners entails.

It is also important to clarify the time frame and how the participants should answer. As a result, you might introduce the items in this way: "For each of the following items, please indicate how frequently you have engaged in those behaviors during the past week using a scale from 'not at all' to 'every day.'" Then you could include some of the following items: "Have conversations with people I consider my good friends"; "Discuss non-work-related issues with a coworker"; and "Talk about local issues with a stranger." Of course, you would need to define the type of conversation and the target discussants based upon your conceptual definition of interpersonal discussion. More broadly, there are many ways to measure a given variable. Often, it is better to ask more questions in a simple and precise way rather than asking one question that fully measures your concept but does so using language that reflects the academic literature instead of everyday conversation.

Double-Barreled

Individual items that tap into more than one indicator, dimension, or concept are referred to as *double-barreled questions*. For example, consider the following question, which is meant to measure the effectiveness of communication with a romantic partner: "Do you feel that you are easily able to see your partner's point in arguments and that s/he is easily able to see your point?" This question is actually asking two separate questions—whether you think your partner understands you and whether you think you understand your partner. As such, the question does not effectively capture either concept. If someone answers yes, does this mean he or she agrees with both ideas or just one? If a participant answers "no," does this mean he or she agrees with neither or only one? The researcher might guess, but any such guess would be a measure of researcher bias more than the attitude of the respondent.

Effective questions focus on a single indicator—that is, they address just one idea at a time. For example, the question regarding partner understanding could be split into two separate questions: (1) "Do you feel that you are easily able to see your partner's point in arguments?"; (2) "Do you feel that your partner easily sees your point in arguments?" This provides separate measures of the respondent's assessment of self-understanding and of partner understanding. Even if these are later combined into an index, it's important to clearly measure only one thing at a time.

| dimension |
| → Unit 5 |
| **concept** |
| → Unit 5 |
| **researcher bias** |
| → Unit 9 |

Reflect & React: Thinking About Question Wording

At their core, problems with question wording threaten the validity of your measures, which, in turn, threatens your confidence that your data are telling you something meaningful. Because of this, it is essential to minimize question wording problems. A good approach to doing this is to read the questionnaire out loud with a group of people. Often, reading questions out loud will reveal some of the subtler problems that are easily missed when reading in your head. Further, reading in a small-group setting allows different people to hear the questions and increases the likelihood of catching problems. This is particularly important when it comes to bias and clarity.

Try this with a group of your friends and some questions from another class or from a study you are working on for this class. See whether they think any questions obviously lead them toward a particular answer regardless of their knowledge or opinions. Ask them whether any questions seem to reflect two different ideas at once. Have them let you know whether there are too many conjunctions ("and," "but," and "or" are key examples) that make it hard to recognize the focus of the question. Let them explain what they think the question means, then consider whether that is how you understood it. If this was a questionnaire you devised, think about how to fix it. If these were questions from another class (such as from an exam), think about how you would have worded them to make them work better.

Types of Items

Many standard approaches to measuring variables are available for researchers. Approaches such as semantic differential scale and Likert-type items allow researchers to assess where individuals fall in their assessment of a particular item while also allowing for comparisons across items. Although there are many ways to measure variables, knowing these standard approaches can make the process simpler and allow you to better assess other measurement approaches. These scales can make it easier to combine items and form indexes—that is, measures that reflect the combined information from multiple individual questions (i.e., indicators). Of course, to form an index, you must also assess the reliability of the indicators through a measure such as Cronbach's alpha.

Likert-Type Items

range
→ Unit 14

indicators
→ Unit 5

dimension
→ Unit 5

concept
→ Unit 5

Questionnaire items that employ a 5-point range of response options from "strongly agree" to "strongly disagree" are typically referred to as Likert-type measures or Likert scales. These types of measures provide study participants with a series of statements and ask them to indicate how much they agree or disagree with those statements. The range of responses usually includes the following choices: "strongly disagree," "somewhat disagree," "agree some/disagree some," "somewhat agree," and "strongly agree." In some cases, researchers may omit labels outside of the extreme ends of the range of possible responses (also called *anchors*) to reinforce the idea that the scale is an interval-level measure. The general idea is to use a series of statements (i.e., indicators) that tap into a single dimension or concept in order to develop a fuller understanding of the study participant's attitudes or beliefs on a particular issue.

Semantic Differential Items

closed ended
→ Unit 7

range
→ Unit 14

Similar to Likert-type items, other common scales used by researchers are semantic differential scales, which use words with opposite meaning as the anchor points (i.e., the two ends of the scale) and ask participants to select the word that best describes their feeling about a particular item. These types of items are closed ended. Typically, these scales use a 5- or 7-point scale, with the antonyms at each end of this numerical range allowing the participant to select various points along the continuum of a particular word pairing. For example, researchers interested in people's satisfaction with their interpersonal communication with romantic partners might present the following statement: "Thinking of how I feel about communicating with my partner makes me feel ___." The participants could then be presented with "happy" and "sad" or "satisfied" and "unsatisfied" as anchor points. Participants whose communication with their romantic partner makes them quite happy might select "happy" or "satisfied" as a response. Those who are less happy with that communication—or even made sad when thinking about it—will select some other point on the scale. The most important key with semantic differential scale items is that the anchor points must truly be antonyms—words that have the exact opposite meaning. Consider the following alternative anchor points to the communication happiness item: "happy" and "confusing." It might be that happiness is somehow related to confusion, but these would be poor anchor points for a semantic differential scale because they are not opposites.

Activities

Activity 7A: Develop a Questionnaire

See terms: indices; Likert-type items; operationalization; semantic differential items.

The goal of this activity is to develop a questionnaire to gain practice with question writing. For this activity, select two concepts that you could measure using a questionnaire. Feel free to use concepts you have previously worked with or look to the literature for ideas on new ones.

Part 1: Start by developing a clear conceptual definition to help guide you through question creation. Next, create a questionnaire that you could use to measure those concepts. Specifically, for each concept, develop the following:

- Four Likert-scale items
- Two semantic differential items
- Two open-ended items.

Part 2: After creating your questionnaire items, consider the strengths and weaknesses of the different types of items and the challenges you might face in using the question wording you have developed. After completing the questionnaire items for each concept, address the following issues:

- Which items are likely to be the strongest/best indicators of your concept?
- Which items do you have the most concerns about as indicators of your concept?
- What challenges might you expect to face with evaluating the open-ended items?

Part 3 (optional): Give the questionnaire to a few friends or co-workers and get their feedback. Compare their feedback to your answers from Part 2. Did they notice similar things in terms of strengths and weaknesses of the questionnaire?

Activity 7B: Bad Questionnaire

See terms: bias; clarity; double-barreled; exhaustive; mutually exclusive.

Your objective for this activity is twofold. First, for each of the poorly written questionnaire items listed below, identify the specific problem (or problems) with the item. Second, develop an alternative way of presenting the item that fixes the problems you have identified. For this activity, don't try to replace the use of closed-ended questions with a completely different method—just suggest better items to replace any flawed measures you identify in the information given next.

Questionnaire Items About Media Use and Environmental Attitudes

Mostly hippies like Willie Nelson and college professors drive a car like a Prius. How would you characterize your support for extending tax credits for hybrid vehicles?

Weak   ___   ___   ___   Strong

How would you characterize your support for mandatory recycling programs?

Strong   ___   ___   ___   Enthusiastic

It is important to recycle and use high-efficiency appliances and use low-energy lightbulbs.

Strongly disagree   ___   ___   ___   Strongly agree

It is important to recycle waste and compost food products.

Strongly disagree   ___   ___   ___   Strongly agree

Plastic bags are overtaking the earth and going to smother us all to death. How would you characterize your support for programs that promote the use of reusable bags?

Not at all important   ___   ___   ___   Very important

How many times have you recycled something in the past year? ___

If you don't do more to help the environment, you are a horrible person.

Strongly disagree   ___   ___   ___   Strongly agree

Indicate how many days a week you use a smartphone or similar device by circling the appropriate response:

0   1   3   5   6   7

Indicate how many days a week you watch televised news:

0–1   1–2   3–4   4–5   5–6   7

Media content can help us understand the environment.

Strongly disagree   ___   ___   ___   Strongly agree

My media use habits relate to my environmental attitudes.

Strongly disagree   ___   ___   ___   Strongly agree

How do you feel about television in relation to the environment?

Activity 7C: Observation

See terms: observation; reactive measures.

The purpose of this activity is to develop an approach to research that uses observation while specifically exploring both direct and indirect approaches. For this activity, we will use the topic of conversational gestures in public places while attempting to answer the following research question: "Do men and women differ in the conversational gestures they use while conversing in public?"

Part 1: For the first part of this activity, the goal is to brainstorm different ways of answering the research question using both direct and indirect observation techniques. In doing so, consider the different locations where you might conduct your observations, the samples you might use, and the specific things (i.e., gestures) you would observe.

Part 2: Select one of the approaches that you developed in Part 1 of this activity. Conduct a pilot test of your research using a small sample or a small number of observations to test out the approach. What patterns did you notice in your observations? What would the answer to your research question be?

Part 3: Provide some critical analysis of your research. Specifically, consider some of the following questions: What worked well? What didn't? What things would you change if you were going to do a full-fledged version of the study? What were specific challenges you faced in carrying out your observations?

Activity 7D: Identify and Critique the Parts of a Questionnaire

See terms: bias; clarity; filter questions.

The goal of this activity is to evaluate the effectiveness of the design of a questionnaire. To do so, seek out a questionnaire from an online source, through extra credit, or use one provided by your instructor. Once you have read through and completed the questionnaire, use the following prompts to more thoroughly evaluate the questionnaire:

■ Is the questionnaire organized effectively? Are there any potential order effects of questions?

■ Are the instructions clear and concise? Do separate sections have clear headings and instructions? Does the introductory section provide any useful information?

■ Does the questionnaire use filter questions at all? Are they necessary? Are there instances in which a filter question would have been useful but was not used?

■ If there was one specific thing you would change about the questionnaire what would it be? Why would you prioritize this change?

Suggested Readings for Further Exploration of Unit 7 Topics

Examples and Cited Works

Dylko, I. B. (2010). An examination of methodological and theoretical problems arising from the use of political participation indexes in political communication research. *International Journal of Public Opinion Research*, *22*(4), 523–534. doi:10.1093/ijpor/edq032

Lang, A., Kurita, S., Rubenking, B. R., & Potter, R. F. (2011). MiniMAM: Validating a short version of the motivation activation measure. *Communication Methods and Measures*, *5*(2), 146–162. doi:10.1080/19312458.2011.568377

Lasorsa, D. L. (2003). Question-order effects in surveys: The case of political interest, news attention, and knowledge. *Journalism & Mass Communication Quarterly*, *80*, 499–512. doi:10.1177/107769900308000302

McLendon, M. J., & O'Brien, D. J. (1988). Question-order effects on the determinants of subjective well-being. *Public Opinion Quarterly*, *52*, 351–364. doi:10.1086/269112

Moy, P., Scheufele, D. A., Eveland, W. P., Jr., & McLeod, J. M. (2001). Support for the death penalty and rehabilitation: Question order or communication effect? *Journal of Applied Social Psychology*, *31*(11), 2230–2255. doi:10.1111/j.1559-1816.2001.tb00173.x

Price, V., & Tewksbury, D. (1996). Measuring the third-person effect of news: The impact of question order, contrast and knowledge. *International Journal of Public Opinion Research*, *8*(2), 120–141. doi:10.1093/ijpor/8.2.120

Schuldt, J. P., Konrath, S. H., & Schwarz, N. (2011). "Global warming" or "climate change"? Whether the planet is warming depends on question wording. *Public Opinion Quarterly*, *75*(1), 115–124. doi:10.1093/poq/nfq073

Schuman, H., & Presser, S. (1996). *Questions and answers in attitude surveys: Experiments on question form, wording, and context*. Thousand Oaks, CA: Sage Publications.

Tewksbury, D., Althaus, S. L., & Hibbing, M. V. (2011). Estimating self-reported news exposure across and within typical days: Should surveys use more refined measures? *Communication Methods and Measures*, *5*(4), 311–328. doi:10.1080/19312458.2011.624650

Vandewater, E. A., & Lee, S. J. (2009). Measuring children's media use in the digital age: Issues and challenges. *American Behavioral Scientist*, *52*(8), 1152–1176. doi:10.1177/0002764209331539

Advanced Discussion

Greenberg, B. S., Eastin, M. S., Skalski, P., Cooper, L., Levy, M., & Lachlan, K. (2005). Comparing survey and diary measures of internet and traditional media use. *Communication Reports*, *18*(1–2), 1–8. doi:10.1080/08934210500084164

Moore, D. W. (2002). Measuring new types of question-order effects: Additive and subtractive. *Public Opinion Quarterly*, *66*(1), 80–91. doi:10.1086/338631

Smyth, J. D., Dillman, D. A., Christian, L. M., & Stern, M. J. (2006). Comparing check-all and forced-choice question formats in web surveys. *Public Opinion Quarterly*, *70*(1), 66–77. doi:10.1093/poq/nfj007

Tourangeau, R., & Smith, T. W. (1996). Asking sensitive questions: The impact of data collection mode, question format, and question context. *Public Opinion Quarterly*, *60*(2), 275–304. doi:10.1086/297751

unit 8

sampling

When trying to find out the answer to a question, who you talk to can make all the difference in the world. For instance, let's say you want to understand how Americans feel about new technologies such as smartphones, iPads, e-book readers, and other mobile devices. If you ask a group of twenty-somethings, you will likely get enthusiastic responses about how great all of these new technologies are and emerge with a sense that these technologies are heavily used and that we, as a society, are dependent upon them. On the other hand, if you ask a considerably older group of people who did not grow up using these technologies, you may get wildly different answers and thus draw different conclusions about the state of emerging technologies. Older people tend to read the print version of the newspaper at higher rates and use social media and other smartphone technologies at somewhat lower rates than younger people and may express skepticism about the impact of these new technologies. This example isn't meant to suggest that one answer is right or wrong but rather to demonstrate that who you ask will affect the answers that you get.

It would be great, of course, to be able to talk to everyone so that you could be certain that all opinions are accounted for. However, this is highly unlikely in most circumstances. Unless you are incredibly efficient, have unlimited financial resources, and have lots of free time, it would be next to impossible to talk to every single American to ask their opinions about new technologies. Instead, you have to select a subset—or sample—of that population to interview in order for the research project to be feasible. This unit covers the different ways that we can go about selecting units of analysis to observe. It discusses how to carry out various sampling strategies and how to assess the quality of the samples that you select.

Sample

polls
→ Unit 10

survey research
→ Unit 10

Most research designs involve drawing a sample, which is a selected group of individuals who make up a subset of a larger **population**, chosen with the expectation that the characteristics of the sample can be used to describe the traits of the overall population. Not all samples are equally **representative**, but any time a portion of the total number of relevant individuals is considered, that constitutes a sample. In rare cases in which all relevant individuals in a given population can be included in the study, that is called a **census**. You have probably seen information about samples in newspaper stories about public opinion polls, as polls rely on being a good representation of the public, but understanding sampling is important to all research. By grasping the logic of sampling, we can understand other important ideas that are commonly discussed in polling coverage, such as **confidence levels**, **confidence intervals**, and **margin of error**, all of which are based on the logic of a complex but critical concept: the **sampling distribution**.

The most critical question for any sample is whether it is **representative** of the population. A representative sample is similar to the larger population in ways that matter for the study, and conclusions based on that sample are likely to more accurately describe the population than samples that are not representative. The most basic way to obtain a representative sample is by using a **simple random sample**, a kind of **probability sample** in which all members of the population are equally likely to be selected. For example, suppose you work for a company with 1,000 employees. You might get a list of all of the employees and number the employees from 1 to 1,000. Then, you could have a computer generate 100 random numbers and contact the people on the list corresponding to those numbers. However, drawing a simple random sample can be challenging, as it often requires a **sampling frame**—that is, a list of all of the individuals in the population. With a sampling frame, a random sample can be obtained using a computer or even a basic **random number table**. Often, though, researchers use other approaches to random sampling, such as **systematic sampling**, or variations such as a **cluster sample** or a **stratified sample**. While these can largely be treated like simple random samples, there are some consequences for data analysis.

As a rule, the larger the **sample size**, the better the sample will reflect the population, although this is not guaranteed. For any random sample, you must also consider the **response rate**, or the share of those selected who actually take part in the study. A random sample may not be representative if there is a systematic pattern of refusals; decreasing response rates have alarmed many survey researchers and marketing professionals in recent years.

In situations in which getting any kind of random sample is too difficult or not important to the research goals, researchers may instead use a nonrandom (or **nonprobability**) sample. Examples of these kinds of samples include **convenience, deliberate** (or purposive), **quota, snowball** (or network), and **volunteer samples**. A common type of nonrandom sample is one you probably have seen many times—people handing out questionnaires at the student union or a local shopping center to anyone who walks by. Any nonrandom sample may induce greater levels of **sampling error**, in which the sample characteristics deviate from those of the entire population, but we cannot easily calculate this error for nonrandom samples.

For example, consider a situation in which you want to assess the extent to which playing video games affects the work or study habits of adult Americans. In this case, you have defined the population you want to understand as adult Americans. This suggests that any American who is over age 18 could conceivably be considered eligible to be part of the sample. If you truly want to generalize your findings to the population of American adults, then you would use one of the probability sampling techniques. But maybe you don't really want to know about all Americans but rather some segment of the adult population; in that case, you would be better off finding a way to include only certain types of individuals, such as women, youth, or the working poor. Further, you may have little interest in generalizing your findings—suggesting that you would be okay with using one of the nonprobability sampling techniques. This illustrates the importance of clarifying not only *who* you want to study but also *what* you plan to do with the results.

Representative Sample

A key goal in sampling from a population is to ensure that the sample is as representative as possible—that is, the characteristics of the individuals in the sample are consistent with those of the larger population. Another way to understand this is that the individual statistics for the sample should be as close as possible to the equivalent parameters for the population. This includes descriptive statistics for individual variables as well as for measuring relationships between variables. For example, suppose you are studying the effects of playing violent video games on school performance. If, in the population, the average child spends 10 hours a week playing such games, then a representative sample would also spend an average of 10 hours a week playing these games. Furthermore, if those who play such games are 5 percent more likely to fail algebra, then in your sample, you should also find this 5 percent difference. Of course, you won't know the values for the population—if you did, you wouldn't need to gather a sample. But if you have a representative sample, then you can expect that the results for these statistics will be similar to those in the population.

No sample can perfectly mirror the population in every way because of random sampling error, but several techniques can help ensure a reasonably representative sample. In particular, using a random sample is generally the best way to effectively represent a large and diverse population. Other types of nonrandom samples, such as a quota sample, can ensure that the sample is representative of the population at least for specific characteristics. Even a random sample will be less representative if the response rate is low and the individuals who actually participate in the study are not representative of the population. The selected pool of individuals would have been representative, but the final sample is not.

It is important to note that researchers are not always concerned with the representativeness of a sample. For instance, researchers conducting experiments typically use nonprobability sampling techniques and rarely have samples that are representative of the public. Survey researchers, on the other hand, would almost certainly want to have a sample that is representative of the population they are studying. In making decisions about sampling, it is important for the researcher to have a clear understanding of the ultimate goals of the research. The goals and outcomes of the research should guide the researcher in making decisions about the research process, including those of sampling and the representativeness—or lack thereof—of the sample. If one of

population
→ Unit 8

descriptive statistics
→ Unit 14

sampling error
→ Unit 10

random
→ Unit 8

quota sampling
→ Unit 8

response rate
→ Unit 8

experiment
→ Unit 9

survey research
→ Unit 10

the goals is to understand the public and to be able to generalize, then having a representative sample should be a priority. If, on the other hand, the goal of the research is focused less on extrapolating to a population and more on understanding the effects of a particular variable, then having a representative sample becomes less of a priority relative to other needs.

Response Rate

The percentage of those people selected to participate in a study who actually complete the study represents the response rate. Depending on the manner of recruitment and contact, there are different ways to compute the exact number. The simplest approach is to compare the list of people chosen from the sampling frame to the number of participants in the study. For example, suppose you have a sampling frame listing all of the students at your university, and from this you randomly choose 100 students. After sending out multiple e-mails to contact these students and to ask them to take your survey, 60 of them take part. This would make your response rate 60 percent.

The response rate is important for studies that use some kind of random sample and are meant to provide a representative sample because it provides an indication of whether the sample is truly representative. The higher the response rate, the better. Lower response rates open up more potential for random error in the sample. The expectation that a random sample is representative is based upon the idea that all individuals in the population are equally likely to be included in the sample. If some types of people are more likely to refuse to respond, then the sample no longer reflects all types of individuals equally well. On the other hand, if refusal is random, then lower response rates have no effect on the representativeness of a survey. Because the study only includes data about those who participate, it's impossible to know for sure whether those who opt out are different in a systematic way. Some studies have compared those who most readily participate in surveys with those who have to be actively persuaded, and in general, it appears that nonresponse is not a major source of systematic error. Nonetheless, you should try to minimize refusals and obtain as high a response rate as possible to give the best chance of having a representative sample.

Higher response rates help produce a larger sample size, giving your study more power and a narrower confidence interval. Certain types of studies, such as mail surveys, tend to have lower response rates because throwing away a letter is easier than hanging up a phone. Techniques such as providing monetary incentives can help increase response rates. Over the past few decades, response rates for most types of surveys have steadily fallen. This can be attributed to changes in technology as well as more broadly negative attitudes toward the media and opinion polls, along with other factors.

For example, consider the study of how playing video games affects adult Americans' work and study habits and assume a response rate of 60 percent.

This means that 40 percent of the people in the original sampling frame did not participate in the study. If people who play a lot of video games are more likely to decline to participate in the study, they would make up a disproportionate number of the 40 percent who did not participate in the study. Consequently, the sample—the 60 percent who agreed to participate—would include a smaller portion of heavy video game players than exists in the "real world." Therefore, the sample would no longer be representative.

Incentive

Often, researchers will offer participants something to encourage them to agree to participate in the study and complete the study. These incentives help boost response rate and therefore can improve the quality of the sample. Researchers can use many types of incentives to attract participants, although the particular incentive tends to vary based on the type of research and the sample. For example, if you are conducting an experiment in a university setting, a likely incentive would be to offer extra credit. This works because students are often motivated to perform better in their classes, and participation in a research study allows them to earn some extra points toward a class. However, if you are going to use focus groups to assess how medical professionals use new media technologies to communicate with their patients you would likely have to offer a different form of incentive.

In the case of focus groups, it is common to offer participants some kind of monetary reward that is commensurate with the money they might be giving up by missing work to participate in the focus group. Therefore, you might offer $25 to $50 (or more) for nonstudent participants in focus group research. Survey researchers commonly offer a smaller individual incentive, often $5 or even less (as a note, the incentive for many online subject pools is even smaller). However, they typically supplement that incentive by offering to enter respondents into a drawing for a larger prize, such as a cash prize. In many cases, survey researchers offer no individual incentive and rely only on the larger prize to serve as incentive enough to boost response and completion rates.

From an ethics standpoint, it is important that the incentive not be seen as coercive to the potential participant. The goal is to design the incentive in such a way that participants do not feel a great loss or anxiety if they decide not to take the opportunity. The incentive is there as a way of thanking the participants for the time they have given you. In most cases, the Institutional Review Board at your university or place of employment will review the details of your incentive and ask you to make adjustments if it is viewed as too coercive. For example, consider a situation in which you offer 50 points of extra credit added to the participant's grade (out of 100 total points for the course) for participation in a study. This is such a large percentage of the grade and can have such a meaningful impact on performance in the class that it would be difficult to refuse to participate in the study. Therefore, respondents may

response rate
→ Unit 8

sample
→ Unit 8

experiments
→ Unit 9

focus group
→ Unit 12

ethical research
→ Unit 4

institutional review
→ Unit 4

participate in a study they ultimately are uncomfortable with. The same would hold if you were to present the opportunity in a way that would suggest they would fail (or otherwise be punished) if they did not participate in the study. Participation must be voluntary, and incentives that are too coercive take away this aspect of individual choice.`

Reflect & React: Appropriate Incentives

In thinking about your interest in participating in research studies, consider what kinds of incentives would inspire you to want to take part in a research study. Keep in mind that using too much of an incentive could be construed as coercive. What would you use as an effective incentive to produce a high response rate without being coercive? What kind of incentive would you find impossible to ignore (i.e., coercive)? What kind of incentive just wouldn't interest you?

---

sample
→ Unit 8

confidence interval
→ Unit 8

representative sample
→ Unit 8

nonprobability sampling
→ Unit 8

sampling error
→ Unit 8

relationship
→ Unit 2

variable
→ Unit 2

random error
→ Unit 6

Sample Size

The number of individuals who take part in your study constitutes the sample size. All else being equal, a larger sample is more powerful than a smaller sample, as it allows for greater confidence in the results. Sample size directly relates to the calculation of confidence intervals, with larger samples allowing for narrower confidence intervals. However, merely having a large sample does not ensure a representative sample. Nonrandom samples can produce large samples quickly, but they are often not representative.

Additionally, the value of increasing sample size diminishes as the sample grows larger. For example, suppose you are studying students at your university. If you talk to just 50 students, you probably won't be very confident in the results, even with a random sample. With so few participants, it only takes a few atypical individuals to distort the results. If you manage to interview 500 students, you could be much more confident in your findings thanks to those additional 450 participants. But if you recruit an additional 450 participants, increasing your sample to 950, the increase in confidence would be much smaller. Even with 500 students, you already have a fairly precise estimate. And even with 950 students, there would still need to be some allowance for possible sampling error.

In general, identifying an appropriate sample size reflects the need to balance study power with the cost and effort required to recruit and interview additional participants. In some cases, this decision also needs to consider the strength of the relationship you are testing. If you expect that the variables will be strongly related, even a small sample will still provide effective evidence. If you are trying to detect a weak relationship, you will need many participants to be confident your findings aren't attributable to random error.

Research in Depth: Statistical Power

A recurring theme throughout this book is that the goals of our research should guide us in the decisions we make for how to proceed with the different steps of the research process. Another recurring theme is that we should be prepared and plan ahead so that we know what relationships we are testing and what statistical techniques we will use before we collect our data. One reason for this is that certain statistical tests have minimum requirements for sample sizes. A second reason is that as we test more complex relationships, we need a larger sample to compensate for the many tests that we will run. For example, consider a project in which we are studying whether people who take a public speaking training course do better in their speeches than those who do not. In this case, there are only two groups to compare. However, we might add more groups, such as a group that receives positive feedback throughout training, a group that receives no feedback, and a group that receives negative feedback (i.e., criticism). If we compare those groups to a group of people who receive no training at all, we are now comparing four groups. Such a comparison necessitates a larger sample size to have the same power to find relationships as a comparison involving only two groups. In many cases our decisions will have financial implications or affect what we tell our clients. As such, we want to make the correct decision based on the data we have and be confident in having made that correct decision.

Statistical power is a term that describes the ability of our analyses to avoid making what is called a type II error—that is, we erroneously conclude that no relationship exists even though one is actually present in a population. Power is generally expressed as a percentage. For example, a test with a power of .5 will correctly identify a relationship as present in half of all samples (.5 equals 50 percent). While scholars focus on making sure they do not incorrectly report relationships that are not present in the population, having adequate statistical power is always a concern. Statistical power depends on multiple factors, including the type of analysis employed. The two most important factors are the strength of the actual relationship in the population and the size of the sample. Stronger relationships are easier to detect; even a small study will consistently identify relationships in which two variables are highly correlated. However, many effects in communication research are subtle, and larger samples are needed to achieve the power to reliably identify them in research.

Tools exist to help scholars evaluate how large a sample they will need to reliably detect the effects of a given size based upon the type of analysis that will be used. One of these is the statistical power analysis program

G*Power, which can be downloaded for free at www.psycho.uni-duessel-dorf.de/abteilungen/aap/gpower3/. To use such tools, a researcher needs to know what kind of analyses will be run to test the hypotheses and have a rough estimate of the expected effect size. If prior studies or even meta-analyses have been published, these can offer a guideline for likely effect sizes and it is useful to explore these previous studies to get a sense not only of effects sizes but some of the types of tests commonly used. But with more exploratory studies, a scholar may not be sure how large of an effect to anticipate. Most tools offer some basic guidelines about small, medium, and large effects to suggest possible sample sizes, but these are just rough estimates with no firm statistical basis. In general, the more power you can obtain, the stronger your results will be.

Scholars sometimes report post hoc power analyses. This type of analysis indicates the power of the study to detect various effects based upon the actual sample size and characteristics. Such analyses can give a sense of whether the study is likely to have missed important relationships, but in general, statisticians oppose the use of post hoc power analysis. As they point out, if the study found significant results, then it had adequate power. If it did not find significant results, post hoc analyses cannot tell us whether a relationship is actually present in the population or whether we simply lacked power to identify it. Thus, it is always better to plan your study in advance, determining a threshold for a reasonable effect size and being sure to have an adequate sample size to reliably detect such effects.

Here are some articles for further exploration if you are interested in expanding your understanding of statistical power and its role in hypothesis testing:

Meyvis, T., & van Osselaer, S.M.J. (2017). Increasing the power of your study by increasing the effect size. *Journal of Consumer Research, 44*, 1157–1173.

Morrison, J. (2010). A power primer: The insignificance of significance in communication research. *Florida Communication Journal, 38*, 59–76.

---

population
→ Unit 8

simple random
sample
→ Unit 8

random
→ Unit 8

Sampling Frame

A sampling frame is a list of all of the individuals in a population. A sampling frame makes it possible to draw a simple random sample by using a random number generator or similar mechanism. You can number all of the individuals on the list and then use the list of random numbers to select as many individuals as needed for the sample in a way that meets the standards for true randomness. In many cases, though, you may not have access to a sampling frame. For example, if you are carrying out a poll during an election, your ideal sampling frame would be a list of all registered voters. While some states keep such lists, others do not, or they do not include the necessary contact information.

Other techniques can be used to randomly select individuals. For example, many polling organizations randomly dial telephone numbers (known as random-digit dialing). In this case, the sampling frame would include the entire list of possible telephone numbers. If you are studying the effects of playing video games on the work and study habits of people living in Montana, you would include all possible seven-digit numbers that follow the state's area code (406). If the population of interest is all residents of the United States, then you would need to include all of the US area codes in your sampling frame, followed by any seven-digit number that could follow those area codes. While some numbers will not be valid, all working phone numbers will have an equal chance of being selected, which roughly corresponds to individuals. Random-digit dialing has limits, though; computer-based automatic dialers cannot legally be used to contact cell phones, for example.

Sampling for content analysis is more likely to use an actual sampling frame. If you downloaded all news stories about a specific topic that you want to study, you could list and number those easily. Studies within organizations also tend to have available sampling frames; if a company hires you as a consultant, it should be able to provide you with a list of employees.

poll
→ Unit 10

content analysis
→ Unit 11

Steps to Success: Constructing an Effective Sample

To produce the most externally valid results, you must have an effective sample that represents your population. A few simple steps can help make this possible.

1. Clearly identify your population. To draw a representative sample, you must know who you are trying to represent. If you want to generalize to college students, then a sample of college students is appropriate. But if you want a diversity of ages, focusing on college students won't work. In some cases, you may specifically want to target particular types of individuals. In those situations, trying to sample broadly from all Americans won't produce the characteristics you want.
2. Decide how important representativeness is. In some cases, particularly experimental research, you may be more interested in the internal validity of your findings than external validity. While any study will benefit from a more representative sample, you must decide whether the trade-off is worth it.
3. If using a random sample, determine whether a sampling frame is available. For example, if you are studying a specific set of companies, then you may be able to

get a list of all employees at each company. A true sampling frame that includes contact information makes random sampling relatively easy and worthwhile.

4. If a sampling frame is not available, consider whether a cluster-based approach is possible. Can you divide your population into groups that can be randomly chosen? This can help save time and energy and get you to a point that individual sampling frames can be obtained. At the same time, the effects on representativeness are minimal.

Population

The population represents the group of individuals about whom we want to draw conclusions. This does not have to be a particularly broad group, such as all the people in the United States. It could be all people who watched a specific television show or who work for a particular company. In addition, "individuals" does not have to refer to people at all. For example, we might be studying individual companies to see how all companies manage their corporate image through public relations. Or we might be studying individual newspaper stories in a content analysis to see whether the news presents an inaccurate representation of a particular issues. Any group of "things" that can be divided into individual units of observation or analysis constitutes a population. Numerical descriptions of the population are known as parameters, whereas those that describe the subset of individuals selected for a study are known as statistics. The latter are based upon the sample of all individuals in the population used in most studies (except when a complete census is obtained).

For example, if the U.S. census from 2010 reveals that 50.8 percent of the population is female, this would be a parameter for the U.S. population. Alternatively, if we conduct a study of U.S. residents using a random sample, we might produce a sample that is 52 percent female. Thus, 52 percent is a statistic for our sample. In most quantitative studies, a core goal is to infer an accurate description of the population based upon the more limited information in our sample while making appropriate adjustments for sampling error—the extent to which our sample and our population differ. This means that we use the statistics we obtain to make estimates of population parameters.

In the case of the percentage of people who are male or female, we can easily compare our sample to the census data and see whether our statistic is close to the parameter. However, in most cases, we are estimating parameters that are not collected by census takers and therefore are unknown. For instance, the census does not collect information on how often you play video games, how often you watch reality television, how much you fear public speaking, or how much attention you pay to online advertising. Therefore, much of what we know about different populations comes from research that uses samples from those populations to estimate population parameters.

Census

When a study attempts to include all individuals in the population of interest, it is a census of that population. A census differs from a sample in that all individuals are meant to participate, instead of a subset of individuals. Because of this, a census will not produce sampling error. Furthermore, we don't necessarily have to employ inferential statistics when evaluating a census. The purpose of inferential statistics is to estimate whether the sample findings would be present in the population. Because a census includes the whole population, no such estimation is required.

For example, suppose you are studying the ways in which Fox News and CNN covered the 2012 presidential election. If you obtained footage of every relevant story aired and counted the number of seconds dedicated to each candidate, you would be able to say *exactly* what portion of stories on each network focused on each candidate. You would not have to test whether small differences might be attributable to chance; any difference would be "real," although it might not be considered practically important.

A census can still include systematic error created as part of the selection and recruitment process. For example, certain groups of people within the population may be leery of sharing information with the government and therefore avoid participating in the census data collection. If some factor—such as an invasive or concerning question—leads to a low response rate, this factor will distort the overall results. Even if there is no systematic error, a study with a low response rate should not be viewed as a perfect census, as the individuals who did participate are being treated as representative of the larger population of individuals who did not. True censuses are rare in communication research. While it is sometimes possible to obtain all examples of media content for content analysis, it can be difficult and time-consuming to code all of this material. It is even more challenging to identify all individuals within a large population, never mind successfully recruiting them. Consider the logistical nightmare of contacting each of the 300+ million people across the entire landscape of the United States, for example. Therefore, most studies rely upon the logic of random sampling to allow a good approximation of the true population rather than a complete census.

Estimation

A central goal of sampling is to allow researchers to form *estimates* about the population from which the sample was drawn. This goal has both conceptual and statistical aspects. Conceptually, we talk about a representative sample in situations in which the design of the sample allows us to feel confident that it is similar to the selected population. As much as possible, researchers try to develop representative samples. Even when nonprobability sampling is used, we

population
→ Unit 8

sample
→ Unit 8

inferential
statistics
→ Unit 15

systematic
error
→ Unit 6

response rate
→ Unit 8

representative
sample
→ Unit 8

content analysis
→ Unit 11

coding
→ Unit 11

probability
sampling
→ Unit 8

population
→ Unit 8

representative
sample
→ Unit 8

nonprobability
sampling
→ Unit 8

probability
sampling
→ Unit 8

simple random
sample
→ Unit 8

still take steps to match the population. For example, if we are studying the use of technology, we want to make sure to include people with different levels of comfort and skill and to have demographic diversity as well.

The statistical aspect of estimation relies upon using a probability sample, such as a simple random sample. When such samples are drawn, we can use statistics to quantify our estimate, indicating both the likely values for the population as well as the confidence we have in those values. The likely values form a range known as the confidence interval, and the amount of confidence we have in that range of values is known as the confidence level. Both ideas depend upon understanding the idea of a sampling distribution and the associated standard error. While these can be complex topics, making sense of them will equip you to gain needed insights into the validity of polls, the logic behind experiments, and ultimately the process of inferential statistics.

Confidence Level

For any random sample, it is possible to estimate the value of a parameter within the population given the known value of a statistic calculated for the sample. The portion of such estimates that will be accurate for the population is known as the confidence level. These levels are typically expressed as percentages. For example, you have likely encountered a newspaper story about an opinion poll that noted that the results should be accurate 95 percent of the time. This implies that if you carried out 100 surveys using exactly the same sampling technique, 95 of them would provide an estimate for the population that included the true value of the parameter for the population. It does not mean that the result is somehow 95 percent correct; either the estimate includes the parameter or it does not, but we have no way of knowing from a single study which case our sample falls into.

As the confidence level increases, the confidence interval necessarily grows larger. After all, if you want to be more certain that your estimate includes the true value, you need to include more possible values in your estimate. Selecting an appropriate confidence level requires a trade-off between how important it is that your estimate is correct and how narrow you want that estimate to be. You can give a very small confidence interval but be wrong a lot of the time, or you can almost ensure that your estimate is correct but at the cost of precision.

Consider again the example of opinion polls. The 95 percent level is often chosen because this means that the confidence level will be fairly narrow—usually a spread of 6 percent (often reported as +/−3 percent) for a large survey (e.g., a statistic of 50 percent in the sample would generate an estimate that the parameter is between 47 and 53). You could have an even narrower interval (e.g., between 48.5 and 51.5), but then you would be only about 67 percent confident. Or you could have even greater certainty—about 99.7 percent—but your interval would have to be wider (e.g., 45.5 to 54.5). In most cases,

95 percent is a happy medium. However, if you absolutely cannot afford an incorrect estimate, you would want to increase the confidence level used for your calculations.

Confidence Interval

The confidence interval reflects the range of values within which you estimate that the true population parameter will fall given the results of your sample and the confidence level you have selected. All else being equal, your confidence interval will be larger—that is, range across more numbers—when you select a higher confidence level. To be more certain that your estimate is correct, you need to include more potential values within it. The confidence interval is often used as a way to think about whether two groups or values are distinct from one another in the population.

Suppose the confidence interval for the percentage of men in a sample who are likely to purchase a brand of shampoo is between 60 and 70. Now suppose that the equivalent interval for women in that sample is between 55 and 65. Even though the percentages of men and women in our sample do not match (65 and 60, respectively), we still could not be confident that men and women differ in the population. A reasonably likely value for women would be 60, and a reasonably likely value for men would also be 60, for example. Because the population could easily fall into those parameters, we couldn't be confident from our sample that a difference in favor of men actually exists.

The confidence interval is also affected by the sample size. Assuming you are studying the same parameter for the same population, a sample of 500 should yield a more precise estimate than a sample of 50, but a sample of 5,000 would be better still. Finally, the confidence interval is affected by how much the concept being measured varies in the population. If there are bigger differences between individuals, that increases the chance you'll have some individuals in your sample with unusually low or high values.

For example, consider a study of how people feel about a company, using a 100-point scale to measure those feelings. Suppose the company is a widely respected charity. Most people would rate the company very high on this scale, and there would be little variance among scores. Even if your sample included an unusual number of lower scores, they would probably still be in the 80s instead of the 90s. If you based your estimate on those scores, you wouldn't be far off. Now consider asking the same question about a major gun manufacturer (representing a more politically contentious issue in the United States). Some people would have very positive impressions of the company, but others would have very negative impressions. If your sample included too many of the negative people in this case, their scores might be 10s instead of the 90s felt by those with positive views. In this case, your estimate will be much further off. In calculating a confidence interval, we take into account the variation within

| range → Unit 14 |
| population → Unit 8 |
| sample → Unit 8 |
| confidence level → Unit 8 |
| sample size → Unit 8 |
| concept → Unit 5 |
| variance → Unit 15 |
| skew → Unit 14 |
| random → Unit 8 |
| reliability → Unit 6 |
| validity → Unit 6 |

the sample and use it to approximate the variation in the population. From there, we make sure the interval is larger when the variance is greater, to allow for the possibility that our sample was particularly skewed by chance.

Despite these steps, it is important to remember that any confidence interval is just an estimate, and there is a possibility that it does not include the true population parameter. Given an infinite number of samples, the confidence level tells us how often this will occur, but for our sample, all we know is that our estimate is likely but not guaranteed to be correct. Furthermore, the confidence interval and confidence level both rely on the assumption that a true random sample has been used and that the measure employed is reliable and valid.

Margin of Error

The margin of error is closely related to the confidence interval, and it is most often referred to in media stories about polls and other surveys in which more complex statistics are not provided. The margin of error represents the amount added to and subtracted from the statistic found in a random sample to produce the confidence interval for the selected confidence level. The margin of error thus roughly conveys how much allowance for sampling error should be made in thinking about the results. It can also be used to calculate the confidence interval when one is not provided. For example, a story about a political poll might state that 47 percent of voters, +/–3 percent, support a law legalizing marijuana. It would also note that this reflects a 95 percent confidence level. Based on this, the confidence interval at the 95 percent confidence level would be between 44 percent and 50 percent. It doesn't seem likely that a majority support the law, even allowing for sampling error.

We should be careful about interpreting the margin of error. Because it relates to the confidence interval and standard error, it is true only for the specific sample described and not for subgroups within that sample. For example, if a survey as a whole has a margin of error of +/–3 percent, then the margin of error would have to be larger if you wanted to consider just the women in that sample, as there would be fewer of them and the confidence interval would necessarily be larger.

Sampling Distribution

Sampling distribution is an abstract statistical concept that is used to compute confidence intervals and related values. It represents all of the possible values of a given statistic for a sample of a particular size drawn from a population with known parameters, as well as the frequency with which each value would occur. This is a key concept in the logic of estimation through sampling, as well as in inferential statistics.

confidence interval
→ Unit 8

polls
→ Unit 10

survey research
→ Unit 10

descriptive statistics
→ Unit 14

random
→ Unit 8

confidence level
→ Unit 8

sampling error
→ Unit 8

standard error
→ Unit 8

population
→ Unit 8

inferential statistics
→ Unit 15

sampling error
→ Unit 8

The sampling distribution represents an application of the so-called law of large numbers. This law states that many events that are random on an individual basis are predictable over a large number of iterations. For example, consider flipping a coin: assuming a fair coin, with a large enough number of flips, you should see 50 percent heads and 50 percent tails. But if you flip the coin only a few times, odds are, you won't have a perfectly even distribution. The more times a random action occurs, the more "smooth" the overall pattern becomes, as each individual case becomes a smaller and smaller portion of the total.

In the context of random sampling, the random event is the selection of participants. Suppose you are drawing samples of 100 students from the population of your university and asking each student what his or her major is. Further suppose that you are specifically interested in the percentage who are communication majors. One sample might include 15 communication majors, or 15 percent of the total. A second sample might instead find that 20 percent of participants are communication majors, and a third sample could find that 25 percent are communication majors. This minor variation among samples is called sampling error, and it occurs even with perfect random sampling. Just by chance, you happened to include a few more majors in one sample than another.

Imagine, though, that you have all the time in the world and can draw thousands and thousands of samples. Eventually, a pattern would emerge. Most of the samples would have very similar values for the percentage of students who are communication majors, while a few samples would have much higher or lower numbers. In fact, if you drew a graph of all the answers and how often each showed up, it would look familiar, taking the shape of a *bell curve*. If you determined the exact mean of the percentages you found in each sample, it would fall right in the middle of that curve. What's more, if you checked that mean against the school's record for major enrollment, it would match exactly. Given a large enough number of samples, the individual sampling errors cancel out. After all, the sample was random, with everyone having an equal chance of being selected, so it's just as likely that you would have selected too many communication majors as too few.

Of course, in practice, we don't have the time to carry out thousands of different samples—if we had anywhere near those resources, we would just conduct a census. And if we can't conduct a census, then we can't know for sure the parameter of most values. But because of the idea of a sampling distribution, we know that a large enough number of samples *could* be averaged to find the parameter. Furthermore, we know that most samples will produce a statistic close to the parameter, while few samples will be further away. In fact, for many statistics, we know exactly what percentage of samples will generate values every possible distance from the parameter.

census
→ Unit 8

descriptive statistics
→ Unit 14

confidence interval
→ Unit 8

confidence level
→ Unit 8

201

For example, with a given sample size, we might be able to calculate that only 5 percent of samples will produce a mean that is greater than .5 away from the population parameter. In other words, in 95 percent of cases, if we take the mean from our sample and both add and subtract .5 to generate a confidence interval, we will include the parameter in that interval. This results in a confidence level of 95 percent. If our survey asks people how many hours they spend on Facebook each day, and the mean is 4 hours, then we would calculate a confidence interval of 3.5 to 4.5 hours. Even if our sample is at the far edge of those 95 percent of samples and a full .5 higher than the parameter it would still be included in our estimate; the same is true if it is at the low end of that range. Of course, there will always be a few samples that are at the far ends of the sampling distribution, and we might happen to draw one of those. That's why we always express our level of confidence as well, reflecting the possibility that we have one of those unusual samples.

Sampling Error

Sampling error most often refers to the mathematically predictable, random error that comes from using a random sample to estimate a parameter instead of carrying out a complete census. Because we have not included the entire population in our study, there is always a chance that we have included people who don't perfectly match the overall population in some way. Maybe, for example, in the population there are 35 percent Democrats, but in our sample, we have 38 percent Democrats because by chance we happened to include a few more Democrats and fewer Republicans in our sample than in the population as a whole. This sampling error is random, so we cannot know how much or in what direction error is present within our sample. However, by taking into account the sampling distribution, we can calculate a confidence interval that adjusts for the likely amount of sampling error present.

Most references to sampling error focus on this narrow, random error. However, more broadly, any factor that creates differences between the values found in our sample and the true values for the population can be thought of as a source of sampling error. Thus, factors such as low response rates and nonrandom samples that are not representative can also create error. It's important to remember that calculations of confidence intervals only account for the first, formal type of sampling error and not other potential sources of error in a study.

Standard Error

The standard error is a reflection of the average or typical amount of sampling error expected for a simple random sample based upon the sampling distribution. The standard error applies to any sampling distribution that is normal, and

random measurement error
→ Unit 6

probability sampling
→ Unit 8

census
→ Unit 8

population
→ Unit 8

sampling distribution
→ Unit 8

confidence interval
→ Unit 8

response rate
→ Unit 8

nonprobability sampling
→ Unit 8

sampling error
→ Unit 8

it is equivalent to the standard deviation for that distribution. It is calculated based on the size of the individual sample and the standard deviation for the population, or it is estimated from the standard deviation for the individual sample. Expressed in simpler terms, the standard error reflects the idea that your estimate for a parameter would be more precise if you had a larger sample and if there was less variation in the population.

These same factors contribute to the size of the confidence interval, and in fact, there is a direct relationship between confidence intervals and the standard error. Depending on the chosen confidence level, the confidence interval will range one or more standard errors in both directions from the statistic obtained from the sample. You may sometimes see standard errors reported in tables and reports instead of confidence intervals, but some simple math can allow you to compute an appropriate confidence interval. In general, for a 95 percent confidence level, the confidence interval will be very close to two standard errors in each direction.

Nonprobability Sampling

Any sampling process that does not meet the standards for random selection of participants is a nonprobability (or nonrandom) sample. Some samples are considered *quasi-random*, in that they use randomization as part of the sampling process and produce a sample that can be compared with a random sample, given certain statistical adjustments. Other types of probability sampling, such as cluster sampling and stratified sampling, are not simple random samples but generally avoid the problems of true nonrandom samples.

On the other hand, sampling techniques such as convenience sampling, deliberate sampling, quota sampling (to a lesser degree), snowball sampling, and volunteer sampling fall short of simple random samples in some important ways. Most notably, they are unlikely to be effective, representative samples. Because participants in these samples are not chosen randomly, there is a much greater likelihood of systematic error. If a sample is more likely to include particular types of individuals for any reason, then the results will overestimate how much those types of individuals or the relationships they reflect occur within the population. This means that attempts to use inferential statistics with such samples may produce biased, inaccurate results. In addition, even if a nonrandom sample is fairly representative, it is impossible to know with any mathematical certainty what its sampling distribution would be. That means that although we might expect sample statistics to be similar to the population parameter, we don't know how far off we expect the average sample to be from that parameter. Because of this, we can't calculate an accurate confidence interval. Our estimate may be close, but we don't know how close it would be over a large number of samples.

---

sampling distribution
→ Unit 8

standard deviation
→ Unit 14

population
→ Unit 8

confidence interval
→ Unit 8

relationship
→ Unit 2

confidence level
→ Unit 8

---

probability sampling
→ Unit 8

cluster sampling
→ Unit 8

stratified sampling
→ Unit 8

simple random sampling
→ Unit 8

convenience sampling
→ Unit 8

deliberate sampling
→ Unit 8

quota sampling
→ Unit 8

snowball sampling
→ Unit 8

volunteer sampling
→ Unit 8

However, nonrandom samples have some benefits. They are often much less complex, expensive, and time-consuming to obtain than random samples. In cases in which external validity is less important than internal validity, this can mean that nonrandom samples are more sensible. Additionally, many relationships between variables are fairly consistent for all individuals—that is, there are no moderating variables that will distort the results for a nonrepresentative sample. Thus, although not statistically ideal, such samples can still give a good sense of how variables would relate in a diverse population.

For example, consider a study measuring the relationship between watching television and volunteering. We might hypothesize that people who are heavy television viewers are less likely to volunteer, as their time is taken up by watching TV. A random sample of all people would provide a good estimate of this relationship. Every individual would have an equal chance of being selected. If there are few people who watch lots of TV and volunteer, there would be few of them in our sample. A nonrandom sample, however, might not be as representative. People who volunteer might also be more likely to be at the location we choose to select our convenience sample, or they might be more likely to volunteer to be part of our sample. However, if those people are no more likely to watch TV than volunteers as a whole, this would not greatly bias our overall results: we would still see a pattern between watching TV and volunteering.

In general, it is best to gather a representative sample through random selection because without this, we cannot know whether our nonrandom sample might actually deviate from the population. For example, suppose that people who volunteer are more likely to be captured in our sample, but so are people who watch TV. We would see only the few people who score high on TV viewing and volunteering and think that the relationship holds in the population. Our estimate of the population would be incorrect. In general, you should be skeptical of results that rely on nonrandom samples that don't use random assignment as part of an experimental design.

Convenience Sampling

A convenience sample is a type of nonrandom sample in which individuals are selected purely based on their availability, with no attempt to choose a representative group or to seek out specific types of individuals. Convenience samples are sometimes referred to as "mall-intercept" samples, reflecting one approach to convenience sampling that is often used: seeking individuals in a public setting, such as a mall, and asking them to participate in a study. Convenience sampling can be efficient, minimizing both cost and time to collect data. In situations in which the representativeness of the sample is not as important, such as an experiment or focus group, this can be useful. However, convenience samples normally do not represent the broader population well.

Think about conducting a survey on your campus. You might want to use a convenience sample to quickly recruit student participants. Even if your intended population is simply students at your university, though, you probably won't get an accurate cross-section by using a convenience sample. For example, if you set up outside the library, you will capture the types of students who use the library to study or conduct research—omitting plenty of students who do neither, at least during the chosen hours. If you set up outside the student union, you'll get a different group—but you can probably think of plenty of friends who never visit the union. If you recruit people outside specific buildings, you'll get a disproportionate number of majors in the types of classes held in those buildings. You could address this problem by broadening the settings in which you recruit potential participants, but you will never be able to say with mathematical precision how well your sample represents the population because you can't know who was left out, only who was included. Convenience samples are similar to volunteer sampling but critically involve the researcher targeting individuals and asking them to take part rather than simply putting out a general call to anyone who might be interested.

Deliberate Sampling

Also referred to as *purposive* sampling, deliberate sampling attempts to target specific types of individuals to include within the study but selects them in a way that doesn't ensure those individuals represent the larger population of interest. For example, suppose you are interested in studying whether new car buyers used the Internet to help research their purchases. If you decide to carry out a true random sample of all individuals, such as through random-digit dialing of all possible telephone numbers, you will find few recent car buyers. This would greatly increase the time and cost required for your study with little benefit. Even a typical convenience sample would still produce few car buyers if the location or mechanism chosen is selected for ease and nothing more.

Instead, you might choose to hand out surveys to individuals who are actually visiting car lots or even get a list of recent buyers from several local car dealerships and distribute surveys to those individuals by mail. These approaches would not draw from a sampling frame of all car purchasers in your population, and so you would not have a true random sample. In some cases, the sample would include people coming to the dealership for other reasons, who would then have to be removed from the analysis if your population is meant to be only new car buyers. However, deliberate sampling can generate a greater number of individuals with the trait of interest than any other efficient sampling approach. As with all nonrandom samples, if the primary purpose of the study is not to draw broad inferences to a diverse population, then this can be an effective way of recruiting participants.

> **population**
> → Unit 8
>
> **random**
> → Unit 8
>
> **convenience sampling**
> → Unit 8
>
> **sampling frame**
> → Unit 8

205

Another use of purposive sampling is to intentionally seek out a diversity of participants. Instead of taking steps to make sure that many of the participants fall into one group, the researcher can intentionally solicit participants from distinct locations and social circles, hoping to ensure greater variation in their sample. Ultimately, this can help generate findings that are true for a broader spectrum of individuals, especially when sampling is intended to produce a relatively small number of participants for more intense qualitative measurement.

Quota Sampling

A nonrandom sample that recruits specified numbers of individuals with specific traits is a quota sample. Such an approach better ensures a diverse and somewhat representative sample, but because the approach is nonrandom, any traits that are not used to create the quota may not be well represented. Many Internet-based surveys use quotas, assembling a sample from an established pool of willing volunteers. Most often, the quotas used focus on basic demographics, such as gender, age, and race.

For example, an advertising company may want to test a product message with a typical group of Americans. By setting quotas to reflect the normal population distribution for income, age, and gender, the company can be sure that it tests the effects of the ad on the range of people who are likely to view the ad once it hits the market. The study would recruit individuals on a voluntary or convenience basis, but once the expected number of people with a given trait is reached, additional individuals with that trait will not be able to take part.

Say that your study wants to include men and women in roughly equal numbers to the population, and you want a total of 1,000 participants. Because women make up just over half the U.S. population, once you have 500 men, you won't allow any more men to participate, but you would continue to recruit women. If the company relied on a convenience or volunteer sample, it might miss out on the fact that women would actually respond negatively to the ad, depending on how those samples were gathered. Quota sampling, on the other hand, will at least ensure representative diversity on that trait. However, quota samples are still not true random samples. They normally start from a group of people who have already agreed to take part.

In some cases, a quota sample may actually draw upon a random sample but use the quota to help ensure a more diverse pool, avoiding some issues with response rate. When the first sample is recruited, however, the normal issues with volunteer samples may still apply—the kind of person who agrees to take part in the study may not be a good reflection of the population as a whole. For example, a quota sample might help make sure that all ages are reflected, but there is no guarantee that the older individuals in the sample

representative sample
→ Unit 8

population
→ Unit 8

convenience sampling
→ Unit 8

volunteer sampling
→ Unit 8

response rate
→ Unit 8

deliberate sampling
→ Unit 8

are like other older individuals. In fact, they may be especially unusual if they choose to participate in this type of study, while most elderly people would not.

An important goal with quota sampling is to identify traits that are relevant to the study being conducted. You can ensure you have representative numbers of people whose absence would distort the results. If you are studying attitudes toward drinking, you could be sure to include nondrinkers so that you don't report unusually favorable opinions. Alternatively, quota samples can serve as a kind of deliberate sample by recruiting specific types of individuals more heavily. Suppose your product is specifically aimed at women. You might set the quota for women to be 80 percent of your total sample instead of being more representative.

Snowball Sampling

Snowball sampling, also known as *network sampling*, is a kind of nonprobability sampling technique in which potential participants are identified by other participants in the study. For example, suppose you are studying online social networks. You might start by recruiting a small group of individuals through some other sampling technique. Then, you would ask those participants to give the names of five other people in their social network whom you would attempt to recruit. You could continue to ask for additional participants from those initially identified until the sample has the desired size and characteristics.

Snowball samples can be useful when you want to study groups or relationships among individuals, as you will have data about multiple people who are connected with one another and, potentially, about those connections as well. In addition, snowball samples may help encourage sampled individuals to participate, as you can refer to the participation of their friends in requesting participation. However, snowball samples tend to be nonrepresentative because you get groups of people who know one another and are likely to be similar. People who are different from those initially recruited will probably not be identified and included in the final study.

relationship
→ Unit 2

nonprobability sampling
→ Unit 8

Volunteer Sampling

Perhaps the most flawed type of sampling is volunteer sampling, in which researchers open the study to anyone who sees a call for participants and chooses to take part, with no attempt to directly contact and recruit individuals. This approach is very similar to convenience sampling, in that it will only include those who happen to come in contact with the means of recruitment. However, with a convenience sample, the researcher at least exerts some effort to collect specific participants, and the potential to create rapport and connect with those who might not otherwise take part can generate some diversity in the sample.

convenience sampling
→ Unit 8

rapport
→ Unit 10

polls
→ Unit 10

<hr>

Reflect & React: Nonprobability Sampling "Polls"

Nonprobability sampling is something we generally encounter on a regular basis without realizing it. For example, when news programs conduct "person-on-the-street" interviews to ask people their opinions on issues, this is a form of nonprobability sampling. Unfortunately, such opinions are often presented as representative of the population from which they come. The same goes for comments sections and letters to the editor that appear in newspapers or on news websites. In the case of letters to the editor, these are often deliberately selected by the editors, and they are more likely to represent extreme or intriguing opinions than to be representative of the whole population. In the case of comments on news sites—or even "polls" posted on news sites where every visitor can click to express an opinion—these likely reflect the opinions of those who are motivated enough to give their opinion who actually visited that site. Consider some polls that you have seen on the Internet or presented in the news. How many of them were based on volunteer samples or other kinds of nonprobability approaches? Given what you read earlier, how confident are you in these data?

<hr>

A volunteer sample, however, offers little incentive to take part; even the minimal social pressure that might come from direct contact with a researcher is not present. Therefore, volunteer samples tend to exclusively include people who have strong opinions about an issue. For example, an online poll dealing with opinions regarding gun control would likely draw people who are either strong supporters or strong opponents of control. If many people have more neutral opinions, their views are unlikely to be included. Often, those who feel strongly about an issue do not share the views of those who are less interested. In the case of gun control, public opinion surveys suggest that the average person is in favor of limited restrictions, but those who feel passionately about the issue are more likely to belong to the National Rifle Association or otherwise strongly advocate against any kind of regulation.

Probability Sampling

population
→ Unit 8

confidence level
→ Unit 8

A probability sample requires that researchers can calculate the probability, or likelihood, of the typical member of the population being selected to participate. As such, all units within the population have an equal and known chance of being selected when probability sampling techniques are used. Because of this, researchers are able to produce estimates of sample quality, including the confidence level and the confidence interval of statistics generated by the sample. Beyond being able to assess the quality of the sample, probability sampling techniques also allow for lower levels of sampling error, although it should be noted that sampling error can never be completely eliminated.

The most basic probability sample is a simple random sample, but other approaches, including cluster samples and deliberate samples, also have probability elements and are more representative than nonrandom samples. The critical aspect of a probability sample is that the selection of individuals relies upon a selection process that includes selection at random. This does not have to mean that the selection of individuals completely meets the standard for randomness. It could be that individuals are first divided into groups, and selection from within those groups (or even subgroups) is random. The basic logic of inference and confidence intervals may not be perfectly applicable to all kinds of probability sampling. However, the presence of some random selection element helps ensure that all probability samples of a reasonable size are at least somewhat representative. Furthermore, for samples in which the selection of individuals involves some kind of systematic approach as well as a random element, it is normally possible to adjust confidence intervals to reflect this approach and the potential for additional random error.

Random

The term *random* has a specific meaning in sampling and quantitative research and should not be taken to mean "haphazard" or "without plan." Instead, *random* refers to a process of choosing individuals that meets two criteria: each individual has an equal chance of being selected, and the selection of each individual is *independent* from that of all other individuals.

Ensuring that each individual has an equal chance of being selected is relatively straightforward. If you have a sampling frame—a list of all individuals in the population—then by numbering that list, you can use a random number table or a computer-based random number generator to pick the desired number of recruits from that list. Suppose you have a roster of every student in a large introductory class with 1,000 students enrolled. A random number generator could produce 200 unique numbers, representing your sample. Each student, then, would have a 1 in 5 chance of being selected, meaning that the probability of being chosen is equal for all students. Meeting the independence requirement can be more complex. This implies that the selection of any given individual does not help us predict which other individuals will be chosen.

Consider again the sample drawing from a large course. Suppose there are five sections, each with 200 students. It might seem convenient to choose one section at random. This would meet the "equal chance" criterion. Because each student is in one of the sections, and his or her section has a 1 in 5 chance of being chosen, each student would have that same 1 in 5 chance of being picked. But this selection would not be independent. If we know that one student in the section has been chosen, then we can accurately predict that every other student in the section is guaranteed to be picked. This may not seem like a big deal, but it can greatly distort how representative a sample is. Suppose the sections meet on different days and at different times. If we choose the class that meets at 8:00 a.m. on Fridays, these students would probably be very different from the students who signed up for a class meeting at 5:00 p.m. on Tuesdays. Meeting both requirements for randomness ensures that our sample is as representative as possible. Any time you see the term *random* referred to in the context of research, it implies that both standards for randomness have been met.

random
→ Unit 8

sampling frame
→ Unit 8

Random Number Table

Many textbooks and other references include a random number table—a list of numbers that meet the requirements for being random. These numbers can be used in place of a more structured way to generate random choices, and if you have a sampling frame that is numbered, you can use the random number table to pick individuals from that list while meeting the standards for randomness. Although you may think that you can simply generate random numbers off the top of your head, research suggests that people are not very good at truly random number generation. We tend to favor certain numbers or types of numbers. For example, which of the following sets of numbers is more random: 1, 2, 3 or 12, 33, 50? You might think the latter is more random, but in fact, each set of numbers is equally likely to be generated by chance. People often overcompensate for apparent patterns and avoid numbers they think wouldn't occur by random chance, such as round numbers and very low or high values. Thus, a random number table or random number generator is a better way to randomly select individuals.

Reflect & React: Human Bias and Sampling

Using a random number table or random number generator is one way of taking the human influence out of the selection process. As indicated, it is nearly impossible for humans to behave—and therefore select study participants—in truly random ways. Because of this, in most cases, when we are left in charge of selecting study participants, some kind of bias will insert itself. Imagine that you are studying the opinions of employees at the large multinational corporation described in the discussion of cluster sampling. The company has provided you with a full list of all employees, with name and employee identification number, that is unique for each employee; it also includes race, gender, and age for each person. Think about the types of biases that might be introduced if you were to go through the list on your own and select names. In what ways would the quality of the sample be affected? What approach could you use to reduce those biases?

Simple Random Sampling

The most basic type of random sample is a simple random sample, which selects individuals from the population in a way that meets the requirements for randomness. That is, each individual should have an equal chance of being selected, and the likelihood of an individual being selected must be independent of that of other individuals being selected. Simple random samples often require a sampling frame to be sure the requirements for randomness are met. A simple random sample provides a representative sample. Statistics calculated from data collected through a simple random sample follow a known sampling distribution. Because of this, confidence intervals can be easily calculated.

In many cases, the units of analysis in populations that we wish to study will already have a number attached to them, allowing for fairly easy simple random sampling. For instance, consider trying to study employees of a major multinational corporation. It is likely that the employees in this corporation have two easily accessible identification numbers that can be used for selection: (1) employee identification number and (2) Social Security number. As long as each of these numbers is unique to each unit of analysis, then they can be used as the numbers in the sampling frame. To conduct simple random sampling of this population of employees, we would simply need to generate a list of random numbers the same length as the employee or Social Security number we are using to identify participants. Any employee whose employee identification number matches a number from the list generated by the random number table would be selected for the sample. Once we have matched enough numbers to reach our intended sample size, we are done. Such examples cut across a number of arenas. For instance, at schools most students have a student identification number that is unique, nearly all households have a unique phone number (although some have more than one, which complicates things), and registered voters typically have a voter identification number.

| population |
| → Unit 8 |

| random |
| → Unit 8 |

| representative sample |
| → Unit 8 |

| sampling distribution |
| → Unit 8 |

| confidence interval |
| → Unit 8 |

| unit of analysis |
| → Unit 2 |

| random number table |
| → Unit 8 |

Cluster Sampling

A cluster sample is a type of sample in which entire groups of individuals are first identified and randomly sampled before individuals within those groups are sampled. This process can involve several levels of grouping variables before

| random |
| → Unit 8 |

| variable |
| → Unit 2 |

face-to-face survey
→ Unit 10

sampling frame
→ Unit 8

confidence interval
→ Unit 8

sampling error
→ Unit 8

the final selection of individuals. For example, suppose you want to conduct detailed, face-to-face interviews with individuals to learn their reasons for supporting a specific political candidate. If these interviews were scattered across the entire country, it would be almost impossible to conduct them efficiently. You might, therefore, get a list of zip codes and randomly select 30 of those zip codes as an initial cluster. Then, within the zip codes, if you could obtain a proper sampling frame for each, you could randomly sample individuals to recruit for your study. Interviewing 20 people within each zip code would give you a total study size of 600 while reducing your travel to just 30 locations. In general, the results from a cluster sample will mirror those from a true random sample, but the use of clusters increases the confidence interval, meaning that more random sampling error will be present and you will be less confident in the precision of your findings. The use of clusters violates the *independence* requirement for a truly random sample. As another example, consider again studying a large multinational corporation. If we want to carry out our interviews face-to-face, we may not want to sample from every single branch of the company. If we chose five locations at random and then sampled employees at random from the list of workers at each location, we would still have a reasonably representative sample and would find it much simpler to visit those locations and carry out the interviews.

Research in Depth: Cluster Sampling

Although simple random samples provide an easy way to produce a representative sample and generally result in the least sampling error, many national studies rely on alternative probability sampling approaches. Identifying a sampling frame for the nation as a whole is nearly impossible, and although random-digit dialing can approximate such a frame, it has its own flaws. One example of a major, ongoing national study that uses a different approach to sampling is the National Election Study (NES), which is carried out by the University of Michigan in conjunction with a broader consortium and widely used by scholars interested in political attitudes and behaviors. As described by the organization, the NES sample is obtained through a multistage process. First, a set of communities is selected from all of the metropolitan statistical areas (MSAs) listed by the U.S. Census Bureau, as well as certain counties not included in an MSA. After this, individual locations (normally census blocks) are selected from within those areas and counties. From there, researchers obtain lists of all housing units in those smaller areas, selecting some at random. Finally, all adults within those housing units are listed, and one is chosen at random. Thus, the NES represents a multistage cluster sample.

This process allows the NES to carry out data collection face-to-face. By limiting the number of geographic locations, researchers can more easily canvass those selected. The process also better ensures that all individuals may be chosen, rather than relying on telephone contact that may miss individuals who are unlisted, use cell phones, or otherwise do not wish to be reached. But a consequence of cluster sampling is that the statistics used for simple random samples are slightly inaccurate when applied to the NES. Some sophisticated studies adjust for this, but most accept that the minor difference is not meaningful enough to distort otherwise strong results.

Stratified Sampling

A stratified sample is a variation of a simple random sample in which the population is first divided into groups, or strata, and then a predetermined number of individuals in each group are selected randomly. For example, if you are studying how men and women respond to advertisements, you might want to be sure you have equal numbers of each gender. If you have a sampling frame that identifies individuals by gender, and you want a total sample of 500, you could randomly select 250 men and 250 women. If the strata chosen match the distribution of individuals in the population, the overall sample will be representative.

In some cases, though, you may wish to sample a larger portion of certain individuals. For example, if you are developing an ad campaign targeting younger individuals, you might want to sample 500 individuals between ages 18 and 30 and then 250 individuals who are older than 30, even though this doesn't match the age distribution in the population. In any case, probability sampling techniques—simple random or systematic sampling—are the foundation of stratified sampling.

In a basic sense, you are using those techniques to select units but identifying some specific characteristic or criteria you will use to guide the overall makeup of the sample. For instance, in the advertising example used in this unit, you would use probability sampling techniques to select each unit, but you would not include anyone between 18 and 30 years of age once you reached the target number of 500 and anyone over 30 years of age in the sample after you reached the target of 250. Stratified sampling could also be a great way to study that large corporation described in the discussion of simple random sampling. Instead of having every employee in our sampling frame, we might want to first stratify the company based on the type of job performed. For example, custodial staff, office workers, people who work on the manufacturing floor, and managers might all be categories of workers we want to include. By setting a quota for each of these categories, we would be sure that we have an adequate number of each (still chosen randomly from within the strata).

simple random sample
→ Unit 8

population
→ Unit 8

representative sample
→ Unit 8

simple random sampling
→ Unit 8

systematic sampling
→ Unit 8

sampling frame
→ Unit 8

Systematic Sampling

This approach to probability sampling uses a sampling interval to select units of analysis from the sampling frame. For example, suppose that we want to study the employees of a multinational corporation with 50,000 employees. To use stratified sampling, you would simply follow these steps: (1) Ask for a full list of employees—perhaps in alphabetical order by last name. (2) Compute the sampling interval by dividing the sampling frame by the sample size. If we want a sample size of 1,000 people, then we would divide 50,000 by 1,000, giving us a sampling interval of 50. (3) Use the sampling interval to select units of analysis until you have the determined number in your sample. In this case, we would select a random starting spot and then select every 50th person from the list. Just like simple random sampling, the goal is to remove the human influence from the selection process. By determining a sampling interval and using a random starting spot, the potential for the researcher to insert his or her own personal biases into the selection process is much less than if the researcher personally went through the list and selected people.

Although this approach is reasonably straightforward to carry out, systematic sampling does have one potential drawback, the phenomenon known as *periodicity*. This occurs when the sampling interval aligns with some pattern in the sampling frame. For example, consider a situation in which you are conducting a content analysis and want to select random months of television content to analyze over a period of 20 years. In theory, each year would give you a randomly selected month, so you would have a good chance of having each of the 12 months represented in some way. However, suppose that the sampling interval ended up being 12. Because there are also 12 months in a year, you would end up selecting the same month for every year, say, January. The end result would be 20 years of content analysis of January, which is highly unlikely to be representative of the rest of the year's content. For instance, January may represent a lull in new programming, or perhaps it is the most violent month for televised content. The problem in this case is that you would not have other months to compare to in order to determine whether January is unique or not. To guard against periodicity, then, it is useful to know whether the list of units in the sampling frame is organized in a meaningful way, such that a pattern or cycle might occur throughout the list. In the current example, periodicity could be avoided by using a sampling interval that does not align with the cycle of the months.

Sampling Interval

In situations in which a sampling frame is available, a sampling interval is a way to randomly select from that list by choosing every *n*th individual on the list. It is typically associated with systematic sampling. Here, *n* refers to a number that will allow you to select a sample of the desired size. For example, suppose you have a list of 5,000 companies, and you want to select 100 of them to study their corporate communication techniques. You would need to select one in every 50 companies. If you choose a random number between 1 and 50 to start and then pick every 50th company after that, you will end up with a random sample of the desired size. (For example, if you generate a random number using an online program, and that number is 15, you would then include the 65th, 115th, 165th, etc., companies on the list.)

In rare cases, a sampling interval may not effectively provide a true random sample. If the list is ordered in such a way that it repeats in a pattern that matches your sampling frame, then you will introduce systematic error due to periodicity. For example, suppose your list of companies is ordered so that it includes a company from each state, in order, then repeated. If you chose the 15th company, it would be located in Iowa. So would the 65th company, as the list would repeat states every 50 companies. In general, though, the odds of such a pattern occurring are very small, and avoiding this issue should be simple.

Activities

Activity 8A: Sampling Strategy

See terms: nonprobability sampling; probability sampling.

In this activity, you will evaluate how the use of probability or nonprobability sampling potentially influences the findings for research and the confidence you have in those conclusions.

Part 1: Locate a research article that uses nonprobability sampling techniques. After you have read the article, use the following prompts to guide your analysis of the sampling approach:

■ What type of nonprobability sampling is used?
■ Do the researchers provide enough detail that you would be able to replicate the study?
■ Is this particular sampling technique appropriate for the research questions or hypotheses?
■ In what ways could the sampling approach be improved?
■ To what extent do the authors adequately address any weaknesses or limitations in their sample?

Part 2: Locate a research article that uses probability sampling techniques. After you have read the article, use the prompts listed previously to guide your analysis of the sampling approach.

Activity 8B: Reporting on Poll Data

See terms: probability sampling; sample quality.

For this activity, locate a newspaper article that reports on poll data. The objective of this activity is to critically assess how the poll data are reported and, specifically, whether the sampling information is presented clearly and accurately. The following are questions that journalists should ask, as suggested by the American Association for Public Opinion Research. Assess the extent to which each of these questions is answered in the news article.

- Who paid for the poll, and why was it done?
- Who conducted the poll?
- How was the poll conducted?
- How many people were interviewed, and what is the margin of sampling error?
- How were those people chosen?
- What geographic area or what group were people chosen from?
- When were the interviews conducted?
- How were the interviews conducted?
- What questions were asked? Were they clearly worded, balanced, and unbiased?
- In what order were the questions asked?
- Are the results based on the answers of all of the people interviewed, or only a subset?
- Were the data weighted, and if so, to what?

Activity 8C: Sampling Strategies

See terms: probability sampling; nonprobability sampling; sample.

The following is a list of research situations. For each situation, your objective is to develop an appropriate sampling strategy to effectively carry out the necessary research. Describe your approach in the column to the right of each research strategy. Be sure to indicate whether you would use probability or nonprobability sampling, your sampling frame, and the size of the sample you would use.

Research situation	Sampling strategy
You have been tasked by the governor's office of California to assess Californians' attitudes toward renewable energy. The governor's office is particularly interested in voters' attitudes toward this issue.	
Your employer is interested in making changes to the vacation and sick leave policy. You have been tasked with determining the best course of action based on the attitudes of the roughly 250 employees. Your bosses are more interested in getting highly detailed responses than in getting limited information from a large number of people.	
You are working for a marketing firm and need to pre-test a few poster designs before making major changes. Your firm can only go with one of the designs and needs some feedback in making the selection as well as tweaking the design. You have a limited budget for the pre-test, but you live near two mid-size universities.	
You are working for a community nonprofit organization that provides job training and skill-building opportunities to homeless people. The nonprofit just received a sizeable grant to make improvements to its services. The director would like to hear directly from homeless people in the area regarding how the money should be spent.	
You are doing some freelance work as a focus group moderator. Your current client is producing a new line of organic sanitizing wipes that are safe for use on skin as well as most household surfaces. They are struggling with deciding on a name and slogan for their new product. However, they have a very specific target audience—middle- to upper-class new moms—in mind and want to hear directly from this group.	

Activity 8D: Practicing Simple Random and Systematic Sampling

See terms: simple random sampling; systematic sampling.

The following is a list of 100 responses to the question, "What is your preferred method of communication?" Use simple random and systematic sampling procedures separately to see how close you can get to producing a sample that is representative of the population. Start with a sample of 10 and then see whether you get better (or worse) results with a sample of 25. As you finish gathering your sample, consider what factors would influence the quality of the sample and might explain why your sample turned out the way that it did.

written letter	social media	text	text	phone call
written letter	social media	text	text	phone call
written letter	social media	text	text	phone call
written letter	social media	text	text	phone call
written letter	social media	text	text	phone call
social media	social media	text	text	phone call
social media	social media	text	text	phone call
social media	social media	text	text	phone call
social media	social media	text	text	phone call
social media	social media	text	text	phone call
social media	social media	text	text	e-mail
social media	social media	text	text	e-mail
social media	social media	text	text	e-mail
social media	social media	text	text	e-mail
social media	social media	text	text	e-mail
social media	social media	text	text	e-mail
social media	social media	text	text	e-mail
social media	social media	text	text	e-mail
social media	social media	text	text	e-mail
social media	social media	text	text	e-mail

Population distribution for each preferred communication method: e-mail, 10 percent; social media, 35 percent; text, 40 percent; phone call, 10 percent; written letter, 5 percent.

Suggested Readings for Further Exploration of Unit 8 Topics

Examples

Fiedler, K. (2000). Beware of samples! A cognitive-ecological sampling approach to judgment biases. *Psychological Review, 107*(4), 659–676. doi:10.1037/0033-295X.107.4.659

Katz, D. (1944). The polls and the 1944 election. *Public Opinion Quarterly, 8*(4), 468–487. doi:10.1086/265704

Yeager, D.S., Krosnick, J.A., Chang, L., Javitz, H.S., Levendusky, M.S., Simpser, A., & Wang, R. (2011). Comparing the accuracy of RDD telephone surveys and Internet surveys conducted with probability and non-probability samples. *Public Opinion Quarterly, 75*(4), 709–747. doi:10.1093/poq/nfr020

Advanced Discussion

Brick, J.M. (2011). The future of survey sampling. *Public Opinion Quarterly, 75*(5), 872–888. doi:10.1093/poq/nfr045

Fan, D.P. (2013). Reconceptualizing survey representativeness for evaluating and using nonprobability samples. *Survey Practice, 6*(2).

Kubey, R., Larson, R., & Csikszentmihalyi, M. (1996). Experience sampling method applications to communication research questions. *Journal of Communication, 46*(2), 99–120. doi:10.1111/j.1460-2466.1996.tb01476.x

Meltzer, C.E., Naab, T., & Daschmann, G. (2012). All student samples differ: On participant selection in communication science. *Communication Methods and Measures, 6*(4), 251–262. doi:10.1080/19312458.2012.732625

unit 9

---

experiments and threats to validity

One of the topics in communication research that students often hope to understand involves the representation of "ideal" body types in media. It's widely perceived that many media outlets present idealized and unrealistic images, suggesting body types and appearances that few people can actually attain. The prevalence of image adjustment software further contributes to this perception. In addition, many of these images are targeted at teens and young adults, who are especially concerned with their appearance and how others view them.

You may have discussed this idea in communication classes and heard that such images can affect a variety of attitudes and behaviors. For example, young women shown "thin-ideal" images of models in magazines may come to believe that's how they should look, and for a certain subset of people, this can lead to unhealthy attitudes toward oneself and food, as well as disordered eating behaviors such as anorexia. Others believe these concerns are overstated or even inaccurate. After all, they argue, the media presents what sells, and we have always been drawn to attractive models and celebrities. What's more, those who are already concerned about their appearance are probably more likely to read fashion and fitness magazines and to notice body types that differ from their own.

You probably have an opinion of your own about this controversial topic. But how do you know whether you are right? Research offers a way to test whether such images actually *cause* changes in attitudes and behaviors. One of the best ways to test whether exposure to media content influences the people who consume it is through experimental research. By using a carefully designed study, we can rule out many alternative explanations, quantify the size of the effect, if any, and see whether the effect is universal or holds only for a small subset of all media users.

Experiments

Experiments are ideal for testing causality because they involve directly manipulating the independent variable—also known as the **stimulus**—to determine its effects on the dependent variable. By using **pre-tests** and **post-tests**, researchers are able to determine whether study participants changed as a result of exposure to the stimulus material. For instance, a team of researchers might want to study whether the types of models shown in a fashion magazine affect readers' self-esteem. They might consider a photo spread with only "normal" body types, a spread with equal numbers of normal and "ideal" body types, and one with only ideal body types. They would use these three **treatment** groups (so named because they receive a treatment or **stimulus**) to compare the effects of the various types of images, measuring responses from those exposed to each condition.

In addition, researchers often employ a **control group** to establish a baseline. For example, you might have a condition in which no images are viewed

independent variable
→ Unit 2
dependent variable
→ Unit 2

to see whether any exposure to models affects people. Researchers can then compare scores from the treatment groups to those of the control group to determine whether the treatment had any effect at all. Although experiments often have a limited scope of phenomena they are exploring, and concerns may be raised about external validity (i.e., generalizability), they have a high degree of internal validity, and their concise design allows for **ease of replication**.

Experimental designs can range in complexity and rigor from **quasi-experimental designs** to a **Solomon four-group design** that employs multiple pre- and post-test groups in addition to a control group. Researchers often explore more than one **factor** (i.e., stimulus or treatment) at a time, leading to more complex multi-factorial designs. For example, you might study both the body types of models and the gender of models to see whether the effects of body type are the same when male and female models are shown. Most basic experiments use a **between-subjects design** where each participant is assigned to just one condition, and comparisons are made between conditions scores. In contrast, **within-subjects designs** are often employed to increase statistical power (or at least to avoid losing statistical power) when there is a large number of factors (or a limited number of participants). This design exposes people to multiple conditions and compares their scores for each. The particular design of the experiment depends on the goals of the research as well as the resources available to the researchers.

Experimental designs face a range of **threats to validity**, which ultimately affect the extent to which the researcher is confident in drawing conclusions from the data. Often, small changes in the structure of the design can minimize threats such as the **Hawthorne effect, interparticipant bias, history, maturation**, and experimental **mortality**. Similarly, care and attention when developing measures and procedures and conducting analyses can address **regression toward the mean, researcher bias, sensitization**, and **testing effects**.

Researchers employing experiments can use several approaches to address these threats to validity and thus improve the quality of their experimental design. Primary among these is using **random assignment** when assigning participants to treatment and control groups. An alternative to random assignment is using **matched (or paired) assignment**, whereby each person in a group has an equivalent in another group. For instance, individuals are typically paired with others who share some characteristic such as gender, race, or age. These approaches help achieve **group equivalence** and allow researchers to avoid situations such as unbalanced groups or **selection bias**. Ultimately, if the groups are not equivalent before the study begins, the researcher will have limited confidence in the data. **Double-blind** studies are those in which neither the researchers nor the participants know the condition to which they have been assigned.

Researchers can also improve how realistic the study is by making the situation like one the participant would encounter in the real world, thus improving the **ecological validity**. **Field experiments** can be used to achieve this because the study occurs in a more naturalistic setting than an academic building: participants' responses are captured in an environment in which they are more comfortable.

Random Assignment

A critical aspect of a true experiment is the use of *random assignment* to treatment conditions. Random assignment requires that the determination of which condition each participant falls into meets the standards for randomness. Specifically, each participant must be equally likely to be placed into a given condition, and the placement of any one participant should not be related to the placement of another participant. For example, random assignment means that you could not assign all people in a class to a single condition and treat them as separate individuals. The members of the class are not *independent* from one another, increasing the likelihood they will all respond in a similar way, which may lead you to overestimate the effects of the stimulus. Random assignment is critical to why experiments can show evidence of causality.

In particular, random assignment helps address two of the three requirements for causality: the establishment of time order and the elimination of alternative explanations in the form of confounds. This occurs because random assignment helps make sure that the characteristics of each experimental group are approximately equal prior to the administration of the stimuli.

Because all individuals have an equal chance of being in a given condition, all individual characteristics also have an equal chance of being in a given condition. For example, if we have two experimental conditions and use random assignment to place subjects within those conditions, we should find roughly equal numbers of women in each condition. Each woman has an equal chance of landing in either group, and, just like flipping a coin, it would be very unlikely for all of the women to land in one condition (or, likewise, for the coin to come up heads every time). This helps address third variables because it means that no alternative variables account for why a person was exposed to a particular stimulus. In a non-experimental study, people with certain personality characteristics, backgrounds, or attitudes might seek out specific types of media. If we find that users of those media have different thoughts, feelings or behaviors, we can't be sure that it wasn't because of the other factors that caused them to seek the content in the first place. For example, if women are more likely to seek out fashion magazines and more likely to believe thinness is desirable, then it might just be gender and not the fashion magazines that account for this pattern. But in an experiment, women are no more likely to see thin-ideal vs. non-thin-ideal content, if they have been randomly assigned to view one or the other. This means we can be reasonably confident that it was the content, and not those other characteristics, that account for any differences between people.

inferential statistics → Unit 15
randomness → Unit 8
causality → Unit 2
time order → Unit 2
confound → Unit 2
stimulus → Unit 9
random sample → Unit 8
inferential statistics → Unit 15
population → Unit 8
quasi-experimental designs → Unit 9
variable → Unit 2

The characteristics that should be equal between conditions include those that you hope to influence by your experimental manipulation. So, prior to exposure to the stimulus, those measures should be equal. If they aren't equal after exposure, you can be reasonably certain that is because of the stimulus and not another factor. For example, random assignment means the people seeing the thin-ideal and non-thin-ideal media should have equally high levels of self-esteem, since low self-esteem people had an equal chance of being in either condition. We know this approximate equality was true *before* participants consumed the stimuli. If it stops being true *after* they were exposed to a treatment, we know the exposure came before the lower self-esteem, helping show time order. If a study does not use random assignment or employ a random sample, then inferential statistics cannot provide an accurate reflection of whether the relationships found should generalize to the population. Quasi-experimental designs in which random assignment is not used can provide some helpful insights, but they are almost always inferior to a true experiment.

Matched (or Paired) Assignment

Sometimes, researchers are not able to use random assignment. Another way to try to make groups with equal characteristics is by intentionally linking similar people into a pair or group, then making sure one member of each group is assigned each condition. When researchers deliberately ensure that individuals in one condition correspond with individuals in the other experimental condition(s) in terms of key variables, this is known as *matching*. This method is used as an alternative to random assignment when it is essential that experimental groups match up in some meaningful way. For example, if you are testing whether a new website is more effective than an existing one for e-commerce, you might want to be sure that you have equal numbers of prior site users in each group. You could ask participants whether and how often they visited the old site and identify pairs of individuals who made roughly equal use of the site. Then, you would randomly assign one of those individuals to each condition. Or consider the example of reactions to body image. You might think it is important to match individuals based on their race, sex, or existing attitudes about their bodies. After matching individuals based on those characteristics, you would then randomly assign one individual to each condition. If you have three conditions, you will need to find trios of people prior to assignment. Because this process involves random assignment, it still meets the requirements for a true experiment.

In most cases, random assignment alone is enough to ensure approximately equal groups, and the extra time and complexity of matching is unnecessary. Additionally, matching alone is not enough to ensure equal groups in each condition, and it should not be considered a sufficient substitute for random assignment. Even if you match individuals on several variables, they

random assignment
→ Unit 9

quasi-experimental
→ Unit 9

dependent variable
→ Unit 2

causality
→ Unit 2

may still differ in other, unmeasured ways. Without a random component to assignment, those unmeasured variables might still lead to differences between groups that can't be attributed to the effect of the stimulus. Matching is also used sometimes in quasi-experimental designs, in which researchers do not have the ability to assign individuals to conditions in advance, randomly or otherwise. In such circumstances, you can match similar individuals in each condition and compare those individuals. This helps increase the similarity between groups and makes it more likely that differences in dependent variables are attributable to the stimulus and not to those other factors. However, this does not ensure that causality is present, as matching may miss important differences, and it may not be possible to perfectly match many individuals in one group to those in the other group(s).

Between-Subjects Design

An experiment in which each participant is assigned to just one condition and comparisons are made between the groups exposed to each condition is called a between-subjects design. That is, researchers look for patterns showing that the average value for the dependent variable is different in a group exposed to one stimulus instead of another. Or they consider if the treatment and control groups have different scores. This design relies upon random assignment to ensure that the groups are roughly equal prior to exposure to the treatment. Thus, if differences between groups are found after exposure, they can be attributed to the effects of the different conditions, and not pre-existing variables. This contrasts with a within-subjects design, in which individuals are exposed to multiple levels of the treatment, and their responses after each exposure are compared with their responses after other exposures.

control group
→ Unit 9

between-subjects design
→ Unit 9

random assignment
→ Unit 9

within-subjects design
→ Unit 9

random error
→ Unit 6

Reflect & React: Selection Bias and Its Impact on Experimental Findings

Imagine that you are the communication director for a political candidate who is considering running one of three advertisements—an attack ad, a positive biographical ad, and a mixed ad that attacks the opponent but also has positive messages about your candidate. If are going to conduct an experiment comparing the three different advertisement types, it is important to make sure those groups are equal to one another before any advertisements are shown.

For instance, suppose that one group consists entirely of friends of the candidate, and the other two groups consist of friends of the opponent.

227

Although this scenario is extremely unlikely, it is easy to see that the ad shown to the group of friends of the candidate would receive a positive response, and the ads shown to the friends of your candidate's opponent would likely receive a negative response. If you were unaware of this selection bias, you might mistakenly conclude that one ad is better than the other two. Such a decision could be disastrous if the ad that is chosen has a minimal or even a negative effect on your candidate.

This example presents a real-world situation in which failing to use random assignment or taking other measures to guard against selection bias can have negative effects. It also illustrates some of the potential challenges to the process. What steps could you take in this case as the communication director to ensure that you reduce selection bias and achieve high group equivalence?

A between-subjects design helps minimize the possibility of fatigue and of sensitizing participants to the study questions or intention. However, there is also a greater likelihood that some differences between conditions are due to random error, as participants are not directly compared to themselves. That is, while on average the participants in each condition will be similar, that's not as precise as comparing two scores from the same participant. In the latter case, we know that the participant is a perfect match to themselves on possible third variables. Between-subjects designs are necessary when exposure to any one treatment would prevent other treatments from being valid experiences. For example, consider the experiment described in the introduction, in which you have three versions of magazine content showing different types of models. You might measure changes in eating behavior by having participants choose from different snack options after viewing the images. You could compare how many people in each condition choose healthy versus unhealthy snacks. Each person would see only one of the three layouts, but you would have three groups of people whose eating behavior could be compared. This is a between-subjects design. You would have a hard time getting a person to ignore the first layout they saw and focus only on a second if you tried to use a within-subjects design. And you'd have people getting pretty tired of whatever snacks were available—not to mention they would probably catch on to the goals of the study.

between-subjects design
→ Unit 9

Within-Subjects Design

In contrast to a between-subjects design, a *within-subjects design* focuses on comparing participants with themselves. To do this, a within-subjects design presents participants with multiple stimuli and compares their responses for each dependent variable after each stimulus is delivered. For example, consider again the experiment testing eating behavior after viewing a magazine layout, with three different conditions. As described earlier, you could have three separate groups of people, each of which sees only one version of the layout. Random assignment should ensure these groups are roughly equal, but some variation in eating habits or personal attitudes may persist.

On the other hand, if you have each participant view all three of the layouts, you would still randomly assign the order in which the layouts are shown. But now you could compare participants to themselves. For example, if a person chooses an unhealthy snack after seeing the attractive models because of low self-esteem but a healthy snack after seeing the mixed-model layout, you could eliminate some typical confounds. You know that this person has the same personality and experiences across both conditions. If he or she changes eating behaviors, that change can't be attributed to normal behaviors and habits. After all, you're considering the same person in both conditions.

The challenge facing within-subjects designs is that participants become sensitized to the questions and focus of the study. Once they are asked a battery of questions about how much they like a layout or given the option of choosing foods, they know those elements are an important part of the study. When the next layout is shown, they will be thinking about how it is different, how they might be expected to respond, and what it specifically shows that might relate to diet and related issues. This may lead them to behave in an unnatural fashion, compromising external validity. In addition, some questions simply cannot be asked multiple times.

Suppose, in this case, you have participants watch one of two advertisements for a new type of taco, and one of your key dependent variables is whether the participants have heard of this new taco before. After the first exposure to an ad, you can't expect them to completely forget the ad or the product before they view the next ad. So, of course, they will remember the product much better after the second ad, but not because of the ad. Randomly assigning the order of stimulus exposure helps with this, but in the end, there is little reason to ask about basic knowledge and recall after the first exposure. The remaining time would be better spent on a between-subjects design to show how each participant reacts after seeing just one version of the ad.

Quasi-Experimental Design

A quasi-experimental design involves comparing responses to different treatments, but it does not include random assignment to treatment conditions. Instead, researchers may use matching or statistical controls to compensate by equalizing the groups as much as possible. However, these techniques do not substitute for true random assignment, and a quasi-experiment does not offer the same evidence of causality as a true experiment. In a quasi-experiment,

variable
→ Unit 2

random assignment
→ Unit 9

sensitization
→ Unit 9

external validity
→ Unit 6

dependent variable
→ Unit 2

random assignment
→ Unit 9

matched assignment
→ Unit 9

statistical control
→ Unit 16

causality
→ Unit 2

stimulus
→ Unit 9

field experiment
→ Unit 9

229

individuals may differ in important ways prior to exposure to the treatment, creating differences between groups that are not caused by the stimulus.

For example, you might want to study the effectiveness of a new approach to teaching media literacy. One instructor might use this approach, while other classes at the university do not. You could give the students in every class a test on media literacy at the end of the semester. If those in the class using the new approach score better, that might be because of the new approach. But it could also be that this group of students was more skilled to begin with, or that there were other differences between the classes, such as the time they meet or the interpersonal style of the instructor. These third variables might be the real cause of any differences between classes. Sometimes researchers have to rely on a quasi-experimental design when naturally occurring differences in the experiences of groups provide an opportunity to make some kind of comparison, and the researcher cannot practically or ethically recreate such differences through random assignment in a laboratory or real-world setting.

Voices from Industry

Lisa Scott—Chief Creative Officer & Managing Director at OneMagnify

Lisa brings energy to everything she touches. An engaging brand advocate, Lisa's dynamic personality resonates within our offices and beyond, and that vitality can be seen and felt in the brands she manages. In her early career on Madison Avenue, Lisa cut her teeth at storied agencies like Young & Rubicam, Saatchi & Saatchi, and Rapp Worldwide, developing successful campaigns for prominent clients like Miller Brewing, Bristol-Myers Squibb, AT&T and DuPont. Lisa would go on to become Global Marketing Manager for DuPont Tyvek before bringing her talents to OneMagnify.

Why are good research skills important in your field?

We develop brand strategies for very large companies across many very competitive industries. Good research helps us gain powerful insights about the industries, the competition, the prospective target audience and helps us develop a strong and differentiated brand proposition.

What specific method or methods do you encounter most?

Online surveys, focus groups and one-on-one interviews.

Can you name specific instances where you have used data collected from research?

We use data and insights in everything that we do. We look to identify media strategies that directly connect prospects with our client's products. Through research we determine which media outlets and vehicles perform the best. For instance, when we run a media campaign, we have all of the outlets and vehicles tagged so that we can see how the target prospect engages with the brand, the supporting websites and what actions the prospect takes. Another way we use research is to understand how our brand concepts appeal to the target audience. Often times we test concepts through focus groups and online research. We are always in search of the most differentiated and compelling brand proposition.

How did research you conducted help inform your decision?

Research allows us to make the best decisions about our brand strategies. Are they compelling? Will they make the prospective target audience take action? Did they generate awareness? Trial? Purchase?

What are one or two pieces of advice or insights you would give about research to students in a communication research methods course?

Research is only as good as the project objectives. Meaning, before engaging in any research study, be sure that your objectives are very, very clear. What are you testing for? What are you seeking to find out? Who, specifically, is your target audience (and be definitive about your target audience—what are their current media behaviors? What are they concerned about? How do they currently use/consume similar products, etc.).

Field Experiment

A field experiment is a true experimental design that takes place outside the laboratory and manipulates the independent variable in a way that individuals encounter the stimulus in a natural environment. This helps increase the external validity of the design, but the loss of control makes it harder to know for certain whether all participants actually experienced the same stimulus.

For example, you might want to test a fund-raising campaign in which postcards are sent out requesting donations. You could identify the population of individuals you hope to persuade and then randomly assign half of them to receive one version of the postcard and the other half to receive another version. Then, you could track which group sends in more money. The results would be more generalizable to the real-world process of fund-raising. However, it might be harder to accurately detect and explain any effects. So many people would not even read the postcard that the effects on those who did would be diminished and hard to observe. Moreover, you would not have the same opportunity to measure attitudes and motivations immediately after exposure, as you would with a laboratory study.

Field experiments are also complicated in many circumstances because ensuring that individuals receive only one version of the stimulus can be challenging. Suppose you want to test the effects of viewing violent television programs. If you could vary which version of a program is broadcast to each individual, this would be a helpful test, but most researchers cannot persuade television channels to air two different programs, targeted by household. Even if you did manage such a design, you would still have a hard time knowing who actually watched the show. You could send out thousands of surveys to people in each condition and receive only a handful back. And then you might still worry that people somehow encountered the "wrong" version of the show—perhaps they watched it at a friend's house or incorrectly recalled seeing the program and actually watched something else.

In addition, field experiments sometimes violate the independence requirement for randomness. Consider a situation in which researchers want to evaluate the effectiveness of an ad campaign that aired in one community but not another. While there are large numbers of individuals in each community, you are comparing just two "clusters" of people. Those in one community may be systematically different from those in another, and the differences you attribute to the advertisement may instead stem from those community-level influences.

In some cases, researchers try to take advantage of existing differences in potential independent variables between communities or other groups to test whether they create changes in dependent variables. For example, if one state implements a ban on alcohol advertising, researchers might try to match individuals in that state with individuals in a similar state where such a ban is not in place. By analyzing differences between the two sets of individuals, researchers can see whether the ban affected attitudes and drinking behavior.

However, this is not a true experiment because it lacks random assignment. Instead, this would be a kind of quasi-experimental design, and the analysis would try to account for as many potential confounds as possible to still give some evidence for causality.

Treatment Groups

All experiments involve manipulations in which participants are exposed to one (or more) of multiple possible treatments—specific versions of stimuli along with any other guidelines or procedures that vary between conditions. In all true experiments, individuals are randomly assigned to a group that represents their experimental conditions. For the most part, these groups are referred to as *treatment groups*, and the particular conditions they experience represent *treatments*, sometimes called stimuli or experimental conditions. For example, as discussed earlier, you could develop a study of the effects of thin-ideal models by comparing layouts with (1) only thin models, (2) only normally proportioned models, or (3) a mixture of the two. Each of these would be a treatment condition.

The treatment groups reflect each unique condition. If a multi-factorial design is used where there are multiple manipulated IVs, then a treatment group will entail the people assigned a specific combination of factors. The one exception is a control group. In the case of such a group, which doesn't receive any treatment, researchers often refer to this as a control condition and thus wouldn't label it a treatment group. Aside from cases of a true control group, in a between-subjects design all participants are assigned to a single treatment group. Analyses of the findings will consider whether the scores for participants in one treatment group are different from those in another group. This comparison allows researchers to see if the variable representing the differences between groups had an effect on the dependent variables.

> **between-subjects design**
> → Unit 9
>
> **independent variable**
> → Unit 2
>
> **hypotheses**
> → Unit 2
>
> **variable**
> → Unit 2
>
> **external validity**
> → Unit 6

Stimulus

The stimulus is the specific experience presented to participants in a given condition of an experiment. In the example of testing the effects of different types of models, the stimulus would be the specific layout of the magazine that is shown to the participants. In general, a good stimulus will be ecologically valid, appearing like the actual type of media content or other experience it is meant to represent. The difference between different stimuli reflect the variable or variables in the study. Where two stimuli differ, they vary. As such, the goal is to create stimuli that are clearly different in terms of the independent variables but otherwise similar. For example, in the magazine study, you would need to make sure that, other than the model body types, everything else is constant. Among other things, you would need to be sure that the number, race, poses, and approximate ages of the models match across all conditions. In multi-factorial designs, the

> **independent variable**
> → Unit 2
>
> **ecological validity**
> → Unit 9
>
> **factor**
> → Unit 9

233

stimuli will differ from one another in terms of each variable. Two stimuli that have the same value for one factor should match perfectly for that factor, and differ only for the factor that distinguishes them. For example, consider if you introduced a second factor to the study of models in magazines representing the presence of a label stating the image was edited. If your other factor was how thin the models shown were, then your conditions would include stimuli showing thin models with labels, thin models without labels, typical bodies with labels, and typical bodies without labels. The models would be exactly the same in both thin-model conditions, for example, and the wording and placement of the label would be exactly the same in both label conditions.

The stimulus reflects the entirety of material presented to study participants, not just those specific details that vary between conditions. For example, if participants are viewing a movie that has had a few scenes altered, the stimulus is the entire movie. This is important because unintended differences between stimuli or even aspects of the stimuli that are not meant to affect the findings can still influence the results. One solution to this is to use *stimulus sampling*. In this approach, many different stimuli that all reflect the same intended variable are chosen. For example, if you want to compare the effects of viewing violent and nonviolent films, you might identify 30 films for each category. Then, you would randomly choose one nonviolent film to show each person in the nonviolent condition and one violent film for each person in the violent condition. This would increase your confidence in the external validity of the results because they hold across a diversity of stimuli, and any specific differences between two particular stimuli could not account for the findings. However, finding many different versions of the chosen factor can be challenging, especially if researchers have to edit or modify the original content in some way to make it work as a stimulus.

Factor

| independent variable → Unit 2 |
| confederates → Unit 4 |

In experimental research, the independent variables are often referred to as *factors*. Thus, each variable that is manipulated represents a factor. In a basic single-factor design, just one variable is manipulated. For example, if you are studying the effects of attractiveness on interpersonal interactions, you might use two confederates, with one who was rated more attractive than the other in a pre-test. Your factor would be attractiveness, and you would have two specific conditions or "cells" (attractive/less attractive).

In many experiments, researchers consider more than one factor at the same time. For example, maybe you think that the effects of attractiveness depend upon the gender of the conversational partner. This would introduce a second independent variable: gender. Now you have a two-factor design. Because in this particular case each factor has two possible values, this would be referred to as a 2 × 2 design, and you would have a total of four possible conditions to which to assign participants. You would have an attractive male partner, an attractive female, a less attractive male, and a less attractive female.

Research in Depth: Body Image

The examples given several places in this unit involve how depictions of models, celebrities, and other figures in media affect self-esteem, attitudes, and eating behaviors among those who view them. Not surprisingly, this topic has been explored in depth in the communication literature. Not every study has reached the same conclusion, but a good summary of the findings can be found in a meta-analysis by Grabe, Ward, and Hyde (2008). These authors examined both experimental and correlational (typically survey-based) research on the link between exposure to media and various measures of body-related outcomes. These include attitudes such as body dissatisfaction and self-objectification, as well as indicators of potential behaviors and even tendency toward disordered eating such as bulimia. In total, their results combined findings from 141 studies.

Although not every published study reached the same conclusion, on average, the results showed clear but small to moderate effects on body dissatisfaction and eating behaviors. The results were present across both experimental and correlational studies, suggesting that this is truly a causal relationship. The results were also consistent over time, indicating that the problem has not gone away. This does not mean that the media is necessarily the primary cause of various issues related to body image and disordered eating. Indeed, plenty of evidence points to other physiological and social contributors. Nor does it mean that all individuals will necessarily respond negatively to thin-ideal images; for example, in a study by Harrison, Taylor, and Marske (2006), only those individuals who felt that there was a discrepancy between the kind of body they wanted to have and the kind they had reacted to slender (or muscular) images by changing their eating behavior. Moreover, the study showed that men and women responded differently, although both were affected. But overall, the evidence definitely suggests that some people are harmed by exposure to idealized and unrealistic images of models and others presented in mainstream media.

Factors can have more than two possible values, of course. Perhaps you identify three confederates with low, moderate, and high levels of attractiveness. If you cross this with the gender factor, you have a 3 × 2 design, for a total of six conditions.

Some researchers reserve the term factor for manipulated independent variables. *Measured* characteristics of the participants, such as their age, ideology or gender, can also serve as independent variables in hypotheses and analyses. But because the researcher isn't able to assign participants to a particular value for that variable, we are less able to speak with confidence about whether any relationships involving those variables are causal. However, you will still sometimes see studies in which measured factors are also presented as part of the design. For example, a study in which the manipulated gender of the confederate conversation partner and the measured factor of participant gender identity were both considered could be described as a 2 × 2 factorial design.

Factorial designs provide quick notation for the number of groups in an experimental design while also indicating the number of independent variables being explicitly tested by the experiment. A 2 × 2 design has four possible conditions (two independent variables, each of which has two attributes). For example, you might be interested in assessing whether model attractiveness (high/low) combined with gender (male/female) has an effect on the self-esteem ratings of people who view the ads. The possibilities are endless, but the number of groups can add up quickly, thus affecting the decision to use a between- or within-groups design.

Figure 9.1 presents a graphical display of the 2 × 2 condition described earlier. Figure 9.2 presents a graphical display of a 2 × 2 × 2 design. In the latter case, there are three independent variables, each with two attributes, for a total of eight different groups needed. In this case, we could consider model attractiveness (high/low) crossed with gender (male/female) crossed with the color of the photograph (color/black and white). The cells are numbered so that you can see how many groups each design would require.

	Gender: Male	Gender: Female
Attractiveness: Low	1	2
Attractiveness: High	3	4

Figure 9.1 Example showing a 2 × 2 factorial design (group number is indicated in each cell)

Color photograph			Black & white photograph		
	Gender: Male	Gender: Female		Gender: Male	Gender: Female
Attractiveness: Low	1	2	Attractiveness: Low	5	6
Attractiveness: High	3	4	Attractiveness: High	7	8

Figure 9.2 Example showing a 2 × 2 × 2 factorial design (group number is indicated in each cell)

Double-Blind Design

When both the researchers and the participants in a study are not aware of their treatment group, this is called a *double-blind* study design. One major concern in experimental research is that the expectations and existing beliefs of either the participants or the researchers can bias the findings. Participants may think they know the purpose of the study and deliberately give answers that are either in line with the study goals or in contradiction to them. Further, researchers may unintentionally cue participants about desired answers or subtly change their observations to fit their hypotheses.

The double-blind study design addresses these concerns by ensuring that neither participants nor researchers know which condition they are in, preventing them from changing their behavior to fit that condition. Double-blind studies are common in medical research, in which a placebo may be given that mirrors the appearance of an actual medication. In communication research, they are relatively uncommon because the differences between conditions are often obvious or impossible to disguise. Deception about the purpose of the study can help minimize bias attributable to participant expectations, in the absence of blinding. And the use of computer-based testing or the distribution of questionnaires that include the stimulus hidden within the packet can keep researchers from knowing the assigned condition during the study. After data are collected, researchers often take steps to ensure that the individuals coding or making sense of recorded observations and open-ended answers are not aware of the condition each response came from. That way, the processing of those data cannot be influenced by researcher bias.

The classic example of a double-blind study is a medical study in which the effectiveness of a drug is being tested. In such cases, the treatment group receives the medicine (the treatment), and another group, the control group,

bias
→ Unit 2

hypotheses
→ Unit 2

deception
→ Unit 4

coding
→ Unit 11

open-ended
→ Unit 7

researcher bias
→ Unit 9

receives a placebo pill. The use of a placebo ensures that everyone in the study is taking a pill of some sort, but only some of the participants receive the actual medicine. This allows the researchers to minimize any differences between the control and treatment groups. The participants in the study do not know whether they are receiving the medicine or a placebo, so their own assumptions about the treatment will not affect the results—this solves the problem of demand characteristics. The doctors giving the medicine are also unaware of the treatment conditions, ensuring that they will not treat the people receiving the "real" pill any differently, thereby eliminating researcher bias.

Control Group

treatment group
→ Unit 9

variable
→ Unit 2

A control group represents a specific condition in a study in which no amount of the treatment is applied or in which the participants are exposed to an unmodified version of something that is otherwise modified in the treatment conditions. Control groups can help establish exactly how large an effect the treatment has. Consider again the study looking at body image and media content. It may be that *any* images of models, regardless of body type, affect attitudes and behaviors. To know whether it is specifically thin-ideal media, and not simply showing pictures of other people, that has an effect, we need a control group for comparison. By having a group that views no images, or images with no models present, we could establish the baseline influence of simply reading a magazine or watching TV even when no images are shown, or even sitting in a lab and consuming no content. As another example, suppose you want to know how much viewers learn from watching *The Daily Show*. Your treatment condition might involve viewing a single episode of the show, then measuring knowledge about the issues found in the program. Meanwhile, those in the control group would simply answer the knowledge questions. The difference between the two would indicate the total amount of learning from the show.

However, there are many situations in which a true control group may not be possible. Suppose you want to measure how happy people feel after viewing *The Daily Show*. If you compared your measure of happiness to those who simply came in and answered the survey, you wouldn't get a good indication of the effects of the show. Maybe people grew less happy simply because they spent a half hour in the lab, even though they were watching TV. You might want to make the nonparticipants wait for 30 minutes before they answer the questions, but then your control condition would reflect the unhappiness that comes from being in an empty room for 30 minutes, which is hardly a perfect baseline. In some cases, you might use a different, irrelevant piece of media content as a comparison. For example, if you want to know how much people enjoy watching *The Daily Show*, it wouldn't make much sense to ask people who watched nothing how much they enjoyed it. Instead, you could show them 30 minutes of a different program, but it would be hard to know which show to choose that would be a fair comparison. If the other program is a fun movie or a boring documentary, that will make a big difference.

Because of these challenges, many studies of media don't include a true control condition. Instead, they simply use multiple treatment groups, each of which has some level of exposure to a relevant stimulus, and the differences between those levels reflect the variable of interest. For example, maybe you think that enjoyment of *The Daily Show* is attributable to the presence of jokes in which the host makes fun of himself. You could take an episode with those jokes and use it as one condition, then create a different version with the jokes removed and use that as the other condition. Neither of these is a true control condition, but the comparison would still be informative.

Pre-Test and Post-Test

Any measures assessed before the stimulus materials are administered are part of the *pre-test*, whereas those evaluated after the stimulus are part of the *post-test*. The post-test is where the key dependent variables are typically measured. In many experiments, researchers include a measure of certain key variables prior to exposure to the stimulus. Sometimes, these are general demographic characteristics or personality traits that are not likely to be influenced by exposure to the stimulus or expected to serve as moderating variables. In other cases, researchers want to establish a baseline measure of the dependent variable prior to treatment.

A design in which the same variable is measured before and after exposure to a stimulus is known as a *pre-test/post-test* experiment, where the measurement occurring after exposure is the post-test. For example, in evaluating the effects of thin-ideal media, you probably would want to measure beliefs about ideal body image. You could simply compare those assigned to view applicable media with those assigned to a control condition. However, you might worry that people taking your study will have a diversity of existing attitudes (perhaps created by prior exposure), creating a lot of random error. If you want to know exactly how people's attitudes changed as a result of exposure, you could measure those attitudes before and after image viewing. By comparing the two scores, you could see the average change in individuals instead of looking only at between-group differences. In this way, a pre-test/post-test design allows some of the same benefits as a within-subjects design, letting researchers compare participants with themselves.

However, pre-testing can create problems as well. In particular, pre-tests run the risk of sensitizing participants to the purpose of the study. By asking participants about specific topics, researchers alert participants to the importance of those topics for the study. For example, a pre-test asking about emotions might lead participants to be more attentive to emotional content or suspect that they are supposed to experience some strong emotional response. One potential but complicated solution to this problem is to use a Solomon four-group design.

dependent variable
→ Unit 2

stimulus
→ Unit 9

control group
→ Unit 9

random error
→ Unit 6

within-subjects design
→ Unit 9

sensitization
→ Unit 9

Solomon four-group design
→ Unit 9

sensitization
→ Unit 9

random assignment
→ Unit 9

239

Another possible approach is to use a post-test-only design—although it is not as rigorous as the four-group design, it eliminates any sensitization effect. In addition, pre-tests are not a substitute for random assignment. While a pre-test can show that people's responses changed over time, it does not guarantee the change was attributable to the treatment. If other factors differed between the treatment groups, those might also explain the changes.

Solomon Four-Group Design

The Solomon four-group design offers many of the advantages of including a pre-test while also testing for the possible effects of that pre-test due to sensitization. In this design, the use of a pre-test is included as an additional manipulated factor, so that half of all participants are assigned to a treatment group that receives a pre-test, while the other half take part in a post-test-only design. In the simplest version of this design, in which there is one factor with just two possible values, individuals are assigned to one of four groups (hence the name), including both pre-test/post-test and post-test-only versions of the design. For example, if you are testing the effect of a conversational partner's gender, you would assign people to converse with either a man or a woman. For both groups, you would further divide them between a pre-test/post-test version in which they answer the questions related to the dependent variable twice, or a post-test-only version in which they answer the questions only after the stimulus. In this case you would have four conditions: pre-test, male partner; pre-test, female partner, post-test only, male partner; and post-test only, female partner.

By comparing the pre-test and post-test-only conditions, you can determine how much of an effect including the pre-test had on the findings and adjust the results accordingly. By comparing the two pre-test groups, you can see how much the average individual changed and use the information about the pre-test and post-test designs to divide that change between experimental effects and sensitization effects. By comparing the post-test-only conditions, you can confirm that the stimulus had an effect even in the absence of pre-test sensitization. Of course, this design is complicated, as it doubles the total number of conditions and thus the total number of participants needed for an adequately powerful test. Because of this, the Solomon four-group design is rarely used, but in situations in which a pre-test is desired by researchers worried about sensitization, it can be helpful.

Advantages and Disadvantages of Experiments

Experiments tend to be noted for their elegance and straightforward designs, although researchers can create quite complex designs with many variations in stimulus materials. This elegance allows for experiments to be replicated fairly

---

pre-test
→ Unit 9

sensitization
→ Unit 9

factor
→ Unit 9

easily, with researchers replicating the stimulus materials used by others to consider further variations quickly and easily. Beyond ease of replication, the success of an experiment is a function of its design. A carefully designed study that meets the requirements of a true experiment—especially random assignment—is typically high in internal validity. That is, researchers can be confident that the relationship between a manipulated and measured variable truly occurred in the study and that it is causal and otherwise occurs in the manner expected. This derives in part from the high degree of control researchers exert over all circumstances of a survey, with as little accidental variation within treatment groups as possible. However, such strict control often comes with a sacrifice in external validity, since the strictly controlled experience of an experiment may not match more natural settings. This represents a lack of ecological validity, and is a component of external validity. Experiments are often weak in external validity in general. The need to recruit participants for a study that may take place at a specific location and to quickly obtain samples for replications creates an incentive to rely on less representative sampling techniques. As such, it is common for experiments to be considered a trade-off between internal validity and external validity, with the former the main emphasis of experimental designs.

Ease of Replication

One of the positive features of typical laboratory experiments is that by using specific stimulus materials with a standard procedure and set of questions, they are easy to replicate. That is, the same research team or other researchers with access to a description of the study could carry out a similar study quickly and efficiently, allowing comparison of the results. Many journal articles that describe experiments report on the results of multiple studies, each with minor variations that replicate and clarify the initial findings.

content analysis
→ Unit 11

convenience
sample
→ Unit 8

internal validity
→ Unit 6

For example, if you are studying the effectiveness of a new advertisement, you might first compare it to the existing advertisement for the same product. If you find that the new ad worked better, you could then carry out a partial replication, using the same measures to compare the new ad to another version of the ad with different music or using a different slogan. Other types of studies, such as content analysis or surveys, can be much more time-consuming, expensive, or both, making it more challenging to carry out a quick replication.

As an additional example, consider testing the effects of thin-ideal media. You might first want to establish whether the use of thin versus average models has an effect. If your results show this is the case, it would be simple to add a condition including models of both types or to further modify the images in other ways. By adding a few additional participants and adjusting the measures slightly, you would be able to both replicate and expand upon your findings. Similarly, you could shift to a different medium simply by creating new stimuli, without making major changes to the measures or having to carry out an elaborate sampling process. Of course, this assumes that you are relying upon a convenience sample in each case. However, because the focus of experimental research tends to be internal validity, this would likely be the case.

Ecological Validity

ease of replication
→ Unit 9

relationship
→ Unit 2

variable
→ Unit 2

external validity
→ Unit 6

While experiments tend to excel in ease of replication, they often suffer in terms of ecological validity—that is, how well the conditions of the study replicate naturally occurring experiences of the type being studied. Ecological validity is a specific component of external validity, or how well the results of a particular study are likely to apply to the larger population of interest. As much as possible, researchers try to capture the relationship between variables in a way that reflects what would happen under ordinary circumstances. For example, a study of television viewing would have greater ecological validity if participants watched TV in a comfortable environment with other people, on a large screen, and with snacks and other possible distractions. If instead participants viewed a small monitor, wearing headphones, in a brightly lit lab, this would probably have less ecological validity. (Of course, as television viewing habits diversify, no one setting perfectly matches how everyone watches television.)

Surveys tend to present few concerns with ecological validity, as individuals are asked to report behaviors that occur in their ordinary lives. Experiments, however, often have flaws in ecological validity. Researchers want to exert careful control over the nature of the treatments. If researchers gave participants a choice about which television show to watch, for example, they wouldn't be able to say that individuals were randomly assigned to view a specific program. But under normal circumstances, people can choose which program to watch, when, and for how long. Because of this, one common criticism of experimental research is that it does not capture natural behaviors. This is part of a larger issue with external validity, which reflects how closely the results for participants within the study match the experience of the larger population to which the results are being applied.

Researchers can take steps to increase the ecological validity of the study. For example, if you are studying the effects of advertising, you could insert the advertisements within a clip from a television program, occurring at the natural commercial breaks. This would be more valid than simply showing the ad to participants, as that would create an atypical focus on the ad and possibly sensitize participants.

Threats to Validity

population
→ Unit 8

sensitization
→ Unit 9

All research faces challenges to validity. Many of these challenges are especially pronounced in experiments—not because they are necessarily more likely to occur in an experiment but because experiments rely on strong internal validity to offset the natural sacrifices to external validity necessitated by the design. However, most of these threats can affect both internal and external validity. A threat would compromise internal validity if it created the impression of a relationship of a particular nature between two variables when that relationship, in fact, was not present. But sometimes it would simply create the impression that a relationship found in a study would occur more broadly when, in reality, the specific conditions of the study generated by the threat created the situation. The latter would be a lack of external validity. Either way, these threats can seriously undermine the usefulness of an experiment and should be addressed as much as possible.

Hawthorne Effect

The *Hawthorne effect*, also known as the *observer effect*, refers to the tendency of people to change their behavior when they are being observed, participating in a study, or otherwise receiving additional attention. The term comes from a series of studies conducted at the Hawthorne Works, a plant near Chicago where changes in the work environment all seemed to lead to increases in productivity. Gradually, the researchers realized that the participants weren't necessarily reacting to the specific changes, such as increased lighting. Instead, they were simply responding to the extra attention and scrutiny. It may be that they wanted to please the researchers, or they may have been worried about being criticized for a lack of productivity.

external validity
→ Unit 6

internal validity
→ Unit 6

double-blind
→ Unit 9

stimulus
→ Unit 9

Observer effects can manifest in a variety of ways. The critical idea is that the mere act of being in a study can alter behavior, and we should not attribute that change solely to the stimulus unless we have an appropriate control group for comparison. When participants specifically change their behavior to match what they think are the expectations of the researchers, this is an example of responding to *demand characteristics*. Sometimes, though, participants may actually behave in the opposite way that researchers expect, or they may become less engaged, productive, or motivated because of the added stress of being observed. Any of these outcomes would be observer effects.

In the context of communication research, study participants may behave differently for a variety of reasons. For example, participants watching a television program in a laboratory setting may focus more intensely on the program than they would at home, knowing the researchers are monitoring (and rewarding) their participation. This would lead to more pronounced effects of the stimulus. Thus, the presence of observers in general can undermine the external validity of a study by creating an artificially intense environment.

Observer effects can also undermine internal validity. If participants are responding to the observer and not the stimulus, then our conclusion about the effects of the stimulus will be in error. Additionally, in some study designs, we may pay more attention to certain conditions. For example, suppose researchers are comparing the effects of watching people play video games to actually playing the games. Those playing the games might receive direct tutoring from the researcher, and the researcher may remain present to help them deal with any in-game challenges. All of this would distort the responses of the players compared with those who only viewed the game. Thus, it's important for researchers to make sure that they observe and treat all participants as equally as possible. Using a design in which researchers are blind to the assigned condition can help address this.

external validity
→ Unit 6

internal validity
→ Unit 6

dependent variable
→ Unit 2

independent variable
→ Unit 2

History

When events take place during the course of a study that represent outside factors not meant as part of the stimulus or design, this constitutes a *history effect*. As with any component of a study not accounted for by the researchers that would not ordinarily occur, this can compromise the external validity of the study. More important, history effects can undermine the internal validity of the design. If these events affect all participants, they still account for some of the change in the dependent variable, and our analyses will mistakenly assume these changes are attributable to the stimulus. A pre-test/post-test comparison would lead to incorrect conclusions about the actual size of the effect, if any. More troubling, history can affect one treatment group and not another, leading the researcher to conclude that between-group differences are attributable to the independent variable when they are not.

For example, suppose you are studying the effectiveness of interpersonal discussion as a way to solve problems and comparing people who meet face-to-face versus those who meet online. But on the night you schedule your sessions, which take place at the library for the face-to-face groups, there is a fire alarm. All of the face-to-face participants have to file out of the building and stand in the cold for 20 minutes before completing their task. This disruption would obviously affect their performance, but the reason would have nothing to do with the relative merits of face-to-face versus online interaction.

Extended from there, history can refer to any situation in which differences between conditions exceed the intended elements of the independent variable. Even something such as the advertisements appearing alongside different body image manipulations could constitute history—if one ad is for a snack food and the other for a gym, this could affect participants in an unintended and unequal way. Researchers can minimize the potential for history effects by ensuring that the conditions under which each participant takes part in the study are as controlled and equivalent as possible and by eliminating from the study any cases in which unusual events occurred.

Interparticipant Bias

Researchers often assume that each participant in a study is individually influenced by the stimulus. When participants affect one another in some way, violating this assumption and potentially meaning that the results no longer reflect random assignment, this is known as *interparticipant bias*. This can occur in a many ways. Suppose you are studying the effects of viewing a movie and comparing a humorous movie to a frightening one. If you have a group of participants view the movie in a theater together, the reactions of some members of the audience may affect the experience of others. For example, if one person who is viewing the frightening movie starts laughing at inappropriate moments, this could cause others to view the film more negatively as well. Of course, watching movies in a theater is ecologically valid, but the assumption of the scholars is that if a person finds the scary movie ineffective at creating fear, this is because of their own reaction and not others in the room. Otherwise, the types of statistics used would have to be changed.

Even when participants don't take part in a study together, their behavior can still create interparticipant bias. For example, consider a study in which participants are told that they will receive money for completing a challenging task using a new Internet tool, but this is actually intended to see whether the added motivation will change how they complete the task. At the end of the study, perhaps the researchers give all of the participants the money regardless of performance or withhold the money from everyone. In this case, the researchers are using a form of deception, and the validity of the study rests on this deception working. But if one of the participants in the study walks out and tells the next person waiting that the money promised is a trick, the next participant won't react in the intended way. Any information that participants reveal to one another about the study can harm the results, even when deception isn't used. For example, a study might look at how much participants learn from watching a 5-minute segment from the news. If a participant in the study tells others the answers to the knowledge questions used to measure learning, subsequent participants will perform better on the test because of that inside knowledge.

Maturation

When participants change over the course of a study for reasons that have nothing to do with the stimulus or study experience, this is often an issue of *maturation*. This occurs because participants "grow up" and become more mature over the course of a long study. For example, a researcher might want to know whether introducing computers into the classroom helps student performance. The researcher might compare scores on a pre-test to those on a post-test to see

stimulus → Unit 9
random assignment → Unit 9
ecologically validity → Unit 9
inferential statistics → Unit 15
deception → Unit 4
validity → Unit 6

control group → Unit 9
internal validity → Unit 6

245

how much learning occurred. However, over the course of a semester, students would inevitably learn anyway, so the total change cannot be attributed to the use of computers. The researcher could partially solve this problem by using a control group that did not use the computers, but the design would have to be developed carefully to ensure the comparison is appropriate.

Another example can illustrate why simply including a control group doesn't ensure internal validity when maturation is a problem. Suppose you are testing the long-term effects of reading newspapers and have a design in which participants are asked to attend weekly sessions to ensure that they are reading. You would want to use a group of people who don't already read the newspaper so that you can focus entirely on the effects of your laboratory sessions. A natural comparison might be with participants who aren't assigned to read the newspaper. If you ask the control group the same items you want to use to measure the effects on the treatment group at the start of the study, then your comparison won't account for any other changes in the participants. The newspaper readers will have undergone several months of maturation, becoming more knowledgeable and worldly regardless of the reading. But if you compare the two groups at the end of the study, some of the nonreaders in the control condition may have started reading newspapers or otherwise paying more attention to news as their lifestyles and personalities changed. In this case, the control group would still have some newspaper exposure, meaning that it isn't a true control group, and the findings would underestimate the effects of readership.

Mortality

external validity
→ Unit 6

population
→ Unit 8

internal validity
→ Unit 6

relationship
→ Unit 2

population
→ Unit 8

sample
→ Unit 8

Any loss of participants during the study constitutes *mortality*. If those participants differ systematically from the individuals who remain in the study, this can harm validity. For example, you might be studying voters' opinions before and after the election, asking them how they feel about each candidate, whether they intend to participate, and how much media they have consumed. Prior to the election, members of both parties might be excited to share their views. But after the election, people whose candidate lost might be less enthusiastic, and many of them could refuse to take part in the second wave. As a result, their views would not be reflected in the overall study, affecting the external validity of the results because the intended population is no longer represented.

Mortality can be an even bigger problem when it affects the internal validity of a study. Consider a study of the relationship between interpersonal interaction and subsequent hostility in which one group of participants is subjected to verbal abuse, while the other receives praise. The intent of the study would be to test whether abused participants become more hostile toward other participants by the end of the study. But suppose that some of those in the abuse condition became frustrated and quit, while only the people who liked arguing stayed with the study. These argumentative types might have given more hostile responses anyway, while the sensitive people who left might have been more friendly. Because all participants were equally likely to remain in the other condition, this would distort the final results. When large numbers of people quit a study, especially if they disproportionately quit from one or more specific conditions, this is likely to distort the results.

Certain study designs are more likely to cause mortality, such as especially lengthy, dull, or difficult procedures. Mortality occurs whenever participants leave a study or stop providing data. In addition to refusing to participate, individuals can also become unavailable for a study because researchers lose track of them or don't collect needed contact information. And mortality can actually involve death, in cases in which a study focuses on an at-risk population. For example, a study of health communication that looks at how people with cancer use discussion forums would inevitably struggle with the loss of participants due to the strain of treatment or even death.

Regression Toward the Mean

In general, individuals who report extremely high or low scores on a scale at one point will later report a score that is closer to the average. That is, even without any outside influence, a person who has an extreme score when first observed will have a less extreme score when he or she is later observed. This tendency of individuals with extreme values to later report more moderate scores is known as regression toward the mean. For example, suppose you are studying the effectiveness of an advertisement for a brand of soda. You might think it makes sense to see whether the ads can persuade people who don't already like the soda to drink it and therefore sample only from people who say they "hate" the soda for your study. After viewing the advertisement, some of these people might merely "dislike" the soda. This increase in scores would make it appear as if the advertisement was effective.

But consider what would happen if you did the same study with people who already "loved" the soda. Some of them, after viewing the ad, might reconsider and decide they only "like" the soda. It would look like the average effect of the commercial was actually to create negative feelings, at least among fans of the beverage. Neither of these results would really show the effects of the ad. For the soda haters, the only direction to go was up, and naturally some of them would moderate their opinions on reflection. For the soda lovers, they could only trend downward, and a few would decide that maybe just "liking" was a more accurate reflection of their opinions. Depending on which group you studied, the results of the ad would appear to be the opposite, but, in fact, the ad had no effect. People were just naturally "regressing," or moving back toward a more typical value.

Another example of the tendency toward such regression can be found in studies of educational media. A teacher may think that a video game is a great

concept
→ Unit 5

mean
→ Unit 14

random
assignment
→ Unit 9

prediction
→ Unit 2

way to convey some important concept and assign those scoring at the bottom of the class to play the game as a way to improve their scores. But people with the worst scores in the class were likely to improve anyway. This doesn't mean they will suddenly earn A's, but the odds are that by the next exam, these same individuals will have surpassed some others in the course, regardless of the educational game.

In general, regression toward the mean won't lead to incorrect comparisons between conditions, assuming that random assignment and not prior score is used to put people into treatment groups. But regression can distort the apparent size of effects if individuals on one end of the spectrum are the focus of a study. And if a moderating variable predicts people being very high or low on a scale at time 1, then naturally at time 2 those individuals will move toward one another, regardless of the intervening experience.

Ceiling and Floor Effects

regression toward the mean
→ Unit 9

moderation
→ Unit 2

sample
→ Unit 8

dependent variable
→ Unit 2

Related to regression toward the mean are ceiling and floor effects, both of which make the tendency toward moderate values more pronounced. A ceiling effect describes a situation in which initial scores are already high, making it unlikely they can increase further. For example, suppose you are studying the effects of thin-ideal media on concern with appearance. You might think that it makes sense to focus on people with low self-esteem who already worry about their appearance. But in an experiment, these individuals would be unlikely to show major increases in concern with appearance because they would already be near the top of the scale. In comparison, floor effects involve situations in which initial scores are so low that further decreases are unlikely. Consider again the effects of thin-ideal media. Suppose you hypothesized that exposure to such media reduces willingness to eat unhealthy snacks, and again you focus on people who are already highly concerned with diet. Those individuals would probably already resist the option to choose unhealthy snacks in a laboratory environment. Showing them thin-ideal content could not lower their selection of such snacks.

A further aspect of ceiling and floor effects, beyond reducing the apparent effects of media, is that they can distort tests of moderation. Suppose you are comparing individuals with high and low levels of concern with diet, using eating behaviors as your dependent measure. The low-concern individuals couldn't do much to further reduce their intake, so any effects of media on them would be masked. High-concern individuals may actually be less affected, but because they actually show a bigger decrease in eating, it would appear as if the content had as strong an effect, if not stronger, on this group. Thus, it's important to be sure that all groups within the sample have moderate levels of the dependent variable as it is measured, to allow for variation created by the stimuli.

248

Researcher Bias

double-blind design
→ Unit 9
focus group
→ Unit 12

Any situation in which the actions or attitudes of the researcher distort the results reflects *researcher bias*. This bias does not have to be intentional; a researcher might unknowingly cue participants to act a certain way without meaning to influence the results. This is why double-blind studies are sometimes used, ensuring that both the researchers and the participants are unaware of their specific condition and eliminating the potential for any kind of bias.

Researcher bias can, at times, be intentional. For example, suppose a researcher for a peanut butter company is carrying out a focus group on what consumers want in peanut butter. That researcher might read out a series of traits that he or she says the participants found important, but these traits would be those that best match the chosen brand of peanut butter. The researcher would ignore the participants who said, for example, that they like chunky peanut butter, and instead mention that "many" people said they like smooth peanut butter. Then, having established that the participants "agree" that these traits are important, the researcher would lead the participants to naturally conclude that the chosen brand of peanut butter is best. This result is obviously invalid.

However, unintentional bias is more common and more problematic because the researcher will report results that he or she *believes* are valid. Consider a study of video game violence in which a researcher assigns participants to play either a violent first-person shooter game or a nonviolent puzzle game. The research team may have chosen the games to be as similar as possible, aside from the violence, and designed the study to ensure equal amounts of playing time and other relevant factors. The researcher has to instruct the participants on how to play the game. The researcher may carry his or her bias against violent games into the instructions, telling those in the violent game condition that they must "be violent," "shoot to kill," and "be aggressive." Meanwhile, in the puzzle condition, even though competition is also a factor, the researcher may not use such violent words. At the end of the study, when the participants show greater aggression in the violent game condition, the words used to instruct them may have been a factor, beyond the game itself.

To avoid the possible influence of the researcher, scholars try to take themselves out of the picture. Double-blind studies are one option, but this isn't always possible. Another option is to use scripts to ensure that all interactions with participants are standardized. For example, in the video game study, the researcher could have written a more balanced description of each game and simply handed it to participants, making sure their personal feelings didn't interfere with the instructions. Or he or she could have read that same script aloud if some interaction was required. One of the main benefits of experimental research is the control that investigators have over the experience; creating very specific and detailed instructions helps add to that control and avoid any potential bias.

bias
→ Unit 3

random
assignment
→ Unit 9

random
→ Unit 8

Selection Bias

Any researcher behaviors or design features that lead to the systematic distortion of study results because certain individuals were more likely to be chosen or assigned to specific conditions constitutes *selection bias*. In some cases, this simply reflects the bias created by the sampling approach. For example, suppose you are running a study to examine how people respond to physical contact during interpersonal discussion. You might advertise for people to take part in a "hugging study." Even if you use random assignment, you may still end up with biased results showing unusually positive results for physical contact. If people who don't like being touched saw the study advertisement, they probably chose not to take part. Thus, while you might think your results apply to a diverse population, they would actually be more limited than you expect. As another example, if you are conducting a study on body image and advertise it as such, you might not draw people who feel uncomfortable with their bodies. This could lead to underestimating the effect of any images because of the omission of vulnerable individuals who are likely to be influenced by certain types of images.

In situations in which selection to specific groups is biased, this creates a much stronger effect on the findings. Random assignment should mean that all participants have an equal chance of being in each condition. But when researchers don't pay careful attention to this requirement, they may inadvertently create unequal groups. For example, a researcher may allow a group of friends to sign up together, ending up with a situation in which all those friends are in the same condition. This would violate the independence requirement for randomness. Researchers might even subtly direct participants into specific conditions in ways that align with personal characteristics. For example, in a video game study, a researcher might let inexperienced participants stay in a control condition in which they only watch a game. This would distort the results, creating an apparent difference between groups that is attributable to game experience and not the treatment.

deception
→ Unit 4

pre-test
→ Unit 9

Sensitization

Any time participants change their behavior because pre-testing, direction, or other information changes how they process and respond to stimuli, this represents *sensitization*. For example, consider a study in which researchers want to know how much participants learn from political comedy shows such as *The Daily Show*. They might decide to use a pre-test/post-test design, asking participants how much they know about current political events both before and after viewing the show and comparing them to a control group that watches a show with no political information. Undoubtedly, the group watching *The Daily Show* would perform better, but it's not clear that this reflects the influence of viewing the show. Once participants take the first test of knowledge, they will realize which political issues they are meant to understand. If the test is the same after viewing the show, then they will have made a point of learning the answers. Even if the test changes, they will know that they are supposed to pay attention to political information and feel bad about having struggled on the previous version. Either way, we would expect participants to do better just because they were *sensitized* to the fact that knowing about current events was important to the study. After all, no one likes to feel stupid or ill-informed. When participants are specifically able to get better at answering questions, this is a *testing effect*. For example, if you ask the exact same knowledge questions before and after showing clips of *The Daily Show*, then participants will naturally make sure they remember the information about those questions displayed on the show. But sensitization can also involve other influences. When participants know to pay attention to political information even though the specific questions change, this also reflects sensitization.

Sometimes sensitization simply alerts participants to the purpose of the study, creating demand characteristics and leading participants to want to answer in specific ways. For example, suppose a study is focused on how individuals respond to conversations with people of different races. Further suppose that the researchers give an initial questionnaire that asks participants about their attitudes toward and exposure to people of different races. A participant might realize the study is about race and naturally decide that he or she should be careful to respond more favorably when interacting with someone of a different race. Avoiding sensitization is one reason why deception and not using a pre-test design are both helpful. Telling participants that the study involves a topic other than the actual focus can help ensure that participants don't focus on the aspects of the study related to the actual research question. And not using a pre-test means participants can't use that test to get better at answering questions or learn what they are "supposed" to do, believe, or focus on.

Steps to Success: Avoiding Threats to Validity

While no study can completely anticipate all possible threats to validity, a few easy steps can minimize the most common issues, giving far greater confidence that the results accurately reflect both the true relationship and effect size for a typical population.

1. Select the most representative sample possible, in a way that gives as little information about the study design as you can. While experiments tend to focus on internal validity, many issues with validity can be minimized by selecting a diverse

pool of individuals and avoiding any cues that would sensitize them to the study design and goals.

2. Be sure to follow strict random assignment procedures. Most concerns with internal validity can be solved simply by making sure that every participant has an equal chance to be assigned to each condition. Even if participants are sensitized, atypical, or at the extreme end of the scale, the internal validity threats these issues represent are largely solved through random assignment. Because all groups are equal, the distortion caused by these factors will not affect the between-group comparisons. You may still have an incorrect estimate of effect sizes or miss subtle effects, but the results generally will be more valid.

3. Minimize differences between conditions. A critical aspect of experimental research is that the only variation between conditions should be the actual independent variable. If showing people media clips, for example, it's important that things such as length, content, volume, screen size, and all other features not directly related to the variable remain constant. Avoid using different rooms for different conditions, for example. Ensure that if data collection is occurring at multiple times of day or in multiple locations, each time and location is used repeatedly and randomly linked to all possible conditions. Consider designs in which a pool of individuals participating at one time can be randomly assigned to all possible conditions instead of placing groups of people in a single condition.

4. Avoid pre-testing or use a Solomon four-group design. Although it can be tempting to use pre-tests to better quantify change in individuals, this is rarely necessary with a true experimental design. If a pre-test must be used, consider a four-group design, in which a non-pre-test group can be compared with a group that took a pre-test. If a pre-test must be used without such a comparison, be sure that the questions do not directly measure those used in the post-test, and do not directly cue participants to the study topic. If consistent measures are needed, administer the pre-test far in advance of the main study and mask the relationship between the two.

Activities

Activity 9A: Designing an Experiment

See terms: experiment; stimulus; strengths of experiments.

For this activity, you will need to start by developing a research question you would like to answer or a hypothesis you would like to test. Once you have done so, your objective is to develop a basic experiment that would allow you to answer your research question (or test your hypothesis). Specifically, consider the following questions as you work to develop your experiment:

- What materials would you need to serve as the stimulus? How difficult would it be to create them?
- How many treatment groups would you need to answer your question?
- How would you address ecological validity?
- What things would you need to measure to assess your dependent variables?
- How would you recruit participants for the study?
- What challenges would you face in carrying out this study?

Activity 9B: Critiquing an Experiment

See terms: experiment; strengths of experiments.

For this activity, you will need to locate a research article that uses an experimental design. Once you have read the article, you should locate the key parts of an experiment as they are discussed in the article. Use the following questions to guide your assessment of this article:

- Why was an experiment an appropriate method for this particular research problem?
- To what extent do the authors address the strengths and weaknesses of the experimental design?
- What are the biggest strengths of the design as carried out by the authors in this article?
- What do you see as the biggest weaknesses with the design? What might you have done differently if you were conducting this study?

Activity 9C: Threats to Validity

See terms: external validity, internal validity.

For this activity, you should identify the particular threat—or threats—to validity described and determine how you would minimize that threat. The table shown next lists a series of scenarios describing threats to validity in the left column. In the space next to each scenario, identify the primary threat described and indicate how you would go about dealing with that particular threat.

You are conducting an experiment designed to assess the effectiveness of a 30-second radio commercial on attitudes toward a local nonprofit. To do so, you have all of the participants report to a large classroom where you play the spot over the speaker system and then have them fill out a post-test.	
You are conducting an experiment that tests whether fitness training affects performance in public speaking courses. The fitness training program you have devised is quite rigorous, and more than 50 of the 100 people you recruited for the treatment group dropped out of the study after the first training session.	
You are conducting an experiment that assesses whether participating in a workshop on building teamwork skills improves the performance of work groups. To assess this, you sit in on the meetings of the groups to observe whether the group members are truly behaving in the ways the workshop demonstrated they should.	

Activity 9D: Developing Stimulus Materials

See terms: experiment; stimulus.

The objective of this activity is to develop stimulus materials that you will then pilot test to determine whether they are working as expected. Specifically, your goal is to determine whether characteristics of news headlines (either for printed newspaper stories or online news stories) affect responses to the articles. For instance, you might assess the difference between headlines that are biased and those that are more objective. There are many possibilities, so be creative! Use the following prompts to complete this activity:

Part 1: Developing stimulus materials

- What aspect of news headlines would you like to manipulate? Why?
- How many variations will you need? Why?
- As you develop your idea, consider looking at other research that has covered a similar topic. What approach was used by those researchers?

Part 2: Pilot testing stimulus materials

- Once you have developed your stimulus materials, you will need to create post-test measures to assess responses to the various manipulations you have created.
- What questions or other measures will you need to use to assess whether the different treatment conditions resulted in any meaningful differences?
- Based on your pilot test, what changes will you need to make?

Activity 9E: Random Assignment

See terms: group equivalence, random assignment, random number table.

For this activity, you will practice using random assignment to achieve group equivalence. We have provided two research scenarios as well as a pool of participants who can be used in these research studies. For each scenario, devise an approach to selecting participants that will maximize the likelihood of group equivalence. Descriptive information about each participant is provided so that you can check afterward how effective your approach was. However, keep in mind that such information would not always be available to you before the study begins!

Scenario 1: This experiment is designed to assess the effectiveness of personalized feedback in performance on public presentations. There are two conditions: (1) a group that receives personalized feedback about their practice performance (e.g., "I really liked the introduction and how you used the example of your family"); and (2) a group that receives feedback that is not personalized in any way (e.g., "I really liked the introduction"). There is no control group.

Scenario 2: This experiment is designed to determine whether the use of color in presentation slides affects retention. There are three conditions: (1) a group that sees slides using a limited color palette of two colors; (2) a group that sees a larger color palette of four colors; and (3) a group that sees an even larger color palette of six colors.

Participant pool (50 total; 25 male and 25 female)

Abbie (F, 21)	Bonnie (F, 31)	Donnie (M, 20)	Greg (M, 22)	Larry (M, 48)
Al (M, 21)	Bort (M, 20)	Doug (M, 53)	Gregor (M, 21)	Lisa (F, 47)
Allie (F, 23)	Brody (M, 44)	Drew (M, 21)	Heidi (F, 49)	Martin (M, 51)
Annie (F, 19)	Carl (M, 31)	Ella (F, 18)	Henrietta (F, 20)	Merry (F, 49)
Art (M, 27)	Carly (F, 52)	Ellie (F, 33)	Hilda (F, 19)	Nancy (F, 21)
Arthur (M, 52)	Chuck (M, 22)	Fred (M, 29)	Ingrid (F, 22)	Neo (M, 20)
Bart (M, 19)	Connie (F, 29)	Frida (F, 50)	Jim (M, 19)	Oscar (M, 19)
Bill (M, 47)	Dan (M, 49)	Fritz (M, 19)	Joy (F, 20)	Paul (M, 48)
Billie (F, 51)	Dana (F, 19)	Gary (M, 51)	Kelci (F, 22)	Reba (F, 19)
Bonita (F, 49)	Daryl (M, 21)	Gina (F, 49)	Kelly (F, 21)	Sara (F, 21)

References

Grabe, S., Ward, L. M., & Hyde, J. S. (2008). The role of the media in body image concerns among women: A meta-analysis of experimental and correlational studies. *Psychological Bulletin*, *134*(3), 460–476. doi:10.1037/0033-2909.134.3.460

Harrison, K., Taylor, L. D., & Marske, A. L. (2006). Women's and men's eating behavior following exposure to ideal-body images and text. *Communication Research*, *33*(6), 507–529. doi:10.1177/0093650206293247

Suggested Readings for Further Exploration of Unit 9 Topics

Examples

Berger, C. R., & Di Battista, P. (1993). Communication failure and plan adaptation: If at first you don't succeed, say it louder and slower. *Communication Monographs*, *60*(3), 220–238. doi:10.1080/03637759309376310

Mook, D. (2004). *Classic experiments in psychology*. Westport, CT: Greenwood Press.

Sengupta, J., & Dahl, D. W. (2008). Gender-related reactions to gratuitous sex appeals in advertising. *Journal of Consumer Psychology*, *18*(1), 62–78. doi:10.1016/j.jcps.2007.10.010

Velez, J. A., Mahood, C., Ewoldsen, D. R., & Moyer-Gusé, E. (2014). Ingroup versus outgroup conflict in the context of violent video game play: The effect of cooperation on increased helping and decreased aggression. *Communication Research*, *41*(5), 607–626. doi:10.1177/0093650212456202

Advanced Discussion

Barabas, J., & Jerit, J. (2010). Are survey experiments externally valid? *American Political Science Review*, *104*(2), 226–242. doi:10.1017/S0003055410000092

Druckman, J. N., Green, D. P., Kuklinski, J. H., & Lupia, A. (2006). The growth and development of experimental research in political science. *American Political Science Review*, *100*(4), 627–635. doi:10.1017/S0003055406062514

Dunning, T. (2008). Improving causal inference strengths and limitations of natural experiments. *Political Research Quarterly*, *61*(2), 282–293. doi:10.1177/1065912907306470

McDermott, R. (2002). Experimental methodology in political science. *Political Analysis*, *10*(4), 325–342. doi:10.1093/pan/10.4.325

Tao, C. C., & Bucy, E. P. (2007). Conceptualizing media stimuli in experimental research: Psychological versus attribute-based definitions. *Human Communication Research*, *33*(4), 397–426. doi:10.1111/j.1468–2958.2007.00305.x

Thorson, E., Wicks, R., & Leshner, G. (2012). Experimental methodology in journalism and mass communication research. *Journalism & Mass Communication Quarterly*, *89*(1), 112–124. doi:10.1177/1077699011430066

unit 10

survey research

Imagine that you are working for a local radio station. Management is considering a format change that would radically alter the number of employees and the budget for the station. If the format change is successful, it will be a boon to management and employees alike. However, if it fails, then the station will go under, and everyone loses. Therefore, management wants to be sure they are making the right decision. It is important that management be certain that the format change will be embraced not only by listeners of the current format but also by the community at large. You have been tasked with developing a research study to determine whether the format change will work. What kinds of questions will you ask? Who will you ask the questions? In short, what is the best approach to solve this problem?

An appropriate approach in this case would be to use survey research because it is designed specifically to draw conclusions about a population based on data collected from a sample. Although it would certainly be beneficial to complement your survey approach with other methodologies (remember the importance of triangulation!), conducting a survey would likely provide station management with a large amount of information that could be used to assess the viability of the format change. In this unit, you will learn about the basic types of surveys, common approaches to gathering survey data, and the differences between cross-sectional and longitudinal designs, providing you with the necessary tools to design and carry out survey research.

Survey Research

Survey research involves asking questions of individuals selected from a population (normally through sampling) to measure relationships between variables. Unlike experiments, surveys do not include any manipulation of variables or random assignment. Therefore, the primary value of surveys is their ability to accurately describe a population and the relationships between variables found in that population. Thus, the representativeness of the sample is especially important to surveys, as they are ill-suited to testing causality and instead are valued for their external validity.

Surveys are commonly encountered in the form of opinion **polls**, including **tracking polls,** which are commonly employed during elections. Surveys are widely used because they provide a good way to accurately assess patterns of attitudes and behaviors in a selected population quickly and at a reasonable cost. For example, a survey would be a great way to evaluate how many people watched a new television program and how much they enjoyed it. A television channel might use such information to decide whether to keep a show on the air, as well as whether changes to a show might make it more profitable. Indeed, television ratings from Nielsen are a form of survey research, providing an accurate sample of television viewers and indicating what portion of them

population
→ Unit 8

sampling
→ Unit 8

relationship
→ Unit 2

variable
→ Unit 2

experiments
→ Unit 9

**random
assignment**
→ Unit 9

**representative
sample**
→ Unit 8

causality
→ Unit 2

watched a particular show. Advertisers use these surveys to decide whether to buy time on a specific program, as the survey tells them not only how many people are watching but also what kinds of people watch various sorts of programs.

Several aspects of surveys help categorize their techniques and goals. First, surveys are often divided between **self-administered surveys**, which involve presenting participants with a printed questionnaire and having them record their own answers, and **interview-style surveys**, in which trained members of the research team ask participants questions from the questionnaire and record the answers given to them. In the latter, it is important to establish **rapport**, but the chance to forge such a connection also offers considerable benefits. Interviews tend to be conducted either **face-to-face surveys** or through the **telephone surveys**, while self-administered surveys are typically conducted through the **mail survey** or the **Internet survey. Internet panels** help researchers identify representative polls of individuals with the interest and technology to answer questions online. Regardless of the format details, an effective questionnaire is important, so researchers should also consider the effective use of contingency questions, which filter respondents into relevant follow-up questions, and are designed to avoid response sets.

Another key distinction in surveys involves time. The most common design for survey research is a **cross-sectional design**, in which the researcher pulls a random sample from a population and administers the questionnaire to those participants. These one-shot survey designs are limited in their ability to assess causality. Because of this, other survey designs known as **longitudinal designs**—including **cohort**, **trend**, and **panel** designs—were developed to allow scholars to track whether answers change over time. These vary in terms of whether specific individuals are recruited to take part in multiple studies or whether broader pools of individuals are used to represent specific groups at multiple points in time.

Polls

One of the most common survey formats is the poll. Indeed, there are no strict criteria that differentiate a poll from other types of surveys, although, in general, a "poll" refers to a survey that samples from a large, geographically defined population and primarily measures the overall distribution of public opinion. Polling is especially common during elections. For example, as a single question—candidate preference—is an important and easily measured concept. Polls can capture a snapshot of opinion at a specific moment. They are also a great way to evaluate changes in opinion over time using longitudinal designs, in which the same question is asked of equivalent groups of people at multiple points in time.

Often, the questionnaire used to collect data for a public opinion poll is short and focused on just a few opinion questions related to the selected issue.

These polls are often conducted through telephone interviews over a short time frame, so keeping them simple and brief allows researchers to have a reasonable sample size. For polls to be useful indicators of the public's attitudes and beliefs, they must employ probability sampling techniques—otherwise, the data collected would not be representative of the population being studied. Because polls rarely focus on relationships between variables, having a sample that represents the basic distribution of opinion is especially important.

Quick polls can be useful for businesses such as radio and television stations to assess audience satisfaction with their product. For example, a radio station might conduct a poll of its listener base to determine what listeners like best about the station, as well as what they would like to see changed. Such a poll could also reveal the most common times that people listen, as well as valuable demographic information about the listening audience.

Tracking Poll

In some cases, researchers are explicitly interested in tracking opinion on an issue within a short period of time. To address this, researchers may carry out a series of small polls at regular intervals. These types of polls, known as *tracking polls*, allow for a closer look at shifts in opinion on an issue over a brief period of time. When firms report the results of tracking polls, they often combine the results of the last few "snapshots," or daily samples, to give a more representative picture of opinion thanks to the larger sample size. Small changes between individual samples may not be meaningful because of their limited statistical power, but some pundits and candidates still pay attention to these minor shifts. Because the window of time is typically short and the need for immediate results is high, tracking polls are often conducted using telephone interviews. However, in some cases, Internet panels are used because they also allow for quick access to large and geographically diverse populations.

questionnaire design
→ Unit 7

telephone survey
→ Unit 10

sample size
→ Unit 8

probability sampling
→ Unit 8

relationship
→ Unit 2

variable
→ Unit 2

representative sample
→ Unit 8

Internet panels
→ Unit 10

Research in Depth: Interpreting Polls

The confidence level and confidence interval are often encountered in media reports of public opinion polls, especially during elections. You have most likely seen this in the form of the "margin of error" reported in many polling stories. However, this information is often hidden or poorly explained in such stories. For example, the *New York Times* regularly sponsors polls related to presidential performance or "approval ratings." In one such poll (Stolberg & Kopicki, 2013), the newspaper reported that President Barack Obama received the approval of 42 percent of Americans. The reporters further noted that this was a meaningful increase from a previous poll that showed just 37 percent approval. But what does that 5 percent increase really mean? The process of estimation gives us a way to understand it better.

For the *Times* story in question, the details of the poll are not included in the main text. Instead, the newspaper provided a sidebar with details about "How the poll was conducted." The *Times* tends to be more detailed about its polling than most news outlets, but finding the details about the margin of error is still complicated. This sidebar indicated a 3 percent margin of error in "19 cases out of 20"—that is, with a 95 percent confidence level. Based on that, we can construct appropriate confidence intervals.

For the December 2013 poll described earlier, this means that our confidence interval, with a 95 percent confidence level, would be between 39 percent and 45 percent. Assuming the earlier poll employed a similar sampling procedure, the confidence interval for that poll would be between 34 percent and 40 percent. Right away, you should notice that the two confidence intervals overlap. It is entirely possible, although unlikely, that both samples were drawn from identical populations that both approved of President Obama at a rate of 40 percent. Moreover, as the sidebar notes, the percentages given for subgroups, such as younger Americans or just men, are even less precise, as the corresponding sample sizes are smaller. Comparisons between groups or between surveys for those groups have even more potential error.

This does not mean we should conclude that the president's approval rating did not change. But we should be cautious not to assume that it changed—an insight the reporter missed in this case. This is a common issue in reporting on polls. Small differences between polls or between subgroups within polls may simply reflect sampling error. Other polls taken at the same time as the *New York Times* poll didn't indicate the exact same level of approval. While some of these differences may reflect problems with the questions used or the sample collected, they may also simply reflect random sampling error. Avoid the temptation to read too much into small variations in poll findings. When you better understand the estimation process, you will learn to distinguish between meaningful differences and minor shifts that are likely to occur by chance.

---

variable
→ Unit 2

sample
→ Unit 8

Cross-Sectional Design

Most studies do not factor in time. Instead, these *cross-sectional* surveys simply measure variables for the participants from one time period. This means that once individuals from this sample participate in the study, they are not contacted again. Further, it is likely that the specific questions used in the questionnaire will not be used again either, although they may inform the design of future questionnaires. Cross-sectional studies are so named because they allow for a one-time look at the attitudes, beliefs, or behaviors of a population—a "slice" across time at that moment. For example, researchers might be interested in the public's response to new trends in reporting and thus conduct a poll assessing attitudes toward reporters using Twitter and Facebook. If the questions and sample used to carry out this poll are only used on a one-time basis, then it is a cross-sectional design.

Cross-sectional designs are limited in that assessments about causality cannot easily be made using such an approach. However, they are quite valuable when it comes to describing populations and understanding how a population felt—or what they were typically doing—at a given point in time. Further, the resources associated with conducting a cross-sectional study are less intensive than they are with longitudinal studies.

<aside>
questionnaire design
→ Unit 7

population
→ Unit 8

poll
→ Unit 10
</aside>

Research in Depth: Using Polls to Track Public Opinion

Polls can be invaluable resources when it comes to political, economic, or industry decision making. They can also provide a picture of how attitudes and beliefs have changed (or remained the same, in some cases) over time. For example, consider Americans' support for capital punishment. In 2004, poll data revealed that 64 percent (+/– 4 percent) of Americans supported capital punishment. In 2012, a *USA Today*/Gallup Poll found support to be 63 percent (+/– 4 percent). The highest level of support was found in 2007 (69 percent) and the lowest in 2011 (61 percent). It is reasonable to conclude, then, that support for capital punishment is relatively stable and hovers at just above 60 percent.

Of course, not all attitudes are so stable. Consider shifts in attitudes toward same-sex marriage over time. In 2006, 42 percent (+/– 4 percent) of Americans thought that marriages between same-sex couples should be recognized as valid. In 2009, support had dipped to 40 percent. However, support began to climb after that point, rising to 50 percent by 2012 and to 54 percent (+/– 4 percent) according to a Gallup Poll conducted in 2013.

Finally, polls assessing attitudes toward legalization of marijuana have shown an even more dramatic shift. In 1995, only 25 percent of Americans thought that marijuana should be made legal. However, support has climbed steadily since then, reaching 36 percent in 2005 and 58 percent (+/– 4 percent) according to a Gallup Poll from 2013. Note: Data for these examples are taken from the website PollingReport.com, a good resource for poll data of all kinds.

Interview-Style Survey

One of the two primary approaches to collecting data using a survey question-naire is to have a researcher or research assistant ask the questions and record the responses given by the survey respondent. In this case, the researcher is using an *interview* approach to data collection, as opposed to the other common approach, a self-administered survey. Interview-style questionnaires are com-mon when collecting data face-to-face or by telephone. A common face-to-face survey approach is to use what is called a "mall-intercept" design, in which people who are shopping at a mall are randomly selected and then approached by a clipboard-wielding interviewer.

Interview-style surveys often allow for good rapport-building and for probing, which is used to get more detailed information from study partici-pants. Building rapport can be an essential tool in recruiting participants and getting them to complete the survey. As such, response rates are often higher for interview-style surveys than for self-administered ones. Further, because of the presence of an interviewer to clarify things, researchers can be more confident that questions were interpreted in the way they intended. Finally, interview surveys allow researchers to collect additional observational data during the data collection process. For example, researchers might be inter-ested in assessing the sincerity of the answers given by the participant. In such a case, the interviewer could observe the tone of voice, whether the respondent appeared to be paying attention, and facial expressions that could indicate distraction, dissatisfaction, or boredom. Although these kinds of assessments are not used often, they do hint at the possibilities researchers have when con-ducting interviews as opposed to self-administered surveys.

Although there are a number of advantages to interview-style surveys, there are also some disadvantages. First, interviewers must be compensated, adding to the cost of any project. Additionally, using interviewers adds a time cost as well because they need to be trained to improve reliability in the administration of questionnaires. That is, each respondent should have a nearly identical experience. If one interviewer is exceptionally friendly and another is more subdued, this could have an effect on respondents. The excep-tionally friendly interviewer might generate longer responses to open-ended responses. This is problematic because now a new variable has been added to the mix—interviewer friendliness. Therefore, the training of interviewers should involve going over procedures for interacting with respondents, using probes, and maintaining objectivity and professionalism. Second, the presence of interviewers can affect respondents in that they may answer some kinds of questions differently in the presence of the interviewer. This can be a function of a lack of anonymity as well as social desirability effects that can occur when participants feel embarrassed, shy, or concerned in some way about how their responses will be judged.

Voices from Industry

Erin Hyland—User Experience Leader
(UX Lead Designer)

Erin's official title is "User Experience Leader" (UX Lead Designer) at a marketing- and technology-focused professional service firm called Trellist Inc., headquartered in Wilmington, DE (https://trellist.com/). This requires her to be a strategic thinker, consultant, and problem solver who works closely with digital marketing, brand marketing, clients, and product teams to create world-class digital experiences.

Why are good research skills important to your field?

Without research, the arguments I make as an interpreter and defender of a user's experience with a digital resource (like a website or mobile app) could be interpreted as my own preference. I need to research to generate new ideas, define best practices, and identify industry standards. Before we develop the UX strategy in a website redesign or app under development, we perform a competitive analysis of peers in the industry. This means we gain inspiration of both what to do and what not to do concerning content development and functionality. We also study the metrics of their current site or app usage to gain insights into how users currently use the site to identify red flags or areas for improvement. Finally, we also interview both stakeholders and users to derive business needs and pinpoint problem areas.

What specific method or methods do you use or encounter most?

Content audit, competitive analysis, and stakeholder and user interviews.

Can you name some specific instances for which you have used data collected from research?

For specific examples, we've made "calls to action" buttons on our website more pronounced, created new content avenues and adapted our navigational menus based on user feedback, analytics, and analysis. By noticing patterns on other sites or gaps in current usage, we're able to generate possible solutions to the newly identified problems we uncovered in our research.

What are one or two pieces of advice or insights you would give about research to students in a communication research methods course?

Take your time; it's not wasted. Be patient. Keep digging. Go beyond the expected. Take lots of notes. Use research to problem identify not problem solve.

Face-to-Face Survey

One of two primary interview-style approaches to survey research, *face-to-face* interviews involve the researcher and the survey respondent directly interacting with one another in the same place. The primary advantages of this approach are that the interviewer can develop strong rapport, interpret nonverbal communication for contextual data, and provide clarification or probing when needed. Therefore, face-to-face interviews can be longer or be used with populations for which it is hard to obtain responses or a high completion rate from participants. Although the U.S. Census uses a self-administered questionnaire for most respondents, those who are reluctant to participate are often contacted through face-to-face interviewing, which allows the researchers to explain the purpose of the process and to be sure the answers given are as valid as possible.

This approach has also been used in consumer and market research when targeting shoppers through mall-intercept surveys. Although face-to-face interviews typically involve the interviewer writing down responses from the participant, smart devices allow researcher to add some interesting elements to their research. For instance, using a smart or mobile device would allow the researcher to directly input responses into a database, thus eliminating the step of data entry. Additionally, use of these devices can also allow researchers to incorporate audio and visual elements into the data collection experience. For instance, perhaps a researcher is interested in getting feedback on how a new movie is being marketed. They could use their smart device to show the movie trailer and then enter responses to questions about the trailer directly into the device.

Although there are advantages to the face-to-face interview approach, a potential concern with face-to-face interviews is that respondents might become self-conscious about difficult, sensitive, or highly personal questions because their anonymity is not protected. In such cases, researchers should clarify the procedures they will use to ensure confidentiality as a means to protect the respondents' privacy.

Finally, a primary hindrance to face-to-face interviews is that they are resource intensive and geographically limited. Specifically, they require extensive training, there are high financial costs associated with sending interviewers out into the field, and interviewers working in the field face potential dangers. Further, unlike telephone interviews, the researchers are tied to a particular location, as the cost of sending interviewers all across the country (or the world) would be incredibly high. A few interviewers working in a phone lab could contact respondents across the world in one night, whereas face-to-face interviewers would be limited to a single town or neighborhood.

Telephone Survey

Unlike face-to-face interviews, in which the interviewer and interview subject are in the same exact place and can physically see each other, *telephone interviews* provide a greater sense of privacy while still allowing the interviewer to maximize rapport and engage in probing. Telephone interviews are a common approach for tracking polls, and they are frequently used in public opinion research because they can be carried out quickly, allow for access to a geographically diverse sample, and have relatively low costs once the initial investment of phones and space is covered. For example, a small call center employing roughly 10 people could make hundreds, if not thousands, of calls in a single night for a brief questionnaire. Because of the shortened time period and access to large, geographically diverse samples, telephone survey centers are often used to conduct polls during election season, when the frequency of such research increases dramatically.

Despite these advantages, there are some potential downsides to telephone interviews. First, some people do not use traditional landlines, leading to a rise in cell-phone-only households. Often these telephone numbers are not included in sampling frames. Second, with the advent of technologies such as caller ID and call blocking, some people will not answer calls that come from survey research firms or numbers they do not recognize. These two concerns call into question the validity of the samples that telephone-only approaches produce. For instance, during the 2012 election season, a common concern voiced by researchers was whether the samples for the many polls that were conducted excluded cell phone users and therefore whether telephone interviews were still a valid approach. In general, however, the data seem to suggest that telephone interviews remain a valid way of measuring public opinion and conducting research and, overall, they were reasonably successful in predicting the results of both the 2008 and 2012 presidential elections. Of course, researchers should continue to develop ways to address the emerging concerns of telephone interviews so that they remain a viable approach to collecting data from large, geographically diverse samples.

privacy
→ Unit 4

rapport
→ Unit 10

tracking poll
→ Unit 10

sample
→ Unit 8

questionnaire design
→ Unit 7

polls
→ Unit 10

cell-phone-only household
→ Unit 10

validity
→ Unit 6

prediction
→ Unit 3

sampling frame
→ Unit 8

Cell-Phone-Only Household

As a result of recent technological innovations, some people have moved away from having traditional landlines for their telephone service; these households use only cellular phones. Many of the new phone numbers and extensions resulting from the expansion of cellular phone use are not included in databases and are often unlisted. Additionally, while computer-based auto-dialers can be used to reach landlines, the law generally forbids using such techniques to reach cell numbers. As a result of this, many cell-phone-only households have fallen outside the reach of pollsters and other survey researchers, raising concerns about the validity of the samples collected if they do not include cell-phone-only households. To address this concern, some researchers have explicitly targeted cell-phone-only households or have taken steps to ensure the inclusion of such households in samples alongside traditional landline households. Such techniques have allowed researchers to explore differences between these households and address the impact of new communication technologies on survey research.

validity
→ Unit 6

sample
→ Unit 8

Research in Depth: The Growth of Cell Phones

Not surprisingly, researchers who study public opinion and carry out surveys have focused attention on the growth of cell-phone-only households for at least a decade. In 2007, for example, the journal *Public Opinion Quarterly* published a special issue dedicated to the topic. Among the studies was a piece by a number of prominent members of opinion research organizations (Keeter, Kennedy, Clark, Tompson, & Mokrzycki, 2007). Their findings suggested that while those without cell phones differed in important ways, the absence of cell-phone-only households could be compensated for through weighting. That is, although certain groups were less prevalent than they would be in the population, by counting the input of members of these groups more than the average response, the overall survey findings remained valid. However, they also suggested that for certain subgroups, the quality of estimates was lower.

Similarly, Link, Battaglia, Frankel, Osborn, and Mokdad (2007) found that weighting could partially compensate for important demographic differences, but certain adverse health behaviors would be underestimated in a study that relied only upon landline respondents. Both studies noted that the shift to cell phones was likely to increase, and in 2010, Mokrzycki, Keeter, and Kennedy reported that evidence from the 2008 election showed a major increase in cell-only households and differences in voter preferences among those relying on cell phones, regardless of age. That same year, Peytchev, Carley-Baxter, and Black (2010) reported that adjusting estimates based on weighting not only failed to compensate for certain flawed estimates but actually made them worse. In short, as the number of people relying on cell phones has grown, it seems the differences between those individuals and those who still or only have landlines have expanded as well.

Of course, survey researchers can contact cell phones just as they dial landlines. But laws prevent them from using computerized dialing programs, which are important to the efficient use of random-digit dialing. In the 2012 election, many polls did include a portion of individuals who relied on cell phones, but they often contacted relatively few such individuals and heavily weighted their responses, increasing sampling error. And cell phone owners may be more reluctant to complete surveys because of the cost.

Thus, researchers have begun searching for alternative ways to reach diverse and representative random samples other than random-digit dialing before so many people switch to cell phones that building a representative sample becomes impossible. One option was described by Guterbock, Diop, Ellis, Holmes, and Le (2011), who combined sampling from electronic databases of addresses along with dialing known cell exchanges, reporting a reasonably representative sample that could be obtained at lower cost than other approaches. Similarly, Link and Lai (2011) reported that targeting addresses that researchers were unable to match with telephone numbers through the mail was a reasonable way to find and contact cell-phone-only households without simply dialing random numbers. Thus, while researchers and pollsters continue to worry about the impact of cell-phone-only households, they are also devising new ways to obtain reliable and reasonably inexpensive samples that still produce representative samples.

Rapport

A positive connection and interaction between the researcher and the research participant is referred to as *rapport*. Rapport is a key part of data collection procedures for survey research as well as many qualitative approaches, including focus groups and qualitative interviews. Researchers strive to develop rapport with study participants because this can elicit better data. First, rapport is important in keeping the response rate and completion rate (i.e., whether participants complete the entire survey) high. Participants who feel connected or even obligated to the interviewer tend to want to give honest answers and address every question. Producing rapport is especially important for studies in which participants will be contacted again, such as a panel study, or when the instrument is especially long. Convincing people to stick with a 60-minute survey or complete another interview weeks or months later is especially challenging, so any connection that the researcher can forge helps.

Second, better rapport can help participants feel more comfortable answering personal or revealing questions. Often, more difficult or highly personal questions will be asked later in the questionnaire, after the researcher has had time to develop a greater level of rapport with the participant. Because ensuring higher response rates and more honest answers is important to producing valid data, researchers take many steps to foster rapport. They may ask participants their first names and then call them by those names, or they may share their own names and goals early in the interview process. However, it is important that researchers not go too far in establishing rapport. Researchers who become too friendly with participants risk violating ethical standards or actually reducing honesty, as some participants may not want to share personal details with someone they feel knows them personally.

qualitative versus quantitative
→ Unit 2

focus group
→ Unit 12

depth interviews
→ Unit 12

response rate
→ Unit 8

panel
→ Unit 10

questionnaire design
→ Unit 7

validity
→ Unit 6

interview-style survey
→ Unit 10

Reflect & React: Building Rapport

In any type of interview research, it is important to build rapport with the interview subject. In most cases, particularly with survey research, you must do so quickly. Consider a situation that is common to survey research: you call someone on the phone who does not know you, is not expecting your call, and is likely busy dealing with issues at home. You have a very limited window of time in which to establish rapport with this person and ensure that they convert from a hang-up to "Yes, I would like to answer your questions!" Perhaps you have been the person at home receiving the unexpected phone call or even the person making the phone call. In either case, think about what strategies you might use to quickly develop positive rapport with the prospective respondent. Specifically, consider the following questions: What kind of greeting should you use? What kind of tone to your voice would be most effective? What information is most important to say about who you are, who you represent, and what the survey is about?

validity
→ Unit 6

rapport
→ Unit 10

sample
→ Unit 8

incentive
→ Unit 8

response rate
→ Unit 8

panel
→ Unit 10

incentive
→ Unit 8

interview-style survey
→ Unit 10

Self-Administered Survey

Unlike interview-style surveys, *self-administered surveys* rely on the participants to complete the questionnaire on their own without any assistance. The two most common forms of self-administered surveys are mail surveys and, more recently, Internet surveys. Mail surveys are the more traditional format and ask participants to fill out responses directly on the paper questionnaire. Internet surveys allow for greater flexibility in design and can include the use of filter and contingency questions more easily than mail surveys. Of course, in both cases, the researcher must take care to use clear instructions and descriptions throughout. This is necessary to ensure the validity of responses because the researcher is not there to clarify any questions or address any issues. Further, clear and concise wording is essential in developing positive rapport to keep respondents from failing to complete the questionnaire. If respondents are confused or annoyed, they are less inclined to complete a questionnaire. If they do continue, they may give meaningless answers because they do not understand the wording or intent of the question.

One of the primary advantages of self-administered surveys is that they require few resources relative to interviews. Therefore, a large-scale national survey can be carried out with a fairly small group of researchers. In some cases, even one researcher working alone can conduct a mail or Internet survey using a national sample. In the case of a mail survey, the only cost beyond obtaining the sample from a sampling firm is the paper for printing and the postage—although incentives to offset low response rates can add to the cost. For Internet surveys, the primary cost is the survey software (although inexpensive options are available) and the server space—as well as purchasing a sample or panel.

There are two primary downsides of self-administered surveys. First, response rates tend to be low. It is easy for an envelope received in the mail that contains a survey to be discarded because it looks like junk mail or can easily be forgotten once it is filed away. This is also true of Internet surveys—contacting strangers by e-mail can result in your message being moved to the junk mail folder. Second, responses often take longer to return, particularly for mail surveys. For example, researchers can conduct a phone survey of hundreds of people (or more) in one night and have the data by the end of the night. With a mail survey, it will take a few days for the survey to get to the respondents, a few days for them to answer it, and then a few days for it to be returned. To address these concerns, researchers can use phone calls as a way to remind respondents to complete the questionnaires and can also use telephone contact as a recruiting tool so that participants know that the questionnaire is on its way—but both of these eliminate some of the benefits of mail surveys and significantly increase the cost.

Continuing with the example from the beginning of this unit, a radio station that is considering a format change but is short on resources might think about a self-administered survey. In this case, there is little up-front cost aside from designing the questionnaire and potentially paying for postage or an incentive of some sort. Such an approach could be desirable in this case because it would allow the station to reach a large portion of the audience it is trying to reach while minimizing the time and monetary cost needed to do so.

Internet Survey

Internet surveys are a fairly recent format for self-administered surveys that use a Web-based interface to collect responses from survey participants. An advantage of Internet surveys is that they can be highly interactive, allowing the researcher to include a number of different question formats. This allows researchers to include images or video clips to evaluate, such as sample logos or advertisements from a company. Internet surveys also allow for streamlining through the use of automated filter questions. This can help save respondents time in completing the questionnaire. Further, data collected through Internet surveys are automatically collected in a database, allowing researchers to avoid the additional step of data entry. Finally, Internet surveys provide a strong sense of anonymity for the research participant while also letting participants fill out the questionnaire in the privacy of their own home.

Of course, there are also some disadvantages to Internet surveys. First, the response rate can be low because of advanced junk mail filters and because it

self-administered survey
→ Unit 10

filter and contingency questions
→ Unit 7

questionnaire design
→ Unit 7

anonymity
→ Unit 4

response rate
→ Unit 8

sample
→ Unit 8

is easy for participants to get distracted by their surroundings (e.g., the TV could be on while filling out the questionnaire). This latter aspect can also result in lower completion rates. Second, the researcher cannot be absolutely certain who filled out the questionnaire. Although most people are honest and trustworthy, there is still always a chance that the person filling out the questionnaire is not the intended respondent. Finally, differences across Web browsers and operating systems can affect the usability of the Internet survey by respondents.

Such problems can have a negative effect on confidence in the data collected. For instance, consider your work for the radio station in conducting a survey on a prospective format change. If the response rate is low or a number of questions were not answered clearly or completely, your confidence in the overall responses would be lessened. For example, what if a large percentage of people left the following question blank: "What format would you most like our station to change to?" You would have very little indication of what to recommend to management regarding the change they should make. Therefore, in using any self-administered survey, it is important to be clear and thoughtful in writing questionnaire items and to take additional steps to keep response rate high.

Internet Panels

sample size
→ Unit 8

sampling frame
→ Unit 8

quota sampling
→ Unit 8

mortality
→ Unit 9

representative sample
→ Unit 8

In some cases, study participants are recruited to enroll in long-running research programs in which they are asked to participate multiple times in either the same study or a variety of studies. When such samples are collected and recruited through the Internet, they are referred to as *Internet panels*. A way to think about these panels is that they are stocked with people who have already indicated a willingness to participate in research and are simply waiting for these opportunities to come along. Often times sampling firms or survey research platforms will provide access to these Internet panels. The researcher pays a fee per participant to the sampling firm and the participants themselves get a small percentage of that fee for participating in research. Typically, these panels have large sample sizes and can include up to 20,000 individuals in the sampling frame. In addition, these panels often provide the option of quota samples, whereby researchers can specify the characteristics of the sample. For instance, if researchers are interested in the attitudes of women ages 18 to 49 toward health care reform, they could use an Internet panel database to produce a fairly representative sample of American women from that age group. Although using such panels comes with costs, this method can save time and energy and be more efficient in the long run allowing researchers to collect data from a large sample rather quickly. Importantly, these panels allow researchers to recruit participants for more complex studies with less concern about mortality, as the participants have already agreed to take part in studies and, in many cases, are compensated for their time. Additionally, Internet panel designs can allow researchers to easily embed experiments within their survey design using the technological advantages of an online survey format. For these panels to work and be useful to researchers, the companies that create them have to use good technique in generating their sample and work to maintain a representative sample over time, as some individuals will quit because they grow bored or experience lifestyle changes, among many other factors. As such, it is important to do research on the panel that you plan to use to ensure that the sampling firm that created the panel is using good technique and has a good reputation.

Mail Survey

This traditional approach to self-administered surveys, often called a "paper-and-pencil" survey, involves sending an easily completed questionnaire to sampled individuals. Potential participants are sent a cover letter and a copy of the survey in an envelope that also includes a return envelope. To ensure a higher response rate, the return envelope should be stamped and addressed. The cover letter should provide clear instructions as well as build rapport between the researcher and the respondent. Researchers can achieve this by providing some details about the institution they represent (reinforcing credibility), explaining the importance of the study being conducted, and providing clarification of procedures and how any offered incentives can be claimed.

For example, if you are working for a nonprofit and want to assess the effectiveness of a recent advertising campaign, you could use a mail survey because it could reach a large sample at relatively low cost. The lower cost of the survey distribution might leave some room in your budget to offer a $5 incentive for participants to complete the survey. In this case, the cover letter should clearly indicate what the nonprofit is and what cause it represents, let respondents know how much you value their input, and let them know that you have included $5 in the envelope as a thank you for participating in the study. Of course, in following guidelines of research ethics, the respondent must not be required to participate and, according to the principle of voluntary participation, must be able to withdraw from the study at any time.

As indicated, a primary strength of the mail survey is that it allows for wide reach at a relatively low cost. The expenses include incentives (if any), envelopes, copying costs, and postage, as well as any costs associated with hiring someone to stuff envelopes and/or input data. The last two costs can be avoided if the researchers carry out these tasks themselves.

The primary weakness of mail surveys is low response rate. Mail surveys are also limited in how they can present information and don't have quite the flexibility that electronic versions have—Internet surveys, in particular, allow for the delivery of a far greater variety of media stimuli. Mail surveys can also take a long time to complete because of the time it takes for surveys to arrive

self-administered survey
→ Unit 10

sample
→ Unit 8

response rate
→ Unit 8

rapport
→ Unit 10

incentive
→ Unit 8

ethical research
→ Unit 4

voluntary participation
→ Unit 4

questionnaire design
→ Unit 7

variable
→ Unit 2

panel design
→ Unit 10

275

at the participant's home, the time it takes the participants to complete the survey, and the time it takes for the survey to be returned to the researcher. Further, responses to mail surveys must be manually recorded for computer-based statistical analysis, adding a further step that can increase the time and cost.

Despite these weaknesses, mail surveys remain a viable means to collect data because they allow wide access to large samples at a relatively low cost compared with other survey approaches. Finally, because respondents can complete the questionnaire on their own time in their own home, the questionnaire can be relatively lengthy. For example, market research firms will often use questionnaires with 20 or more pages of questions that measure a wide range of variables. They do this because they may be simultaneously collecting data for a wide array of clients. In some cases, a panel design may be employed to allow the researchers to track respondents over time. Despite all of these advantages, in recent years Internet-based studies have largely supplanted mail surveys.

Longitudinal Designs

causality
→ Unit 2

independent
variable
→ Unit 2

dependent
variable
→ Unit 2

cross-sectional
design
→ Unit 10

cohort
→ Unit 10

trend
→ Unit 10

panel
→ Unit 10

variable
→ Unit 2

response rate
→ Unit 8

questionnaire
design
→ Unit 7

Because basic surveys struggle to identify causal relationships, researchers may be interested in including the element of time within their study. While this does not necessarily control for all possible confounds, it does allow researchers to determine whether a proposed independent variable actually comes before a dependent variable. If researchers want to consider an issue over time, they often opt for longitudinal studies over cross-sectional studies, which are only administered at one point in time. There are three specific types of longitudinal designs: (1) cohort, (2) trend, and (3) panel. In each case, the design includes time as a key variable. For example, market research firms are often interested in tracking consumer behaviors and attitudes over time so that they can adjust their marketing approaches and understand changes in consumer behavior. Unlike cross-sectional studies, longitudinal designs are ideal for this kind of research because they allow researchers to follow changes in variables over a period of time, which can stretch from months to years.

While all studies look to maximize response rates, for longitudinal designs, this can also mean trying to retain participants across multiple questionnaires (referred to as "waves" of the study). If response rate is too low in longitudinal designs, particularly panel designs, the ability to draw conclusions over time is minimized. Even in a nonpanel design, differences in response rates might explain differences between data collections, making comparisons meaningless.

Longitudinal designs can be valuable to businesses as well. Consider your role as the survey designer for the radio station. A longitudinal survey design would allow you to not only answer current questions (e.g., "What format changes should be made?") but also monitor the success (or failure) of the changes that are made. For instance, a longitudinal design could allow the station to track the interests and opinions of its listener base over the course of 5 years. In doing so, you would have a clear sense of any shifts in listener habits, changes in the demographics of your audience, and any increases in listenership. Such information could be incredibly valuable to potential advertisers and local businesses as you sell advertising space.

Cohort

Longitudinal studies that follow the same type of person—or cohort—over time are referred to as *cohort studies*. In these kinds of studies, researchers are interested in following a particular group to see how it changes over time and thus conduct a series of cross-sectional designs using people from a particular group—or cohort—each time. Every person included in a cohort design sample shares at least the group membership characteristic in common. In many cases the shared group characteristic is based on year of birth or similar characteristic. For instance, researchers often look at different cohorts based on the era when people were born, such as Baby Boomers born in the mid-1940s to the mid-1960s and Generation X between the early 1960s and 1980s. As such, the sampling procedures will draw from that particular group each time a follow-up survey is conducted, but the sample will not include the exact same people. For example, consider a situation in which researchers are interested in tracking whether communication styles change over the course of a person's life (e.g., do people become more passive or assertive in their style). Using a cohort design, the researchers could select a particular group—perhaps Millennials (individuals born in the 1980s and 1990s)—and track their communication styles using one survey every year over a 10-year period. To do this each year, the researchers would create a new random sample from individuals that are part of that cohort—that is, people who are in the Millennial cohort (born in the 1980s and 1990s). At the end of the 10-year period, they would then have 10 surveys that were conducted using samples from Millennials. At no point would individuals born before the 1980s or after the 1990s be included in this particular approach. The cohort the researchers are interesting in tracking is only those people who are defined as Millennials.

> **longitudinal design**
> → Unit 10
>
> **sample**
> → Unit 8
>
> **random**
> → Unit 8
>
> **variable**
> → Unit 2

Trend

Longitudinal studies that focus more on following a particular issue or variable over time are referred to as *trend studies*. In this case, the researchers are interested in whether attitudes toward an issue—such as support for or opposition to gun control—have changed over time. In this case, the sampling procedures typically draw from a more widely defined group than in cohort studies. For example, researchers might be interested in further understanding attitudes

> **sample**
> → Unit 8
>
> **population**
> → Unit 8
>
> **cohort**
> → Unit 10

277

toward communication style and whether Americans' attitudes toward different styles have changed over time. To do so, they could conduct a study annually that in each case draws a sample from the broadly defined population of "Americans" and ask the same questions each time. As a note, each sample includes different people who all belong to the same broadly defined group (in this case, Americans); the researchers are not contacting the same people each time. Therefore, the sample would always include Americans, but the researchers are not bound to choose people who were born in the same year, as a cohort study might. That is because the emphasis is on understanding broader attitudes toward the issue and not necessarily how the attitudes of a particular group have changed over time.

Panel

Longitudinal studies that follow the same exact people in a series of studies over a period of time are referred to as *panel designs*. In this case, once the sample is drawn for the first wave of the study, the researchers continue to contact those same exact people for all subsequent waves of the study. Because of this, it is important that the first wave have both a large sample size and a good response rate to improve the chances that the researchers will be able to recruit the same people again for future waves. Typically, participants are informed that they will be involved in a multiwave panel study and are given a sense of how many waves there will be.

Panel designs are quite powerful because they allow researchers to conduct more advanced statistical analyses than either cross-sectional studies or other longitudinal studies. Further, well-designed panel studies also allow researchers to better assess causality and therefore look for more complex relationships than can be done with other methodologies. Panel studies allow researchers to directly compare an individual's answers at one point in time to those at another time. Because of this, they can consider changes in those individuals and see whether the changes are linked to earlier behaviors or attitudes. For example, researchers might want to develop a more detailed understanding of communication styles and understand *why* people develop the styles they do. A panel design would be a useful tool in this particular case. Researchers could employ questions designed to assess the individuals' communication styles and then include other questions about upbringing, media use, relationship satisfaction, and other important variables over the course of multiple surveys that track key variables at each point. For example, does communication style effect relationship satisfaction? Do media use habits shape communication style (i.e., do we model how we communicate based on what we watch on TV)?

Although panel designs are powerful tools, they are relatively uncommon because they are resource intensive. First, they require a considerable time commitment from the researchers as well as the participants. Second, the costs

longitudinal
design
→ Unit 10

sample
→ Unit 8

sample size
→ Unit 8

response rate
→ Unit 8

**cross-sectional
design**
→ Unit 10

causality
→ Unit 2

relationship
→ Unit 2

variable
→ Unit 2

incentive
→ Unit 8

mortality
→ Unit 9

278

of recruitment, maintenance of the sample, and incentives offered to partici-pants can increase rapidly, depending on the size of the sample desired. Finally, poor retention of participants from one wave to the next can make detailed statistical analyses difficult and affect the quality of the panel (this is another example of mortality).

Research in Depth: Panel Studies in Popular Culture

Perhaps the most famous use of a panel design comes from a series of documentary films produced in Great Britain known as the *Up* series. The series started by following a group of 7-year-old British children in 1964 leading to the initial documentary, titled *Seven Up!* The producers of the first documentary have returned to check in with this group every 7 years since then and have thus far produced eight documentary films, each play-ing off of the 7-year premise. For instance, the second documentary was titled *7 Plus Seven*, the third was titled *21 Up*, and so on through the most recent title, *56 Up*, which checked in on the participants at 56 years old. In the case of this study, the documentarians were interested in assessing the role that class plays in how we turn out as adults.

By tracking the same individuals over time, the researchers were able to look directly at the role that different characteristics of each child played in their development. Although this particular study did not employ probability sampling techniques (the children were purpose-fully chosen to represent a range of social classes), it does illustrate the power that longitudinal studies can have in tracking change and provid-ing detailed pictures of the world around us.

279

Activities

Activity 10A: Survey Design

See terms: survey; conceptualization; operational definition.

For this activity, you will need to start by developing a research question you would like to answer or a hypothesis you would like to test. Once you have done so, your objective is to develop a survey that will allow you to answer your research question or test your hypothesis. Specifically, consider the following questions as you work to develop your experiment:

- What population are you interested in studying?
- Which approach would be most useful for this situation—a self-administered or interview-style survey?
- Which survey format—face-to-face, telephone, online, or mail—would be most effective for what you are studying?
- What kinds of questions do you need to ask to measure your concepts? What are some challenges you might face in creating effective measures?
- What are some limitations you might face in using a survey approach to study this issue?

Activity 10B: Survey Research Critique

See term: survey.

For this activity, you will need to locate a research article that uses a survey design. Once you have read the article, you should locate the key parts of a survey as they are discussed in the article. Use the following questions to guide your assessment of this article:

- Why was a survey an appropriate method for this particular research problem?
- To what extent do the authors address the strengths and weaknesses of the survey design?
- What are the biggest strengths of the design as carried out by the authors in this article?
- What do you see as the biggest weaknesses with the design? What might you have done differently if you were conducting this study?
- Did the researchers use appropriate sampling technique for survey research?

Activity 10C: Interviewing Practice

See terms: interview-style survey; face-to-face survey; telephone survey.

The objective of this activity is to gain practice as a survey interviewer and to experience some of the strengths and weaknesses of this approach. For this activity, recruit six people to serve as participants in your practice interview. Conduct half of the interviews over the phone and half of the interviews face-to-face. Be sure to keep notes on both the responses given and your experience as an interviewer. After you finish, assess your findings and consider the following: (1) What would you do differently next time? (2) Do you prefer one format over the other? If so, why? (3) What would you change about the questions if you could?

Here are the interview questions:

1. Of the following media choices, which is most preferable for obtaining news on current events:

Newspaper   Websites   Television   Radio   Social media

2. Of the following media choices, which is most preferable for obtaining relationship advice:

Newspaper   Websites   Television   Radio   Social media

3. Of the following media choices, which has been most influential in your career development:

Newspaper   Websites   Television   Radio   Social media

4. What are the three biggest strengths of social media websites?

5. What are the three biggest weaknesses or criticisms you see for social media websites?

Activity 10D: Longitudinal Designs

See terms: cross-section; cohort; panel; trend.

Five survey scenarios are described next. Your objective for this activity is to determine the type of study (cross-sectional or longitudinal) that is being conducted. Be sure to indicate why you have made your decision.

Study description	Type of study
You are interested in studying whether job skills training programs have long-term effects. To do so, you recruit 500 people who have taken part in a job skills training program and ask them to complete a questionnaire every January for the next 10 years.	
You are curious as to whether people are supportive of a new initiative in your borough to promote recycling. To gauge the level of support for this initiative, you ask 250 residents to complete a questionnaire that they can fill out and mail back to the borough office.	
While working for an online dating company, you are tasked with tracking the public's willingness to engage in online dating as well as their relationship satisfaction. To do so, you decide to take a different random sample from the U.S. population every 6 months and assess the two measures using a telephone poll.	
Your experiences with new technology and social media have spurred an interest in people's changing relationship with technology. To study this, you decide to assess the impact on the millennial generation and do so by taking a random sample of people who were born in the 1980s and 1990s every year for the next 15 years.	
You are working with a client who is thinking of starting a new music festival in a major U.S. city. However, getting too far into developing the festival, your client would like to know whether residents of the city are likely to be supportive of the festival. To assess the level of support, you decide to conduct a brief telephone survey of residents of the city.	

References

Guterbock, T.M., Diop, A., Ellis, J.M., Holmes, J.L., & Le, T.K. (2011). Who needs RDD? Combining directory listings with cell phone exchanges for an alternative telephone sampling frame. *Social Science Research*, *40*(3), 860–872. doi:10.1016/j.ssresearch.2011.01.001

Keeter, S., Kennedy, C., Clark, A., Tompson, T., & Mokrzycki, M. (2007). What's missing from national landline RDD surveys? The impact of the growing cell-only population. *Public Opinion Quarterly*, *71*(5), 772–792. doi:10.1093/poq/nfm053

Link, M.W., Battaglia, M.P., Frankel, M.R., Osborn, L., & Mokdad, A.H. (2007). Reaching the U.S. cell phone generation: Comparison of cell phone survey results with an ongoing landline telephone survey. *Public Opinion Quarterly*, *71*(5), 814–839. doi:10.1093/poq/nfm051

Link, M.W., & Lai, J.W. (2011). Cell-phone-only households and problems of differential nonresponse using an address-based sampling design. *Public Opinion Quarterly*, *75*(4), 613–635. doi:10.1093/poq/nfr040

Peytchev, A., Carley-Baxter, L.R., & Black, M.C. (2010). Coverage bias in variances, associations, and total error from exclusion of the cell phone-only population in the United States. *Social Science Computer Review*, *28*(3), 287–302. doi:10.1177/0894439309353027

Stolberg, S.G., & Kopicki, A. (2013, December 10). Obama sees a rebound in his approval ratings. *The New York Times*. Retrieved from www.nytimes.com/2013/12/11/us/politics/obama-sees-a-rebound-in-his-approval-ratings.html

Suggested Readings for Further Exploration of Unit 10 Topics

Examples

Baker, R., Blumberg, S.J., Brick, J.M., Couper, M.P., Courtright, M., & Dennis, J.M. (2010). Research synthesis: AAPOR report on online panels. *Public Opinion Quarterly*, *74*(4), 711–781. doi:10.1093/poq/nfq048

Helgeson, J.G., Voss, K.E., & Terpening, W.D. (2002). Determinants of mail-survey response: Survey design factors and respondent factors. *Psychology & Marketing*, *19*(3), 303–328. doi:10.1002/mar.1054

Advanced Discussion

Asher, H.B. (1995). *Polling and the public: What every citizen should know*. Washington, DC: CQ Press.

Fowler, F.J. (2002). *Survey research methods*. Thousand Oaks, CA: Sage Publications.

Groves, R. M. (2011). Three eras of survey research. *Public Opinion Quarterly*, *75*(5), 861–871. doi:10.1093/poq/nfr057

Krosnick, J. A. (1999). Survey research. *Annual Review of Psychology*, *50*, 537–567. doi:10.1146/annurev.psych.50.1.537

Smith, T. W. (2013). Survey-research paradigms old and new. *International Journal of Public Opinion Research*, *25*(2), 218–229. doi:10.1093/ijpor/eds040

unit 11

content analysis

A critical focus of media research is the actual content that appears in media. For example, many scholars and critics have remarked on the frequency of negative political advertising. These ads, they say, create cynicism, drive voters away from the polls, and contribute to partisanship in two-party democracies such as the United States. It's an interesting and common idea, but to test this theory, we would need to do research.

Fully exploring this idea would require several types of studies. We might carry out a survey to find out whether the average voter actually thinks that campaigns are negative and to gauge their opinions about the tone. However, such research wouldn't tell us whether ads actually *cause* these attitudes. So, we could use an experiment to test whether negative ads actually affect the people who watch them. This would give us good evidence of causality but wouldn't tell us whether this is really an issue in actual campaigns. The best bet to truly understand the nature of advertising would be to look at the ads themselves—maybe our assumption about the tone of the advertising is wrong, or perhaps there are concerns we have not yet considered. We need a systematic way to consider media content—to look for patterns and trends. We call this approach content analysis.

Content Analysis

Content analysis involves the systematic measurement of variables found within fixed texts or artifacts, as opposed to people. "Text" here refers to any material generated by people through some action and stored in an unchanging form; it does not have to involve written language and could include pictures, videos, or music, among other things. These materials are sometimes known as **social artifacts**. The example of measuring negativity in ads is one case in which content analysis might be used, but there are many others. For example, content analysis could also be used to see whether news programs give more time to Democrats than Republicans, whether advertisements are more likely to show White consumers than those of other races, or whether video games tend to show women as more sexualized than men. Content analysis is even used when researchers want to convert open-ended items from surveys or other research projects into quantitative data describing basic patterns in participant responses.

Content analysis most frequently involves the same basic process as all systematic research. First, you must identify the population of texts you wish to study and then draw an appropriate sample from that population. Next, you must engage in a systematic process of observation to measure the relevant variables within that population and evaluate whether your measurement approach is effective. Finally, you are left with data (most often quantitative) that can be analyzed the same as any other research outcomes, as we will discuss in a later unit.

survey
→ Unit 10

experiment
→ Unit 9

causality
→ Unit 2

systematic
→ Unit 1

variable
→ Unit 2

open-ended
→ Unit 7

population
→ Unit 8

sample
→ Unit 8

qualitative versus quantitative
→ Unit 3

reliability
→ Unit 6

reactive
→ Unit 7

depth interviews
→ Unit 12

transcript
→ Unit 13

Content analysis does have certain characteristics that differ from other types of research, though. First, content analysis requires researchers to pay attention to the **unitizing** of the content, in a way that may be more complex than normal sampling. For example, a content analyst may initially collect political advertisements that aired on television over the course of a week. But the researcher may not want to describe the entire ad as a single unit; instead, he or she might want to consider each time the candidate is mentioned separately, meaning there may be many units of content analysis within a single ad.

Additionally, content analysis requires a specific process to turn the text into data, known as **coding**. Trained individuals must follow a **coding guide** and fill out a **coding sheet** based on their systematic observation of the text. In a survey, we ask participants to provide answers that fit with our specific question formats. In content analysis, the coder must translate the text into the desired format. Sometimes, this is fairly simple; when coders evaluate **manifest content**, they are looking at basic, surface characteristics that require minimal interpretation. At other times, the process is more complex. Coders may be asked to evaluate **latent content** that requires interpretation and "reading between the lines." In some cases, coders are not used and researchers engage in what is called **computer-aided content analysis**, whereby computer software carries out the coding process.

Content analysis also requires researchers to carefully consider **intercoder reliability**. Of course, measurement reliability is always important, but in content analysis, we must consider the consistency between coders. An effective measure and well-trained coders should ensure that each coder evaluates the content in the same way, but we can test this through the use of **intercoder statistics**.

Finally, content analysis can be quite useful in situations in which unobtrusive measures are required. For example, you might be asked to help your employer identify issues with communication and attitudes toward leadership at the place where you work. In such a situation, it could be difficult to get honest and frank answers from people using a survey or depth interview because of concerns about reprisal. However, it is likely that employees and employers are sharing communication in numerous ways, such as intra-office e-mails, letters, memos, and transcripts from staff or team meetings. In each of these cases, you could analyze the content of those different forms of communication, develop a coding scheme, and then make some assessment about the quality of the communication and perceptions of the workplace. As a note, from an ethics standpoint it is necessary to look into the communication policies at your place of employment before reading individual e-mails or other communicated messages.

social artifacts
→ Unit 11

Unitizing

Because there are many different aspects of social artifacts that can be studied using content analysis, it is important to decide which specific piece of the social artifact will be analyzed. This decision to break the social artifact into different pieces—or units—is referred to as *unitizing*. Consider trying to study the tone of election ads. You might decide to focus on the individual ads, selecting and coding each to see how negative it is. However, not all advertisements air an equal number of times. If you had data about when each ad aired, you could choose to look at blocks of time, coding every ad that appeared on television within a sample of 30-minute blocks.

The choice you make about how to unitize the social artifacts determines the sampling strategy, the variables that can be observed, and, consequently, the conclusions that can be drawn. Therefore, any decision to unitize should be determined primarily by your guiding research question. In some cases, it may be necessary to adjust your unitizing decision to help increase the sample size. For instance, if you are studying argumentation patterns in court cases dealing with the legalization of marijuana, there may be only a small number of such documents accessible to analyze. In such a case, you might decide to use a smaller unit, such as the paragraph or even the sentence within the court document.

sample
→ Unit 8

variable
→ Unit 2

research questions
→ Unit 2

sample size
→ Unit 8

Coding and the Coding Process

In content analysis, measurement involves a process of evaluating the units of analysis and assigning a value for each of the variables being observed. This process of assigning values is referred to as *coding*. Once again, suppose you are studying the tone of political advertisements. To study this, you could take a random sample of advertisements that aired during a campaign and then assess whether each is positive or negative in tone. You could assign values to reflect the tone—ranging from 1 for highly negative to 5 for highly positive. The unit of analysis here is the advertisement, and the variable is the tone, which is measured quantitatively. The rules and procedures for how each variable should be coded (i.e., measured) are spelled out in the coding guide, and the assigned values are recorded on a coding sheet. Content analysis does not need to be quantitative— you could also evaluate and describe the tone of coverage—but this begins to resemble other forms of qualitative research addressed elsewhere.

variable
→ Unit 2

random
→ Unit 8

coding guide
→ Unit 11

coding sheet
→ Unit 11

qualitative versus quantitative
→ Unit 3

Coding Guide

All definitions, descriptions, and procedures for a content analysis are provided in the coding guide. This includes the conceptual and operational definitions and, in many cases, examples of how variables are to be coded. The coding guide is a valuable tool for researchers because it becomes the working document that they use to work through the concept explication process for the different concepts that will be assessed in the content analysis. By studying the coding guide, the researcher should have a clear sense of the coding process for the study being conducted. In the situation in which you are coding political advertisements, you would need to clearly explain what constitutes a negative or positive

conceptual definition
→ Unit 5

operational definition
→ Unit 5

variable
→ Unit 2

advertisement and how to assign the numerical values that correspond to each tonal level.

For another example, consider a situation in which you are working for an advertising agency that has just procured a contract with a fast-food franchise. The fast-food franchise would like to do something unique while also tapping into common themes that cut across other ad campaigns by fast-food companies. Therefore, it is necessary to identify how frequently certain themes arise in fast-food commercials. Four possible themes are saving money, fast service, excitement, and escape from the norm, among many other options. The coding guide should clearly state the meaning of each of these themes, provide an example of what the theme looks like in practical use, and give a clear sense of how value can be assigned to that theme. For instance, the "saving money" theme could be defined as "instances in which emphasis is placed on low or reduced costs, money saving, budget eating, or cost comparisons showing lower prices." An example of this would be a commercial indicating that a full meal can be had for under $5.

Finally, the coding guide should illustrate exactly how the coding should occur, such as "score 1 point for the presence of each theme and combine the scores, such that an ad that mentioned all four of the themes would score 4 points and one that only mentioned one theme would score 1 point." A good coding guide should leave no room for guessing: it should be as explicit, clear, and detailed as possible to ensure high levels of intercoder reliability.

Coding Sheet

During the coding process, assigned values are recorded onto a coding sheet that lists all of the variables being coded and provides appropriate space for the recorded values. In most cases, each coding sheet corresponds to the coding for one unit of analysis, thus your total sample size will typically match the number of coding sheets you have completed. The listing of variables on the coding sheet should correspond with the order listed in the coding guide.

For example, if you are conducting an analysis of the themes present in fast-food advertising, then each possible theme that you are coding should be listed on the coding sheet. Next to each theme should be a space for you to record the value of that observation. For instance, if the coding guide indicates that each separate mention should count as 1 point for that theme, then you would total the number of mentions of that theme and record the total on the coding sheet. That is, if the "saving money" theme is mentioned seven separate times, a value of 7 should be placed next to the blank for the saving money theme on the coding sheet. In most cases, each coding sheet will also include a case number to help the researcher keep track of individual units of analysis. In some cases, this can be useful if coding sheets include open-ended responses or notes such as examples or specific details. The researcher can then easily locate such cases and pull them out for further use.

Computer-Aided Content Analysis

coding
→ Unit 11

validity
→ Unit 6

unit of analysis
→ Unit 2

coding guide
→ Unit 11

Computer-aided content analysis is a useful tool that researchers can employ to analyze large and often complicated sets of data, and it works by having a computer analyze digital content looking for patterns in the presence (or absence) of particular words and phrases. There are many applications of this kind of approach and one of the more common uses is in analyzing words or phrases as the unit of analysis. The researcher essentially programs the coding system to look for which words and phrases co-occur together, thus revealing patterns in the data and helping the researcher understand what the content is telling them.

Consider an example of research where you wanted to explore whether protesters were treated differently based on their race. You would then set up the computer-aided content analysis system to look for words or phrases that carried positive or negative meaning as well as words that would allow you to know the race of the protesters. For instance, you might include descriptive words such as "angry," "helpful," "violent," and others to reflect meaning. You then simply need to upload the content you wish to analyze into the coding system.

Note that in computer-aided content analysis there are no concerns about reliability. The computer program will consistently apply whatever rules you dictate it to apply—it does what it is told and thus will produce perfect reliability. However, the primary concern then shifts to the validity of the coding scheme you have created. As such, careful attention must be paid to the construction of the rules for the computer program to follow to ensure that coding of the content is accurate. Consider how subtle shifts in language and word choice can have implications for the meaning conveyed. To account for these issues, the coding scheme must also have rules built in that match the complexity and subtly of language. However, computer-aided content analysis is a fast-growing area with many improvements in coding software in recent years that allow for highly complicated and detailed coding schemes. In any case, it is good practice for researchers to do some coding of their own to compare their results with the computer-aided systems results to get a sense of how well the program is performing and whether any adjustments are needed.

Of course, one of the major advantages of this type of research is the near instantaneous results that can be achieved. Once the coding system is in place massive amounts of data can be run through the system and produce results quite quickly. Consider a situation where you worked for a major company and wanted to analyze social media traffic about the company. In short, you want to know what people are saying on social media about your employer. Tweets and other social media posts could easily be collated and run through computer-aided content analysis to give you a detailed sense of the themes and patterns that are present in social media chatter about your company.

Voices from Industry

Sue McCrossin—Founder of Boomtown Internet Group

Sue McCrossin graduated from Pennsylvania State University and began her programming career at Siemens in 1982 (then called Shared Medical Systems). She worked in information technology in Fortune 100 companies in some capacity until starting Boomtown Internet Group in 2004. She is passionate about exploring the infinite possibilities of Internet marketing, particularly where technology, marketing, and data analysis collide to create new methods of marketing.

Why are good research skills important to your field?

Research is crucial in everything we do, and in digital marketing, we have to substantiate our recommendations before a client will spend a single dollar. We must research market position, the various marketing outlets' return on investment, and actual marketing return on investment in the form of client conversions.

- Not only do we research the market position, competitors, and trends before we make a sale, we also know that our competitors are researching the effectiveness of the work we are doing for our clients each month and are using research data to try to steal them away from us.
- Even after a sale, we need to diligently research the ever-changing digital marketing trends to retain our customers and stay ahead of our competitors. Research is also needed to stay ahead of search ranking penalties.
- Unlike other professions in which "continuing credits" help professionals stay current with trends, Internet marketers rely on research and experiments to determine the most effective marketing methods for various clients and stay current with the ever-evolving digital landscape.

The reason good research skills are important is that digital marketers do not have the luxury of leisurely exploration. The field is cutthroat and fast paced, and if research is done poorly, valuable time is wasted, and the wrong conclusions can have serious detrimental effects on client return on investment. Additionally, many clients insist on implementing a solution as soon as a problem is diagnosed and the solution researched. The initial research can often make or break the outcome of the project.

What specific method or methods do you use or encounter most?

We are most interested in identifying the optimal customer and his or her habits, market position, return on investment, where and how customers find our clients, how customers interact with the marketing material and how they share it, timing and events prior to a sale, customer retention data, reputation management, where and how competitors get leads, and a host of specific research data that individual clients demand.

Can you name some specific instances for which you have used data collected from research?

In online marketing, we must research the search phrases that potential visitors to our clients' websites and social media search before purchasing. In order to determine which specific keyword phrases to focus upon, we use more than seven research tools and show our findings to our clients using shared Google Drive sheets and documents. We use the following tools to share our findings:

- Google AdWords Keyword Tool
- SEMrush keyword ranking tool
- Google search results showing number and value of competitors
- Google Analytics and Google Webmaster Tools to determine current impressions and clicks associated with keywords
- Google+, Facebook, LinkedIn, Twitter, Tumbler, etc., to determine number of followers and social presence (also check Hootsuite)
- Moz on-page grader tool
- Majestic SEO Backlink Report to look at anchor text links.

How did the research you conducted help inform your decision?

If we could not substantiate our recommendations to our clients with well-researched statistics, our clients would not be able to make informed marketing decisions. In the case of keyword research, clients can choose focus keywords only after they can estimate the cost and return on investment for each phrase.

What are one or two pieces of advice or insights you would give about research to students in a communication research methods course?

- Research tools are only as good as the data they are fed.
- Research tools that claim to do everything rarely work for long because the digital landscape changes so quickly.
- Every client is different, and while you may have found the perfect solution for one client after diligent research, you still have to conduct research before drawing a conclusion for another client, no matter how similar.

Intercoder Reliability

Essential to the success of content analysis research is making sure that the coders are consistently in agreement with one another in their coding process. This consistency—known as *intercoder reliability*—is important because most quantitative content analyses use multiple coders. In order for the coded data to be reliable—and also, it is hoped, valid—the different coders must agree on how to code each variable, such that they should independently arrive at the

qualitative versus quantitative
→ Unit 3

reliability
→ Unit 6

validity
→ Unit 6

same conclusions. Intercoder reliability is improved through training sessions in which the coders work closely with the researchers and with each other to understand the coding procedures. Further, clear conceptual and operational definitions make achieving higher levels of intercoder reliability possible. Intercoder reliability is assessed through a range of statistical approaches; the reliability score for each variable is used to indicate the researchers' confidence in the consistency of measurement for that variable.

Consider again the challenge of measuring the tone of political advertising. Different people will see the same advertisement in different ways. If the person viewing the ad supports the candidate, he or she might think the "attack" is justified and fail to code it as purely negative. That is why it is important to clearly define the variables in the coding guide and to make sure all coders are consistent in how they follow that guide. Consider another example: if you are interested in assessing whether the level of violence in video games has increased over time, you could determine this by using a content analysis of the top 10 games over each of the past 10 years. Next, the researchers would need to train the coders so that all of the coders agree and see violence in the same way, such that they assign the same values for each variable for each unit of analysis. If the researchers are using a violence scale of 1 to 5, where 1 equals a low level of violence and 5 equals a high level of violence, then the specific score given for each game in which violence is measured should be the same for all of the coders.

In many cases, perfect agreement among coders is not reached, and there are often minor differences between coders that can still be acceptable to researchers, within reason. In some cases, the coders might differ only slightly—one might assign a 4 and another a 5 for violence. While this would not be perfect reliability, it might still be acceptable. If those same coders concurred that a "less violent" game scored a 1 or a 2, they would still be reasonably consistent, and intercoder statistics would reflect the imperfect but close agreement. The general idea behind intercoder reliability is to have all of the coders be as similar as possible in their coding.

Intercoder Statistics

Acceptable levels of intercoder reliability are determined using an array of statistical procedures that determine a coefficient (i.e., score) based on the strength of the level of agreement between the coders. The specific statistical test that is used depends, in part, on the level of measurement for the coded variables as well as the number of coders used. In most cases, the value of the coefficient ranges from 0 to 1, with scores closer to 1 indicating stronger levels of agreement.

Another difference among intercoder statistics is that some account for chance, while others—such as percent agreement—do not. Chance agreement refers to the possibility that coders will agree in some cases simply by accident.

Research in Depth: Hostile Media Perceptions and the Challenge of Coding

It might seem that agreeing on coding should be relatively simple for coders. After all, most people view media every day, and they are probably confident in their ability to describe it accurately. But that confidence may be false. One domain of media research illustrates why accurate perceptions of certain aspects of content are difficult to obtain: the "hostile media" phenomenon.

The classic demonstration of this finding comes from Vallone, Ross, and Lepper (1985). Those authors showed that pro-Israeli and pro-Arab undergraduates differed in their perceptions of news related to a massacre in Beirut, with both sides seeing the coverage as biased against their own perspective. This reflects the basic pattern found again and again in hostile media studies: People with strong views on an issue tend to see content as biased against their views. If the content is balanced, those on both sides will see it as biased. If the content is biased in favor of one group, that group will often see it as fair, while the opposition will see it as especially unfair. This finding has been replicated in many contexts, such as during a UPS strike (Christen, Kannaovakun, & Gunther, 2002) and in research on primates (Gunther & Chia, 2001). This tendency appears to be specific to judgments of media, with partisans not having the same perceptions of bias in student essays (Gunther & Schmitt, 2004).

This research may sound interesting but unrelated to content analysis. However, many of these studies seem to confirm that this is a fundamental psychological tendency, and one that is difficult for people to overcome. Coders are subject to the same psychological biases as others, and they must work to make sure those biases do not compromise the validity of their results. If a conservative and a liberal coder evaluated the same news content, they might assign very different values on a number of variables. This is why clear, objective definitions that minimize personal judgment are so important. Critics of quantitative content analysis often complain that it misses subtle elements, but those subtle elements may be artifacts of personal bias rather than meaningful features of content.

This is more likely to be true when specific answers are common. If positive advertisements are rare, for example, we would expect most coders to assign negative scores to most ads. The ability to identify the rare cases of positive ads thus becomes more important. Because of this, statistics that account for that possibility are more stringent and typically better measures of intercoder agreement than those that do not.

variable
→ Unit 2

range
→ Unit 14

statistics
→ Unit 14

Steps to Success: Preparing for Intercoder Reliability

There are numerous approaches to measuring intercoder reliability as well as debate over the best approach to use in each circumstance. However, the most common approaches include percent agreement, Scott's pi, Cohen's kappa, and Krippendorff's alpha. The first of these—percent agreement—is the easiest to compute, but it does not account for chance agreement. For instance, if you and a friend code whether the people you see are "happy" or "sad," there is a high probability that you will agree by accident in some cases simply because there are so few choices (only happy or sad). If you add a third category—"neutral"—the likelihood of agreeing by chance becomes less (a 1 in 3 chance as opposed to a 1 in 2 chance). However, percent agreement does not account for such differences. To compute percent agreement, you simply divide the number of agreements by the number of observations. If you observed 20 people and agreed on 16 of them, then the percent agreement value would be 80 percent (16/20).

Although Scott's pi, Cohen's kappa, and Krippendorff's alpha all account for chance agreement, Krippendorff's alpha also accounts for the magnitude of differences between coders. Further, Krippendorff's alpha is a highly versatile approach in that it can be used for nominal, ordinal, interval, or ratio measures. In a basic sense, Krippendorff's alpha works by comparing each of the coders for a given observation. Therefore, you would set up your data in a spreadsheet (or table) by putting the case number in the first column and then the names (or identification numbers) of the coders in the second column.

For instance, if you and a friend are coding happiness/sadness ratings for each of your coworkers, you would set up the file with the names (or IDs) of the coworkers in column 1, your and your friend's names in column 2, and the happiness/sadness rating of each in column 3. In this way, the analysis will compare how close your and your friend's ratings were for each of the observations you shared and then devise a score. The more consistently you agree with one another, the closer the value is to 1. The less consistently you agree with one another, the closer the value is to 0.

Types of Content

open-ended
→ Unit 7

latent content
→ Unit 11

manifest content
→ Unit 11

A central question in content analysis is what constitutes "content"—that is, what sorts of material are subject to content analysis, as opposed to some other observational or measurement approach. In general, we classify content as a type of social artifact, or a fixed record of existing communication. Content for analysis can also be generated through open-ended measures, such as thought-listing questions on surveys. Arguably, these types of content are also social artifacts, as the act of taking a survey is a form of communication, but in general, researchers tend not to consider them in those terms. Furthermore, we divide the specific aspects of these artifacts into two broad categories. Manifest features are those that are self-evident and easy to objectively define, while latent features require some interpretation and understanding of the practices that produced the specific artifact and tend to focus on definitions that are intersubjective but not necessarily objective.

In considering the content of political advertisements and their potential negative effects, it is likely that you would be concerned with both surface-level characteristics and latent content. For example, manifest content could include characteristics of the candidates such as race, their body type (e.g., thin or heavy), their sex (male or female), and any specific descriptive words that appear on the screen. Latent content could include measures such as how friendly and credible the candidate appears to be as well as what primary strategy the ad employs (e.g., attack ad or character-building ad). After some practice coding, it would likely be very easy to code the manifest variables of race, body type, sex, and presence/absence of descriptive words as each are easily observed. Although body type might be somewhat more challenging to code, a number of validated measures exist to allow you to compare the body type in the ad to an array of images in order to determine how thin or heavy the model is. As for the latent content in this case, coding friendliness and credibility of candidates will be somewhat more challenging to code and will take considerably more practice. In either case, it is essential that final coding not begin until acceptable levels of intercoder agreement have been established.

Social Artifacts

In much the same way that an archaeologist would study art, pottery, and other artifacts left behind by cultures and societies, communication researchers study social artifacts, such as music lyrics, films, diaries, letters, newspaper articles, news reports, and many other possibilities. Any material left as the result of communication processes, in a fixed and observable state, constitutes a social artifact. In order to render social artifacts usable in quantitative analysis, they must be subjected to systematic content analysis. For example, political advertisements constitute a social artifact. They are produced as part of the process through which candidates communicate with voters through mass media. If recorded, they can be analyzed, but this analysis will never alter the content of the advertisement. To know whether these advertisements show internal patterns or relationships with other variables, such as voter behavior or candidate characteristics, they must be carefully coded.

Social artifacts are valuable when researchers are interested in difficult-to-access populations or when historical comparisons are needed, as in historical analysis. For example, consider a situation in which researchers want to know about Americans' attitudes toward a topic such as trust in the news media and whether such attitudes have changed from the early part of the 1900s to the present day. Perhaps researchers could find records of early polls and subject

variable`
→ Unit 2

qualitative versus quantitative
→ Unit 3

relationship
→ Unit 2

variable
→ Unit 2

population
→ Unit 8

historical analysis
→ Unit 13

polls
→ Unit 10

secondary analysis
→ Unit 3

them to secondary analysis. But this approach has its own shortcomings; for example, perhaps the questions were not asked consistently over time, making statistical claims about change suspect. An alternative approach would be to study letters to the editor in newspapers and news magazines over the course of that time period and assess levels of trust toward the media through a content analysis of those letters. Further, researchers could also look at internal memos from media outlets and evaluate any discussions of the public's perceptions of the news media discussed in those letters.

Social artifacts are also valuable as units of analysis simply because they provide useful insights into the attitudes, beliefs, norms, and behaviors of different societies and cultures. For example, we could conduct a content analysis of the highest-rated television shows in different countries with the intent of assessing levels of violent and sexual content in the top shows of those countries. Such an analysis would provide key insights into which countries are more (or less) tolerant of sex and violence in their viewing preferences.

Latent Content

manifest content
→ Unit 11

intercoder reliability
→ Unit 11

coding guide
→ Unit 11

indicator
→ Unit 5

intersubjective and replicable
→ Unit 1

reliability
→ Unit 6

validity
→ Unit 6

In contrast to manifest content, latent content refers to meaning that is implied or hidden beneath the surface. Latent content is typically much more challenging to code than manifest content. As a result, intercoder reliability tends to be more difficult to achieve. Because of this, it is important for the coding guide to be explicit in the description of coding procedures for latent content. In many cases, researchers use a series of manifest content indicators to help improve reliability in assessing latent content.

For example, latent content might include the idea of differentiating character and issue attacks in a political advertisement. Consider an advertisement that claims a candidate cannot be trusted because he took money to support a bill. Is this a character attack because it focuses on honesty, or is it an issue attack because it mentions the bill? Researchers would need to arrive at a shared, intersubjective definition for each idea before they could be effectively coded.

Another example would be a study of violent media content. A latent measure such as intent to harm would be challenging to code, but this could be a useful measure because it would seem important to know whether the aggression was done in an angry manner or perhaps in a more humorous way, such as cartoon violence that causes no lasting harm to the character. At the same time, though, it could be difficult to consistently evaluate whether the person committing the aggressive act is acting out of anger or some other motivation. To help in coding this, you might instruct the coders to look for cues that help distinguish angry aggression from other types, such as facial expressions, the intensity of the act, and the outcome of the act. Ultimately, latent content can be very important to understand because it can help researchers get at the true meaning of a concept. However, there are real challenges to doing so in a reliable and valid way.

298

Reflect & React: Manifest and Latent Messages in Everyday Life

We often hear the phrase "read between the lines." This phrase refers to the idea of interpreting meaning that is below the surface—that is, latent content. For instance, a friend might tell you something (e.g., he or she likes your new car), but you conclude that the person actually feels differently (e.g., he or she does NOT like your new car) based on the body language used when expressing his or her feelings. Perhaps the person sounded flippant, bored, hostile, or insincere in what he or she said. However, it might also be that you were misinterpreting your friend's body language.

Consider situations you have encountered in your own life in which you have "read between the lines" and reflect on how differences in coming to agreement on latent meaning pop up in everyday life and can affect the conclusions we draw. Specifically, consider the following questions: What was different about the manifest and latent content that caused a change in your interpretation? What could you do to improve your ability to interpret latent content that is encountered on a regular basis (e.g., gestures, body language, or tone of voice)?

Manifest Content

Content that is surface level and easily observable is referred to as manifest content. Unlike latent content, manifest content tends to be easier to achieve higher levels of intercoder reliability, and the coding process tends to be less time-consuming. The agreement is easier to achieve because there is little room for interpretation when it comes to coding. A manifest aspect of political advertising might be whether the name of the opponent is included in the ad. This is a clear, objective feature that anyone should be able to identify with minimal training. Another example would be violent behavior shown in media: manifest examples of violence could include punching, kicking, and pushing. As long as conceptual and operational definitions for manifest measures are clear, the coding is generally straightforward simply because the content being coded is visible to observers. It should be noted that researchers often measure both latent and manifest content to give a more well-rounded understanding of the content that is being analyzed. For instance, it might be useful for the researchers to also include latent measures of violent behavior, such as the intensity or intent of each violent act, to give a more nuanced sense of context.

latent content
→ Unit 11

intercoder reliability
→ Unit 11

coding
→ Unit 11

conceptual definition
→ Unit 5

operational definition
→ Unit 5

Activities

Activity 11A: Designing a Content Analysis That Answers Your Research Question

See terms: coding; coding guide; conceptualization; operationalization.

The goal of this activity is to take two concepts of interest to you and develop ways to measure them using a content analysis approach. It is likely that you may not have initially conceived of these concepts as being used in a content analysis—perhaps you are more interested in surveys or experiments. However, part of the challenge of the activity is considering different approaches to measurement. Please follow the prompts and questions given next to complete this activity.

- Select two concepts and write down a conceptual definition next to each concept.
- How will you have to adjust the conceptual definition and/or dimensions to measure these concepts using a content analysis?
- What specific social artifacts will you analyze as part of this content analysis?
- Develop at least four indicators for each of your concepts.
- Apply your indicators to a sample of at least five different units of analysis.
- After conducting this basic coding, assess how effective your coding scheme was. What adjustments would be needed if you were to go forward with this project?

Activity 11B: Evaluating Content Analysis in Research Articles

See terms: coding guide; content analysis; method section; operationalization.

For this activity, find an article that uses content analysis methodology. Follow the prompts given next as you work through the article and critically assess its quality.

- Evaluate the quality of the presentation of coding procedures in the article: Would this research project be easy or difficult to replicate based on the detail provided?
- Evaluate the clarity of conceptual and operational definitions: Are the conceptual and operational definitions both clear and appropriate for content analysis methodology? In what ways could they be improved?
- Evaluate the authors' discussion of intercoder reliability: Do all items meet acceptable levels? What procedures did the authors employ?
- Evaluate the conclusions and limitations discussed: Do the authors draw clear and reasonable conclusions based on their methodology and data? Do the authors clearly present limitations of their measurement approach and methodology?

Activity 11C: Evaluating Media Content

See terms: coding; content analysis; intercoder reliability; operationalization.

For this activity, you will work with a partner to develop a research question about media you use on a regular basis. The research question should be one that can be answered using a content analysis and thus be something that entails evaluating social artifacts of some kind. After developing your research question, use the following steps to guide you through this activity:

- Work with your partner to create a brief coding guide that has at least five manifest variables that you will observe. Be sure to create clear definitions for each measure.
- Select a small sample of media content that you can analyze to answer your research question.
- Watch, read, or listen to the media content and apply your coding scheme—be sure to do this *separately* from your activity partner (but make sure it is the *same* content; that is, you should could the same television show, for example)—and record all of your coding on a coding sheet.
- After conducting the coding, draw conclusions about what you have observed and write a brief summary of your findings.
- Meet with your partner to discuss your findings and to do a basic assessment of intercoder reliability such as percent agreement. How reliable were you?
- Consider what aspects of the research would need to be improved if you were to move forward with the project.

Activity 11D: Evaluating an Existing Coding Scheme

See terms: coding; coding guide; validity.

For this activity, you are to evaluate a coding scheme designed to determine whether there are race and gender differences behind the treatment of television characters on dramatic television shows. Start by applying the coding scheme shown next to four main characters from a television show that you watch. After doing so, evaluate the coding scheme's effectiveness and then work to improve the coding scheme. Specifically, consider the following:

- What indicators would you consider removing from the coding scheme? Why?
- What indicators need minor improvements such as more expansive lists of attributes? What is ineffective about these items?
- What would you want to code in order to address things that are completely missing from this coding scheme? How would adding these items improve the coding scheme?
- What limitations still remain for your revised coding scheme?

For each character, code the following items:

- Character gender: Male Female
- Character age: Older Younger
- Character race: Black White Other
- Character's primary role: Antagonist Protagonist Comic relief Leader
- Character's occupation: Blue collar White collar Other
- Character as aggressor: Yes No
- Character as victim of aggression: Yes No
- Character as joking toward others: Yes No
- Character as "butt" of jokes: Yes No
- Amount of screen time for the character (by percentage of scenes appearing): 10 percent 25 percent 50 percent 100 percent

References

Christen, C. T., Kannaovakun, P., & Gunther, A. C. (2002). Hostile media perceptions: Partisan assessments of press and public during the 1997 United Parcel Service strike. *Political Communication, 19*(4), 423–436. doi:10.1080/10584600290109988

Gunther, A. C., & Chia, S. C. Y. (2001). Predicting pluralistic ignorance: The hostile media perception and its consequences. *Journalism & Mass Communication Quarterly, 78*(4), 688–701. doi:10.1177/107769900107800405

Gunther, A. C., & Schmitt, K. (2004). Mapping boundaries of the hostile media effect. *Journal of Communication, 54*(1), 55–70. doi:10.1111/j.1460–2466.2004.tb02613.x

Vallone, R. P., Ross, L., & Lepper, M. R. (1985). The hostile media phenomenon: Biased perception and perceptions of media bias in coverage of the Beirut massacre. *Journal of Personality and Social Psychology, 49*(3), 577–585. doi:10.1037/0022–3514.49.3.577

Suggested Readings for Further Exploration of Unit 11 Topics

Examples

Riffe, D., & Freitag, A. (1997). A content analysis of content analyses: Twenty-five years of *Journalism Quarterly. Journalism & Mass Communication Quarterly, 74*(3), 515–524. doi:10.1177/107769909707400306

Williams, D., Martins, N., Consalvo, M., & Ivory, J. D. (2009). The virtual census: Representations of gender, race and age in video games. *New Media & Society, 11*(5), 815–834. doi:10.1177/1461444809105354

Advanced Discussion

Herring, S. C. (2010). Web content analysis: Expanding the paradigm. In J. Hunsinger, L. Klastrup, & M. Allen (Eds.), *International handbook of Internet research* (pp. 233–249). Dordrecht, Netherlands: Springer.

Holsti, O. R. (1969). *Content analysis for the social sciences and humanities*. Reading, MA: Addison-Wesley.

Krippendorff, K. (2004). *Content analysis: An introduction to its methodology*. Thousand Oaks, CA: Sage Publications.

Lacy, S., & Riffe, D. (1996). Sampling error and selecting intercoder reliability samples for nominal content categories. *Journalism & Mass Communication Quarterly, 73*(4), 963–973. doi:10.1177/107769909607300414

unit 12

qualitative research

Imagine that you are working for the marketing department of a regional restaurant chain that has a few franchises in the Northeastern United States. You are considering expanding into the Southwestern market, but you want to know what aspects of the restaurant your company will need to adjust in order to be successful in this new market. For instance, certain menu items may need to be removed for the new market, others might need to be renamed or slightly modified, and even a few items will likely have to be added to the menu. Additionally, visual elements of the restaurant menu and food presentation may need to be adjusted as well to demonstrate sensitivity to and awareness of local cultural customs. Finally, prices for menu items and other special offerings may need to be changed as well. However, company management likely will only be persuaded to make such changes if they hear firsthand accounts from potential customers. These are potentially detailed changes that require detailed responses from potential customers.

To get this kind of feedback, you could employ one or more of the qualitative research methods discussed in this unit. Qualitative methods are ideal in this case because they are suited to producing highly detailed information, and they allow for greater interaction between the researcher and the study participant. Using these methods, you would provide excellent opportunities for research participants to interact with your menu, food items, and other aspects of the restaurant. This would likely produce the detailed feedback that management is looking for.

Qualitative Research

Qualitative research methods include an array of approaches that allow researchers to collect detailed, descriptive information from a (typically) small number of units of analysis relative to quantitative methodologies. In most cases, qualitative methods entail much more interaction with the unit of analysis than quantitative methods do. In-depth, multi-method exploration of only one or two examples is known as a **case study**. Often, such as in the example leading into this unit, qualitative methods take the researcher out of the lab and into more **natural settings** where **field research** can be conducted. When such an approach considers the context of the situation, the biases of the scholar, and the perspective of the units of analysis, it is referred to as **ethnography**. As researchers consider these issues and further analyze how their own biases might affect the relationship between the researcher and those they study, they engage in a process of **reflexivity**.

When studying people—or other units of analysis—in such settings, scholars often engage in **participant observation**. When doing so, the role of the researcher can range from a **complete observer** to a **complete participant**. Within that range of roles, researchers can more subtly vary the extent to which they observe or participate, such as taking on the role of **observer-as-participant** or

qualitative versus quantitative
→ Unit 3

exploration
→ Unit 3

bias
→ Unit 3

rapport
→ Unit 10

becoming more involved with their research target as **participant-as-observer**. When engaging in field research, researchers have to take care in deciding on a process for **exiting** the field by doing whatever they can to maintain the relationships they have developed and consider how their presence will have affected the people they observed.

Qualitative or **depth interviews** are a common form of qualitative research. They can take many formats, but a common approach is the **funnel** format, whereby researchers start with broad questions and then focus on more specific and detailed questions that get at the heart of what the researcher is trying to understand. Within that format, the interviewers can also utilize multiple frameworks to organize the interview, including **fully structured, semistructured,** and **unstructured approaches**. These approaches vary in the extent to which the researchers follow a scripted (or not) set of questions.

Beyond individual-based interviews, researchers can also employ **focus groups**—a common method in marketing, politics, and public relations—in which multiple participants are gathered to engage in discussion at one time. Focus group size typically ranges from 6 to 12 participants, but in some cases, mini-focus groups can be used with only 3 to 5 participants. The discussion is overseen by a trained professional known as the focus group **moderator**.

Central to these varied approaches is the relationship between the researcher and the participant, known as rapport. Researchers should ask a wide array of questions to gain a full picture of the topic of study. Improved rapport helps the researcher have greater success when asking more detailed and personal questions. In all, these methods are designed to produce highly detailed data based on interviews, **field notes**, and observations undertaken by the researcher. Typically, qualitative researchers stay in the field conducting observations until they see similar patterns recurring—referred to as the **saturation** point.

Reflexivity

Reflexivity refers to the process by which researchers consider their own biases, backgrounds, and attitudes and how those elements can affect both their relationship with the subjects they are studying and the conclusions they draw based on their interactions with those people. Reflexivity is commonly associated with qualitative interviewing and ethnography, but it is an important consideration in most qualitative research methods. One of the reasons this process is so important to qualitative research but is not often considered in quantitative research is that qualitative researchers tend to have more involved interactions with the people they are studying. Consider a situation in which you are conducting qualitative interviews to understand consumer attitudes toward descriptions of food items on a menu. You could spend an hour or more engaging in a detailed conversation with each person. Further, in each case, you strive to build rapport and ask personal questions of the research participant. You then have to make sense of the information given by analyzing the results.

Because of the more personal relationship you have built with the participants and the data you are analyzing, it is important to understand how your own biases could influence that process. For instance, it could be that you personally developed the menu-item descriptions, causing you to react strongly to comments that critique those items. Or perhaps the items were written by the person previously in your position—therefore, you may be predisposed to want to change those items. Contrast this with quantitative data collection approaches, such as survey research, in which the researcher uses a questionnaire as a means to collect data and therefore has minimal contact with the participant (and little chance to influence participants because of their own biases). Of course, many qualitative researchers would argue that it is still valuable for researchers to consider how their biases affect both the data collection and data analysis process and would urge quantitative researchers to reflect on their own biases when interpreting data.

questionnaire
design
→ Unit 7

Case Study

Research that involves in-depth exploration of one or two units of analysis in great detail is referred to as a *case study*. Case studies often employ multiple qualitative methodologies to provide a thorough assessment of the issue or topic under study and focus on one particular "case" for illustrative purposes. For instance, a researcher might analyze internal papers such as minutes from board meetings or company e-mails, and conduct interviews with current and past employees, to develop a thorough understanding of an issue that occurred within the company. Typically, case studies are used as a means of highlighting particular aspects of an issue, and the units of analysis for a case study are chosen because of the particular characteristics they represent by using deliberate sampling techniques. For example, researchers interested in how corporations use public relations to handle crisis events (e.g., an explosion at a factory, customer deaths from food contamination, or pollution leaking into the water supply) could study this topic in a number of different ways. They could conduct a content analysis of all press releases dealing with crisis events released in a given year, or they could conduct qualitative interviews with numerous corporate communication people to understand the process and procedures used to deal with crisis events.

A case study approach focuses on how *one* company handled *one* particular incident. For instance, researchers could study how BP (British Petroleum) used crisis communication to respond to the April 2010 oil rig explosion that led to the deaths of 12 workers as well as billions of dollars in land and property damage. Using the case study approach, researchers would closely study the particular decisions that BP made, when those decisions were made, why

exploration
→ Unit 3

qualitative versus
quantitative
→ Unit 3

unit of analysis
→ Unit 2

deliberate
sampling
→ Unit 8

content analysis
→ Unit 11

depth interviews
→ Unit 12

those decisions were made, and whether they were the correct decisions to make. In a case study, researchers often use various methods to gather the information needed to fully understand the case. This might include analyzing internal memos and e-mail messages, conducting interviews with employees and management, as well as assessing press coverage to determine the effectiveness of BP's response to the crisis. The key is to focus on the one "case" to provide the basis for understanding the topic you are exploring.

To that end, any time that researchers engage in a case study, it is essential that they fully recognize and discuss specific characteristics of the unit being studied that could affect what happens. For example, a corporation such as BP has incredible levels of resources, political connections, and, more than likely, in-house legal counsel and crisis communication teams. Therefore, it is better prepared to respond to crises than smaller companies (or individuals) with fewer resources and less experience. It is also likely that the public has assumptions about the company that are firmly in place, as BP has an international reputation and has been in existence for a number of years. In such a case, it would be important for the researchers to recognize that BP's response—and the subsequent success or failure of that response—may be unique to the company and may not apply equally to all other crisis communication events. Consider, for example, a local pizza shop that serves contaminated food to its patrons. This event could lead to patrons getting sick, and local news media may end up covering the event. In most cases, a small, family-owned pizza shop will not have an on-staff crisis communication expert or legal counsel to help it navigate the crisis. Therefore, the owners may handle a crisis much differently than a corporation such as BP would. As such, it is also unlikely that the local pizza company would gain much benefit from using BP as a case study and would likely select a company with similar characteristics for a case study helping them determine an appropriate response. This demonstrates why not only being selective with sampling but also conducting multiple case studies can be a fruitful way to provide a more detailed and broad-based understanding of a particular issue.

Reflect & React: Assessing Strengths and Weaknesses of Case Studies

In thinking about the case study approach, what do you see as the biggest strengths of this approach? What about the biggest weaknesses? To help with this assessment, locate some scholarly research that employs the case study approach. What do the authors of the study say about the strengths and weaknesses of this approach? Why do you think the case study was an effective approach for their research questions?

Field Research

field experiment
→ Unit 9

survey research
→ Unit 10

field notes
→ Unit 12

reactive measures
→ Unit 7

triangulation
→ Unit 3

In many instances, communication research is conducted in laboratory or university settings, requiring participants to visit a college campus (or be students there) or other research facility. However, in other cases, researchers are interested in studying people in their natural environment. Field research involves the researcher conducting observations in settings that are appropriate to the topic being studied. For example, a cultural anthropologist might study a tribe from the Amazon rainforest by living with that tribe for a month, or a biologist could study primates by living among them. Both of these are instances of field research. Each of these topics could conceivably be studied in the lab but there are great possibilities and opportunities to going into the field instead.

Field research is an important part of communication research as well. For example, you might be interested in understanding how regional cultural differences in the United States affect how managers and their employees in the restaurant industry interact with one another. It could be that a traditional top-down model, in which the bosses call the shots in an authoritarian way, is the norm in certain geographic regions, whereas in other regions, the norm is shared decision making, with bosses consulting their employees before making major decisions. Field research could be a good way to understand this issue because it would enable you to observe these kinds of interactions as they occur in real-world situations. This approach would also allow you to gather considerable detail about how people interact in these settings, providing useful insights for developing company policy.

A resulting strength of field research is that it allows the researcher to see things as they normally occur and to capture incredible detail that would not be so easily observed or measured using other techniques. In some ways, this approach is similar to field experiments in that the study is taken out of a controlled environment, but field research tends to be even more focused on detailed observation and avoiding intervention. Consider how, in conducting field research, you could take note of the body language of the employees in addition to noting their conversations. Such detail would be difficult to measure using a survey or depth interviews because those methods often take the participants out of their natural habitat. Because of the incredible amount of detail that the researcher can observe, it is important to take good field notes so that analyses conducted at the completion of data collection are certain to be accurate.

Although there are major strengths of field research, there are also some weaknesses to consider. The primary concern is reactivity—that is, the presence of the researcher can influence how people behave. It might be that employees are more likely to behave in a more subservient way when they are being observed. Or it could be that they are more likely to speak out because they feel emboldened by having someone other than their employer in the room.

In either case, the researcher cannot be certain, so it is important to acknowledge this limitation when discussing the findings of field research. Of course, using triangulation by studying the topic using other methods that confirm the observations made in the field can strengthen the researchers' confidence in what they have observed.

Ethnography

field research
→ Unit 12

focus groups
→ Unit 12

survey research
→ Unit 10

reflexivity
→ Unit 12

In the case of ethnographic research, the focus is on studying a particular group in its natural habitat (i.e., naturalistic settings), with the goal of developing a nuanced and detailed cultural understanding of the group under study. There are many aspects of a group that can be assessed through ethnography, including communication habits and patterns (e.g., how communication changes over the course of a relationship), norms, roles (e.g., how bosses or employees define who they are and what they do; how corporate culture is developed), expectations (e.g., the role of culture in defining career aspirations), and other such elements that provide a detailed picture of what the group being studied is really like. Therefore, ethnography is a particular type of field research that considers how culture and other types of context influence the attitudes and behaviors of the people under study. In many research methods, such as focus groups or surveys, researchers attempt to home in on a particular attitude or behavior, often at the expense of developing a full understanding of who the participants are and how they are shaped by their culture and background. Ethnography is a more developed and typically time-consuming approach that requires the researcher to develop a better and fuller understanding of the culture being studied and how that culture might influence attitudes and behaviors of the people under study simply because these elements are an important part of the picture of *who* is being studied.

For example, a national nonprofit organization that helps immigrants and refugees find job training and counseling services may be interested in expanding its services to include some new locations. All of its previous locations have been in big cities with established immigrant populations, yet the new locations are slated to be in rural and typically underserved areas. It would be useful for the nonprofit agency to have a developed cultural understanding of the norms, ideals, and cultural practices of the immigrant and refugee groups that will call these new rural locations home. It might be that the cultures established in these rural locations are quite different from those established in large urban locations such as New York City. Ethnography would be a useful approach for the nonprofit agency to better understand the needs of the new community it is trying to reach.

By entering into the field, researchers working with the nonprofit could experience firsthand the distinct ways members of the culture—or subculture—live, work, communicate, and share knowledge. This approach could provide key insights into how best to reach members of the group, such as whether face-to-face discussions are more effective than e-mails or phone calls. It could also provide insights into decision-making processes, such as whether the men or women hold special decision-making powers in a relationship or whether such decisions are shared. In each case, these insights can have a direct impact on the strategies the nonprofit uses to reach members of the group and carry out its mission. As a note, given the considerable amount of time that researchers could spend with the people they are studying while conducting an ethnography, they must consider reflexivity. Specifically, they need to address the extent to which their presence has had an influence on the people being studied and the conclusions drawn from observations made.

Exiting

Exiting refers to the process of leaving the research field to begin the process of qualitative data analysis and writing reports on the observations you have conducted. Typically, researchers use the saturation point as their cue to begin the exiting process. When you begin hearing the same stories over and over and noticing the same patterns again and again, it is time to begin the process of exiting the field. However, exiting the field is not as simple as packing up and leaving. Just as researchers give thought to how they enter the field and work to develop rapport with the people they are studying, they must put similar thought and care into how they leave the research field.

For instance, consider a situation in which you have spent months building relationships with a group of people, and then you suddenly disappear from their lives. Months later, they may find out that you have written research articles about them, and thus the purpose of your visit was simply to study them. This could result in those relationships being fractured, exacerbating any negative effects caused by your abrupt departure. If you needed to return to the field to gather more information, it would be difficult to do so because the relationships you had built might be fractured beyond repair.

Therefore, it is important to consider where you are in the research process when deciding the best approach to exiting the field. For instance, if you are certain that data collection is complete and you will not need to return to the field as a researcher, then you can fully exit the field by debriefing the people that you have interacted with and letting them know any details of the study that you wish to share. However, if you would like to maintain the ability to return to the field as a complete participant or similar role in the future, you would likely not want to reveal any details about what you are doing. Yet it would be valuable to maintain the good relationships that you have built. In this case, you would want to find a way to exit the field that would allow you to maintain those relationships without damaging them by abruptly leaving without explanation.

qualitative data analysis
→ Unit 13

saturation
→ Unit 12

rapport
→ Unit 10

debriefing
→ Unit 4

complete participant
→ Unit 12

research ethics
→ Unit 4

field research
→ Unit 12

informed consent
→ Unit 4

voluntary participation
→ Unit 4

In any type of research, it is important to consider the ethics of what you are doing as a researcher. Field research is no different and can often lead researchers into gray areas in terms of informed consent and voluntary participation. Therefore, exiting is a critical step in the research process to make sure that you as the researcher are not leaving the people you have been studying worse off than when you arrived to study them.

Field Notes

Throughout the course of field research, it is essential that the researchers keep track of their observations through the use of field notes. These notes are detailed descriptions of what the researchers observed during their time in the field. They should be written down or recorded as soon as possible so that the researchers do not forget or misremember any of what they observed. Often, these notes are recorded in a field log or journal. Field notes are an invaluable piece of the data analysis process in qualitative research, and they are useful to the researchers in looking back over what they experienced during the course of the study.

In some cases, such as observational research, the researchers are able to record notes during the course of data collection. Because this process can sensitize those being observed to being studied, researchers need to find a less distracting way to record information. However, it must still allow them to still collect data as they go. In other circumstances, such as participant observation, recording notes during data collection becomes more difficult because the researchers are focused on carrying out the activities they are studying. In such situations, the researchers should develop a system for keeping track of information, such as by developing a notation system that allows them to quickly and briefly note details about what they are doing. They should then write down their fully developed field notes as soon as possible using the notation system to help them remember what they observed. Of course, the advent of new technologies allows for a variety of ways to record field notes, including audio recordings, texting information to yourself during the observation, writing notes in a traditional journal, and using photos or video to complement any notes that you might take. During the analysis process, qualitative researchers will revisit their field notes a number of times as they work through the process of coding and evaluating the data.

Consider a situation in which you are involved in a research project that is focused on understanding how alcohol consumption affects conversation style in mixed-sex dyads (e.g., a conversation between a man and a woman). Qualitative field research would be an ideal way of studying this topic, and one approach would be to engage in some observational research at a local bar. As a complete observer, you could find a place to observe the goings on at the bar from a quiet and, perhaps, dimly lit corner. In such a case, you could sit quietly with a notebook or other recording device (perhaps a tablet) and

QUALITATIVE RESEARCH

keep track of the things you see. To people in the bar interacting with friends and having a good time, you likely wouldn't be noticed or wouldn't raise suspicion, as it is common for people to interact with mobile devices nowadays. In recording your observations, you would want to keep track of the different patrons at the bar and note how much alcohol they consume, whom they talk to, and any other behavioral changes you notice in them throughout the course of the night. In many cases, there may be varied and even unexpected events, such as a live band, crowding patrons, or even a fight, so you would be able to record all these developments in your notes. These detailed notes would be useful to review at the end of the observation process and would give much more nuanced information than simply using a standardized format such as a questionnaire.

Alternatively, you could carry out your research as a complete participant, becoming a part of the very thing you are studying. Because in this case you would be directly interacting with the people you are studying, it would be more difficult to keep detailed field notes during the observation period. Therefore, you might find moments to "excuse yourself" from the observation to quickly record some notes on your phone or in a small notepad. However, as soon as the observation ends and you leave the situation for that evening, you would want to record as much detail about the evening as you could, saving those notes for further analysis.

Natural Settings

One of the most valuable aspects of field research is that researchers are able to observe their subjects in their own environment. These natural settings often make it likely that research subjects will behave in more normal ways than they might if taken out of their natural environment. Consider, for a moment, animals at the zoo. Although many zoos strive to create "naturalistic" environments for their animals, in reality, these environments are quite different from the natural world. For example, the zebras and giraffes at the zoo typically have a nice little space with some trees and fresh water that also happens to not be populated by crocodiles or lions (not to mention the hyenas). The lions, on the other hand, have their own space where the keepers toss in a few pounds of meat every day or so to keep them happy (and well fed, of course). Although zoos and other captive exhibits can be valuable ways for scientists and the public to learn about animal behavior, they also impose some limitations on our ability to draw conclusions about what we observe simply because the environments are not fully realistic.

In much the same way, research that brings human participants into a research lab could affect the observations simply because the participants have been taken out of their environment. Field research cuts through this issue by observing participants in their own environment on their terms. Of course,

field research
→ Unit 12

depth interviews
→ Unit 12

qualitative versus quantitative
→ Unit 3

field notes
→ Unit 12

the downside of this approach is that the researcher has less control over the research situation, and many things can occur that might interfere with the data collection process. For example, in conducting research on workplace satisfaction and communication style, it would be useful to study participants at work. However, during the course of observation, there could be a workplace argument, some repair work going on at the office, a particularly needy customer who takes up a lot of time, or many other distracting events. The trade-off is that the researchers gain valuable insights by studying people in their natural settings, but they recognize that they lose some control over the setting and the experience that they will observe.

Consider an example of conducting research on the culture of sports fans. One effective approach would be to study fans of a particular team and develop an understanding of their norms (e.g., which teams they see as rivals and which players they like or dislike) and rituals (e.g., chants or taunts yelled at games, tailgating behaviors, and popular spots to watch "away" matches). This could be done by inviting some fans to your office and conducting depth interviews. However, such an approach would not allow you to capture these fans in the moment, and some valuable details could be lost. Simply put, they may answer questions in a laboratory setting differently than they would in the field before, during, or after a game.

Of course, an advantage of conducting these interviews outside the context of the game or tailgate is that the interview subjects are more likely to be sober and have the time and focus to give you more detailed responses than they might during a game. Yet a field research approach would also yield valuable insights into fan culture. Walking through the tailgating area prior to the game; interacting with fans before, during, and after the game; and then observing the norms and rituals you are studying in real time would provide a tremendous amount of detail and would give access to naturally occurring events. These events may not be entirely typical—observations made during a snowstorm, for instance, will be distinct from those made on a clear, sunny day. However, each of these things becomes part of the qualitative researcher's field notes and research report.

Saturation

exiting
→ Unit 12

relationship
→ Unit 2

variable
→ Unit 2

research questions
→ Unit 2

A common question in qualitative research is, "how many people do I have to interview/observe/study before I start the process of exiting the field?" The answer to that question is when you reach *saturation*—that is, the point at which you are no longer observing new or different things and continue to see the same patterns emerging in your observations. Researchers are looking for patterns in relationships between variables. When those patterns become clear and begin to repeat over a series of observations, this means the researchers have identified the relationship and must now work to unpack the patterns and develop an understanding of what is going on in order to answer their research question.

The question of how many people to interview/observe/study can be an important one because qualitative research can be very time-consuming. For example, depth interviews could take up to an hour or more for each interview. Focus groups could range from 60 minutes to 120 minutes. Field research can be even more time-consuming because it involves going out into the field on multiple occasions over a period of time. Because researchers often have limited resources (e.g., time and money), they want to maximize their time in the field but also leave adequate resources for data analysis and writing a research report. Further, discussing the saturation point in the research report shows that the researchers have collected an adequate amount of data and have not left any stone unturned in answering their research question.

Consider the example from the beginning of this unit in which you are working for a restaurant that is considering expansion but needs to better understand regional differences before fully committing to the expansion. It would be valuable to know when to stop collecting new data and focus on analyzing the data you have collected and making an informed decision. If you have completed five interviews so far and each has provided you with a different reaction and possible set of solutions to your problem, then it is likely that more data collection is needed. The same would hold if you have conducted two focus groups and left them both with a wide array of options but no clear consensus as to what decision to make. Ultimately, what you are looking for is confidence that you are interpreting the data in a meaningful way and making good decisions based on the data you have collected. Therefore, repetition of themes and ideas is a good thing because it suggests that you are heading in the direction of identifying the underlying patterns. As a note, saturation does not require a series of identical responses, so long as you see clear patterns emerging. For example, all of your interview respondents might indicate that they are unhappy with the dinner specials offered on the menu. Two of them may indicate they want fuller meals, and another may specify that he or she wants more meat-based options. Overall, there is a clearly a pattern that suggests that larger meals are needed and it appears that meat-based meals would be a useful way to resolve this problem.

Focus Group

This type of qualitative research employs many of the techniques of depth interviews but applies them to a group setting, in which a moderator leads a group discussion. In most cases, focus groups have 6 to 12 participants, although the number can vary based on the goals of the researchers and the nature of the topic. For instance, if the researchers would like to get more in-depth responses from each participant, a smaller number of participants would be necessary. However, if the researchers are interested in getting a wider range of responses, but are less concerned with depth, then a larger focus group could be used. In

qualitative versus quantitative
→ Unit 3

depth interviews
→ Unit 12

focus groups
→ Unit 12

field research
→ Unit 12

qualitative data analysis
→ Unit 13

themes
→ Unit 13

depth interviews
→ Unit 12

moderator
→ Unit 12`

incentive
→ Unit 8

research questions
→ Unit 2

some cases, researchers even use mini-focus groups that have as few as 3 to 5 participants. Focus group sessions typically last 60 minutes to 120 minutes, and participants are often provided with an incentive to compensate them for their involvement in the focus group. The nature of the compensation depends on the composition of the group. As such, research will often adjust the compensation or incentives offered based on the amount of time and travel they are expecting participants to give. Further, in some cases, researchers will compensate participants based on perceived salary if they are asked to give up time at work to participate in the focus group.

One of the most valuable components of the focus group is the group dynamic and the idea that a group of people can produce a greater range of ideas and bring a greater range of perspectives on a topic than a single interview subject. One reason is the time savings: researchers can conduct two focus group sessions with 12 to 24 people in the same amount of time that it takes to conduct in-depth interviews with only 2 to 3 people. Of course, the trade-off is in the depth of information gained from each participant; it will be less from each participant in a focus group. However, the overall depth and variety of information could be greater in focus groups, as participants are able to hear and respond to one another. The discussion may generate ideas that would not have come up in a one-on-one interview.

Focus groups are commonly used in advertising and market research, although they are useful for many research questions and topics. For example, an advertising agency may have produced two versions of an advertisement for a client. A cost-effective way of helping the client determine which advertisement will be most effective is to conduct focus group sessions in which participants watch the advertisements and then react to them. The moderator can direct the discussion to elicit details about what the participants like and dislike about the ads, as well as what they would like to see changed.

A similar procedure could be used to determine the best slogan or catchphrase for a new product. In this case, the researchers could conduct a focus group early in the process to generate initial ideas. For instance, an up-and-coming fragrance company may be interested in reaching a younger demographic and therefore would want to develop a slogan that appeals to that demographic. In this case, the researchers would put together a focus group made up of people from that target demographic and engage in a discussion with them about the product, with the aim of generating ideas that could be used as the basis for the new slogan. The researchers would then take those initial ideas and develop them further into two or three possible slogans. A follow-up focus group could then be conducted to help decide which of the three slogans the ad agency should use.

One of the downsides of focus groups is that some of the participants may be excessively influenced by more vocal members of the group. For instance, in some cases, a dominating personality could affect the group dynamic and the quality of the discussion by making others in the group feel less interested in speaking. Consider the situation in which you are assessing customer feedback before your restaurant expands to a new location. If one person in the group adamantly suggests that no changes are needed and that he or she "loves everything about the restaurant," this could result in others taking on this same theme if they feel uncomfortable disagreeing (or simply lack strong opinions of their own). On the other hand, overly timid or quiet people can also have a negative effect because the discussion is then dominated by a small number of participants. The end result in this case is that only a few people have actually contributed ideas when you were hoping to hear from all members of the focus group.

In other cases, participants can get "stuck" on one idea, when members of the group continually build on an earlier response and fail to offer original ideas. Researchers may value discussion that leads to true consensus, but they also want participants to explore a range of topics. Therefore, in focus group research, the moderator plays an important role in generating discussion in which each of the participants makes a meaningful contribution. This enables researchers to capitalize on the ability of focus groups to generate a range of ideas. Given this, focus group moderators have to be creative and continue to develop their skills at leading effective discussions that will help their clients.

Research in Depth: Uses of Focus Groups

Focus groups can be used for a wide variety of research topics. Here are some examples of focus groups used to study different communication phenomena—in certain cases alongside other methods to provide for triangulation:

1. Sayed (2011) used focus groups—in conjunction with survey data—to study social media use among activists in Egypt.
2. Weber, Dillow, and Rocca (2011) used focus group data to better understand effective strategies for developing anti-drunk driving public service announcements.
3. Childs (2005) used focus groups and depth interviews to explore black women's attitudes toward black-white interracial relationships.
4. McLaughlin and Vitak (2012) used focus groups to assess the ways in which norms have evolved on social networking sites and the impact of violations of those norms.

Consider topics that are of interest to you. In what ways would focus groups be a useful research tool in the study of those topics?

Voices from Industry

Connie Morris—Focus Group Expert

Connie Morris earned a master's degree in education from Wichita State University, where she has also taught communication courses for 40 years. She is a past member of the National Communication Association, International Listening Association, Popular Culture Association, and the Kansas Speech Communication Association, which awarded her its University Teacher of the Year Award. Connie is experienced in marketing research, group facilitation, and speech coaching for professionals.

What specific method or methods do you use or encounter most?

I taught communication classes for 40 years at a local university. For the past 15 years, I also have conducted hundreds of focus groups as a consultant for an agency that counseled clients in advertising, marketing, and public relations. The clients included churches, nonprofits, banks, and an automobile leasing company, to list a few. The clients wanted to know how to improve customer service, introduce a new product or program, focus fund-raising, and learn their customers' concerns.

How did the research you conducted help inform your decision?

In one case, a local nonprofit was concerned about meeting its local fund-raising goals while the national office was facing major accusations of making questionable decisions and mishandling money. This was casting an unfavorable light over the entire charity. Focus groups were conducted locally to determine the opinions of charity givers. How would this impact local fund-raising? Three specific issues emerged as concerns. Participants wanted to know that the majority of dollars donated locally would stay local; they wanted minorities to be shown as givers, not just receivers; and they wanted to see true stories of local families being helped.

The agency used this information to produce ads for television addressing these points. The ads were on target—informative, humorous, and warm and fuzzy. The nonprofit exceeded its fund-raising goal that year.

What are one or two pieces of advice or insights you would give about research to students in a communication research methods course?

Focus group research produces rich results. The bottom line is if you want to know what people think, ask them.

Moderator

The person who is responsible for guiding the focus group and ensuring that all participants contribute to the discussion is the moderator. The role of the moderator is to guide the participants through the discussion and keep it focused on the topic at hand. That can be a real challenge, particularly in larger focus groups in which the moderator has to balance a range of personalities and generate input from all of the people in the group. Because of this, a good focus group moderator is adept at dealing with different personality types and will keep more assertive personalities from dominating the group discussion while also drawing out contributions from more timid personalities.

Further, a good moderator will use probing to generate more detailed responses and thoughts from participants, but he or she should refrain from making value statements or giving responses that would either encourage or discourage discussion in any way. The moderator is there to get information out of the participants, not to have his or her individual perspectives or ideas color the nature of the discussion. Because of the complexities of dealing with different group dynamics and the challenge of remaining neutral in leading group discussions, focus group moderators are often highly trained. Therefore, experienced focus group moderators may charge a hefty fee for their services.

In most cases, focus group sessions are documented on either video or audio recordings. However, the moderator will also typically take notes during the course of the discussion. This allows the moderator to make decisions about what questions to ask, when to probe, and whom they need to generate more responses from within the group. For example, if one idea generates a lot of positive nonverbal response from group members (such as head nodding and smiling), the focus group moderator would likely want to delve further into why that idea was so well received. Without active note taking, it would be easy for the moderator to forget to follow up and instead move on to the next question on the list. By actively taking notes, the moderator is more involved in the discussion and better able to make any necessary adjustments to the initial plan, allowing him or her to respond to what the group is saying or doing.

Participant Observation

Participant observation is a type of field research in which the researcher conducts observations of the topic being studied. In this type of research, the researcher does not engage in interviews with study participants but instead studies the subjects through either passive observation or active engagement in the behaviors under study. The different types of participant observation research fall along a continuum ranging from complete observer to complete participant. Taking the role of complete observer, the researcher does not directly interact with the people or situation being studied. On the other hand, taking the role of complete participant requires the researcher to engage directly with the people or situation being studied. Along this continuum are varying degrees to which the researcher

field research
→ Unit 12

depth interviews
→ Unit 12

complete observer
→ Unit 12

complete participant
→ Unit 12

observer-as-participant
→ Unit 12

triangulation
→ Unit 3

acts as observer, participant, or both. These other roles often include observer-as-participant and participant-as-observer. These terms reflect the extent to which the primary role is either observer or participant. For instance, when acting as observer-as-participant, you would function more as an observer but engage in some of the participatory activities of your research subjects. On the other hand, the participant-as-observer is further involved and takes more of an active role with the research subjects.

For example, consider a situation in which you are interested in studying how people interact with one another in a public setting such as a community park. Specifically, you might be interested in understanding particular activities that people engage in, as well as how they communicate their interest in participating in those activities to others. Participant observation is a method that is uniquely suited to studying this issue. As a complete observer, you might study the situation from a distant part of the park where there are not many people. In doing so, you could easily take notes and would not interfere with or participate in the activities you are observing.

Over the course of your study, however, you might gradually increase the extent of your participation in your research. The next day, you might move closer to the central activities and perhaps sit on a bench near the action, pretending to have lunch or read a book. In such a case, you are still acting as more of an observer, but you are now much closer to participating in the action. After noticing some of the activities people engage in, you might decide to further increase the level of participation in your research. On the third day of your observations, you could bring along another researcher and engage in one of the activities that you previously observed. For instance, perhaps people who hang out at this park toss a football around or play guitar and sing. In this case, you have now crossed over to being a participant-observer rather than a complete observer or an observer-participant. On the fourth and final day of your research, you might become a complete participant by directly engaging and interacting with the people you are studying. In this case, you could invite some of the people you are studying to throw the football around with you or even invite yourself to hang out with a group of people.

As you evolve through these different roles, the nature of the experience you have with whom and what you are studying changes. You become much closer to the people you are studying, which can provide valuable detail about the activities they engage in and the ways they interact with one another. However, you may also affect how they act toward one another by taking an active role in their lives. For instance, perhaps inviting yourself to participate in a group activity resulted in a conflict between group members. It might be that such a conflict would not have occurred if you had not been present. Ultimately, such issues reinforce the value of triangulation—using multiple methods to study the same topic.

Complete Observer

reactive measures
→ Unit 7

The role of complete observer is one in which the researcher is able to observe whom or what they are studying but is removed from the situation so as not to create reactivity—a situation in which the presence of the researcher influences the activity being studied. The upside to being a complete observer is that the researcher has greater confidence that the observations made are not a result of his or her influence on the research subjects. However, the downside to being a complete observer is that important details could be missed. This can occur because the researcher is keeping a distance from those being studied. For example, consider observing human interactions at a park. If you choose to be a complete observer and study interactions between people from afar, you will feel confident that your presence has not caused them to act differently. However, although you will be able to observe general patterns of behavior, it may be difficult to get highly specific details, such as what people are saying to one another, facial expressions people make during conversations, and other behaviors they may exhibit that are difficult to distinguish from afar. You may also miss out on direct experience with the behavior or the opportunity to hear from participants about their motivations and feelings.

Complete Participant

reactive measures
→ Unit 7

complete observer
→ Unit 12

The role of complete participant is one in which the researcher inserts himself or herself into the situation being studied. As such, instead of observing from afar, the researcher engages directly with the people being studied and participates in the same activities as those being studied. A strength of this research approach is that the researcher is able to access an incredible amount of detail and truly get a sense of the experience the participants are having. The researcher can easily see facial expressions, hear side comments and conversations, directly feel the joy or despair that may result from that activity, and otherwise gather useful details about who or what is being studied. On the other hand, such research runs the risk of creating reactivity, whereby the presence of the researcher has a direct impact on the behavior of those under study. For example, in studying human interactions at a park, the researcher—acting as complete participant— might introduce himself or herself to people, offer to participate in activities, or even be the person who initiates action. However, it is possible that such things would not have occurred without the presence of the researcher. Further, the outcomes of these activities may be altered by the presence of the researcher. In both cases, the researcher should recognize the strengths and weaknesses of the roles of complete participant and complete observer before making a decision about how to proceed.

complete observer
→ Unit 12

complete
participant
→ Unit 12

Observer-as-Participant and Participant-as-Observer

Although it is useful to understand the two ends of the spectrum—complete participation and complete observer, there is middle ground and the role of the researcher can be further broken down based on the extent to which the researcher acts as a participant or an observer. In some cases, the researcher will lean more toward being a participant in the activities being observed and, as such, would identify his or her role as participant-as-observer. In this way, the researcher is distinguishing what he or she does from what a complete observer or complete participant is doing. Taking a role that blends the level of participation and observation can allow the researcher to balance the strengths and weaknesses of being a complete participant or a complete observer.

For example, consider a situation in which you want to better understand how strangers interact with each other in a public setting such as a park. You may start as a complete observer by watching the activity from afar and not letting on to anyone that you are present—thus acting as a complete observer. However, you may realize that you are missing key details about how people are interacting with one another because it is difficult to hear what they are saying and you can't see everyone's faces when you are interacting. Therefore, you would want to enter the field in some way to be able to capture some of that detail. One approach would be to find an area of the park that is heavily trafficked with people and set up in that area to conduct your observations. By placing yourself closer to the middle of the action, you are now part of the field that you are observing, and thus you might have people come up to you and introduce themselves or have similar opportunities to interact with strangers. Yet if you do not take on an explicitly active role, you are not acting as a complete participant. By moving closer to the action and sometimes being a part of that action but not initiating or otherwise leading the action, you take on a role that puts you in the middle of the continuum from observer to participant. As a note, there are not always clear lines between someone acting as observer-as-participant or participant-as-observer, so it is not important to get caught up in how you might label yourself as a researcher. What is important, however, is to have a clear understanding of how you as the researcher may affect the people that you are observing and what implications that could have for the conclusions you draw.

survey research
→ Unit 10

rapport
→ Unit 10

Qualitative/Depth Interviews

Interviews in qualitative research differ from those in survey research in that they capture much greater detail and typically take a longer amount of time to complete. In most cases, qualitative researchers using the interview methodology take an approach whereby they gradually build toward developing an understanding of the concepts being studied. Because of this, rapport building becomes a central focus of the qualitative interview. As the interviewer builds rapport, he or she is able to ask more personal questions and gain more honest and detailed responses. As such, it isn't recommended practice to start with the most challenging or important questions. Typically, these types of interviews follow a funnel format in which general questions are asked early on, allowing the interviewer to circle around a particular topic by asking more and more focused questions as the interview progresses. Qualitative interviews can be a valuable research tool, particularly when researchers are interested in understanding a concept in a highly detailed, ideographic way. Because of this, they are an excellent companion to survey research, which can provide a wide range of information but misses out on key details and subtext.

For example, researchers interested in understanding the role that communication style plays in relationship satisfaction could start with a survey that identifies that people with certain communication styles tend to experience greater relationship satisfaction. However, such a study may not fully explain *why* certain communication styles fare better than others. Qualitative interviews could then be used to further explore this relationship. The researchers could conduct interviews with people who have different communication styles and ask questions specifically designed to get the respondents to talk about their own communication style and how it affects their relationships. In doing so, the researchers would be able to get specific examples of how people with different communication styles handle different aspects of their relationships, including issues such as conflict, romance, and work—life balance. In such cases, the researchers have to be specific about the particular things they want to study. Often there is a desire to throw everything but the kitchen sink into a questionnaire or interview, but the reality is that they must be highly focused to maximize the quality of the information obtained. To obtain this information, interviewers use different types of questions to tap into different aspects of how the respondent sees the world around them. Finally, researchers convert all of the interviews into transcripts that are then used to analyze responses given.

funnel
→ Unit 12

relationship
→ Unit 2

questionnaire design
→ Unit 7

transcript
→ Unit 13

Funnel

The qualitative interview process is like a funnel. Consider how a funnel is wide at the top and narrows down to the bottom, such that there is a much smaller hole at the bottom of the funnel than at the top. In much the same way, qualitative interviews typically start with a broad set of questions that allow the interviewer to develop a base for understanding the issue but also allow for rapport building. Although the goal of the interviewer is to get to the bottom of the funnel—where the most specific questions will be asked—it often takes time to get there as the interviewer and the participant move gradually through their conversation.

depth interview
→ Unit 12

rapport
→ Unit 10

research question
→ Unit 2

qualitative versus quantitative
→ Unit 3

For example, consider a research project in which your goal is to understand the role that music plays in how people form their identities. You might be tempted to simply ask people, "What kind of music do you like and what does that say about you?" Although this might be your guiding research question, it would be more effective to gradually work your way toward understanding that question. In fact, it may be that you never directly ask that question. You could, for instance, start off by asking a very general question about the music the respondent currently has on his or her phone, computer, or other device. You might then ask a follow-up question that gets the respondent to indicate their current favorite songs. A further follow-up question might then ask, "What is it about those artists or songs that sets them apart from the others you like?"

Note that the questions are progressively more specific, building on the participant's previous responses. Of course, it would be necessary to use probing to encourage the more detailed responses that make qualitative research so valuable. The funnel metaphor demonstrates how the qualitative interview is a process that builds on itself, in that each question and response informs subsequent questions and responses. The hallmark of a good interviewer is that he or she follows the flow of the conversation and allows room for the respondent to provide detail and explore areas in depth, all the while focusing on the particular goal or research question that is at the bottom of the funnel.

Interview Structure

Qualitative researchers conducting depth interviews have a range of options in determining how closely—or loosely—they plan to follow their interview script, ranging from fully structured to unstructured interviews. The particular approach that the interview takes is largely dependent on the research goals and guiding research question. For example, in exploratory research, the interviewer may employ a more unstructured approach simply because much is still unknown about the issue under study. The unstructured approach would allow considerable room for the participants to provide insights into the key concepts and potential relationships for the topic under study. However, as more is known and a clearer sense of expectations is developed, a more structured approach should be used. This would include more standardized questions to help further focus the data. Generally, it is valuable for qualitative interviewers to leave some space for the interview subjects to develop answers in their own way and for the interviewer to be able to adapt to the responses given by the interviewee. As a result, semistructured interviews can be a valuable tool because they allow the researcher to strike a balance between ensuring that key questions or topics are covered and allowing room for new ideas that may arise during the interview session.

Fully Structured Interview

Fully structured interviews employ a clearly defined list of questions that are meant to be presented in a specific order during the interview. In using such an approach, the interviewer will work through the list, asking each question after the interviewee has completed answering the preceding question. Using this approach, the researchers ensure that specific questions will be answered and that the experience of each interviewee will be as similar as possible. The downside to such an approach, however, is that the conversation between the interviewer and interviewee may feel stilted and lack flow. Additionally, fully structured interviews often leave little room for moving away from the script and capitalizing on new ideas mentioned by the interviewee. Fully structured interviews are commonly used in the hiring process as well as in exit interviews (when an employee leaves a company).

Semistructured Interview

Semistructured interviews typically have a set of questions or items that must be covered, but they allow more room for the interviewee to expand on the ideas he or she presents. Using this approach, the order of questions and amount of time spent on each will largely depend on the answers given. The interviewer will often allow the interviewee to expand on answers and work to gradually move the interviewee toward the next specific item or question to be discussed. This helps maintain the flow of the conversation but also allows for new information and ideas to be captured as part of that process. Of course, such an approach can be challenging for an interviewer, so it is important that interviewers schedule practice interview sessions to work out probing strategies and other techniques to help guide the interviewee through the process. In a semistructured interview, each of the interviewees is likely to have a somewhat different experience in terms of how much time he or she spends discussing the different questions and in what order. For quantitative research, the threat to reliability that this approach poses would be unacceptable. However, for qualitative researchers, this is viewed as a benefit for validity that outweighs reliability concerns simply because it recognizes the differences in experiences that people may have and creates a more natural conversational flow.

For example, consider again the example from the introduction in which you are conducting research on the viability of a market expansion for a restaurant. A useful data collection approach would be to conduct interviews with employees and managers of other restaurants in the region into which you are hoping to expand. In such a case, you could gain valuable insights into the business practices of restaurants that are currently successful. Using a semistructured interview approach, you would likely prepare a few main questions ahead of time. For instance, you might ask about the following:

qualitative versus quantitative
→ Unit 3

reliability
→ Unit 6

validity
→ Unit 6

research questions
→ Unit 2

rapport
→ Unit 10

semistructured
→ Unit 12

reliability
→ Unit 6

validity
→ Unit 6

what customers like most about the restaurant, what the best-selling items are, what specials are offered, and what the typical customer is like. By setting a reasonable number of key questions, you leave yourself plenty of space to ask follow-up questions. For instance, one respondent might indicate that the typical customers are "families with kids." It would be valuable to follow up on this observation with some questions about what such customers like in particular about the restaurant, what those customers commonly order compared with other customer types, and what efforts have been made to reach out to other types of customers.

qualitative data analysis
→ Unit 13

Unstructured Interview

An unstructured interview is one in which the general topic and guiding research questions are known but the specific questions and structure of the interview are not determined ahead of time. In such a case, the interviewer may start with a general question to build rapport and get the conversation started but then follow the flow of the discussion, as dictated by the responses given by the interviewee. This approach ensures that each interviewee will have a decidedly different experience in terms of the specific questions discussed as well as the order and amount of time spent on each question. As with semistructured interviews, this may pose a threat to reliability, but the perceived benefit to the validity of the experience and responses given is thought to outweigh those concerns. It may seem that such an approach is "easy" to carry out. However, when the interview process is less structured, the success of the interview depends upon the skill of the interviewer. The skill of guiding an interviewee through a fruitful and meaningful conversation comes with practice. Therefore, interviewers should schedule practice interviews to hone their technique in preparation for the "official" interviews used for data collection and qualitative data analysis.

Steps to Success: Preparing for an Effective Qualitative Interview

Preparation is an important part of a successful qualitative interview. Here is a checklist of items to consider before going into the field to conduct a qualitative interview:

1. I am clear on whether I am using a fully structured, semistructured, or unstructured interview approach.
2. I have conducted practice interviews to assess the quality and flow of my questions.
3. I have a strategy for building rapport.

4. I have necessary supplies to record the interview and take notes, including a working audio recorder (with sufficient memory and fresh batteries!), notepad, and two pens.
5. I have reviewed any necessary literature, and I am confident that I am not missing any key questions.
6. I have selected good interview locations that are quiet, comfortable, have adequate seating, and will have minimal influence on the participants.
7. I have sufficient knowledge of my interview subjects to enable rapport building and appropriate question asking.

Reflect & React: Assessing Interview Structures

Locate some scholarly research that uses qualitative interviews. To what extent do the authors discuss the strengths and weaknesses of the particular approach they used? Do they use a fully, semistructured, or unstructured approach? What would you have done differently in studying that same topic? What differences do you notice in how the articles are organized and structured compared with quantitative articles?

Activities

Activity 12A: Developing a Qualitative Research Project

See terms: focus groups; ethnography; qualitative/depth interviews; participant observation.

For this activity, identify a research question or hypothesis that interests you and that you think could be effectively explored through qualitative research. Then, perform the following steps:

- Choose a specific research method that would be appropriate for your topic. Explain how this method could be used in exploring it.
- Explain why you chose this approach instead of other qualitative research options. What are the strengths and weaknesses of your chosen approach?
- Identify what you think the main challenges would be in using your selected approach. For example, what kind of sample would you need? Do you need to develop interview questions? Would observation opportunities be difficult to arrange?

Activity 12B: Reading Qualitative Research

See terms: abstract; discussion; literature review; method section; results section.

For this activity, find a research article that uses one of the qualitative methodologies described in this unit. Then, for comparison, identify an article on this same topic that uses a quantitative approach. Read both and address the following prompts to construct an essay that compares the two approaches:

- In what ways are the parts of the two articles similar? For example, are the organizational structures similar? Do the two articles share the same section headings (e.g., methods, results)?
- In what ways are the parts of the articles different?
- Does the qualitative approach omit any information found in the quantitative study that you consider vital? What about the other way around?
- Which of the papers is the strongest in terms of its presentation of material—clarity, organization, and so on?
- How would you characterize the writing style of each article—accessible, challenging to understand, jargon filled, or something else?
- Which approach do you prefer (quantitative or qualitative)? Why are you drawn more to this approach than the other?

Activity 12C: Conducting Participant Observation Research

See terms: complete observer; complete participant; participant observation.

For this activity, find a group or organization that you are interested in knowing more about and observe that group's interactions. In particular, focus on differences in use of nonverbal communication techniques across members of the group. To carry out this research project, you should attend meetings or events sponsored by the group and take notes on what you see. As a note, please be mindful of the group you are observing and consider ethical principles of voluntary participation and informed consent. In working through your observation data, consider the following questions:

- What conclusions would you draw about how members of this group interact with one another? Are there differences in how members interact with each other compared to how they interact with nonmembers?
- What other research methods would be useful in helping you better understand this group?
- What might you do differently with more time and energy put into preparation? Be specific in considering the improvements you would make to your research approach.

Activity 12D: Using Focus Groups in Applied Settings

See terms: focus group; moderator.

For this activity, imagine that you are a program director for a television network, and you are interested in perceptions about a particular show (to facilitate this activity, identify a show that you and some friends regularly watch). Conduct a series of mini-focus groups using friends, classmates, and others to find out what they like and dislike about the show. Evaluate the session and draw conclusions. Use the following prompts and questions to guide you through this activity:

- Use your guiding research question—what do people like and dislike about the show—to help you develop a few (four or five) specific questions that you can ask your focus group.
- Consider what approaches you need to use to balance the discussion and ensure participation from all members of the focus group. For instance, how do you build rapport with the focus group participants while also helping them feel more comfortable with each other?
- Be sure to take notes during the discussion (don't worry about an exact transcript but just detailed notes on what folks are saying).
- Use your notes and other observations you make during the focus group session to draw conclusions about their feelings toward the show. Are there specific exemplars that illustrate the conclusions you have drawn?
- Consider ways that you could improve your performance as focus group moderator. What would you do differently next time?

Activity 12E: Comparing and Contrasting Interview Structuress

See terms: interview structure; fully structured; semistructured; unstructured.

For this activity, you will compare and contrast two different interviewing approaches—fully structured and unstructured. To facilitate this, take on the role of a corporate communication consultant who is tasked with improving employee-to-employer communication. In doing so, interview one person using a fully structured approach and another using an unstructured approach. Compare and contrast your experiences and outcomes. Use the following prompts and questions to guide you through the process:

■ Use the guiding research question to help you develop a list of four or five questions for the fully structured interview (note: for the purpose of the activity stick to your script for the fully structured interview so you have a good point of comparison with the unstructured approach). For the unstructured interview, develop one broad question to start the discussion and then go from there. Note: It may be helpful to do the unstructured interview first.
■ Be sure to take good notes, recording both what the interviewees say and what goes well or poorly in the process.
■ Compare and contrast your findings, focusing on both the process, results, and conclusions you draw from your interviews.
■ Consider which approach was most effective and whether you prefer one approach to another. In thinking about your preference consider why you prefer one approach to the other.

References

Childs, E. C. (2005). Looking behind the stereotypes of the "angry black woman": An exploration of black women's responses to interracial relationships. *Gender & Society*, *19*(4), 544–561. doi:10.1177/0891243205276755

McLaughlin, C., & Vitak, J. (2012). Norm evolution and violation on Facebook. *New Media & Society*, *14*(2), 299–315. doi:10.1177/1461444811412712

Sayed, N. (2011). Towards the Egyptian revolution: Activists' perceptions of social media for mobilization. *Journal of Arab & Muslim Media Research*, *4*(2–3), 273–298. doi:10.1386/jammr.4.2-3.273_1

Weber, K., Dillow, M. R., & Rocca, K. A. (2011). Developing and testing the anti-drinking and driving PSA. *Communication Quarterly*, *59*(4), 415–427. doi:10.1080/01463373.2011.597285

Suggested Readings for Further Exploration of Unit 12 Topics

Examples

Carbaugh, D., & Hastings, S. O. (1992). A role for communication theory in ethnography and cultural analysis. *Communication Theory*, *2*(2), 156–165. doi:10.1111/j.1468-2885.1992.tb00035.x

Gitlin, T. (1981). *The whole world is watching: Mass media in the making and unmaking of the new left*. Los Angeles, CA: University of California Press.

Jacobs, S. (1990). On the especially nice fit between qualitative analysis and the known properties of conversation. *Communication Monographs*, *57*(3), 243–249. doi:10.1080/03637759009376200

Whyte, W. F. (1993). *Street corner society: The social structure of an Italian slum*. Chicago, IL: University of Chicago Press.

Advanced Discussion

Ellingson, L. L. (2009). Ethnography in applied communication research. In L. R. Frey & K. N. Cissna (Eds.), *Routledge handbook of applied communication research* (pp. 129–152). New York, NY: Routledge.

Lindlof, T. R., & Shatzer, M. J. (1998). Media ethnography in virtual space: Strategies, limits, and possibilities. *Journal of Broadcasting & Electronic Media*, *42*(2), 170–189. doi:10.1080/08838159809364442

Lunt, P., & Livingstone, S. (1996). Rethinking the focus group in media and communications research. *Journal of Communication*, *46*(2), 79–98. doi:10.1111/j.1460-2466.1996.tb01475.x

Yin, R. K. (2009). *Case study research: Design and methods*. Thousand Oaks, CA: Sage Publications.

unit 13

approaches to qualitative analysis

Imagine that you have finally completed your last interview! You have been working with a social work agency in a major city to study how people in inter-racial relationships address racial identity through conversations with their partners. You've spent more than 5 hours conducting depth interviews with five different couples and have completed and printed your transcripts. You are ready to start analyzing your data. Yet looking at a stack of transcripts from hours of depth interviews may feel overwhelming. Where to begin? Of course, you recognize that within all of those pages of your transcript is important information providing you answers to your driving question about how folks address racial identity in their relationships. It will take work to discover the answers within your data, but all of the work will be worth it to better understand the unique communication challenges that interracial couples face. Unlike quantitative research, in which data analysis programs do much of the heavy lifting, qualitative data analysis requires the researcher to do the work to discover the true story buried within the data. All it takes is preparation, good technique, patience, and an interest in discovery.

Qualitative Data Analysis

Qualitative data analysis allows the researcher to discover rich detail and depth of information. The approach to analysis can vary in terms of the extent to which the researcher is looking for objective analysis—such as in analyzing focus group data for a client, or more subjective analysis—such as when the researcher wants to provide critical analysis of a popular film or song. As discussed in Unit 12, qualitative research typically focuses on a small number of cases—relative to quantitative research—but provides extensive observation and exploration of those cases. Qualitative research also is often an iterative process, in that the researcher makes observations, analyzes data, and then repeats that procedure to develop a more thorough and extensive understanding of the topic being studied. Such theoretically and methodologically integrated approaches are often guided by **grounded theory,** which allows the researcher to develop a theoretical understanding through an in-depth and iterative data analysis process. Think of the process you might go through to make a decision about buying a new cell phone. While some may simply spontaneously buy a phone model, others will engage in a more extensive process. This could involve trying out some different phones, talking with friends and family members, reading up on current models, and keeping an eye on popular phones you notice others using and then going back and trying out the phones again now that you have developed a more detailed understanding of them.

The analytical approaches that qualitative researchers take are necessarily rooted in the distinction between quantitative and qualitative data collection. Quantitative researchers often take complex and abstract concepts, such

exploration
→ Unit 3

qualitative versus quantitative
→ Unit 3

concept
→ Unit 5

transcript
→ Unit 13

as personality, emotion, or happiness, and create measures to observe those concepts with just a few items. Qualitative researchers, on the other hand, often consider the full breadth of information and insights that come along with observing concepts. The result is that while quantitative researchers end up with numerical responses to items, qualitative researchers often have long, detailed notes (or transcripts) based on their observations. Such in-depth analyses should reveal **themes** that help you draw conclusions and tell the story of the data. Standout examples—or **exemplars**—are used when you report your findings and want to provide clear-cut instances that demonstrate what your data show. The challenge, however, is that there is more information to make sense of, and that information isn't always neatly organized and self-contained, as it typically is in quantitative research.

Qualitative researchers can analyze many different types of source material, such as discussions between two or more people in **conversation analysis** or written materials (such as letters, books, etc.) in **textual analysis**. In some cases, researchers are looking to more critically evaluate their data providing a more subjective analysis. As such, **rhetorical criticism** encompasses a more involved analysis of texts of different kinds (e.g., movies, music, or books), affording the researcher the opportunity to deeply explore not just the meaning behind a text but also other aspects such as motivations, varied interpretations, and the creation of that text. Researchers focused on the history behind texts—or changes over time in how a text is presented—can pursue **historical analysis**. In any case, qualitative data analysis provides detailed and extensive interpretation of data collected through qualitative methodologies.

Conversation Analysis

themes
→ Unit 13

transcript
→ Unit 13

variable
→ Unit 2

application
→ Unit 3

qualitative versus quantitative
→ Unit 3

Conversation analysis involves a highly detailed exploration of patterns and recurring themes in conversations, most often between two people. Researchers using conversation analysis rely on accurate transcripts that detail all aspects of the conversation, including pauses, repeated words, and utterances (such as "um" or "uh"). The actual analysis of the conversations can focus on a number of things, but the central objective is to identify recurring patterns and themes. For example, researchers could focus on studying turn taking, whereby the researcher analyzes how people in a conversation negotiate who will speak when. You can likely recall a time when you struggled to interject your opinion into a conversation or when you kept talking to block someone else from inserting his or her opinion.

Conversation analysis can allow researchers to identify different types of conversational styles, such as people who are prone to interrupt as well as those who wait for a clear opening before deciding to speak. Through conversation analysis, the researcher can then determine the type of style a person exhibits by looking for clues in the transcript. Someone who is more apt to interrupt others would be characterized by starting to speak in the middle of someone else's sentence. Someone who is inclined to wait his or her turn would be characterized by only speaking after the previous person has completed a sentence or left a noticeable pause.

Apart from identifying conversational styles and patterns, conversation analysis can also be a valuable analytical approach to understand how contextual characteristics influence conversational patterns. For example, a researcher might focus on employer-employee interactions, specifically considering how employers address performance reviews with their employees. In such a case, the nature of the relationship (employer to employee) becomes a key contextual variable, as does the nature of the topic (going over the employee's performance evaluation). The researchers would then record conversations between employees and employers discussing this topic. As a note, in most cases, conversation analysis researchers are not present during data collection. The conversations are recorded either through video or audio recording and then transcribed for analysis.

Reflect & React: Observing Conversational Styles in Everyday Life

The next time you are having dinner with friends or family, take note of the different conversational styles present at the dinner table. Who is most likely to interrupt? Who is patiently waiting his or her turn? Are there other characteristics (e.g., personality) that you notice about these people that help explain why they employ the styles they do? Are you surprised by anything that you observe?

Consider locating a research article or book chapter that discusses conversational styles. What are some of the main styles that are discussed? Now consider the different conversation styles that you encounter on a regular basis in your conversations with friends, family, coworkers, teachers, and so on. Can you identify any exemplars of those different styles based on the people that you know and communicate with regularly?

In analyzing the transcripts that result from these employer-employee conversations, the researchers would be able to develop a better understanding of the types of strategies that employers use to discuss both positive and negative attributes of their employees. For instance, is it more effective to start with good news and then transition to bad news? Should bad news be delivered quickly, as if ripping off a bandage, or is a more deliberate approach effective? The researchers can also simultaneously evaluate how the employees respond to what their employer is telling them.

Ultimately, researchers can learn a considerable amount about people, the distribution of power in relationships, and the influence of context on how we communicate, all based on the conversations that people have. The insights gained from this type of research also have numerous practical applications as well. Research using conversation analysis has made important contributions to the legal profession, to workplace communication, to interactions between medical providers and patients, and to relationship counseling, among other things.

As a note, the basic premise of coding transcribed conversations also lends itself to quantitative analysis, and some interpersonal communication scholars take such an approach. For instance, the frequency of utterances can be coded, as can other characteristics about each occurrence using quantitative techniques. Ultimately, it all comes down to the method the researcher is comfortable with and the ultimate goal of the research. These similarities underscore that at their core, all research methods are rooted in an organized and systematic approach to collecting and interpreting data.

Exemplars

In discussing the patterns and themes present in qualitative data, researchers often provide a very specific, concrete example that demonstrates that theme or pattern very closely. Described as *exemplars*, these highly specific examples are essential to qualitative data reporting because they provide a concrete instance for the theory or theme that is being described. For example, consider a research study in which you evaluate the audience's reaction to a test preview for a new horror movie that is coming out. In this case, focus groups would be a useful method to gain feedback on the preview because you can hear input from many people at once. The general sense of the discussion from the focus groups might indicate that people are excited about the movie and also clearly felt the suspense and fear that the preview generated.

Although such a succinct analysis is good for the client to have (and the client should feel good that the audience responded appropriately to the preview), a qualitative report can provide much more information and play to the strengths of the method. Therefore, the researchers would want to locate quotes from the interviews that clearly exemplify those themes. For instance, after indicating that the audience that saw the preview was now excited for the movie, the researchers might add, "As one respondent indicated—'I can't wait . . . just cannot wait to see this movie now!'" Such a quote is a perfect exemplar for the finding that the audience is excited because it clearly demonstrates the theme that is being discussed. The researchers would also want to identify an exemplar to support the conclusion that the audience felt suspense and fear. For instance, perhaps one of the participants said, "That movie looks scary as hell!" and another said, "That looks scarier than *The Shining*. Totally scary!" Both of these statements from the focus group participants would be excellent exemplars in that they provide a concrete and unambiguous example of the theme discussed.

Exemplars are common and, frankly, essential to reporting results from qualitative data analysis. Often, research reports can seem heavily theoretical and abstract in their presentation of information. Exemplars help provide simple and straightforward examples of what the researchers think the results suggest. Statistics serve a similar purpose in quantitative research in that they boil down potentially complex relationships into a clear-cut sense of what is going on. The importance of exemplars also reinforces why it is necessary for qualitative researchers to take highly detailed field notes or take great care in preparing transcripts. Each of these things provides the source material for accurate presentation of exemplars.

Consider the research example in the introduction to this unit in which you are studying communication patterns in discussing racial identity in interracial relationships. A theme that might emerge from such research is that newer couples talk more frequently about issues of race and racial differences between the partners, whereas older couples in interracial relationships talk less about racial differences between themselves and their partners. Exemplars would be valuable to those reading the research to understand what those patterns look like in real life. For instance, one of the partners in a newer relationship might have said, "We talk a lot about it [racial differences], not always in serious ways. I mean, it is something we deal with especially when we hear comments from people when we are out in public." On the other hand, one of the partners in a more established relationship might have said, "We used to talk more about it but now we just, you know, we just don't think of it as much as we used to." Both of the statements reflect the central theme—that there are differences in how newer versus more established couples deal with racial differences and similarities in their relationship.

Grounded Theory

This research approach involves a high level of interactivity with the data and the coding process. Specifically, the researcher makes multiple passes through the data to refine coding categories and identify relationships between those categories. Ultimately, through identifying concepts and understanding the nature of the relationships between concepts (e.g., positive relationships versus negative relationships), a relevant theory that can guide your understanding of observed relationships will emerge. One process through which grounded theory can be carried out is the constant comparative technique, which involves continually returning to observations and reassessing them as new interpretations and understandings of the data are developed.

coding
→ Unit 11

relationship
→ Unit 2

concept
→ Unit 5

theory
→ Unit 2

341

The broad approach to grounded theory primarily uses inductive reasoning to develop a theory based on the patterns that emerge from the data, although, as more is known and understood, some deductive reasoning is employed as well. Successfully using a grounded theory approach requires that the researcher develop a high level of familiarity with the data being analyzed. The researcher must also be open to adjusting the approach as new information and interpretations of the data are discovered with each pass through the data. Because of this, initial passes through the data may simply involve understanding or identifying broad themes, key concepts, and key events. The researcher can then work to refine those broad ideas into more specific categories in subsequent passes. As the main coding categories clearly emerge, the researcher can then focus on looking at relationships between these categories.

You may be wondering how a researcher using a grounded theory approach knows when to stop analyzing the data. The answer to this is similar to that for other qualitative approaches—saturation. In the case of grounded theory, when the researcher is no longer identifying new coding categories and a more focused sense of why the patterns are occurring emerges, then the process is nearing completion. The final pieces of the process would be to look for exemplars to help flesh out the story that the data are telling and to clarify relationships between categories.

Suppose you want to understand the different types of advice given in commencement speeches at high school graduations. Grounded theory could be a useful approach in this case because it would allow you to develop coding categories through a process of interacting with the data. This means that clear-cut categories do not need to be established ahead of time. The first step would be collecting some transcripts from graduation speeches. After the transcripts have been collected, you would then want to read through these transcripts, taking some initial notes along the way and making sure to note key passages and themes that stand out. You could then take a second pass through the transcripts, this time more explicitly focusing on possible categorization schemes for the different ideas presented in the speeches. During this second pass, you might identify the following categories of advice: career planning, keeping family connections, and looking forward not backward.

A follow-up pass through the data would allow you to determine whether these categories are sufficient. If you are able to fit all of the different types of advice into one of these three coding categories, then you have reached the saturation point. If certain types of advice do not fit, then it is likely that additional coding categories are needed. Perhaps another common category of advice in graduation speeches is getting to know oneself. If such a category emerges during the third or fourth pass, an additional pass through the data would be necessary to ensure that you have now covered all possible coding categories. As the coding categories take shape and solidify, you should then begin to identify relationships between these categories and determine whether certain types of advice tend to occur together or not. Such relationships would help you then identify a theory—whether new or preexisting—that could explain what is occurring.

Constant Comparative Technique

Constant comparative technique, also referred to as *constant comparative method*, is a process of qualitative analysis that involves working through transcripts and field notes to home in on the meaning of key concepts. This approach is often associated with grounded theory as a means of analyzing qualitative data and developing a theory to explain findings from that analysis. As the term implies, this approach involves returning to the transcript (or other text) to develop meaning through a two-step process that is repeated as many times as is necessary. The first step is to break the data into units—sometimes referred to as unitizing. These units are basically smaller pieces within the transcript that allow for easier assessment of the story within the data. For instance, each sentence or paragraph could be a unit. Once the decision has been made about what the unit of analysis will be, the researcher then codes each of the units into categories. This allows for the identification of distinct categories (also known as attributes) but also helps in the process of determining the meaning of a particular concept.

The constant comparative technique uses more of an inductive approach in which the categories and their respective meaning are not set ahead of time. The categories and their meaning emerge through the process of repeatedly going through the data—each time getting closer to determining the "true" meaning of a particular concept. In this approach, each time the researcher goes through the data, he or she is looking at it in a slightly different way as the interpretation and sense of meaning evolves with each pass. Because of this, a concept that may have seemed unique on the first or second pass may work better being split into two or more concepts based on perspective gained on the third and fourth reads through the data.

The general process of the constant comparative technique has some similarities to the content analysis method in that the researcher must determine units and then code those units into appropriate categories. However, in content analysis, the coding categories are firmly set ahead of time, and the researcher works from a coding guide that spells out clear definitions and coding categories such that the way a term is defined at the start of the study will be the same as it is defined (and measured) at the end of the study. The constant comparative approach, on the other hand, leaves considerable room for adjustment, and it is often the case that coding categories (and even the unit being observed) will shift throughout the course of the study.

For example, consider a situation in which you are analyzing focus group data on the effectiveness of a new marketing campaign for a community library. In the initial read through the transcripts, the concept of "likeability"

| transcript |
| → Unit 13 |

| field notes |
| → Unit 12 |

| concept |
| → Unit 5 |

| grounded theory |
| → Unit 13 |

| unitizing |
| → Unit 11 |

| attribute |
| → Unit 5 |

| inductive versus deductive reasoning |
| → Unit 2 |

| content analysis |
| → Unit 11 |

| coding guide |
| → Unit 11 |

| focus group |
| → Unit 12 |

| dimension |
| → Unit 5 |

343

continues to come up, such that people indicate how much they like the library staff, how much they like the new building, and how much they like services offered by the library. However, after a second (or third pass) through the data, it may be clear that these concepts are distinct things, such that people form separate opinions on the likeability of the staff, the building, and services offered. Therefore, these three themes would emerge either as distinct concepts on their own or as dimensions of the larger likeability concept. Subsequent passes through the data would then use the lens of having discrete categories of staff, building, and services as a framework for interpreting the data, allowing you to focus your analysis on further distinguishing those dimensions and considering the distinct ways that people assess how much they like or dislike these aspects of their community library.

Research in Depth: Grounded Theory

Grounded theory has been used by researchers in numerous settings to develop a fuller understanding of a wide range of phenomena. As you review the examples provided here, consider how you might use a grounded theory approach in your own research. Citation information is provided should you wish to locate these articles and read them on your own.

- Benoit (2013) used grounded theory to analyze texts of political debates and derived four dimensions of personality traits that arise in debates: sincerity, empathy, morality, and drive.
- Dillon (2012) used grounded theory to analyze depth interviews, looking at how attending physicians communicate with patients about medical errors, as well as how they help trainees deal with this process as well.
- Cardillo (2010) used grounded theory to analyze narratives written by people dealing with chronic conditions, developing an understanding of the active role that people can take in redefining and reconstructing understanding of themselves.

---

concept
→ Unit 5

depth interviews
→ Unit 12

themes
→ Unit 13

Historical Analysis

Historical analysis is an approach that is not necessarily limited to a single analytical approach but rather explicitly considers the historical aspects of an issue. For example, researchers could study the evolution of video games over time or look at shifts in communication style in the American workplace from the 1950s to present, among many other possibilities. There are many directions that researchers conducting historical analysis can go, but the emphasis rests on conducting the research with a focus on a defined period of time or in looking at how characteristics of a particular period of time shaped an issue or topic. As a result, in conducting historical analysis, the researcher is interested in two broad issues: first, understanding in what ways the concept under study has shifted over time and, second, understanding the extent to which shifts in things such as social norms, ideology, and other major cultural or historical changes have had an impact on the concepts under study.

panel
→ Unit 10

transcript
→ Unit 13

For instance, in considering changes in video games over time, the researchers would want not only to explore the extent to which video game content has changed—such as becoming more or less violent, more or less realistic, or more or less challenging—but also to consider factors that may have helped shape those changes. In the case of video games, it could be that important technological advances were made that improved quality. Or perhaps social norms shifted to become more accepting of violent and sexual content in games. Historical research involves not just looking at the specific content under study but also analyzing other materials to develop the historical context needed to fully interpret the data. For instance, researchers studying video games over time might also look at internal communications generated by video game manufacturers as well as magazines and websites catering to video game players or to the industry. Further, the researchers could also conduct qualitative interviews with key players in the gaming industry, such as programmers, designers, or executives. These different approaches could provide valuable contextual information for understanding why video games have evolved the way that they have.

Historical analysis could also provide valuable insights into the recurring topic in this unit—interracial relationships. For instance, if you are studying this topic from a historical perspective, you might look at media representations of interracial relationships and identify key themes for how those relationships were presented. Alternatively, you could analyze diaries written by people in interracial relationships, which would give you particularly good insights into what those people were thinking and how they dealt with any problems they may have faced. Ideally, it would be beneficial to use both of those methods in order to develop a broader understanding of the issue, and even to look at other sources of data. In either case, your approach would want to include a broader understanding of important contextual factors. For example, in looking at media coverage over time, you might also discuss broader cultural changes, such as the civil rights movement or major cultural events (e.g., the first televised interracial kiss was on the original *Star Trek* series).

These examples illustrate some of the unique aspects of historical research. In particular, one unique aspect is the use of archival data that, in some cases, may not have been available at the time. These data may include documents that were saved from earlier time periods but were not publicly available when first created. Examples include communication between employees at

345

a company, letters from journalists to political sources, and personal diaries or records. By using these kinds of data, a historical analysis is more than just a look across time, such as a panel study might be; it is a way to look at how a particular time period may have influenced a topic while also giving a fuller picture of what that time period was like. For example, in further considering the topic of interracial relationships, it could be useful to look at media coverage of court cases involving the legality of interracial relationships. In addition, it would add further depth to the issue and relevant context to read transcripts from any legal proceedings as well as internal memos and other documents shared by lawyers, judges, and other people involved in legal aspects of the process.

Rhetorical Criticism

textual analysis
→ Unit 13

unit of analysis
→ Unit 2

social artifacts
→ Unit 11

sampling
→ Unit 8

representative sample
→ Unit 8

Rhetorical criticism is an approach that provides in-depth critical analysis of a piece of communication (often referred to as an *artifact*) that focuses on the extent to which the artifact being studied works as intent (or fails to work). Further, part of what makes this approach unique and interesting to scholars and critics alike is that it takes a subjective approach to analyzing a communication artifact. As such, it is an approach that goes beyond textual analysis, which is more concerned with the content that is present as opposed to how that content works (or doesn't work) to affect the people who encounter it. For instance, consider conducting rhetorical criticism on a popular film. A researcher using rhetorical criticism (also referred to as *rhetorical analysis*) would engage in a detailed analysis of the different elements of that film—images, interactions between characters, words both spoken and written on the screen, and other signs and symbols—while also interpreting the goal and purpose of the film. In doing so, the rhetorical critic makes an assessment about the quality of the film. That is, the rhetorical critic strives to answer what works and does not work about the film in terms of its goals (e.g., inform, persuade, or entertain), its cultural impact (e.g., implications for attitudes toward race or gender), and its theoretical relevance, among other things.

In many cases, the rhetorical critic will analyze texts from a particular perspective, focusing on issues such as culture, race, gender, or religion. Using these perspectives, the rhetorical critic can then assess the success or failure of a text based on how it would be received or interpreted by different groups. In the case of film analysis, the rhetorical critic might consider the positive and negative implications of the film for different groups that might watch it, such as men, women, ethnic minorities, and so on. This could lead to analysis that breaks down why a film is offensive or does a poor job of representing a particular racial group or sexual identity. Alternatively, the analysis might highlight what a film does right (i.e., how it works) in providing nuanced

Bob Ford—Sports columnist for the *Philadelphia Inquirer*

A 1976 graduate of the University of Maryland's Philip Merrill College of Journalism, Ford has been twice nominated for the Pulitzer Prize in commentary. His work has been cited by the Associated Press Sports Editors, the Society of Professional Journalists, and the Keystone Press Association. He is a six-time winner of the Pennsylvania Sports Writer of the Year as selected by the National Sports Media Association.

Why are good research skills important in your field?

In any nonfiction writing, and especially journalism, accuracy is king. The reader has to trust the information being put forward, or he or she will not return to that source for information in the future. Gathering facts is simply research, although it can take many forms.

What specific method or methods do you encounter most?

On a day-to-day basis, the most common form of research is personal interviews. We talk to the subjects of our stories, or we talk to those with knowledge of those subjects.

Can you name specific instances where you have used data collected from research?

My specific field is sports writing. I began my career as a news writer, covering police, courts, and municipal government. There are very few stories I write that do not involve data that I have researched. Usually, in my field, that means statistics. I recently wrote a column that compared the national championship basketball teams of Villanova University from 2016 and 2018. Which team would win if it were possible for those two teams to play? I used statistics from each season to compare them and make an argument.

How did research you conducted help inform your decision?

I am an opinion columnist, so often I go into research with the goal of confirming a decision rather than making one. In other words, if my contention is that the 2018 Villanova team would have beaten the 2016 Villanova team, then I am looking for research results that back me up. It happens, however, that sometimes the research will change my mind on a topic, and lead me in an unexpected direction. In the end, the facts have to be respected.

What are one or two pieces of advice or insights you would give about research to students in a communication research methods course?

I have always enjoyed digging around to find stuff. I'm not sure that can be imparted on someone who doesn't share the same interest. It really helps if you like going down a rabbit hole looking for something. The best little piece of advice also applies to other aspects of life: Don't assume. OK, you're positive that so-and-so said such-and-such. You remember it clearly. Doesn't matter. Look it up. Turn all the pages, even the ones you don't think hold anything for you. It might be that you come across something that leads you in another of those unexpected directions.

and accurate portrayals of minority characters that avoid common tropes or stereotypes. Rhetorical criticism therefore plays an important role in critical cultural explorations of topics and issues helping to provide perspective on topics and issues that is often otherwise ignored.

There are many options for what, specifically, a rhetorical critic can analyze, but the primary unit of analysis for this kind of research is the social artifact. For example, classic studies of rhetoric focused on speeches and other public displays, but more current rhetorical criticism has broadened its focus to include advertisements, popular music and film, and other media messages. Further, from a sampling standpoint, the researcher typically selects one or two texts for analysis, such as a movie, music video, or graphic novel, among other things.

For example, consider a situation in which you are interested in answering questions about how popular media reinforces gender roles. Using rhetorical criticism, you would select a representative text to analyze, such as a popular music video, television episode, or film. You would want to select a text that addresses gender roles in some way and consider the particular perspective from which you will conduct the analysis. You might focus on gender roles in the context of African American sitcoms or in shows that deal with workplace relationships. The particular perspective will focus the criticism by providing a lens through which the analysis is developed. For instance, if your criticism focuses on African American sitcoms, you will want to consider both the text's effectiveness for that particular group—African Americans—but also how it fits into a broader cultural context.

Through this perspective and the analytical approach, you would identify various signs and symbols (e.g., words, images, or clothing) that demonstrate how the text is attempting to present its message. The analysis can then address why these signs and symbols were used, why others were not used in their place, and whether the use of these signs and symbols is appropriate and/or effective for the various audiences that may be exposed to the message. It could be that certain aspects of the sitcom will resonate well with African American audiences, and other aspects will resonate with a white audience as well. Rhetorical criticism would identify such instances but also develop an understanding of *why* that is.

---

qualitative versus quantitative
→ Unit 3

content analysis
→ Unit 11

social artifacts
→ Unit 11

Textual Analysis

Textual analysis is the qualitative counterpart to the typically quantitative-oriented content analysis and involves the in-depth analysis of the content of various kinds of social artifacts, referred to as *texts*. Texts can encompass many different things, such as movies, magazines, websites, books, speech transcripts, and more. In textual analysis, the researcher is exploring both manifest—surface-level

Reflect & React: Critically Analyzing the Media We Consume

The next time you settle down to watch your favorite television show, imagine yourself watching the show from a perspective that is different from your own. For instance, if you are a man, you might try to imagine how a woman would react to what you are watching and consider why she would react that way. Do you notice anything different than you normally do? What things stand out to you as you watch from this different perspective? What key symbols do you use to draw these conclusions? How did watching this show using this different mindset affect your enjoyment? For even more research fun, consider asking friends or family members what they think of when they watch this same show. In what ways are your reactions similar or different?

observations and meanings—and latent—more hidden and interpretive meaning—content. This will allow the researcher to understand characteristics of the text and develop a more thorough understanding of the different themes present in the content of that text. The focus is less on whether and how these different pieces work (and how users are affected), as in rhetorical criticism, and more on what is present or not in various types of texts.

Consider working for a nonprofit agency that works with local communities on drug prevention. This nonprofit may be interested in creating some public service announcements (PSAs) that deliver an antidrug message to the community. To do so, it may be valuable to evaluate the content of existing antidrug PSAs so that the nonprofit can get a better handle on the types of images and phrases that it should consider using in its own PSA. Textual analysis would be a useful approach in this case and could be accomplished by collecting some notable anti-drug PSAs from years past. To carry out the textual analysis, you would watch the ads and look for the presence or absence of various types of themes, images, and symbols. For example, many of the PSAs may include dramatic music that could be used to represent dread, foreboding, or general feelings of seriousness. Further, many of the PSAs may also include close-ups of sad, angry, or frustrated loved ones to represent the negative consequences of drug use on families. By determining the presence or absence of various themes, as well as when and where they are used within the PSA, you could develop a good understanding of the key pieces you would need to help the nonprofit create its own PSA.

To be clear, textual analysis is not focused on whether or how these different themes work. Therefore, the analysis is not concerned with how certain visual devices might persuade or inform, so there is much less process- and

transcript
→ Unit 13

manifest content
→ Unit 11

latent content
→ Unit 11

themes
→ Unit 13

effect-oriented discussion in textual analysis than there is with other approaches such as rhetorical criticism.

Themes

In conducting qualitative analysis, researchers are looking for patterns that emerge across the various observations—whether through depth interviews, field notes, focus groups, or other approaches—that have been made. These patterns—referred to as *themes*—are the essence of qualitative research because they provide the core sense of what the findings indicate and a useful way to characterize relationships between variables. Qualitative researchers identify these themes using an approach that is typically more interactive and iterative (i.e., one that repeats a process a few or more times) than what is often employed in quantitative research. However, there is great variety to these approaches. In some cases, the researcher will use a more structured approach with set coding schemes guided by prior research and theory. In others, such as when using a grounded theory or constant comparative approach, the themes will emerge as the researcher interacts with the data.

Identifying the key themes can take some time because, as is often the case, numerous themes will emerge on the first or second pass through the data. Once this initial wide array of themes is identified, the researcher should work to narrow that list down. This can be done by grouping similar themes together. These groupings can then be used to identify main themes and any relevant sub-themes that are present. Subthemes fit within the main themes in much the same way that dimensions fit under the broader umbrella of concepts. As a note, it is important that the researcher not rush to determine the themes. This is because once themes are in place, they can affect how any additional data are interpreted. For instance, once you identify a particular theme, you may be predisposed to fit things into that theme, which might stop you from identifying additional original themes. Preventing new themes from being identified could, ultimately, have a negative impact on the validity of the data. As themes and any relevant sub-themes are identified, the researcher should identify appropriate exemplars as a way to illustrate the themes in a concrete way.

Consider a situation in which a researcher conducts a series of focus groups designed to explore differences in how male and female employees communicate with their superiors in the workplace. In reading through the transcripts, the researcher will want to identify any key similarities and differences in how men and women communicate. These similarities and differences will help the researcher identify any key themes. For example, perhaps women indicate that they find face-to-face interactions to be more effective in communicating with their boss. On the other hand, men may find e-mail a more effective communication approach. Further, both men and women may indicate that their bosses are not as responsive to their communication attempts as they would like them to be. In this case, there are two key themes. One is in a lack of satisfaction with workplace communication. A second theme is the difference in the communication medium used (face-to-face versus e-mail). Further analysis within those themes could identify reasons for the differences and lack of satisfaction, as well as provide suggestions for how both men and women can more effectively communicate at work.

The unique challenge of analyzing themes—as well as other qualitative approaches—is in the process of understanding the meaning of potentially complex and highly detailed texts. For example, comments that research subjects make, actions that they take, and decisions that they make can have varied meanings depending on context, motivations, and other circumstances. Further, the interpretation of themes can be shaped, in part, by the theoretical perspective taken by the researcher conducting the analysis. In the foregoing example, using a gender-specific theory might result in different conclusions than an approach that puts more attention on race, class, or other underlying factors.

Transcript

depth interviews
→ Unit 12

focus group
→ Unit 12

conversation analysis
→ Unit 13

In most cases, depth interviews, focus group discussions, and conversations used for conversation analysis are recorded. The typed version of that full recording is referred to as a transcript, created through a process called transcription. The transcripts allow researchers to look more closely at the responses provided by the research participants. This is important because researchers should not rely only on memory to draw conclusions about what they have observed. Field notes and transcripts can therefore be incredibly important resources that allow for more in-depth exploration of what respondents have said. It is much easier to search through a printed transcript for patterns, keywords, or other indicators than it is to continually listen to recordings or rely on memory.

Steps to Success: Preparing the Transcript

Before analyzing interview or focus group data, the audio recordings must be transcribed. This allows the researcher to work from a hard copy of what the respondents have said allowing them to make notes, highlight, and otherwise mark up the printed data. Follow these steps in preparing your transcript for analysis:

1. At the interview, do a recording check to make sure sound levels are accurate and that you can hear all of the participants clearly. Additionally, make sure par-

ticipants identify themselves in some distinct way—this is particularly important in focus groups, in which you could have up to 12 different people talking!

2. Whether you use transcription software or pay someone to transcribe the interviews, it is important to check the transcripts against the original recordings to verify quality. Any inaccuracies in the transcription process will result in inaccuracies in the data.

3. Review the transcripts while listening to the recording. Although your specific procedures will be determined by the questions you are trying to answer, listening to the interviews while reading and noting the transcript can reveal a great deal of information. For instance, you will be able to note lengths of pauses, changes in tone, overlaps in conversation, and many other details that will likely not have been present in the initial transcription.

4. Be prepared to review your transcript multiple times—learning something new each time. As themes begin to emerge, be sure to note segments of the transcript that will serve as exemplars in your final report.

5. If multiple researchers are looking at the transcripts, make sure that you are consistent in the style of notation used on the transcript. Approaches such as conversation analysis have established notation styles, so be sure to consult the literature for insights into how to note your transcript. Any adjustments to a previously established approach should be discussed by all members of the research team.

6. As you prepare segments of your transcript to include in any published reports, determine what steps need to be taken to protect the privacy of participants in the study. This could entail changing names and other identifying details, such as age, race, type of employment, and any other personal details that could reveal who the person is.

In some cases, researchers will use computer software to transcribe conversations or focus group sessions. When doing so, it is important to check the transcripts and correct any misspelled words or other mistakes, especially if the researchers will also use computer software to analyze the transcripts. As such, the transcriber should plan on listening to the recording again while reading along with the transcript. This will allow the transcriber to correct any mistakes and add any notes or contextual information. In other cases, researchers will hire an assistant to transcribe interviews or focus group data. It is also necessary to check the transcript against the original recording in this case, as the person doing the transcribing could have made a mistake. For example, in some cases, it is difficult to tell the voices apart when there are multiple participants, as in a focus group. If the person doing the transcribing attributes responses to the wrong participant, this could have a serious impact on the interpretation of the data and the conclusions the researchers are able to draw.

Although typing up a transcript can seem like a daunting task, it is a necessary one. Further, it can also be a useful way for the researchers to begin to understand the data they have collected. Typically during interviews or focus group sessions, it is hard to see the big picture, as there is a tendency to focus on specific responses so that the interviewer or moderator can effectively prepare for the next question. When typing up the transcript while listening to the recording, the researchers can begin to acquaint themselves with the data in a different way and begin the process of understanding key patterns that will emerge from the data. Finally, having a completed transcript will allow the researchers to easily pull out exemplars that stand out as ways to express the themes and patterns they have observed.

Activities

Activity 13A: Interview Transcript and Analysis

See terms: depth interview; transcript.

For this activity, you are to conduct an interview, transcribe the interview, and then analyze the interview to draw conclusions about the research question provided. The guiding research question is as follows: *How do people use social media to communicate with romantic partners?* Specifically, you should recruit two participants for the interview and conduct an interview with each of them. In doing so, be sure to follow good technique as described in Unit 12 and make sure to determine which interview structure you will use before you begin. As you conduct the interview, take notes on the process so that you can assess your performance as an interviewer beyond simply analyzing the responses provided by the interviewees. Consider the following questions as you go through this process:

- Would you characterize the interview process as a success? Why or why not?
- What would you change about the interview process if you could do it over again?
- What conclusions were you able to draw about how people use social media in romantic relationships?
- How helpful was the transcript? What challenges do you see in using a transcript as the basis for your analysis?

Activity 13B: Rhetorical Criticism

See terms: rhetorical analysis; rhetorical criticism.

The main objective of this activity is to apply the rhetorical analysis approach to a real-world situation. For this activity, you should watch 1 hour of commercial television (broadcast television with commercials) and focus on the ads. In doing so, use the following questions to guide you through the process:

- What themes are present across all of the ads?
- What exemplars can you identify that represent the general themes present in the ads? Why have you determined those particular themes to be important?
- What conclusions can you draw about the audience based on the ads?
- What conclusions can you draw about the state of advertising based on these particular ads?
- How does your perspective on the ads change as you consider different perspectives (e.g., race, gender, sexuality)?
- Would some perspectives see the ads as "good" and others see the ads as "bad" (or offensive)? If so, why?

Activity 13C: Using Grounded Theory

See terms: coding categories; exemplars; grounded theory; saturation.

Visit YouTube or another online video website and seek out some commencement speeches (whether from a university or high school graduation) to help you answer the following research question: *What techniques do speakers use to provide inspiration for life after graduation?* Once you have located three or four speeches, use a grounded theory approach to identify the different inspirational techniques that are used. Keep track of your thoughts as you work through your analysis and continue to review the commencement speeches. In particular, consider the following questions: What are the key types of inspirational techniques? What are exemplars that clearly show those types of inspirational techniques in action? Be sure to look for relationships between categories, considering which of the categories of inspirational techniques tend to go together.

References

Benoit, W. L. (2013). Candidates' personal qualities in political leaders' debates. *Human Communication*, *16*(2), 87–94.

Cardillo, L. W. (2010). Empowering narratives: Making sense of the experience of growing up with chronic illness or disability. *Western Journal of Communication*, *74*(5), 525–546. doi:10.1080/10570314.2010.512280

Dillon, P. J. (2012). Educating medical trainees to disclose medical errors. *Florida Communication Journal*, *40*(2), 43–52.

Suggested Readings for Further Exploration of Unit 13 Topics

Examples

Bishop, G. F. (1992). Qualitative analysis of question-order and context effects: The use of think-aloud responses. In N. Schwarz & S. Sudman (Eds.), *Context effects in social and psychological research* (pp. 149–162). New York, NY: Springer.

McLeod, D. M., & Hertog, J. K. (1992). The manufacture of "public opinion" by reporters: Informal cues for public perceptions of protest groups. *Discourse & Society*, *3*(3), 259–275. doi:10.1177/0957926592003003001

Advanced Discussion

Birks, M., & Mills, J. (2011). *Grounded theory: A practical approach*. Thousand Oaks, CA: Sage Publications.

Braun, V., & Clarke, V. (2008). Using thematic analysis in psychology. *Qualitative Research in Psychology*, *3*(2), 77–101. doi:10.1191/1478088706qp063oa

Tompkins, P. K. (1994). Principles of rigor for assessing evidence in "qualitative" communication research. *Western Journal of Communication*, *58*(1), 44–50. doi:10.1080/10570319409374483

unit 14

descriptive statistics

Suppose you have just finished a major survey of Americans' news use. You have assembled your data, and among the measures you have a set of items that reflect how people feel about news. You've asked ratio-level questions about frequency of news use, interval-level measures that indicate how much participants agree that news is useful, ordinal-level measures in which participants rank their favorite news sources, and nominal-level measures in which they indicate whether they use a particular source. In short, you have lots of data about news use and attitudes toward news.

But what do you do with your data? That is, how do you go about understanding the meaning of the data you have collected? You know that the data should be representative of the larger population and that you can use information from these data to form estimates about that population. But estimates based on what? Before you can draw conclusions based on quantitative data, you have to understand how best to summarize those data through the use of descriptive statistics. In doing so, you will take the first steps toward telling the story of your data, from how often people engage in various behaviors to how they feel about different issues and topics.

Statistics

Statistics provide a numerical summary of some characteristic of a set of data. Statistics can describe any kind of quantitative data. For example, advertisers use statistics such as CPM (cost per thousand) and audience demographics to know where to buy ads. Journalists talk about statistics such as the unemployment rate or the average cost of housing to explain how the economy affects people in their community. Our data about media use measure things such as hours of cable news viewing and preferences for the Internet as a news source. Statistics are increasingly common, as the computer software used to calculate them becomes more powerful and available and as students increasingly learn about statistics as part of their education. Understanding the different types of common statistics is a critical part of what's called *numeracy*, or the ability to make sense of numbers.

For researchers, most statistics are used to describe a sample. Because each individual in a sample is a separate case, statistics allow researchers to condense information about how every individual case responded to each measure, summarizing all those data points with a few key numbers. Many of these statistics are common and will be familiar from even basic math classes. Others are more unusual, but once you understand them, you will be able to explain all the important aspects of your data numerically.

In general, statistics used to describe individual variables—called descriptive statistics—are divided into a small number of categories. Measures of **central tendency** are used to describe the typical or "average" value for a given variable. Examples of these statistics include the **mean, median,** and **mode**. Other

ratio-level measure → Unit 7
interval-level measure → Unit 7
ordinal-level measure → Unit 7
nominal-level measure → Unit 5
representative sample → Unit 8
population → Unit 8
qualitative versus quantitative → Unit 3
sample → Unit 8
variable → Unit 2

statistics describe how widely individual scores are spread out in the data; these are known as measures of **dispersion**. Examples of these statistics include the **standard deviation, variance,** and **range**. Finally, many statistics are used to describe the distribution of data. That is, they consider how often each possible value for the variable occurs. This is represented as the **frequency distribution** of the data, and it is often depicted as a **histogram**. Many times, data approximately follow a **normal distribution**—the so-called bell curve that is used to graphically represent measures such as IQ, height, and SAT scores. Other statistics explain how much the data fail to match the normal distribution. For example, **kurtosis** is used to explain how "pointed" or "flat" a distribution is, while **skew** describes how nonsymmetrical the data are. Some other important aspects of the distribution are more difficult to quantify but are still important to researchers. The presence of **outliers**—cases that aren't similar to most of the values in the data—can indicate problems with data collection and distort the conclusions that researchers reach. All of these are important in research. Even if two variables have the same means, they may differ in other important ways. By using the full set of appropriate statistics, researchers and professionals can make better decisions and more fully understand what their data show.

Descriptive Statistics

sample
→ Unit 8

variable
→ Unit 2

relationship
→ Unit 2

population
→ Unit 8

inferential
statisticas
→ Unit 15

estimation
→ Unit 8

description
→ Unit 3

In general, this unit focuses on what are known as descriptive statistics. Technically, all statistics *describe* the characteristics of a particular sample. But most sources distinguish statistics that simply give information about a single variable from those that are used to quantify relationships between variables—and, by extension, to test the generalizability of those relationships to a population. The former are what we consider here as descriptive statistics. The primary purpose of descriptive statistics is to evaluate the measures of variables in a study, identifying abnormal or interesting distributions—such as how frequently some values occur compared with others—and ensuring that subsequent inferential statistical tests meet assumptions. But descriptive statistics are also a first step toward estimation, as most estimates are simply an extension of the description of a given sample to a larger population. For example, if we find out the mean number of hours that the respondents in our sample reported watching Fox News, we would have not only important descriptive information about our sample but also an insight into roughly how much time the average American spends watching Fox News.

Central Tendency

mean
→ Unit 14

median
→ Unit 14

One way to describe variables is to present information about the most typical or "average" values for a variable. Statistics that provide information about a typical or normal value are known as measures of central tendency, and they include the mean, median, and mode. All these measures are ways to represent a normal or common value for a variable within a sample. For example, consider an exam taken in one of your communication courses. After you take the exam, you want to know how well you did. Your score on the exam will help you understand your performance, but you probably also want to know how your score compared with those of other students in the class. In such a case, the instructor would likely provide you with information about the overall scores for all the students enrolled in the course, such as giving you the mean score for the class. Even if your score wasn't outstanding in an absolute sense, knowing that you did much better than the mean would help you understand your performance on the exam.

Measures of central tendency are important because they give a sense of what typical members of a group said or how they did on a task. Many statistics involve comparing measures of central tendency, most often the mean, to see whether members of different groups seem to differ from one another *on average*. All the measures of central tendency reflect typical or average values, but they vary in important ways related to the appropriate level of measurement, the robustness of the test, and the variety of statistics that can be calculated based on the chosen measure.

mode → Unit 14
sample → Unit 8
levels of measurement → Unit 5
central tendency → Unit 14

Mean

The mean is one of the most common statistics. As a measure of central tendency, it reflects the typical value of a group or sample for a given variable. More specifically, it reflects the value calculated by summing all of the individual scores on a measure and then dividing that total by the number of people in the group. For example, suppose you ask five people how many friends they have on Facebook, and you receive the following replies: 55, 100, 150, 300, 900. The mean of those responses is 301, as the sum of the five numbers is 1,505, and 1,505 divided by 5 equals 301. The mean is widely used and most people understand it, so it can be a helpful way to present information about central tendency. The mean is also useful because many other statistics rely on comparing means between groups. For example, one type of statistical test addressed in the unit on inferential statistics is t, used to compare two means to see whether they are sufficiently different from one another—for example, did Republicans watch more hours of Fox News on average than Democrats? Such a comparison can only be made by calculating means to compute this test.

The mean has several shortcomings. Because it requires you to be able to logically add up values, the level of measurement for the variable must be an interval or ratio. That is, you can only calculate the mean when the increase between one level and the next level of a variable is constant. Additionally, the mean is strongly influenced by skew or outliers. If there are a few cases in your data that have notably higher or lower values than the remaining cases, this will dramatically

sample → Unit 8
variable → Unit 2
levels of measurement → Unit 5
interval-level measure → Unit 5
ratio-level measure → Unit 5
skew → Unit 14
outliers → Unit 14
population → Unit 8
median → Unit 14

increase or decrease the mean in deceptive ways. Think about the example of the number of Facebook friends given previously. The mean is 301, but that number is higher than four of the five cases. The one person who said that he or she had 900 friends strongly distorted the overall finding. If that person hadn't been included in your sample, then you would have come away with a much different conclusion. Because of the influence of outliers, we say that the mean is not *robust*.

When reporting many commonly measured statistics, researchers avoid reporting means because they are similarly distorted. For example, measures of the typical income in a population tend be presented in terms of the median rather than the mean. Consider what would happen if you reported the mean income in your community. A small number of well-paid individuals—maybe the university president, the football coach, or a locally based CEO—would dramatically increase the mean wage. It would look as if most people in your community make a lot of money, when in reality, nearly everyone is getting by on far less. Therefore, when government agencies report typical income levels, housing prices, or other values that could be distorted by a few unusually high cases, they tend to present the median rather than the mean.

Median

In contrast to the mean, the median is a much more robust statistic, which is why it is often used to represent a typical or central value when describing data. The median is defined as the middle value when all values for a variable are listed in order. Consider again the example of a question in which five people listed the number of Facebook friends they had as follows: 55, 100, 150, 300, 900. The mean is 301, which doesn't seem to represent the central tendency well because it is higher than all but one of the answers. The median is the midpoint in that list, 150. That's a better reflection of the typical value. The median represents the point at which half of all values are above and half are below that point. Two answers for the Facebook question are higher than and two are less than the median value of 150. (In cases in which you have an even number of responses, you will be left with no exact "middle" value, so you simply find the mean of the two middle cases. For example, if you want the median value for 10, 20, 30 and 40, it would be 25—the mean of the two middle values, 20 and 30.)

Because the median is more robust, it better reflects the central tendency in data that have strong outliers or skew. However, the median does not have the same statistical utility that the mean does. Few statistics involve comparing median scores, and calculating a confidence interval for the median is not as simple or widely done as for a mean. However, the median can be calculated for a greater diversity of scores than the mean. As long as you have at least an ordinal level of measurement, such that you can logically sort the scores in order from lowest to highest, you can calculate the median. But it still can't be used for every possible measure, and it is less familiar to many people.

variable
→ Unit 2

central tendency
→ Unit 14

outliers
→ Unit 14

skew
→ Unit 14

confidence interval
→ Unit 8

ordinal-level measure
→ Unit 5

sample
→ Unit 8

levels of measurement
→ Unit 5

nominal-level measure
→ Unit 5

One additional benefit of the median is that it provides a natural point at which to divide a sample into two equal groups. By definition, the median is the point at which half of all individuals will report greater and half lesser scores. Think about this in the context of an exam. If your instructor says that the median score was 75, and you earned an 80, then you know that you outscored at least 50 percent of the class, as your score was above the median. If this division of scores continued, the instructor might slice the values into still smaller chunks. Perhaps the instructor would identify *quartiles*, dividing the answers into four equal groups. The median would divide the second and third quartiles. The instructor might then say that the division between the first and second quartiles (the first quartile is the highest quarter of the scores) was 85. You would realize that while you did better than at least half of the students in the class, you also did worse than at least a quarter, as you fell below that cutoff.

Data can be divided into any number of groups. We're used to seeing *percentiles*, which indicate which of 100 equal groups a given score falls into. The SAT, for example, often reports that an individual's score was in, say, the 95th percentile, meaning that the person did better than roughly 95 percent of all test takers but worse than about 5 percent. Any such divisions follow the same logic as the median, identifying a cutoff point at which some portion of scores will be higher or lower, then reporting that point. As such, these divisions require that the variable be measured at the ordinal level or higher.

Reflect & React: Data Visualization

Most descriptive statistics are a great way to summarize basic information about a manageable set of variables when the audience is familiar with statistics. While that describes typical academic audiences and publications, it may not apply when working with clients or trying to communicate to the public. Thanks to the growing trove of data mined from Internet and mobile users along with the increasing distribution of government and organizational data online there are is a lot of quantitative information available. Along with that boom has come tools that make it easier to not just analyze but also visualize the results.

Data visualization is a broad term for everything from traditional bar and pie charts to more complex infographics to interactive mapping tools and network diagrams. What they share is the use of visuals to convey quantitative information and engage an audience. It's not a new technique. For example, this website curated by a data visualization program lists what they consider 10 of the most notable historic and recent examples of using data to show, rather than tell: www.tableau.com/learn/articles/best-beautiful-data-visualization-examples. Another company runs a blog that compiles numerous examples of data visualization, including their lists of some of the topic examples in given years: www.visme.co. Media outlets like the *Washington Post* and *New York Times* and research organizations like Pew produce numerous visual components to support their data-driven journalism.

However, not all visualization is useful. Sometimes complex interactive tools or an excessive focus on aesthetics can make it hard to see the numbers for the shiny bits. As a research student, you're well equipped to evaluate whether the data part of data visualization actually works.

Find and locate at least two examples of data visualization from these sites, or from an Internet search of your own. Think about these questions while viewing each:

- What kinds of descriptive statistics are the authors representing? Are those appropriate to use for the data they have?
- Are the authors providing any description of relationships between variables, or just describing individual variables? How many variables are they actually including? What kinds of relationships might exist between these variables?
- Are the visual elements effective? Do they help make the data more interesting? Do they actually clarify the information provided?
- Which example do you find more compelling, and why?

---

sample
→ Unit 8

concept
→ Unit 5

frequency distribution
→ Unit 14

normal distribution
→ Unit 14

Mode

The one measure of central tendency that can be used with any level of measurement is the mode. This statistic indicates the most common value among all possible values for a variable. As such, it can even be used with a nominal level of measurement, as it simply indicates which category was chosen most often by participants. In such cases, the mode is a useful statistic.

However, most of the time the mode isn't a great indicator of central tendency. Consider, for example, a study that asks 500 participants their income. Odds are that no more than a few participants make the same amount of money, and so the modal value could easily be far higher or lower than the "average" income for the sample. On the other hand, the modal value is useful to consider for other reasons. In some cases, flawed measures may lead many people to choose a particular value simply because it doesn't require much thought. For example, suppose you ask people to indicate how they feel about a given brand, with answer choices of "very negative," "negative," "neutral," "positive," and "very positive." If 70 percent of the participants answer "neutral," this might suggest some important things. Maybe most people truly feel neutral about the brand. But maybe many participants weren't familiar with the brand or didn't know how to answer the question and chose "neutral" as the safe response. Identifying a modal response can help diagnose situations in which the answers don't make sense or reflect something other than the intended concept.

The idea of modality is also used in talking about the "shape" of a frequency distribution. A normal distribution will have one clear point around which the values cluster, representing the most common answers. Regardless of the exact mode, this basic "clustering" around a point represents a distribution with a single mode. In other cases, the distribution will cluster around multiple values. For example, people's reports of the number of hours they view Fox News might display multiple modes. One cluster would be at or near zero, while a second might be nearer to 2 or 3 hours a day. Democrats probably avoid Fox News, whereas conservative Republicans who choose to watch Fox News may consume this news source for multiple hours each day. This distribution is referred to as *bimodal*; even if there aren't exactly two modes, the presence of two "peaks" in the distribution is enough to be described that way.

Dispersion

In addition to measuring the central tendency of a variable, another important set of statistics focuses on the dispersion of a variable. These statistics measure how spread out the values are. The simplest statistic to measure this is the range, which reflects the difference between the highest and lowest values. Other statistics that give a more precise indication of dispersion are the variance and the standard deviation. These two measures are related—the standard deviation is the square root of the variance—but the standard deviation is more commonly reported.

Dispersion is important for several reasons. In general, having more widely dispersed scores is useful for testing relationships. If there is little variance in a given measure, it will be hard to accurately predict what accounts for those small differences. Suppose that you are studying the effects of an advertisement on feelings toward a brand. If everyone already liked the brand, it would be very hard for any ad to have an effect. Thus, measures of dispersion would show little variation, as all participants already have similar scores. This could suggest that you need to find a way to measure brand attitudes that identify subtler differences among participants. Instead of asking whether people like the brand, for instance, you could ask how much they like specific traits or features of the brand. Careful testing of the measures before carrying out the final study could identify problems such as this.

Measures of dispersion also help place scores in context. Think about an exam in a large class. If 500 students took the exam, and the mean was 75 (out of 100), you have some sense of how the students did. But suppose you earned a score of 80—how would you place that score in context? If the dispersion is

| central tendency |
| → Unit 14 |
| variable |
| → Unit 2 |
| range |
| → Unit 14 |
| variance |
| → Unit 14 |
| standard deviation |
| → Unit 14 |
| mean |
| → Unit 14 |

small, you would know that most students scored close to 75, so your score of 80 may be one of the stronger scores in the class. But if the dispersion is large, you would know that a lot of people did much better or much worse than the mean. You still did better than average, but you would suspect that many students earned a score far greater than the mean of 75, and your score may not be as strong as that for many of your peers.

Range

One measure of dispersion is the range, which represents the difference between the largest and smallest values found in the data. In general, the range is most useful when participants can give a large variety of numerical values. For example, if you are measuring the number of Facebook friends that people have, giving the range would show the diversity of individuals in your sample. One person might have just five friends, while another in the data might list 1,000. The range, then, would be 995; however, most scholars would report the high and low values (1,000, 5) instead of or in addition to the computed range. Showing this would give a sense of the types of answers that were possible. It would also show the degree to which there are unusual or extreme values included in the sample, if presented in conjunction with a measure of central tendency such as the mean or median.

To calculate a true range, the variable must be measured at the interval or ratio level, as subtraction is required. However, you can give the high and low values for an ordinal variable, as the ability to order the variable implies that you can say what the highest and lowest scores were. The range isn't generally used to calculate other statistics, and it doesn't provide a clear indication of the dispersion for *typical* values, so it is less commonly reported and used compared with the variance or standard deviation.

A variation of the range that is sometimes reported is the interquartile range, which is the difference between the values that mark the cutoff points for the lowest and highest quarter of the scores. A simple example can illustrate this: suppose the following 12 values are reported for the number of Facebook friends: 5, 15, 30, 60, 95, 120, 150, 175, 190, 225, 350, and 1,000. The lowest quarter of the values would be 5, 15, and 30, while the highest quarter would be 225, 250, and 1,000. The interquartile range would be between 30 and 225, or 195. This value is sometimes used as a guide to establish whether a value is an outlier if it falls multiple times the interquartile range from the median.

Variance

Whereas the range focuses on the most extreme values as a measure of dispersion, the variance measures the average amount of difference between values for a given variable. Variance is calculated in a series of steps (see Steps to Success: Computing the Standard Deviation), but the basic process involves comparing

Voices from Industry

Daniel Pishock—Creative Digital Solutions Architect

Daniel is a Creative Digital Solutions Architect who specializes in implementing digital solutions that allow businesses to streamline their supply chains and grow their businesses exponentially.

Why are good research skills important to your field?

They are vital for myself and the success of my company. I cannot make well informed decisions and recommendations without the research to back up and support my solutions.

What specific method or methods do you use or encounter most?

Mostly traditional, high-ranking results found in SERPS and from trusted influencers which I then cross reference. In regards to influencers, they are individuals I have followed and tested their theories for years and must be well respected in their industry.

Can you name some specific instances in which you used data collected from research?

There isn't a single thing I doing for a client that isn't based on or supported by research. I use it daily. For example, I recently had a client who was looking for a learning management system (LMS) to implement to assist with company training. The company has about 50 employees but had some budget restrictions. In an oversaturated marketplace, my research allowed me to find the simplest, most affordable solution that allowed their employees to get started in the LMS with virtually no training and begin engaging in training day one.

How did the research you conducted help inform your decision?

The research forced me to look at dozens of alternative products which revealed the strengths and limitations of each product and also the myth of brand recognition which rarely equaled a better product. Bigger brands often came with larger price tags while not providing any additional perks.

What are one or two pieces of advice or insights you would give about research to students in a communication research methods course?

Simple. You need to find reliable, trustworthy resources. That is becoming more and more challenging in a world that wants information quickly with little fact checking; however, it is essential and the foundation of qualitative and quantitative research.

each individual score to the mean, determining how far each score is from the mean, summing those differences, and accounting for the total number of scores. Variance thus provides a measure of how scattered the different cases in the data are. The larger the variance, the more the scores differ.

For example, consider two studies of Facebook users. In one study, the variance for the number of Facebook friends is 10. In the other, it's 100. Clearly, the second study has captured a greater diversity of Facebook users with a much broader range of friends. If you want to explain why people have different numbers of friends, it would be more helpful to consider the individuals in the second study because the bigger differences would allow you more readily figure out the causes of this variance. If most people in the sample differed by only a couple friends, it would be hard to see what accounts for those very small differences. You might think pure chance could easily create such differences. But if people differed by dozens or hundreds of friends, those differences would not be attributable to simple chance, and the relationship between the differences and other variables would be larger and more easily identified.

Variance can also be used to compare two or more variables within the same population. For example, suppose your instructor gave two exams, one of which had a variance of 30 and the other 5. On the first exam, you would expect to find big differences between students. Clearly, some people found the test very easy, and some found it very hard. If you scored a few points below the mean, you would still expect a lot of students to have done worse than you. On the second exam, with such a small variance, scoring only a few points below the mean would be enough to do worse than almost everyone in the class.

Standard Deviation

The standard deviation is closely related to variance, and it is another indicator of how spread out the scores in a distribution are (see Figure 14.1). To compute the standard deviation, you determine the variance and then take the square root of that value. When the variance is computed, the distance from each score to the mean is squared. Therefore, the variance does not use the same scale as the original measure.

Suppose a measure of the number of hours respondents watch television news has a variance of 9. That does not mean that, on average, hours of viewing deviated by 9 hours from the mean. The reason for this is that the scores were squared before adding them up and dividing by the number of people in the sample. Thus, that nine measures "hours-squared," an idea that doesn't mean much on its own. With a variance of 9, the standard deviation would be 3, and that number does represent actual hours as measured using the original scale. Depending on the distribution of scores, the majority of people would ordinarily be within 3 hours of the mean. In fact, with a normal distribution, you could say *exactly* what percentage of people would be one or more

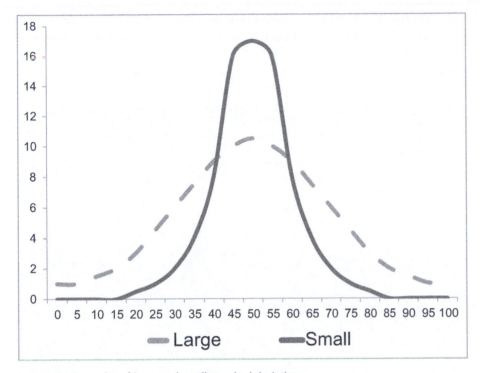

Figure 14.1 Examples of large and small standard deviations

Note: Scores range from 0 to 100 for the large standard deviation and from 20 to 80 for the small standard deviation. Further, note that a larger proportion of the scores are closer to the mean for the small standard deviation.

standard deviations from the mean. Because of this useful characteristic, the standard deviation is reported more often than the variance, even though the two are interchangeable. Furthermore, the standard deviation is also used in calculating many statistics that involve testing relationships, such as a *t*-test, and it is also a component of calculating the standard error, which is used in determining appropriate confidence intervals for a statistic when making estimates for the population.

Frequency Distribution

The frequency distribution represents the range of possible values found for a given variable or statistic within a group of individuals (most often a sample) and the number of individuals who fall into each possible value. A frequency distribution is simply a description of the actual values identified within the data. It can be represented visually as a histogram. Although distributions are conventionally described in visual terms, there is also an underlying numerical

range
→ Unit 14

variable
→ Unit 2

sample
→ Unit 8

pattern to the distribution that is important to keep in mind. For example, when a frequency distribution shows that 12 participants read the newspaper for 35 minutes a week, this is not simply a bar on a chart 12 units high—there are actually 12 individuals within the data who gave the answer of 35 minutes.

Steps to Success: Computing the Standard Deviation

Although most important descriptive statistics, including the standard deviation, can be easily computed using software, it is helpful to understand the process by which they are calculated. Here, we focus on how to determine the standard deviation using a set of 10 numbers: 3, 4, 4, 6, 7, 7, 7, 9, 9, 10.

1. Determine the mean for the data. As discussed elsewhere, the mean is calculated by summing all of the values for a variable and then dividing by the total number of values (see Step 1 in the table below). The mean for these numbers is 7.
2. For each individual case, subtract the individual score from the mean. Then, square the computed difference; this will make every value positive (see Step 2 below).
3. Add all of the squared individual difference scores (see Step 3 below). The sum of squares for our data is 52.
4. Divide this total by one of the following:

   a. If this is a score for an entire population, divide by the number of individuals.
   b. If this is a score for a sample, divide by one fewer than the number of individuals. (For example, if you have a sample of 100 individuals, you would divide by 99.) In our example, we have a sample of 10, so we divide by 9 (10 − 1 = 9). In this case, we divide the sum of squares (52) by 9 to obtain a value of 5.78 for the variance (see Step 4 below).

5. This computed value is the variance. Find the square root of this value, and you have the standard deviation (see Step 5 below). The standard deviation in this case is 2.4.

Table 14.1 Computing standard deviation

Individual scores	Step 2: Score—Mean	Step 3: Square and sum differences
3	−4	16
4	−3	9
4	−3	9

Individual scores	Step 2: Score—Mean	Step 3: Square and sum differences
6	-1	1
7	0	0
7	0	0
7	0	0
9	2	4
9	2	4
10	3	9
Step 1: Compute the mean Mean = 7		Sum of squares: 52
		Step 4: Divide sum of squares by $(N - 1)$ $52/9 = 5.78$
		Variance = 5.78
		Step 5: Square root of Step 4
		SD = 2.4

If a value differs dramatically from most of the other cases in a study, that individual case may be an outlier. It also reflects a real individual, but one who may distort the overall conclusions. Features of the distribution such as kurtosis and skew can be calculated as statistics, just as you can calculate a mean or standard deviation. These statistics also correspond to visual aspects of the distribution.

Illustrating distributions visually can be helpful. Often, this is done by showing an idealized, smooth curve that extrapolates what the distribution would look like if the total number of cases shown were much larger than the number actually present in the sample. However, the statistics describing the distribution still reflect the actual data points and not this smooth curve. One of the most common idealized distributions is referred to as the normal distribution, which you may recognize as the standard bell curve that many scores, such as SAT scores, often follow. Other statistics related to distributions are often based on a comparison to this normal distribution. Kurtosis describes whether the shape of the curve is pointed or flat compared with a normal distribution. Skew reflects whether the distribution is symmetrical or deviates from symmetry, in which direction, and by how much.

Histogram

A histogram is a visual representation of a frequency distribution that shows a bar for each possible value or logical range of values, with the height determined by the portion or absolute number of cases having that value. The primary purpose of a histogram is to provide a visual representation of the frequency distribution. Because many features of distributions, such as skew, have visual aspects, showing the shape of the distribution as a histogram can help diagnose and understand such features.

Histograms are visually similar to bar charts, although a bar chart typically reflects more than one variable. For example, a bar chart might show the percentage of men and of women who voted for a specific candidate or wished to purchase a certain product. A histogram, however, represents only one variable, and the height of each bar represents the frequency of the values of that variable, not percentages or other statistics describing a second variable (see Figure 14.2).

Ordinarily, the x-axis (the horizontal line along the bottom of the figure) is marked to indicate the individual values or value ranges, while the y-axis (the

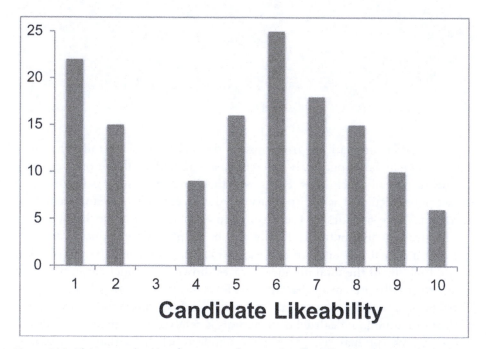

Figure 14.2 Histogram showing frequency of scores for likeability assessment of a political candidate

Note: All scores within the range (1–10) are indicated even if they were not selected. This histogram hints at a bimodal distribution, with 6 being the most common score ($n = 25$), but 1 was also fairly common ($n = 22$). The peaks and valleys of a histogram help tell the story of the data.

vertical line at the far left of the figure) corresponds either to the raw frequency of cases or the percentage of all cases having a given value or range. For variables with few possible values, normally a separate bar is produced for each possible value. Variables with many values will show ranges, but it's important that the width of each bar correspond to an equal-sized range. Values not present in the data but possible for the scale need to be visually represented as well. For example, suppose you asked participants to rate a candidate on a 10-point scale. Perhaps you received answers reporting all numbers except 3 and 9. You would still need bars for 3 and 9 alongside the other values; those bars would simply have a height of 0.

Because histograms represent each increment of a variable, they are generally only used to represent interval or ratio-level variables. With an ordinal variable, it would not be clear how much space would need to be left for missing values or what would constitute "equal-sized" value ranges. For example, consider the histogram below demonstrating scores for a candidate likeability measure. The scores range from 1 to 10, where 1 indicates "very low likeability" and 10 indicates "very high likeability." Note the cluster of scores at the low end, with 1 and 2 being fairly common scores, yet no one in the sample responded with a 3. This suggests that there is a small but noticeable group of people who strongly dislike the candidate. Further, the most common score (also called the mode) is 6, with scores steadily declining toward 10 after that. Overall, it seems reasonable to conclude that there is a group of people who strongly dislike the candidate, a sizeable group with more moderate opinions about the candidate, and a smaller group that has strong positive feelings toward the candidate.

Normal Distribution

Sometimes a smooth curve is drawn over a histogram to estimate the visual representation of the distribution if there were a very large number of responses. These smooth curves can represent a variety of distributions with known mathematical qualities; the best known and most important of these is called the *normal distribution*. Many variables and statistics follow a normal distribution in the population, meaning that their distribution within a sample should be approximately normal. This is important because many statistics used to measure relationships assume that the variables are distributed in a normal or essentially normal way. Testing whether a distribution is close to normal is important to be sure those analyses are appropriate.

Often referred to as a *bell curve*, a normal distribution (also known as a normal curve) has several important features that allow researchers to draw conclusions and make estimates when a variable follows the normal

histogram
→ Unit 14

variable
→ Unit 2

population
→ Unit 8

sample
→ Unit 8

relationship
→ Unit 2

median
→ Unit 14

mean
→ Unit 14

distribution. These stem from two important features of a normal distribution. First, a normal distribution is symmetrical—there will be an equal number of cases and equivalent shape on both sides of the midpoint of the distribution. That midpoint is the median, of course, and a consequence of this symmetry is that the mean and median will be the same. (As a note, the mode is also the same as the other two measures of central tendency in a truly normal distribution, as the peak value will be right in the center of the curve.) If the distribution is not symmetrical, such that the shape on one side of the curve is more stretched, this is known as skew.

More important is the second feature of a normal distribution. The specific bell shape of this distribution means that it follows what is known as the *normal rule*. A specific, known percentage of all cases in the distribution will fall within certain numerical distances of the mean. For example, 68.2 percent of all values will be within one standard deviation of the mean in a normal distribution. Suppose you know that the length of conversations at a party follow a normal distribution, with a mean of 5 minutes and a standard deviation of 2 minutes. If you sat on a couch at a typical party, carefully timing all the conversations, you would find that two-thirds of them (roughly 68.2 percent) took no less than 3 minutes (5 minus 2) and no more than 7 minutes (5 plus 2). Similarly, the normal rule says that just over 95 percent of values in a normal distribution will fall within two standard deviations of the mean. At that same party, you would expect that 95 percent of the time, you would observe conversations lasting between 1 minute (5 minus 4—that is, 2 times the 2-minute standard deviation) and 9 minutes (5 plus 4).

This feature of the normal distribution, along with an important characteristic of large samples, helps explain how we are able to make estimates of population parameters, stating with considerable precision our confidence interval and confidence levels. It turns out that the *sampling* distribution for both means and percentages is normal. (Remember that the sampling distribution describes the frequency curve you would find if you drew a very large number of samples from a population and calculated the same statistic for each one. Each sample in this situation is an individual case, and the frequency of computed statistics is akin to the frequency of values reported by individuals in a single sample.) Even if the variable itself is not normally distributed in the population, the relevant statistic will be.

For example, if you are computing the mean age for a large number of samples drawn from the population, the distribution of those means will follow a normal curve. Age itself is not normally distributed; it has a positive skew because older individuals are rare compared with young individuals. But for a very large number of samples, the mean age computed in each, plotted as a frequency distribution, will follow the typical bell curve shape. The standard deviation of this curve will be the standard error for the statistic,

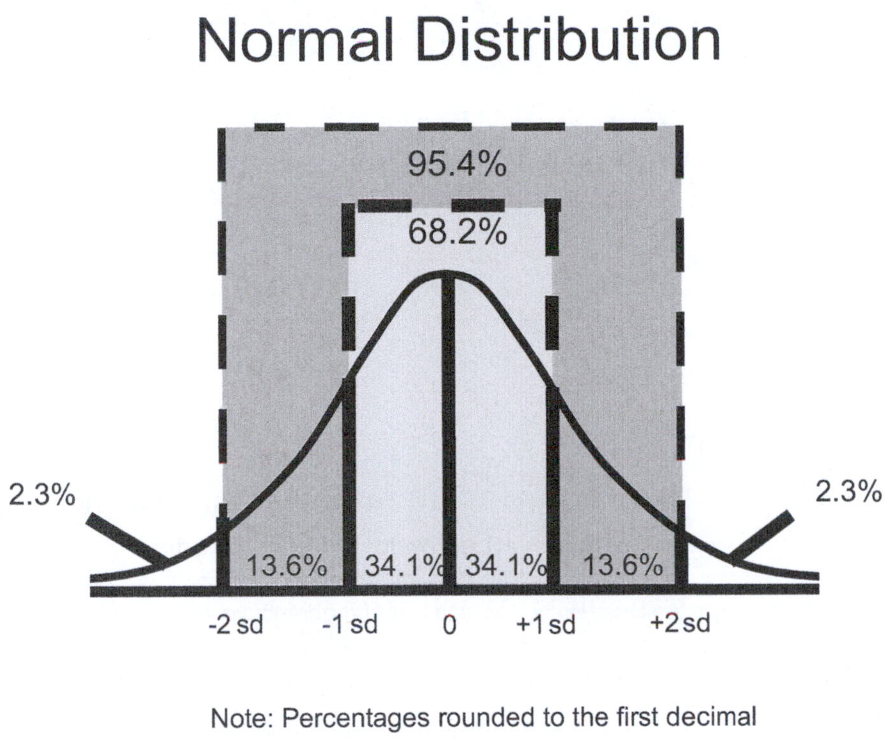

Normal Distribution

Note: Percentages rounded to the first decimal

Figure 14.3 Normal distribution showing percentage distribution of scores within each range of standard deviations

and the mean will be equal to the population parameter—the true mean in the population.

Kurtosis

Although the normal distribution of sampling distributions is linked to estimation, within a given sample, testing whether a distribution is normal is sometimes important to meeting the requirements for other statistical tests. One important measure of a distribution is its kurtosis. A distribution that perfectly matches the shape of a normal distribution is known as *mesokurtic*. If the kurtosis statistic is computed, this distribution will have a value of 0. A distribution that has a narrower, more "pointed" shape compared with the normal distribution is *leptokurtic*, and it will have a positive value for kurtosis. A distribution that is more widely spread and "flatter" compared to a normal distribution is called *platykurtic*, and it will have a negative value for kurtosis. One way to remember this is to think that a leptokurtic distribution leaps into the air, while a platykurtic distribution lays flat like a platypus bill.

normal distribution
→ Unit 14

sample
→ Unit 8

375

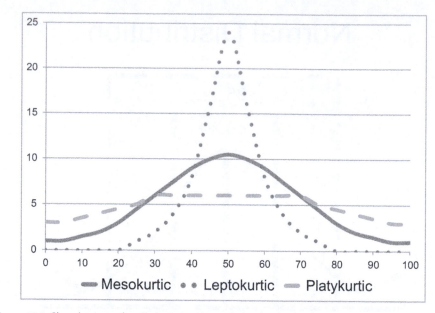

Figure 14.4 Showing mesokurtic, leptokurtic, and platykurtic distributions

<table>
<tr><td>

mean
→ Unit 14

median
→ Unit 14

variable
→ Unit 2

frequency distribution
→ Unit 14

normal distribution
→ Unit 14

</td></tr>
</table>

Outliers

An important feature of normally shaped distributions is that the mean and median are the same. This occurs because the distribution is symmetrical, of course, but minor deviations from symmetry don't usually make much difference in this pattern. The link between the mean and median is important for statistics that rely on normally distributed variables. The mean is generally used to help calculate those statistics, but the mean is not robust and can easily drift away from the true "center" of a distribution. This implies that the mean is easily influenced by outliers—that is, extreme or unusual values that don't fall smoothly into a frequency distribution. Outliers necessarily imply that a distribution isn't normal, but they also can be a distorting influence even when a normal distribution is not assumed. Because outliers are far from most values in the data, they can exert a disproportionate influence on the calculation of statistics such as the mean.

Research in Depth: Outliers

In real-world data sets, in which answers aren't restricted to a limited range of possibilities, outliers can pose serious challenges to the accurate interpretation of data. For example, consider the distribution of population and other important variables across the United States. (These data are from the U.S. Census Bureau in the early 2010s, so some numbers may have changed since then but the example holds.) Most people in the United States live in one of several extremely populous states. If we consider just these 10 states (listed in the table shown later), we find that the mean population is a little over 17 million people. The median is 12.8 million, showing how the extraordinary population of California distorts the results. But even so, none of these 10 states is a clear outlier. In addition to population, we report the mean travel time that people spend getting to work. Not surprisingly, these numbers are generally above the national average, but they are fairly consistent with one another and none would be an outlier. The correlation between state size and travel time is positive but pretty weak (.29).

In the second set of numbers, we introduce a clear outlier in terms of population, Wyoming, which is among the smallest and most rural states in the Union. Clearly, Wyoming's population value of less than 1 million is a strong outlier. The state mean population drops by more than 1.5 million thanks to the addition of this one extreme value, while the median is almost unchanged. Once again, this shows how the mean is less robust against outliers. But consider the results for travel time. Wyoming has a lower than average travel time, but it is hardly an outlier at 18.5. However, the addition of one outlier in the form of population means a major shift in the test of the relationship between population and travel time. Including an outlier for any value when testing relationships can also significantly distort the findings for the relationship.

Table 14.2 Illustrating the effects of outlying values

State	Population	Travel Time	State	Population	Travel
NY	19,651	31.5	NY	19,651	31.5
CA	38,333	27.1	CA	38,333	27.1
TX	26,448	24.9	TX	26,448	24.9
FL	19,553	25.8	FL	19,553	25.8
GA	9,992	27	GA	9,992	27
PA	12,774	25.8	PA	12,774	25.8
OH	11,571	23	OH	11,571	23
IL	12,882	28.1	IL	12,882	28.1
MI	9,897	23.9	MI	9,897	23.9
NC	9,848	23.5	NC	9,848	23.5
			WY	582	18.5
Mean	17,094.9	26.06		15,593.73	25.37
Median	12,828	25.8		12,774	25.8
Population/travel correlation		.290359			.522424

Skew

When a distribution is not symmetrical because the values on one side of the median are more "stretched" toward the high or low end of the scale, this reflects skew. Like outliers, skew can shift the mean relative to the median. Positive skew occurs when the values on the high end (or the right, if graphed) of the distribution are more extreme and far from the mean than those on the low end. Negative skew reflects a situation in which the values on the low end (or the left, if graphed) of the distribution are more extreme and far from the mean. When the distribution has positive skew, those high values will increase the mean relative to the median. That is, the mean for the distribution will be a larger than the median when both are computed. When the distribution has negative skew, those low values will decrease the mean relative to the median. Like kurtosis, skew can be measured on a numerical scale, with negative values indicating greater negative skew, positive values positive skew, and a value of 0 denoting a perfectly symmetrical, nonskewed distribution.

Skew has a similar effect to outliers in distorting certain statistics, but there are some important distinctions. When a distribution is skewed, there are still many cases toward one extreme and a reasonably smooth progression to those cases. It's not a situation in which a very small number of cases (perhaps as few as one) are strongly influencing the results. This may make it seem that skew is less problematic, and mild skew can usually be ignored. But with outliers, a single extreme value can simply be omitted. With skew, dropping one or two cases will not solve the problem and risks ignoring meaningful and important variance. Instead, skew is often addressed by transforming the variable.

Research in Depth: Skewed Data

Although detailed processes for transforming data are beyond the scope of this text, it is important to be familiar with basic approaches to transforming data. Common approaches to transforming skewed data include taking the square root of each of the values, squaring or using a logarithmic function for each of the values in the distribution, or using a fraction of some sort (e.g., 1/4 or 1/3) to alter the distribution. The specific approach used should be determined based on what the researcher needs the distribution to look like. For instance, if a normal distribution is needed for analysis, then the researcher can use a particular type of transformation. Further, if all positive values are needed, then the researcher might square each of the values to remove any negative values.

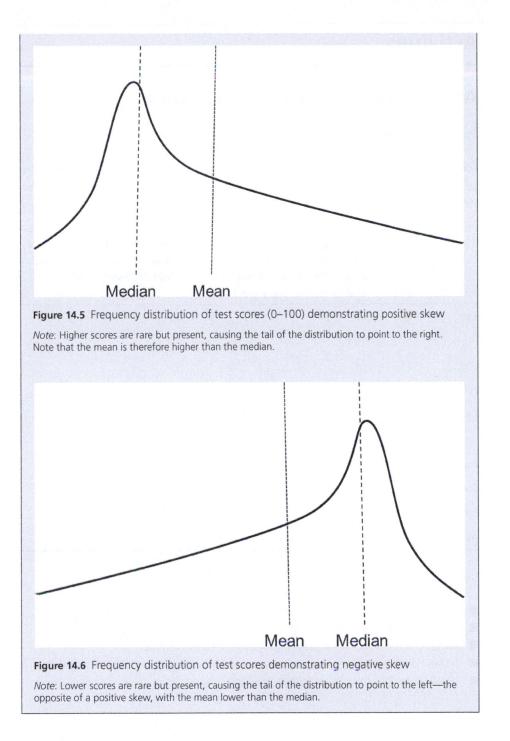

Figure 14.5 Frequency distribution of test scores (0–100) demonstrating positive skew

Note: Higher scores are rare but present, causing the tail of the distribution to point to the right. Note that the mean is therefore higher than the median.

Figure 14.6 Frequency distribution of test scores demonstrating negative skew

Note: Lower scores are rare but present, causing the tail of the distribution to point to the left—the opposite of a positive skew, with the mean lower than the median.

379

Activities

Activity 14A: Descriptive Statistics

See terms: median; mean; mode; range.

For this activity, you should evaluate the data provided and draw conclusions about the sample. Focus only on univariate analysis—that is, measures you can use to describe the samples provided. Use the questions given next the data to guide your analysis.

	Age	Scores on "fear of public speaking" scale, where 1 equals "not at all fearful" and 10 equals "very fearful"	Television-watching measure, where 1 equals "rarely" and 5 equals "every day"
Tom	19	1	3
Harry	21	1	4
Lou	23	2	5
Sven	20	3	5
Kevin	22	4	4
Jaime	21	8	5
Bort	21	9	4
Barry	18	9	5
Leonard	21	9	4
Albert	24	10	5

Guiding questions:

- What measures of central tendency can you compute for each measure?
- What measures of dispersion can you compute for these measures?
- What conclusions can you draw about the age of this sample?
- What conclusions can you draw about how much this sample fears public speaking?
- How often does this sample watch television?

Activity 14B: Critical Analysis of Statistics in Practice

See terms: descriptive statistics; central tendency; dispersion.

The objective of this activity is to assess how well the media presents statistical information. For this activity, locate news articles that present statistical information in them. You are specifically interested in assessing how the news media presents statistical information. Use the following questions to guide your assessment of those articles:

■ What types of statistical information are presented in the articles? (e.g., means, modes, or standard deviations)
■ Is any important information missing? If so, what should be included?
■ Do the journalists draw accurate conclusions from the data? Why or why not?
■ What information is provided about how the data were collected?
■ What is your overall assessment of the quality of the reporting on the data discussed in the articles?
■ Does one article do a better job of presenting statistical information than the others? If so, how?

Activity 14C: Statistics in Everyday Life

See terms: statistics; descriptive statistics.

For this activity, you should locate a statistical report from a noted organization (a great resource for this is the Pew Foundation, which funds a number of efforts to study aspects of civic and media life and makes their data quickly available after collection) or a research article from a scientific journal. After you have read the article, assess the quality of the information presented. Use the following questions to guide your assessments:

- What measures of central tendency are presented in the research report? Are these measures appropriately and clearly presented?
- What measures of dispersion are presented in the research report? Are these measures appropriately and clearly presented?
- Do the conclusions drawn in the report match the data as presented?
- What conclusions would you draw from the data? Do they match those of the authors of the report? Why or why not?

Activity 14D: Visualizing Data

See terms: frequency distribution; histogram.

For this activity, evaluate the histograms presented later and draw conclusions about each. In particular, consider the following questions:

■ What is the main story that the data tell? Why do you draw this particular conclusion?
■ What additional information would be useful to help you better tell the story of these data?

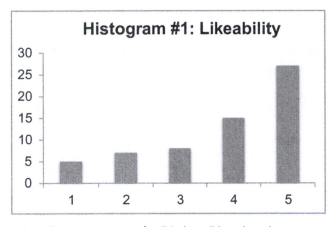

Histogram 1: "Likeability" assessments of political candidates based on exposure to a positive-oriented advertisement about them. A score of 1 equals "very unlikeable," and a score of 5 equals "very likeable."

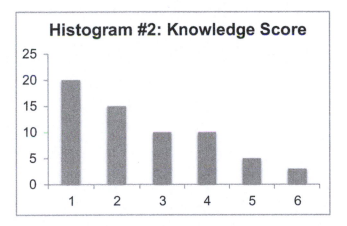

Histogram 2: Scores for a measure of "knowledge of current events". Six items were asked. Each was scored as 0 for "incorrect" and 1 for "correct", for a maximum score of 6.

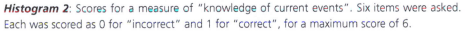

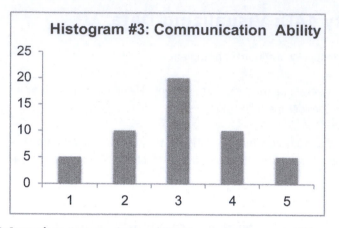

Histogram 3: Scores for a "communication ability" measure assessment skill in communicating interpersonally ranging from a score of 0 indicating "poor skill" to a score of 5 indicating "high skill."

Suggested Readings for Further Exploration of Unit 14 Topics

Examples

Babakus, E., Ferguson, C. E., Jr., & Jöreskog, K. G. (1987). The sensitivity of confirmatory maximum likelihood factor analysis to violations of measurement scale and distributional assumptions. *Journal of Marketing Research*, *24*(2), 222–228. doi:10.2307/3151512

Gould, S. J. (1996). *The mismeasure of man*. New York, NY: W. W. Norton.

Advanced Discussion

Chew, V. (1968). Some useful alternatives to the normal distribution. *The American Statistician*, *22*(3), 22–24. doi:10.1080/00031305.1968.10480473

Harrison, D. A., & Klein, K. J. (2007). What's the difference? Diversity constructs as separation, variety, or disparity in organizations. *Academy of Management Review*, *32*(4), 1199–1228. doi:10.5465/AMR.2007.26586096

Little, R. J. A., & Rubin, D. B. (1989). The analysis of social science data with missing values. *Sociological Methods & Research*, *18*(2–3), 292–326. doi:10.1177/0049124189018002004

Roth, P. L., Switzer, F. S., & Switzer, D. M. (1999). Missing data in multiple item scales: A Monte Carlo analysis of missing data techniques. *Organizational Research Methods*, *2*(3), 211–232. doi:10.1177/109442819923001

unit 15

principles of inferential statistics

In Unit 14, you finished your study and needed to make sense of your measures of news media use. The descriptive statistics presented in that unit were a good start. They gave you a sense of how your sample answered your questions and started telling the story of your data. You noticed whether certain types of news media appear to be used more frequently than others. Perhaps social media is frequently used to gather information, and "feeling smart" is listed as a common reason for doing so. You also noticed whether there were any anomalies with your data that might pose a challenge, and those initial, descriptive analyses even set you on the path toward making estimates about the population.

But suppose you want to know more. Perhaps you want to find out whether different aspects of news media use are related to knowledge about or interest in current events, or whether certain motivations result in more or varied types of media use. Maybe you want to control for any possible influence of factors such as education or partisanship in testing those relationships. By understanding the varied inferential statistics available for evaluating relationships and testing hypotheses, you can better answer these sorts of questions.

Inferential Statistics

Inferential statistics are a special class of statistics that researchers use to make inferences, or estimates, about a larger population based upon the specific sample collected in their study. In practice, there are two steps to using statistics to make inferences. First, researchers must calculate an appropriate statistic to measure a specific quality in their data. Often, these statistics allow for **bivariate analysis**. They measure not one variable but the relationship between two variables. Examples of these statistics include **chi-square, t-tests,** and **Pearson's r.** The last-named statistic measures correlation and accounts for both the **magnitude**, or strength, and the direction of a relationship, providing two critical pieces of information about how the tested variables are related. Other statistics are used for multivariate analysis, which means that they measure the relationship between two variables after one or more other variables have been used as statistical controls (this is explored further in Unit 16).

Once the statistic is calculated, inferential statistical analysis takes an additional step to assess whether the relationship within the given sample is likely to apply to the larger population. That is, researchers ask whether the pattern they found would apply to everyone who shares the traits of those in the sample or whether it is just a fluke of their study. One way this is done is by computing a confidence interval and evaluating the implications of that interval. In this way, researchers make an estimate of the population parameter. For example, if an advertising company found that people who watched ads in an old campaign bought five cans of soda on average and those who saw the new

population
→ Unit 8

relationship
→ Unit 2

multivariate analysis
→ Unit 16

sample
→ Unit 8

polls
→ Unit 10

confidence interval
→ Unit 8

prediction
→ Unit 2

sampling distribution
→ Unit 8

387

campaign bought six on average, it could compute a statistic to measure that difference and to see whether the confidence interval overlapped with 0. If it didn't, the company could conclude the new campaign would work for the whole population, and not just its sample, and proceed to buy air time.

In many academic studies, though, another approach is taken. Researchers test against the **null hypothesis**, which predicts that there is no relationship. By evaluating whether the evidence supports the null hypothesis, researchers can decide whether to reject the null prediction. If the null hypothesis is rejected, this means that the researchers have decided the evidence doesn't indicate a population with no relationship, and instead there must be a **statistically significant** relationship between the variables that extends beyond the sample and applies to the population. When researchers reject the null, they conclude that a relationship likely exists, but they do not say that they "proved" the original hypothesis. Similarly, when they do not reject the null, they say that they "failed to reject the null," not that they accepted the null.

This is related to the basic principle that research is skeptical and cautious. It takes strong evidence to reject the null because it takes strong evidence to support a theory. But it's also too simple to think of a hypothesis as definitively supported (proved) or not supported. Instead, we think about all results in terms of probability. That is, as we accrue evidence and take into account weaknesses in our study, we learn more about the likelihood that any particular claim is true. But unless we could measure the entire population perfectly, we are always balancing the evidence and thinking about the odds, not making conclusive statements. One tool for quantifying these considerations is the **p-value**, which describes the probability our sample comes from a population where the null hypothesis is correct. The larger the *p*-value, the more likely it is that we're studying a population where no relationship exists, and the less likely we are to reject the null. The *p*-value is calculated based on the known sampling distribution for the specific test statistic used to measure the hypothesized relationship in our sample. Of course, not all test statistics have the same distribution, and even the same statistic may have different distributions depending on the number of cases or categories being considered, an idea that is reflected in the notion of *degrees of freedom*. Depending on our hypothesis, we may also decide whether we want a one-directional **one-tailed test** or a more conservative **two-tailed test**.

When deciding whether to reject the null or fail to reject the null, researchers make their best estimate about the population. If we knew the exact relationship in the population, we wouldn't need to use inferential statistics. Think about an election. We use opinion polls to "guess" who will win. As the election gets close, those polls can be accurate within a percentage point or two, but they never perfectly match the actual results. Once the election is over, we don't need opinion polling to tell us who will win; we have the actual results.

Think of inferential statistics as election polling without the election. We will never know the actual "ballots" cast based on our sample; we only have the poll. Because of this, we have to accept that our estimate of the "winner" in the election won't be perfect. If the two candidates are far apart in a poll, though, we're pretty sure who will win. If the poll shows them very close, we aren't confident enough to say that one person is more likely to win. Inferential statistics follow a similar principle: If the relationship is small, we can't be confident it's really there. But no matter how confident we are, there is always a chance that we're wrong, just as there's always a chance that an opinion poll will completely flub the final tally of votes.

We categorize the mistakes we make in inferential statistics into two types. **Type I error** reflects those situations in which we choose to reject the null, but in fact, no relationship exists in the population. We think there is evidence that a relationship exists, but that evidence is just a fluke, and our conclusion is wrong. One major danger in research is that type I error can happen more often than we think. For just one test, a type I error might be rare, but if we run 20 similar tests, the odds are better than 50–50 that one of those tests will appear significant just by chance. To help correct for this, we can adjust our analyses, for example, by using a **Bonferroni correction. Type II error** reflects the opposite case: we fail to reject the null, but a relationship is present in the population. This can happen if we don't have enough statistical power in our study.

Even if our conclusion is right and we find a statistically significant relationship that does reflect a relationship in the population, there is no guarantee that this relationship is important. Consider an ad campaign that increases sales by a few thousand dollars. The relationship between the new campaign and sales might be real, but your client probably wouldn't want to spend millions developing it just to boost sales by a paltry amount. We talk about this in terms of *practical significance*, and as part of inferential statistics, we try to estimate how big the effect of a variable is by computing the **effect size**. Effect sizes are often described in terms of **variance explained**.

Scientific journals and reference styles (such as those of the American Psychological Association or the Modern Language Association) often have specific preferences for the statistical information that should be included when reporting the results of data analysis. In general, the information provided should allow the reader to understand whether the test provides support for the research hypothesis or not. This typically means including the value of the specific statistical test (e.g., t-test or chi-square), the degrees of freedom for that test, the p-value, and a measure of the strength of the effects when possible. However, as problems with the traditional null hypothesis approach have emerged, a growing number of journals are pushing for alternatives to p-values and scholars have highlighted shortcomings with this approach.

389

Shana Steigerwalt—President at Modern Driven Media

Shana is the founder and president of Modern Driven Media, a digital marketing agency specializing in inbound marketing and content creation. She specializes in fostering an environment of comfort, creativity, and exploration to uncover online marketing strategies to grow to achieve business goals. Since the agency's launch in 2015, the team has partnered with clients within a variety of industries, including automotive, hospitality, technology, and business services, to transform their online presence and establish predictable revenue opportunities for their business.

Why are good research skills important to your field?

Data and insights are powerful in any marketing strategy. Being able to conduct research allows you to utilize information to formulate your own viewpoints, recommendations, and thoughts around a specific subject. The ability to do this independently and communicate it effectively with other team members or thought leaders is crucial to business growth and achieving greater results. In addition, it gives you a competitive edge. The more informed you are, the more creative your strategy can be.

What specific method or methods do you use or encounter most?

All of our partnerships start with questionnaires and interviews to learn about our business partners and their customers. These give us the opportunity to cater content specifically to their buyers personas and personalize our approach to marketing communication. We are also consistently mining through data and analytics for all website and online platforms. The more we understand consumers behaviors online, the stronger their online user experience will be. Social media also allows us to find a middle ground between the qualitative data we get on behalf of our clients to use to build relevant and engaging content, as well as the quantitative data needed to make better informed online decisions to reach our intended audience.

Can you name some specific instances for which you have used data collected from research?

We use data collected in our research to adjust and manipulate our digital and content marketing strategies on a consistent basis. Every decision we make is based on some sort of data.

How did the research you conducted help inform your decision?

We are able to adjust all of our campaigns based on best performing content. The more data we are able to collect, the stronger our execution becomes.

What are one or two pieces of advice or insights you would give about research to students in a communication research methods course?

First, continue to ask questions, look for inconsistencies, and predict possible outcomes to provide the best analysis. The more thorough you are, the stronger your analysis will be. Second, as you research and learn, share your information to build your own thought leadership. That could be in team meetings, with clients, on social platforms. Your ability to think critically, utilizing the information you compiled in your research, is irreplaceable.

Logic of Inference

The key to understanding inference is directly linked to the process of null hypothesis testing and to the interpretation of the p-value that this process generates. Ultimately, we wish to make a conclusion about the statistical significance of a relationship. The definitions that follow lay out each of the key pieces of this process in greater detail, but a basic example of the process can help show how they are connected. Consider again testing the relationship between news use and political knowledge. Suppose we are focused on a particularly simple question, asking people whether or not they read news online. Further suppose that our measure of knowledge is only slightly more complex—we ask participants a series of true/false questions about current events, then tally up their scores. Thus, we have a nominal-level measure of news use and a ratio-level measure of knowledge (because scores could include getting zero correct). Now, how do we decide whether the news users and non-users differ?

A logical starting point would be to calculate appropriate descriptive statistics for each group. We could find the mean and the standard deviation for the news users and non-users separately and compare those values. But just looking at the two sets of numbers won't give us statistical confidence in our results. We might think there is a meaningful difference between the two groups, but how can we be sure? We could be more certain if we had a statistic that quantified the difference between the groups, taking into account not just the difference in means but also the dispersion of the scores and the size of our sample, as both would affect our confidence. Fortunately, we have such a test: the t-test. We can calculate a t-test to measure just how far apart our two groups are. Now, we have a way to decide whether the difference is meaningful—specifically, whether we think it is just a peculiarity of our sample or something that would likely persist in the population.

The t-test has a known sampling distribution. That is, even though we don't know the difference between the two groups in the population, we know how often samples like ours will produce a given value of t if certain assumptions

null hypothesis
→ Unit 15

p-value
→ Unit 15

nominal-level measure
→ Unit 5

ratio-level measure
→ Unit 5

mean
→ Unit 14

standard deviation
→ Unit 14

t-test
→ Unit 15

sampling distribution
→ Unit 8

sample
→ Unit 8

population
→ Unit 8

about the population are true. Remember that the sampling distribution for a statistic reflects the idea that if many samples are drawn from a population, and each is used to compute a statistic estimating some population parameter, those statistics will tend to cluster around the true value, with the rare sample turning out particularly high or low. That same principle can be used to decide whether our value of *t* shows a relationship—but with a slight twist.

Instead of focusing on estimating the value of *t* for the population, we form an assumption that the value of *t* in the population is 0. This is the null hypothesis—a value of 0 indicates that the difference between the groups is nonexistent, or null. We know what the likely values of *t* would be in a series of samples just like ours taken from a population in which the null hypothesis is true. As such, we can determine whether or not our value of *t* is probable in a universe in which the null hypothesis is true. In fact, we can quantify this probability in the form of a *p*-value. If, based on the *p*-value, we decide that the null hypothesis is improbable, we will reject the null and declare that we have found a statistically significant relationship. So, at the end of this process, we can look at the scores for our news users and non-users and explain why we think they show a real difference in the population based on statistics, not just our own guess.

Null Hypothesis

The null hypothesis is the opposite of the stated research hypothesis (also called the *alternative hypothesis*); it is the prediction that there is no relationship between the variables being tested. The null hypothesis provides the foundation for one statistical approach to testing relationships and is connected to the larger logic of hypothesis testing as a way to see if a theory can be falsified. That is, instead of proving research hypotheses true, researchers build knowledge by *rejecting* null hypotheses. In a basic sense, researchers have identified a testable prediction from the theory, and if this prediction is wrong it would undermine the theory. Rejecting the null means the researchers have considered the evidence from an inferential statistical test and decided that the evidence suggests the null hypothesis is unlikely to be true in the population. The theory has withstood its test. Specifically, this means that if our sample shows a reasonably strong relationship between two variables, it's highly unlikely that the population would show no relationship. The exact likelihood that our sample would have occurred if the null hypothesis were correct is the *p*-value, so a small *p*-value is more likely to cause researchers to reject the null. Of course, any time researchers reject the null hypothesis, they run the risk of making a type I error, incorrectly concluding that a real relationship exists. Therefore, the strength of the evidence needed to reject the null tends to be high and the corresponding *p*-value low.

For example, consider a situation in which you are comparing those who say they primarily get news from television with those who say they get news

---

hypotheses
→ Unit 2

relationship
→ Unit 2

variable
→ Unit 2

sample
→ Unit 8

population
→ Unit 8

***p*-value**
→ Unit 15

type I error
→ Unit 15

***t*-test**
→ Unit 15

from newspapers in our nationally representative sample. You want to know whether knowledge scores are higher for the newspaper users, as you have hypothesized that *knowledge will be higher for those who rely on newspapers than for those who rely on television*. You could evaluate this using a *t*-test, which would allow a comparison of the mean scores of two groups. In doing so, the *t*-test would be interpreted in part based on whether its results are consistent with the null hypothesis, which you would state as follows: *Those who rely on newspapers and on television will not differ in their level of knowledge*. The null hypothesis predicts that there is no relationship between variables. If this is correct, we will find a *t* value of 0 because the mean scores for the two groups will be equal. If we find a particularly large value of *t* in our sample, we can assume that the null is incorrect and that the population does not have a *t* of 0.

Even though we talk about rejecting or failing to reject the null in somewhat absolute terms, it's important to remember that a single statistical test is not definitive evidence about the relationship in the population. Failure to reject the null can result from having too little statistical power or a flawed measure that generates excessive random error. Rejecting the null in a given study does not necessarily mean the relationship is strong and robust; we might have been deceived by systematic error, or we might have had one of the small number of samples that showed a relationship even though the null was correct for the population. Because of this, it is important that researchers remember the cyclical nature of the process and continue to replicate studies and refine their measurement approach.

p-Value

Our decision about whether to reject the null is traditionally based upon the *p*-value—the probability that an individual sample would produce at least the strength of relationship you observed if the null hypothesis were true (i.e., there is no relationship). This value depends upon the sampling distribution for the specific test used, which may include information about the test statistic as well as the sample size and other details. Typically, when a statistical test produces a larger value, that means your observations deviate more from what the null hypothesis would predict. That is, large statistical test scores reflect a relatively large difference between what you expected (based on the null) and what you observed. Larger statistics, in turn, are reflected by smaller *p*-values. After all, if you found a strong relationship in your sample, the odds that this relationship occurred by chance are correspondingly small. *P*-values range from 0 to 1, with values closer to 0 indicating a smaller likelihood that chance accounts for the relationship and values closer to 1 indicating a larger likelihood that chance accounts for the relationship.

For example, if we perform a test to evaluate the relationship between level of support for the Republican party and number of hours spent viewing Fox News,

null hypothesis
→ Unit 15

relationship
→ Unit 2

standardized coefficient
→ Unit 16

sample
→ Unit 8

population
→ Unit 8

sampling distribution
→ Unit 8

correlation (Pearson's r)
→ Unit 15

chi-square
→ Unit 15

the results may suggest that the measured relationship has a corresponding p-value of .03. Assuming that our measures are valid, this would indicate that there is just a 3 percent chance that a sample would occur that generated such a strong relationship if it was drawn from a population in which the null hypothesis was correct. (Remember, the null hypotheses would state that party support and Fox News viewing are unrelated, meaning that if we conducted a census the statistic measuring this relationship would be 0.) As you can see, 3 percent is a small number, so the likelihood that we would observe such a finding if the null were correct is small, and the researchers can be fairly confident in rejecting the null.

Alternatively, if the p-value produced from a statistical test has a value of .5, this would indicate that there is a 50 percent chance that you would have a sample with a difference as big or bigger than yours if the null were correct. In this case, 50 percent is fairly large and would instill little confidence in the researchers that what was observed is truly distinct from the null. Therefore, the researchers would fail to reject the null and conclude that, in this instance, there does not appear to be a relationship between the two variables. By evaluating the p-value of a given test, the researchers can decide how confident they are in their ability to reject the null, often relying upon a standard guideline to help make this decision.

The p-value for a given result of a statistical test is based on the unique sampling distributions associated with those particular tests. Remember that the sampling distribution refers to the pattern of scores we would obtain for a given statistic if we drew an enormous number of samples, all of the same size and taken from the same population. In null hypothesis testing, we assume these samples are drawn from a population in which the null hypothesis is correct. For example, the distribution of coefficients in a t-distribution looks similar to a normal distribution, with values on either side of 0. More extreme scores (i.e., those further away from 0 in either direction) are less common, and scores closer to 0 are more common, giving the distribution an almost bell-shaped curve. However, the distribution of coefficients for the chi-square and F-distributions skew infinitely away from 0 and only produce positive values. Similar to the t-distribution, higher values for these distributions are less common and, therefore, they are generally associated with smaller p-values.

To determine the exact p-value for a given value of a statistical test, you need three things: (1) the value of the test statistic calculated for your sample, (2) the degrees of freedom for the statistic being calculated, and (3) a table listing the p-values for each possible value. Once you determine the exact p-value for the statistical test that you ran, the next decision is to determine whether that p-value meets the standard for statistical significance. In social sciences, the benchmark is often set at $p < .05$. This means that any p-value of less than .05 would result in a rejection of the null hypothesis.

The area within a given statistical sampling distribution that contains the p-values that are at or below the level of statistical significance is referred to as the *region of rejection*. As the terms suggests, any *p*-value—or corresponding test score—that is within this area will result in the researcher rejecting the null hypothesis. For example, consider using a Pearson's correlation (*r*) coefficient with a sample of 25 students to test the relationship between hours spent studying per day and final exam score. In doing so, you will likely set the acceptable *p*-value at the .05 level, meaning that you would reject the null for any *p*-value *less than* .05. The corresponding value for a Pearson's correlation for the *p* < .05 level with a sample of 25 is .396. This indicates that any correlation coefficient *above* .396 will produce a *p*-value that is less than .05. (Remember that because *p* reflects the level of support for the null, the stronger the evidence of a relationship, the smaller *p* will be.) Therefore, the region of rejection for this particular test is any correlation coefficient above .396. Conversely, any correlation coefficient at closer to zero than .396 would result in a failure to reject the null hypothesis. Because correlation distributions are symmetrical, there would also be a region of rejection below –.396, as addressed in the discussion of two-tailed tests.

Statistical Significance

Statistical significance refers to the judgment that a *p*-value is below a set level and that the null hypothesis may therefore be rejected. Rejecting the null hypothesis means that you are concluding that you have observed a relationship between two (or more) variables. As such, when researchers report that findings are "statistically significant," they are typically indicating that the statistical test they performed produced a score with a corresponding *p*-value of less than .05. Based on this low *p*-value, the researcher is more confident that the relationship is real and unlikely to be attributable to chance (or other extraneous factors).

The traditionally acceptable level in social sciences is a *p*-value of .05. Therefore, any *p*-value under that number—such as .049, .03, or .001—would meet the criteria for statistical significance and result in the null hypothesis being rejected. There is no absolute reason why .05 is a traditional value, and you should not conclude that something particularly important or "magical" happens when a relationship crosses this threshold. But the use of .05 as a benchmark does set a fairly stringent standard for rejecting the null hypothesis and is in place to help guard against a type I error, in which the null is incorrectly rejected. In a basic sense, the .05 value means that if the null were true, there would be only a 5 percent chance (or 5 times out of 100) of a given sample producing a statistical test score similar—or even higher in value—than the one we observed. Certain steps further contribute to how conservative a test is. For example, if we decide to use a *two-tailed test* when available, we account for the likelihood of a relationship between variables as strong as the one we found in either the positive or negative direction.

p-value
→ Unit 15

null hypothesis
→ Unit 15

standardized coefficient
→ Unit 16

relationship
→ Unit 2

type I error
→ Unit 15

one-tailed versus two-tailed tests
→ Unit 15

Researchers can adjust the level of statistical significance to guard against type I error. Common benchmarks that are more stringent are the .01 and .001 levels. For the .01 level, the researchers are allowing for a 1 percent chance (or 1 time out of 100) that the finding they have observed would occur if the null were true. The .001 level is even more stringent, resulting in a .1 percent chance (or 1 time out of 1,000) that the finding would occur if the null were true. Again, this means that we would be more confident in rejecting the null hypothesis because the chance that we are making a mistake (i.e., a type I error) is quite small—less than 1 percent in this case. It is important to note that the acceptable level of statistical significance should be set ahead of time, before the statistical tests are carried out. Often, the acceptable levels are determined by the field within which the researcher is working. For example, natural sciences such as biology and chemistry might set stricter levels than social sciences such as communication or sociology. In either case, it is important to set the acceptable level of statistical significance ahead of time and to plan out the statistical tests that will be run. This helps prevent the occurrence of type I error that can result from running more statistical tests than are necessary.

The level that is set in order to achieve statistical significance and reject the null is typically referred to as the *critical value*. Because every value of a statistical test corresponds to a given *p*-value, researchers can set the level that they are comfortable with and then compare the results of any statistical test with that preset level. For example, if you are testing a Pearson's correlation (r) coefficient using a sample of 25 students, you might set the acceptable *p*-value at the .05 level. The corresponding value for r for the $p < .05$ level would be .396. This means that observing a correlation coefficient *above* +.396 (or below −.396) would result in a rejection of the null hypothesis. In this case, the critical value for this sample and test is .396.

Type I Error

Because null hypothesis testing involves deciding what we think is true of the population, we always face the possibility of making an error in this decision. After all, if we *knew* for certain what the pattern was in the population, we wouldn't need to collect a sample and perform our test. A type I error occurs when we incorrectly reject the null hypothesis. This means that that we have concluded that a relationship exists, but in reality, it does not. This type of error is the opposite of type II error, which occurs when we fail to reject the null, but in fact, a relationship does exist.

Our decision about the threshold to set for determining statistical significance affects the likelihood of making a type I error. When we decide that a higher *p* value is acceptable, we are considering less improbable results to still be considered as not due to mere chance. That is, a greater portion of samples drawn from a population where the null hypothesis is correct will still be considered sufficient evidence to reject the null. Thus, if the null hypothesis is actually correct, the portion of all studies that result in a type I error increases as the *p*-value considered sufficient for significance increases.

A second instance in which type I error occurs is when researchers run a large number of statistical tests, such as a series of *t*-tests comparing dozens of potential dependent variables in an experiment with a simple two-cell design. All inferential statistics involve a small chance of incorrectly rejecting the null, and these chances add up as we perform more tests. Consider trying to throw a football through a hoop. Even if you are not good at throwing a football, there is a good chance that if you throw the football enough times, you will eventually get the ball through the hoop. The same principle applies to running statistical tests—if we run enough tests, some are bound to reach levels of statistical significance. For example, if we use the *p*-value of .05 as our level of statistical significance but run multiple tests, the odds of type I error increase dramatically. If the null hypothesis is correct, then the odds that a single test will result in a value of $p < .05$ is just 5 percent. But if we run five separate tests, those odds go up. Because the odds are 95 percent that we are correct each time, we can compute the odds of being "right" five times in a row—they work out to just about 77 percent, meaning that with just five separate tests, we have a 23 percent chance of making a type I error. Conduct 10 tests, and this increases to almost 40 percent. Again, this assumes the null hypothesis is correct, but of course in our research we don't know whether that assumption is right or wrong. It will be tempting to assume a "significant" result means the null was wrong, but we want to be sure we don't yield to that temptation too easily. To account for this, researchers often use corrective measures to adjust the acceptable level of statistical significance when conducting multiple tests.

Research in Depth: Questionable Research Practices and Type I Error

The logic of null hypothesis testing is vulnerable to abuse. A key assumption behind the idea that a *p*-value of $< .05$ (or some other figure) is that this is a conservative number. Some type I errors will occur, but for every 20 cases where a hypothesis is incorrect and the null is valid, only one should result in a $p < .05$. A careful analysis of a false theory should yield mostly null results.

However, because of publication bias and other factors, scholars have argued that in practice a far higher percentage of tests result in type I errors because of intentional and inadvertent choices made by researchers in search of significance. Terms for these processes vary. Simmons, Nelson and Simonsohn (2011) talk about "undisclosed flexibility" in the research process that masks the real probability of null findings. Gelman and Loken (2013) refer to the "garden of forking paths," while also warning about the even more ominous concept of "p-hacking." Matthes et al. (2015), focusing on communications, describe many of the issues as "questionable research practices," or QRPs.

Although there are subtle differences across these papers and many others, the core problem identified in all is that the logic of null hypothesis testing rests on there having been exactly one way to test a given hypothesis, so that either that one test did or did not deviate significantly from what we would expect given the null. Unfortunately, the complexity of the research process means this is rarely the case, and scholars may not even realize the hidden choices they have made in constructing their analyses.

An important point to remember is that the p-value does not imply that only 5 percent of significant results are in fact type I errors. We cannot know the percentage of type I errors that occur, because we don't know whether the null hypothesis is actually correct. A researcher studying a false hypothesis will find significant results on occasion, and 100 percent of those results will be type I errors. But ordinarily this would be somewhat obvious, because for every one of those errors there should be numerous cases where we failed to reject the null. The preponderance of non-significant findings should tell us something is wrong with the hypothesis.

However, publication bias can undermine this process. Researchers may choose to ignore studies that "didn't work," and move on to another experience. A lack of replication can keep us from having a large enough pool of tests to realize most of them result in large p-values. Journals can even encourage researchers to omit portions of their analyses that resulted in non-significant outcomes in favor of the "exciting" significant results. All of these factors undermine the logic of science, and none of them should be acceptable under ideal research conditions.

Researcher bias also plays a role. Most researchers are confident in their theories and expect their hypotheses to be supported. Given this, it is easy for a scholar to conclude that the selection of variables that produces a significant result must be correct. If analyses including specific control variables or defining outliers in a particular way generate that expected result, that's a good reason to stop testing. But if the results seem "just shy" of significance, a researcher might try to keep cleaning their data. Pushed to the extreme, this is what is sometimes called p-hacking; repeated tests in search of significance, with only the final result reported and no information given about the prior choices. But the "garden of forking paths" argument points out that we may make many of those early choices based on reasonable criteria and without checking the final results, and yet we're still "selecting" our final set of results from a pool of other results not present in the paper.

This is a complex issue, and there is no one simple solution. Following the best practices of research, being transparent about all aspects of the method and results, and avoiding the temptation to "fish" for significance are all important steps. More nuanced forms of data analysis may help as well, as do exact replications that keep all the same choices made by an earlier researcher to make sure it wasn't the specific characteristics of the data that shaped the analyses to find significance. One idea that is gaining popularity is pre-registration of studies, letting researchers clearly indicate the exact method they would follow and statistical tests they would perform. The hope is that this rewards researchers for being transparent and following best practices, and discourages scholars from modifying their studies to chase significance or feeling compelled to ignore non-significant outcomes.

As someone learning how to conduct research, it's important to guard against the biases in favor of your hypotheses and make sure you present the findings as obtained. As someone who reads research, you should pay attention to inconsistencies between studies that claim to be testing the same ideas; it might suggest that the authors made those changes in search of significance. You should also look out for seemingly arbitrary decisions about omitting or including variables or cases for similar reasons. And you should notice more direct indicators of likely type I error, like analyses that conduct a large number of comparisons without correcting for the number of tests.

Gelman, A., & Loken, E. (2013). The garden of forking paths: Why multiple comparisons can be a problem, even when there is no "fishing expedition" or "p-hacking" and the research hypothesis was posited ahead of time. New York, NY: Department of Statistics, Columbia University. Retrieved from www.stat.columbia.edu/~gelman/research/unpublished/p_hacking.pdf

Matthes, J., Marquart, F., Naderer, B., Arendt, F., Schmuck, D., & Adam, K. (2015). Questionable research practices in experimental communication research: A systematic analysis from 1980 to 2013. Communication Methods and Measures, 9(4), 193–207. doi:10.1080/19312458.2015.1096334

Simmons, J. P., Nelson, L. D., & Simonsohn, U. (2011). False-positive psychology: Undisclosed flexibility in data collection and analysis allows presenting anything as significant. Psychological Science, 22, 1359–1366. doi:10.1177/0956797611417632

Bonferroni Correction

An example of a common correction for the increase in type I error is the Bonferroni correction, which works by adjusting the *p*-value considered evidence of significance based on the number of tests performed. Specifically, to use a Bonferroni correction, you would divide the *p*-value normally used to establish statistical significance by the number of tests performed. This would determine the new threshold for significance. For example, if we are conducting five tests and have otherwise set the *p*-value for statistical significance at .05, then we would determine that the necessary *p*-value for significance among these five tests is .01 (.05/5).

As an alternative to adjusting our threshold for significance, we can also correct our actual *p*-values by multiplying them by the number of tests performed. So, for example, if we are running five tests and one of them has a *p*-value of .005, we would multiply that by 5, get a new value of .025, and decide the result is still significant at the .05 level. This correction makes each individual test more stringent but helps protect against making a type I error.

The Bonferroni correction is easy to perform, as we need only account for the number of tests performed and can make the adjustment after the results are produced rather than needing to account for it when calculating our initial statistical tests. But it may overcompensate for the likelihood of type I error. Other tests beyond the scope of this text may be better. The best solution, though, is to be precise and careful in your initial planning, so you have only a few tests in mind and have powerful enough data to detect meaningful effects without "fishing" for results.

Type II Error

Type II error is the opposite of type I error and occurs when the researchers fail to reject the null hypothesis when they should have rejected it. This means that a relationship does exist in the population, but the researchers do not consider their sample's evidence sufficient to expect such a relationship in the population. The primary reason that type II errors occur is not having enough statistical power. This is a result of the sample size not being large enough given the size of the relationship being tested for. Sample size is important for multiple reasons. First, many tests will produce a larger test statistic and correspondingly smaller *p*-value when the sample size is larger. These tests have built into their calculation the idea that a bigger sample size provides greater confidence in the findings. Additionally, the sampling distribution for statistical tests generally depends upon the degrees of freedom. The more pieces of information, in the form of individual observations, and the less complex the test, the more degrees of freedom we have. Typically, the larger the degrees of freedom, the "narrower" the sampling distribution, meaning that when we have more degrees of freedom, a given statistic will typically have a smaller p-value. Conversely, when degrees of freedom are smaller, the p-value produced from a given test will typically be larger. In short, our tests will be more powerful when we have more participants.

Because of this, larger sample sizes are highly desirable to researchers simply because they increase the statistical power and improve the likelihood of identifying statistically significant relationships when they exist. (This doesn't necessarily mean the relationship is important, and with very large samples you can reliably detect even tiny relationships but then have to decide how to use this information.) For example, if you are interested in studying the relationship between the number of hours spent practicing speeches and the grade you receive for the speech, you could use Pearson's correlation to test the relationship between these two ratio variables. The degrees of freedom for Pearson's correlation are determined by the sample size using the following formula: $N - 2$. For a sample size of 12 ($df = 10$), you would need to observe a correlation value of .576 or greater to reject the null hypothesis using the $p < .05$ level of statistical significance. If you increase the sample size to 52 ($df = 50$), the correlation value needed to reject the null drops to .273. If you increase the sample size even further to 102 people ($df = 100$), then the correlation value needed to reject the null drops to .194 at the $p < .05$ level. If the real relationship in the population were .2, and your study actually matched the population value perfectly, then you would have made a type II error in the first and second cases. That is, though you accurately found the correlation in your sample, you wouldn't have been confident enough in a sample with 12 or 52 people to reject the null. With the power from the sample of 102 people, now you can be confident in your result. This is because as the number of people in your study increases, the precision of your result also increases, so it is less and less likely that the test statistic you obtained is dramatically different in the population. But greater precision also means that you may be increasingly confident that the result, though "real" and not equal to 0, reflects a very small relationship. To better quantify this, we should calculate and report information about the effect size.

correlation (Pearson's r)
→ Unit 15

variable
→ Unit 2

One-Tailed Versus Two-Tailed Tests

Another important consideration in many types of inferential statistics tests involves whether a one-tailed or two-tailed version of the test is used. This issue applies whenever the sampling distribution for a given test is symmetrical, reflecting the potential for positive and negative values. For example, when a t-test compares mean scores, the mean for group A can be either higher or lower than that for group B. If the null hypothesis is correct, extreme values in either direction are equally probable. If group A is television news viewers and group B is newspaper readers, and our dependent variable is political knowledge, then the

sampling distribution
→ Unit 8

t-tests
→ Unit 15

mean
→ Unit 14

null hypothesis
→ Unit 15

relationship
→ Unit 2

p-value
→ Unit 15

null hypothesis would predict that these two groups are equally knowledgeable. By extension, it would be just as common for a rare sample to occur such that newspaper readers are more knowledgeable as for one to occur where television viewers are the knowledgeable ones. With a two-tailed test, we account for both types of relationships when computing the *p*-value. That is, if our test found that television viewers were less knowledgeable by 1 point on our scale, the *p*-value would reflect the likelihood of finding a 1-point difference regardless of which group was more knowledgeable. In contrast, a one-tailed test is directional. We would consider any finding in the unexpected direction evidence in favor of the null because it goes against expectations.

Because the distributions of tests in which one- and two-tailed tests are both possible are symmetrical, there is an exact relationship between the *p*-value for each test. Specifically, the one-tailed value will be half of the two-tailed value because it considers results in only one direction (instead of two) significant. Suppose our test for political knowledge found a one-tailed value of .04. A two-tailed test would give a *p*-value of .08. In this case, we would have likely rejected the null using a one-tailed test but not a two-tailed test. Because of this, we say that a two-tailed test is more conservative. Given the same size difference, we will be more reluctant to reject the null when using a two-tailed test.

But remember that a one-tailed test implies that we had a clear expectation of the direction of the relationship before collecting the data. If our study had found that television viewers were *more* knowledgeable, with a one-tailed test, we would not have rejected the null, even if we had found an enormous difference between the two groups. As such, one-tailed tests are only appropriate when we have a very clear theory-based expectation that a relationship will be positive or negative and are prepared to consider any evidence in the opposite direction as meaningless and due to chance. Note in Figure 15.1 how the area into which a critical value must fall for a two-tailed test is smaller than it is for a one-tailed test because it is split to either side. Therefore, the critical value must be more extreme—that is, further from zero. In this case, the example shows a distribution for a *t*-test in which there are 10 degrees of freedom and a total *p*-value of .05. In the case of the one-tailed test, the *p*-value is all on one side, and, as a result, the critical value needed to reject the null hypothesis is 1.812. However, for the two-tailed test, the *p*-value is split, leaving .025 on either side. In such a case, the observed value for the *t*-test must be either lower than −2.228 or higher than +2.228. In either case, a more extreme score is needed to reject the null than is needed for the one-tailed test.

Comparison of region of rejection for one-tailed versus two-tailed test. Using the *t*-distribution for a *t*-test with *df* = 10 and *p*-value of .05.

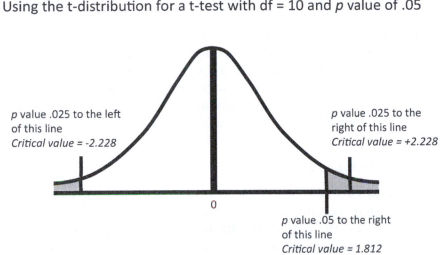

Comparison of region of rejection for one- vs. two-tailed test
Using the t-distribution for a t-test with df = 10 and *p* value of .05

p value .025 to the left
of this line
Critical value = -2.228

p value .025 to the
right of this line
Critical value = +2.228

0

p value .05 to the right
of this line
Critical value = 1.812

Figure 15.1 Example of *p*-value distribution and region of rejection

Effect Size

Although null hypothesis testing is used to measure the statistical significance of a relationship, this only tells us about our confidence that finding a pattern in our study wasn't due to a chance difference from a population where no relationship exists. A statistically significant finding gives confidence that a relationship exists in the population as well. But given a powerful enough test, that relationship may be very small. Thus, we also report a measure of effect size, which tells us how closely related two variables are within our sample.

Generally, a larger effect size offers greater evidence that the relationship is meaningful. A measure of effect size is purely descriptive—it only tells us how strong the link is within our data. As such, it is not a substitute for inferential testing, and it should be viewed with caution if we have a small sample in which considerable sampling error is likely. But especially with larger samples, effect size provides useful insights into the importance of our findings. The specific measure of effect size that should be used varies depending on the statistical test employed. For instance, Cohen's *d* would be used when comparing two means (such as in a *t*-test) and eta-squared (η^2) would be used to estimate effects sizes for ANOVA (analysis of variance). In general, the larger the value of the test statistic measuring the relationship, the stronger the observed effect and thus the larger the effect size measure will be.

null hypothesis
→ Unit 15

statistical significance
→ Unit 15

relationship
→ Unit 2

population
→ Unit 8

variable
→ Unit 2

sample
→ Unit 8

mean
→ Unit 14

t-test
→ Unit 15

one-way ANOVA
→ Unit 15

In some cases, measures of effect size tell the researcher the amount of variance explained. That is, the measure lets us know how much of the difference between individuals for the dependent variable can be accurately predicted with our knowledge of the scores for the independent variable. Not all effect size measures directly reflect variance explained, although the same idea is still expressed. Basically, every measure of effect size shows how strongly related two (or more) variables are, and because we've defined relationships in terms of the ability to make predictions, a measure of effect size will indicate how well we can predict one variable using another within our sample.

Variance Explained

One broad class of measures of effect size are those that assess variance explained. In a basic sense, measures of variance explained tell the researcher how much of the variation in the scores of the dependent variables is accounted for by an individual independent variable. For example, consider the question of how the time spent watching cable news relates to the level of political knowledge. Suppose our measure of political knowledge consists of 10 true/false questions, so that scores could range from 0 correct to 10 correct. Because this is a ratio-level measure, we can compute the variance. This, you will recall, provides a measure of the typical or average dispersion—the difference between individual scores and the mean value. Without any additional information, we would simply predict that everyone would have the mean score for knowledge. The variance explained involves the fact that almost every person's actual score is different from the mean. The more accurately we predict their score by knowing information about the independent variable, the more of this variance from the mean we can explain. Because variance is an actual number, we can quantify just how much of that variance is accounted for by our more accurate estimate.

Reflect & React: Effect Sizes and Society

One benefit of meta-analysis is that it can offer more concrete measures of effect size and variance explained than individual studies. Consider some of the following values from published meta-analyses. Do the effect sizes reported surprise you? Would you have expected them to be larger or smaller? How do they compare with one another? Do you think the sizes reported are large enough to be considered socially important? (Values reported are the percentage of variance explained.)

- Use of computer-mediated communication and time to complete group task: 42 percent (Baltes, Dickson, Sherman, Bauer, & LaGanke, 2002)

- Exposure to expert (versus nonexpert) sources and persuasiveness of argument: 16 percent (Wilson & Sherrell, 1993)
- Exposure to thin-ideal media and body dissatisfaction: 3 percent (Groesz, Levine, & Murnen, 2002)
- Health communication campaigns and seat belt use: 2 percent (Snyder et al., 2004)

For example, suppose that we find a correlation between hours spent watching cable news and the knowledge score of .08. Although this Pearson correlation coefficient might be statistically significant, it is important to assess the variance explained by viewing cable news to get a true sense of how much it affects knowledge. In this case, the researcher would compute r^2, the effect size measure for the Pearson correlation. This is done by squaring the correlation coefficient (.08 × .08 = .0064) and then converting it to a percentage (.0064 = .64 percent). This procedure reveals that viewing only accounts for .64 percent of the variance in knowledge. Compared with the total variance, this is a tiny fraction—less than 1 percent. We would be able to do slightly better than merely guessing that everyone had the mean level of knowledge if we knew how much cable news they watched, but not much. If we subtracted the original variance from the small amount accounted for by our improved prediction, we would still be left with nearly all the original value. As a note, if we could explain all of the variance that would mean a value of 100 percent—or a Pearson correlation of 1 (1 × 1 = 1.00, which equals 100 percent).

Now consider a case in which our value of r is .5. The r^2 in this case would be .25 (.5 × .5). This observed value would allow us to account for 25 percent of the original variance. While there will still be some definite differences between our predicted scores and the true value for knowledge, knowing how much people watch cable news in this case would make us considerably more accurate.

Bivariate Analysis

Often, researchers are interested in moving beyond simply describing variables (sometimes known as univariate analysis) and instead want to consider the relationship between two variables—for example, the independent and dependent variable predicted to be related in a hypothesis. In such cases, in which the focus is on the relationship between only two variables, the researcher is conducting bivariate analysis. There are many bivariate tests that researchers can use to analyze their data, but the decision of which test to use depends primarily on the level of measurement of the two variables. Additional assumptions about the variables need to be met for certain tests. For instance, if both the independent

relationship
→ Unit 2

variable
→ Unit 2

independent
variable
→ Unit 2

dependent
variable
→ Unit 2

405

and dependent variables are nominal-level variables, then the appropriate test would be a chi-square. If you are comparing two groups and have an interval- or ratio-level dependent variable, you would generally use a *t*-test. If you want to consider three or more groups with such a dependent variable, you would probably run an ANOVA, and if you want to see how two interval- or ratio-level measures are related, you would test the correlation. In each case, these tests produce a specific statistic, such as an *F*-statistic, *t*-statistic, or other measure that reflects the clarity of the relationship between the two variables.

Bivariate analyses are commonly used in experiments in which researchers are interested in directly testing whether the different conditions resulted in differences between treatment groups and don't need to adjust for potential confounding variables. For example, the experiment might include two treatment groups to compare the effectiveness of different types of advertisements (the independent variable in this case) on interest in a product (the dependent variable). The researchers could then compare means for the interest variable between the two treatment groups to determine whether exposure to one advertisement resulted in higher levels of interest in the product than exposure to the other—a *t*-test would be a perfect approach to use in this situation.

Like all inferential statistics, bivariate analysis can be used for null hypothesis testing—that is, to determine whether we can reject the null and conclude that a significant relationship exists. You should review that material carefully to fully understand how best to interpret the results of your bivariate analysis. Briefly, though, for a given test statistic, we can determine whether it would be likely to have occurred if our sample were drawn from a population in which no relationship existed. The bigger the between-group differences or the more pronounced the relationship, the less likely it is that the null is correct. This is expressed in terms of a *p*-value, and when that number is small, we are more comfortable rejecting the null and concluding that the relationship we have found is statistically significant—that we would also expect to find a relationship in the population. Furthermore, all bivariate statistical procedures can also generate a measure of effect size, which gives a sense of whether this relationship is large enough to consider important.

Chi-Square

When testing relationships between two nominal-level variables, chi-square is the appropriate test to use. When reporting values for a chi-square test, the Greek symbol chi (χ) is used, so you would give the value as $\chi^2 = 3.14$ (for example). Consider a situation in which you might need to use the chi-square test. For instance, you might compare the snack preferences of sports fans, determining whether baseball and football fans differ in their preference for peanuts or soft pretzels. In this case, you would want to determine whether football fans prefer soft pretzels at a higher or lower rate than baseball fans.

A chi-square test works by determining the difference between what you would expect to find if there were no relationship between variables and what you observed. Therefore, the null hypothesis for this chi-square would state that there is no relationship between sport preference and snack preference. In conducting the observations and running the test, chi-square values will be higher when the difference between observed values and expected values is higher. The greater this difference, the more confident you will be that the relationship exists in the population you are studying.

It is important to note that increases in the number of attributes for each variable will increase the number of cells in a chi-square table. For example, using two variables that each have two attributes produces a chi-square with four cells (2×2). Using two variables that each possess three attributes produces a chi-square with nine cells (3×3). The number of attributes also affects the degrees of freedom for a chi-square. The degrees of freedom are important in determining the p-value for each test. Increasing the number of cells—and therefore the degrees of freedom—also means that chi-square values are likely to be higher when there are more cells. The degrees of freedom act as a check that adjusts the level of the p-value that is acceptable for a given test based on the number of cells. In this way, the chi-square score needed to reach statistical significance for a four-cell (2×2) chi-square is not as high as what is needed for a six (2×3), nine (3×3), or 12-cell (3×4) chi-square.

To demonstrate how chi-square works, let's consider the situation in which you are interested in whether sports fans (baseball and football) differ in their snack preference (peanuts or soft pretzels). You could observe 50 baseball fans and 50 football fans (total $N = 100$) and ask them to choose between peanuts and soft pretzels. In this case, both the independent variable (sport preference) and the dependent variable (snack preference) have two attributes. The first step in computing a chi-square is to record how frequently the different attributes co-occur (see Tables 15.1 and 15.2 and note the observed values). Ultimately, what you are looking for is differences in the rate at which one group does something versus the other. In this case—looking at the first example in Table 15.1—40 of 50 baseball fans chose peanuts, a rate of 80 percent. On the other hand, only 10 of 50 football fans chose peanuts, a rate of 20 percent. The percentages are reversed for soft pretzels—clearly, football fans (80 percent) prefer soft pretzels at a greater rate than baseball fans (20 percent). A chi-square test, then, is a way of determining whether that observed difference is statistically significant.

As indicated, a chi-square works by comparing what you observed with what you would expect to find if there were no relationship. In the current example, if there were no relationship between sport preference and snack preference, then both sports fans would choose peanuts or soft pretzels at about the same rate. In this case, because the sample is divided evenly among the sports fans (50 of each) and evenly among the snack preferences (50 of

variable
→ Unit 2

null hypothesis
→ Unit 15

population
→ Unit 8

attribute
→ Unit 5

tables
→ Unit 3

_p_-value
→ Unit 15

statistical significance
→ Unit 15

independent variable
→ Unit 2

dependent variable
→ Unit 2

attribute
→ Unit 5

sample
→ Unit 8

Table 15.1 Chi-square example 1

	Peanuts	Soft pretzel	Total
Baseball	Observed—40	Observed—10	50
	Expected—25	Expected—25	
Football	Observed—10	Observed—40	50
	Expected—25	Expected—25	
Total	50	50	100

Table 15.2 Chi-square example 2

	Peanuts	Soft pretzel	Total
Hockey	Observed—30	Observed—20	50
	Expected—32.5	Expected—17.5	
Basketball	Observed—35	Observed—15	50
	Expected—32.5	Expected—17.5	
Total	65	35	100

each), we would expect that same even split in preference among fans if there were no relationship. Note that the table indicates that those expected values would be 25 (50 percent of football fans choose pretzels and 50 percent choose peanuts, with baseball fans choosing at the same rate). You might also notice that the expected values (25 for each cell) and the observed values differ greatly. Therefore, we would conclude for this example that there *is* a relationship between sport preference and snack preference, such that baseball fans choose peanuts more than soft pretzels and football fans choose soft pretzels more than peanuts. Indeed, if we computed the exact chi-square value it would be 36.0. The critical value for a chi-square with 1 degree of freedom is 3.84, which is well below the chi-square value based on what we observed. As such, in this case we would reject the null and would conclude that there is a difference in snack food preference for baseball and football fans.

Now let's consider the same general premise but demonstrate an example in which there is not a significant relationship (see Table 15.2). In this case, you conduct observations with hockey and basketball fans on their preference for peanuts or soft pretzels. In this case, note how more people overall prefer peanuts (65 percent) to soft pretzels (35 percent). Among hockey fans, it is observed that 30 (60 percent) of 50 prefer peanuts and 20 (40 percent) of

50 prefer soft pretzels. Basketball fans are somewhat different but follow the same general pattern in that 35 (70 percent) prefer peanuts and 15 (30 percent) prefer soft pretzels. In this case, you can also see how the expected values are different for the cells compared to the previous example, in which each cell had the same expected value. In this case, the expected value of the peanuts cells are higher because more people prefer peanuts overall. Further, the differences between observed and expected are much smaller in this example. This is reflected in the small chi-square score of 1.098. As indicated earlier, for a chi-square with one degree of freedom the critical value would be 3.84 if the pre-determined significant *p*-value was .05. In this case, the chi-square statistic is not greater than the critical value. As such, you would fail to reject the null hypothesis and would conclude that there is no relationship between sport preference and snack preference. Despite a small difference in our sample, it's hard to be confident that a difference exists in the population as a whole.

Steps to Success: Computing Chi-Square

The sum of (observed − expected)^2/expected for each of the cells. df = (number of rows − 1) × (number of columns − 1).

For example, for a 2 × 2 chi-square, there is 1 df [(2 − 1) × (2 − 1)]. To confirm that any observed difference is statistically significant, we can compute the chi-square value by using the previously mentioned formula. Additionally, we need to compute the degrees of freedom. The final step is to determine the p-value for the chi-square score. To achieve the traditional level of significance ($p < .05$), a chi-square with 1 df must be at least 3.84. In the first example (Table 15.1), the resulting value is $\chi^2 = 36.0$. This has a p-value of less than .001, which is below the acceptable level, so we would reject the null hypothesis. However, in the second example (Table 15.2), the resulting value is $\chi^2 = 1.1$ for a p-value of .29. This p-value is considerably above the commonly accepted benchmark of .05, indicating that we would fail to reject the null in this case.

t-Tests

These are a set of statistical tests that are used when the to compare mean scores between two groups or variables. The most commonly used approach is an independent samples *t*-test, used when the independent variable is nominal with two values, and the dependent is interval- or ratio-level. Because of this, *t*-tests are commonly used in analyzing data collected from experiments. This is because experimental designs often pose hypotheses about how two experimental conditions (e.g., control versus treatment) vary on some outcome measure. But *t*-tests are also useful when comparing two naturally occurring groups from a random

independent variable
→ Unit 2

nominal-level measure
→ Unit 5

attribute
→ Unit 5

sample. For example, maybe you want to compare the knowledge level of those who say that CNN is their favorite news source with those who say *The Daily Show*. You would want to know whether the mean knowledge level for viewers of one show is sufficiently different from the score of viewers of the other. In this case, *t* provides a clear measure of this difference that can be further used to compare your result against the null hypothesis through a *p*-value.

Conducting a *t*-test results in a *t*-statistic, which is a value determined by comparing the two groups. The further the value of the *t*-statistic is from 0, the greater the likelihood that the difference in scores between the two groups is statistically significant, all else being equal. A *t* of 0 would indicate that the groups are equivalent, with matching means. This, of course, would support the null hypothesis. As the value of the *t*-statistic deviates further from 0, it reflects evidence of differences, which can lead to rejecting the null. Researchers can use either a one-tailed test or a two-tailed test. One-tailed tests are used when the researcher states a hypothesis and therefore expects a particular finding (e.g., the group that took a public speaking class will perform better in speaking than the group that did not take the class). Two-tailed tests are used when the researcher is not sure what to expect and thus poses a research question.

The degrees of freedom are used to help determine whether the *t*-score for a given test is statistically significant. In the case of the *t*-statistic, the degrees of freedom are computed by subtracting 2 from the total sample size. For example, a sample of 100 would have a *df* of 98. The higher the *df*, the lower the *t*-score that is needed to produce a statistically significant result. For instance, using a sample of 10 (*df* = 8), the researcher would need to reach of *t*-score of 1.86 or higher to reach the $p < .05$ level of statistical significance using a one-tailed test. However, with a sample of 100 (*df* = 98), the researcher would only need to reach a value of 1.66. This is one reason why larger samples are desired when comparing groups, but sample size matters for another reason as well, rooted in the computation of the *t*-score.

To compute a *t*-test, you need three pieces of the information. First, you need the mean scores for the two groups. The greater the difference between the means, the greater the likelihood that the *t*-score will be further from 0 and therefore statistically significant. Second, you need to know the standard deviations of the means for both groups. The smaller the standard deviations— and therefore the greater the confidence in the mean scores—the greater the likelihood that the value of the *t*-score will be further from 0. Third, you need to know the sample size. Larger sample sizes increase the likelihood that the *t*-score will be greater because they increase the power of the test. The resulting *t*-score is then used, along with the *df*, to determine the *p*-value and whether the difference between the mean scores is statistically significant.

If you are reading about or conducting *t*-tests, you will find that multiple formulae exist to compute the value of *t*, connected to specific aspects of the measurement and data. For example, a *t*-test exists to compare individuals' scores on one variable to their scores on another variable—this is known as a *paired t*-test. For *t*-tests that compare group scores on a single variable, different tests will be reported based on whether the groups being compared are equal in size and variance. The details of this are readily available in statistical textbooks, but do not change the basic logic or interpretation of a *t*-statistic.

One-Way ANOVA

Analysis of variance (ANOVA) is a statistical test that is used when the independent variable is a nominal-level measure and the dependent variable is a ratio-level measure. Unlike the *t*-test, however, ANOVA can be used when there are three or more groups (or attributes) in the independent variable. (As we will learn later, there are also versions of ANOVA that allow for more than one independent variable, making it even more flexible.) This makes ANOVA a useful statistical test for experiments when researchers need to compare multiple treatment groups, whether or not a control is included. ANOVA is referred to as an *omnibus* test because it is used to determine whether general differences exist between groups, but it cannot, on its own, determine which of the specific groups are different. Because of this, post hoc testing procedures have been developed to allow researchers to determine which groups are statistically significantly different and which groups are not.

Conducting an ANOVA will produce an *F*-statistic that, along with the degrees of freedom, is used to determine whether the ANOVA has revealed statistically significant differences. The degrees of freedom for an ANOVA are composed of two numbers. The first is derived from subtracting 1 from the number of groups being compared. The second is derived from subtracting the number of groups from the total sample size. As such, an ANOVA that has 20 people in its sample and is comparing 4 different groups would have degrees of freedom of 3 (4 − 1) and 16 (20 − 4), noted as *df* = 3,16. The *F*-statistic produced by the ANOVA is always a positive number, and the larger that number, the greater the likelihood that a statistically significant difference exists between the groups compared for the independent variable.

As with all interferential statistics, the value of *F* is used along with the degrees of freedom to determine the *p*-value, indicating the strength of evidence in favor of the null. If that *p*-value is small, we can conclude that the null is incorrect; the results in our sample showing differences between groups, as a whole, probably reflect a real pattern in the population. With ANOVA, additional post hoc analyses would be necessary to determine exactly which groups are different from one another. Typically, this involves using a *t*-test to compare specific groups, although some variations are available to account for the inflated possibility of a type I error generated by making multiple comparisons.

independent variable
→ Unit 2

nominal-level measure
→ Unit 5

dependent variable
→ Unit 2

ratio-level measure
→ Unit 5

t-test
→ Unit 15

experiments
→ Unit 9

F-statistic
→ Unit 15

sample size
→ Unit 8

p-value
→ Unit 15

population
→ Unit 8

type I error
→ Unit 15

mean
→ Unit 14

variance explained
→ Unit 15

variance
→ Unit 14

null hypothesis
→ Unit 15

theory
→ Unit 2

Consider again our evaluation of whether knowledge differs between those who prefer different news sources. If we are measuring not just two choices, but several, one-way ANOVA would be an appropriate way to evaluate the overall research question of whether people's political knowledge is related to their choice of news source. The exact details of the test can be found in a statistics book, but this example can illustrate the basic logic. Suppose we want to compare those who prefer MSNBC, Fox News, CNN, and *The Daily Show*. At first, it might seem that we could just compare the mean values. But each of the four groups has a mean score—what do we subtract from what to generate a single statistic? Instead, ANOVA compares the ratio of variance explained by group membership to the overall variance in the dependent variable. If the members of each group of viewers are very similar to one another in their knowledge, but there are big differences in knowledge overall, the resulting *F*-statistic will be larger.

For example, suppose the average knowledge score for MSNBC is 3, for Fox News it is 5, for CNN it is 4, and for *The Daily Show* it is 8. We would then need to see how much variance there is in each group's scores. If most viewers for each channel had similar scores, then that similarity, relative to the overall spread in means between groups, would likely create a fairly large, significant *F*-statistic. But maybe despite the apparent difference in means, the variance for each group is quite large. Many viewers of *The Daily Show* might have been among the lowest scorers, while a subset of Fox and CNN viewers scored very high. The more the group scores overlap, the less it seems likely that group membership is an important explanation. In that case, the *F*-statistic would be smaller, and we would be less likely to reject the null.

At first glance, ANOVA may seem frustrating because it only broadly reveals differences between groups. However, this serves an important statistical function in that it prevents researchers from conducting a series of statistical tests without much forethought. Specifically, the use of omnibus tests such as ANOVA helps researchers avoid type I error, whereby they reject the null hypothesis when they shouldn't. If researchers simply conduct a series of tests comparing groups, then the likelihood of making a type I error increases simply because more tests are run. Consider the example from the previous paragraph. Without the ANOVA, the researcher would have to run six separate *t*-tests to compare each of the four groups with one another. Unless every one of these comparisons was equally justified by theory, there is a good chance the researcher might have found a single difference and overstated its importance, potentially committing a type I error. By first running the ANOVA, the researcher can further explore any significant findings revealed by the ANOVA and minimize the likelihood of a type I error.

Many of the post hoc tests that have been developed to work with ANOVA include controls to guard against type I error. At the same time, there are situations in which researchers may want to carry out specific comparisons even when the overall *F*-statistic is not significant. Consider again the comparison of cable news and *Daily Show* users discussed earlier. It may be that the omnibus *F*-test suggests that knowledge does not differ between users of the four news sources. But the score for *Daily Show* viewers is noticeably higher than for any of the cable channels. Perhaps there is a specific difference between these two distinct content formats. If the prior literature and theory support this idea, specific *planned comparisons* between *The Daily Show* and the three other formats would be appropriate even without a significant value for *F*.

Correlation (Pearson's *r*)

Two key pieces of information can be learned from a correlation coefficient: (1) the direction of the relationship and (2) the strength of the relationship. The direction of a correlation indicates whether the values are moving in the same direction or in opposite directions. In a positive correlation, both values increases in one variable predict increases in the other, while decreases in one predict decreases in the other. For example, practicing any activity typically improves your ability in that activity. Therefore, hours of practicing running will improve your endurance, such that as hours of running increases, the distance you can run before getting tired also goes up. Conversely, those who practice less will not be able to run as far. Negative correlations, on the other hand, indicate that the values for each variable are moving in opposite directions, such that as the value of one variable increases, the value of the other decreases. For example, it is likely that sitting on the couch playing video games will have a negative correlation with your fitness, such that as hours of video game playing increases, your fitness level will go down. Keep in mind that while we describe these patterns in terms of individuals, what we're actually considering is the pattern in the sample as a whole. That is, we're comparing people who spend more time playing games to those who spend less time, and looking at how much fit each of those individuals' reports being.

Strength is dictated by how close to or far from 0 the coefficient is. Values closer to 0 indicate weaker relationships, whereas values closer to –1 or +1 indicate stronger relationships. A value of 1 (or –1) would indicate a "perfect" correlation, meaning that that values consistently move together—as one increases, so does the other. For example, if practicing running has a perfect correlation with level of fitness, this means that for every hour of running practice, you will see a positive increase in your level of fitness. For example, if fitness is measured by how long you can run on a treadmill, then every hour you spend running will allow you to stay on the treadmill longer when tested. On the other hand, if practicing running shares a zero correlation with level of fitness, there will be no consistency across hours of practice and level of fitness, such that some people who run a lot will have high fitness, others who run a lot will have poor fitness, some who don't run at all will have high fitness, and so on. People who never run would be expected to stay on the treadmill just as

bivariate analysis
→ Unit 15

relationship
→ Unit 2

interval-level measure
→ Unit 5

ratio-level measure
→ Unit 5

range
→ Unit 14

variable
→ Unit 2

population
→ Unit 8

null hypothesis
→ Unit 15

sample
→ Unit 8

sample size
→ Unit 8

statistical significance
→ Unit 15

***p*-value**
→ Unit 15

independent variable
→ Unit 2

linearity
→ Unit 15

long as people who run daily. In short, there is no clear pattern or consistency in the relationship. Note that the correlation test only reflects a linear relationship. If running becomes less helpful after the first two or three runs a week, a Pearson correlation won't fully capture this information.

In social sciences (e.g., communication, political science, psychology, and sociology), correlations tend to be smaller than they are in the natural sciences (e.g., biology or chemistry). This is largely a function of humans being complicated and inconsistent, as well as the fact that there are often many independent variables that can explain any attitude or behavior. Because of this, perfect and even very high correlations are uncommon, and lower benchmarks are often considered meaningful.

Either way, the exact size of the effect measured by a correlation can be determined. Pearson's r values can be used to calculate $r2$, a measure of variance accounted for. The $r2$ value tells you how much of the variance of a dependent variable is accounted for by a particular independent variable. For example, consider a situation in which hours spent running and fitness level share a Pearson's correlation coefficient of .60 (see Figures 15.2 and 15.3). To compute $r2$, you would simply square the value (i.e., multiply it by itself) to produce a value of .36 (i.e., .6 × .6). This tells you that hours spent running accounts for 36 percent of the variance in fitness level scores. This indicates that hours spent running plays a fairly important role in your level of

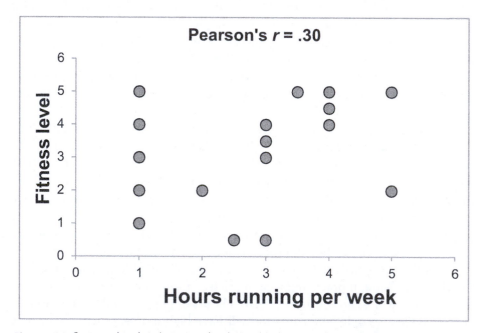

Figure 15.2 Scatter plot showing a weak relationship between hours spent running per week and fitness level

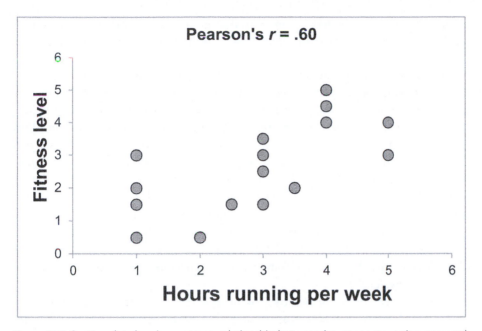

Figure 15.3 Scatter plot showing a strong relationship between hours spent running per week and fitness level

Note: It is much easier to draw a line through the pattern in the distribution for a stronger correlation than it is for a weaker one. The scatter plot for the strong correlation clearly shows that the more you run per week, the higher your fitness level is.

fitness. The remaining 64 percent of the variance in your fitness level might be explained by other independent variables, such as genetics, experience, age, sex, or other exercise behaviors.

Let's now consider an example of a negative correlation. It is likely that hours practicing running will also make you faster, decreasing your time to complete a loop around the track. As such, hours of running practice and time to complete a lap share a negative relationship, in this case, –.30. This is a modest negative correlation. We can extend our understanding of this to r^2 and determine that hours spent practicing accounts for 9 percent (.30 × .30 = .09) of the variance. This suggests that practice time, although somewhat important, is likely only one of many important factors in determining how fast you can run. Because many factors can be important in explaining the variance of a dependent variable, researchers often use multivariate analysis to expand on findings demonstrated through bivariate analysis.

Linearity

An assumption of many statistical tests involving two interval- or ratio-level measures is that the two variables share a relationship that moves consistently

interval-level
measure
→ Unit 5

415

in one direction, such that as one variable increases, the other either consistently increases or consistently decreases. The linearity of a relationship does not directly relate to its strength—it is possible to have a strong but nonlinear relationship or a weak but clearly linear one. Nor is it linked to the direction of the relationship; both positive and negative relationships can be either linear or nonlinear. Rather, the issue of linearity is important because many tests, including Pearson's r, regression, and more, assume the relationship between variables is linear. As a result, these tests may not be able to reveal relationships when they are nonlinear, or they may give results that are meaningless or misleading. Visually, a way to think about linearity is that when two variables share a linear relationship, it is possible to draw a straight line through the plots of the scores for both variables, as demonstrated in Figure 15.4. However, in a nonlinear relationship, there are often bumps or curves in that line suggesting that the relationship is more complicated than simply "as one goes up, the other goes down." Note that Figure 15.5 demonstrates a curvilinear relationship between age and fitness level.

Linearity can be confirmed by looking at a "scatter plot," which shows the scores for the two variables plotted such that each case's values on the independent variable and dependent variable are shown as a single dot or point. The sample charts used here are scatter plots showing the scores for age and level of social media use for each participant (i.e., respondents score 1 point for each type of social media they use, including Facebook, Twitter, Instagram,

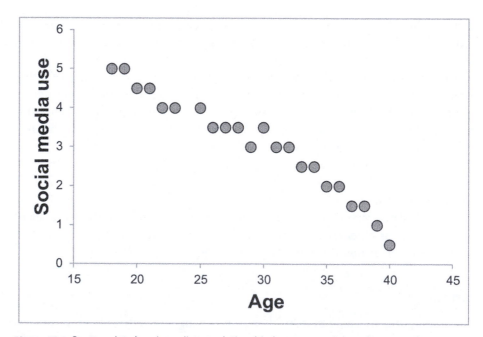

Figure 15.4 Scatter plot showing a linear relationship between social media use and age

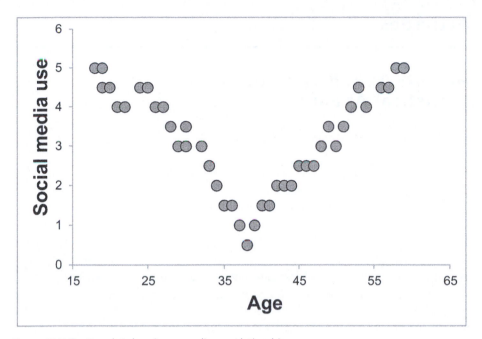

Figure 15.5 Scatter plot showing a nonlinear relationship

Snapchat, and Twitch. For instance, if someone is 50 years old and uses four of the different social media options, they would be plotted at the intersection of 50 (age) and 4 (level of social media use) on the scatter plot. By plotting all of the values in a sample, the researcher can see how those scores are distributed and whether it is a linear or nonlinear distribution. In a linear relationship, it is fairly easy to draw a relatively straight line through the plot. However, nonlinear relationships, as shown in the example, require that line to curve in some way to make its way through the pattern of plots.

Activities

Activity 15A: Preparing for Statistical Analysis

See terms: bivariate analysis; inferential statistics.

For this activity, develop a research question that you would like to answer that considers the relationship between two variables. As you develop this research question, think about how you will measure the variables. Consider the following:

- Based on these initial thoughts, what level of measurement do you expect for each of the variables?
- Given the expected level of measurement of your different variables, what types of statistical tests would you likely run to explore the relationship between the two variables?
- What makes these tests appropriate?
- What assumptions do the tests have? How would you ensure that your data conform to those assumptions?

Activity 15B: Critically Assessing Statistical Analysis

See terms: statistical analysis; bivariate analysis; level of measurement.

For this activity, locate a research article that conducts some type of bivariate analysis. Start by describing the nature of the relationship (or relationships) and the test (or tests) used to assess the relationship. Use the following questions to guide your assessment:

- What particular tests are used in this research report?
- What are the independent and dependent variables? What is the level of measurement for each of those variables?
- Are these particular tests appropriate? Why or why not? Could the researchers have used different tests to test these relationships?
- How would you evaluate the quality as far as how the tests and their results are reported? Do the researchers clearly describe the results of their tests?
- Is there any information missing that would help your evaluation of the data and the results as described?
- Are the conclusions drawn from the data accurate based on the tests conducted?

Activity 15C: Statistical Testing in Experiments

See terms: statistical analysis; bivariate analysis; ANOVA; *t*-test.

For this activity, locate a research article that uses the method of experiment and either the statistical procedure ANOVA or *t*-test. Start by describing the guiding research questions behind the study and determining whether *t*-test or ANOVA were used. Use the following questions to guide further assessment of the research:

- Which specific statistical test was used in this study? Was this test appropriate? Why or why not?
- What information is provided by the authors to allow readers to interpret the findings?
- How do the authors present the information about the statistical test? If any visuals are used, are they effective? Why or why not?
- Do the authors provide any discussion of the limitations of the statistical tests used?
- What discussion, if any, do the authors provide about the necessary conditions to conducting the statistical test they used?

Activity 15D: Chi-Square

See terms: chi-square; *p*-value.

For this activity, you will use the data presented later to answer the research questions provided. In each case, you can use a chi-square test to do so. A sample chi-square table for Research Question 1 is presented after the data to help get you started.

Research Question 1: What is the relationship between conversation style and disclosure level?

Research Question 2: What is the relationship between conversation style and happiness?

Bonus Question: What is the relationship between disclosure level and happiness?

Table 15.3 Data

Subject	Conversation style	Disclosure level	Happiness
1	Assertive	High	Low
2	Assertive	Low	High
3	Assertive	High	Low
4	Assertive	Low	Low
5	Assertive	High	Low
6	Assertive	High	High
7	Assertive	Low	High
8	Assertive	High	Low
9	Assertive	High	Low
10	Assertive	High	High
11	Assertive	Low	High
12	Assertive	High	High
13	Assertive	High	High
14	Assertive	High	Low
15	Assertive	Low	Low
16	Assertive	High	Low
17	Assertive	High	Low

(Continued)

421

Table 15.3 Continued

Subject	Conversation style	Disclosure level	Happiness
18	Assertive	High	High
19	Assertive	High	High
20	Assertive	Low	High
21	Assertive	High	Low
22	Assertive	High	Low
23	Assertive	Low	High
24	Assertive	High	Low
25	Assertive	High	High
26	Passive	Low	Low
27	Passive	Low	Low
28	Passive	Low	High
29	Passive	Low	Low
30	Passive	High	Low
31	Passive	Low	Low
32	Passive	Low	High
33	Passive	High	Low
34	Passive	Low	Low
35	Passive	Low	Low
36	Passive	Low	High
37	Passive	High	High
38	Passive	High	Low
39	Passive	Low	Low
40	Passive	Low	Low
41	Passive	Low	High
42	Passive	Low	Low
43	Passive	Low	Low
44	Passive	High	Low

Subject	Conversation style	Disclosure level	Happiness
45	Passive	Low	High
46	Passive	Low	Low
47	Passive	Low	High
48	Passive	Low	Low
49	Passive	High	Low
50	Passive	Low	High

Table 15.4 Chi-Square Table for Research Question 1 (Conversation Style and Disclosure Level)

	Assertive	Passive	Total
Low disclosure	Observed___	Observed___	
	Expected___	Expected___	
High disclosure	Observed___	Observed___	
	Expected___	Expected___	
Total	25	25	50

References

Baltes, B. B., Dickson, M. W., Sherman, M. P., Bauer, C. C., & LaGanke, J. S. (2002). Computer-mediated communication and group decision making: A meta-analysis. *Organizational Behavior and Human Decision Processes*, *87*(1), 156–179. doi:10.1006/obhd.2001.2961

Groesz, L. M., Levine, M. P., & Murnen, S. K. (2002). The effect of experimental presentation of thin media images on body satisfaction: A meta-analytic review. *International Journal of Eating Disorders*, *31*(1), 1–16. doi:10.1002/eat.10005

Snyder, L. B., Hamilton, M. A., Mitchell, E. W., Kiwanuka-Tondo, J., Fleming-Milici, F., & Proctor, D. (2004). A meta-analysis of the effect of mediated health communication campaigns on behavior change in the United States. *Journal of Health Communication*, *9*(Supplement 1), 71–96. doi:10.1080/10810730490271548

Wilson, E. J., & Sherrell, D. L. (1993). Source effects in communication and persuasion research: A meta-analysis of effect size. *Journal of the Academy of Marketing Science*, *21*(2), 101–112. doi:10.1007/BF02894421

Suggested Readings for Further Exploration of Unit 15 Topics

Examples

Heider, D., McCombs, M., & Poindexter, P. M. (2005). What the public expects of local news: Views on public and traditional journalism. *Journalism & Mass Communication Quarterly*, *82*(4), 952–967. doi:10.1177/107769900508200412

Kenski, K., Hardy, B. W., & Jamieson, K. H. (2010). *The Obama victory: How media, money, and message shaped the 2008 election*. New York, NY: Oxford University Press.

Putnam, R. D. (2000). *Bowling alone: The collapse and revival of American community*. New York, NY: Simon & Schuster.

Advanced Discussion

Levine, T. R. (2011). Statistical conclusions validity basics: probability and how Type 1 and Type 2 errors obscure the interpretation of findings in communication research literatures. *Communication Research Reports*, *28*(1), 115–119. doi:10.1080/08824096.2011.541369

Levine, T. R., Asada, K. J., & Carpenter, C. (2009). Sample sizes and effect sizes are negatively correlated in meta-analyses: Evidence and implications of a publication bias against nonsignificant findings. *Communication Monographs*, *76*(3), 286–302. doi:10.1080/03637750903074685

Levine, T. R., & Hullett, C. R. (2002). Eta squared, partial eta squared, and misreporting of effect size in communication research. *Human Communication Research*, *28*(4), 612–625. doi:10.1111/j.1468-2958.2002.tb00828.x

Levine, T. R., Weber, R., Hullett, C., Park, H. S., & Lindsey, L. L. M. (2008). A critical assessment of null hypothesis significance testing in quantitative communication research. *Human Communication Research*, *34*(2), 171–187. doi:10.1111/j.1468-2958.2008.00317.x

O'Keefe, D. J. (2011). The asymmetry of predictive and descriptive capabilities in quantitative communication research: Implications for hypothesis development and testing. *Communication Methods and Measures*, *5*(2), 113–125. doi:10.1080/19312458.2011.568375

Sun, S., & Fan, X. (2010). Effect size reporting practices in communication research. *Communication Methods and Measures*, *4*(4), 331–340. doi:10.1080/19312458.2010.527875

Weber, R., & Popova, L. (2012). Testing equivalence in communication research: Theory and application. *Communication Methods and Measures*, *6*(3), 190–213. doi:10.1080/19312458.2012.703834

unit 16

multivariate inferential statistics

Although descriptive statistics and bivariate analysis can be valuable to researchers in understanding data, sometimes more is needed. Human attitudes and behaviors can be complicated and difficult to explain. In such situations, we need to use statistical tests and procedures that are designed to account for that complexity. For instance, consider a situation in which you are working for a market research firm. You have a client that wants to better understand not only *who* is interested in its product but also *why* they are interested in that product. In such a case, you have to explain product interest, the dependent variable (DV), using a host of independent variables (IVs) that fall into two broad categories: (1) the *who* variables, which might include things such as demographic characteristics, and (2) the *why* variables, which might include things such as motivations to purchase, exposure to advertising, and brand loyalty.

Bivariate analysis would assess each of these relationships in individuals by looking closely at each variable and its relationship to the dependent variable, one at a time, and indicating whether each alone was a predictor. However, it is likely that the client would like to know which of those variables is the most important predictor when all the variables are considered simultaneously. The statistical tests and procedures covered in this unit provide the basics you need to get started in conducting such tests using multivariate inferential statistics.

Multivariate Analysis

Whereas bivariate analysis focuses on the relationship between two specific variables (most often the independent and dependent variables), multivariate analysis includes more than two variables. The reasons for introducing additional variables are numerous. Perhaps most important, including additional variables allows researchers to use **statistical control**, which cancels out the influence of those variables on both the independent and dependent variables. This ensures that the remaining relationship is not attributable to those factors, allowing for greater confidence in claims that the relationship is causal and not **spurious**. This can also help researchers identify relationships that may previously have been hidden or **suppressed**. Further, accounting for additional or "third" variables can allow for testing whether there is evidence of mediation or moderation. The latter is accounted for by the inclusion of an **interaction** term in the model. If the interaction term is significant, this suggests that the two variables tested with this statistic interact—that is, the relationship between one of them and the DV is moderated by the other.

Many statistical tests are used to examine multivariate relationships. We discuss some of the most common, including **ANOVA (analysis of variance) with multiple independent variables**, **ANCOVA** (analysis of covariance), **MANOVA** (multivariate analysis of variance), and both ordinary least squares **regression** and **logistic regression**. Regression is an especially common

bivariate analysis → Unit 15
relationship → Unit 2
variable → Unit 2
independent variable → Unit 2
dependent variable → Unit 2
mediation → Unit 2
moderation → Unit 2
variance explained → Unit 15
variance → Unit 14

approach, as it bridges several linear modeling approaches to describing relationships between multiple IVs and a DV and generates a greater wealth of information than simpler bivariate statistics. Thus, we consider a number of statistics obtained by regression, including both **standardized** and **unstandardized coefficients**, R^2, and the **odds ratio**, which is used in logistic regression.

Statistical Control

The primary reason to use multivariate statistics is to allow for statistical control. This process ensures that the variance explained by one IV is not actually attributable to shared variance with another IV. By default, all multivariate statistics are designed such that only the unique variance of a given independent variable is accounted for in the resulting statistic. That is, all multivariate statistics provide a result for a given IV that is controlling for all other IVs. Consider, for example, a study in which you want to determine how much of an effect advertising for a political candidate had on votes received by that candidate. That is, you want to explain the variance in votes by the amount spent on advertising. You could simply look at the correlation between the two variables, but you might suspect that other third variables could be inflating this correlation. For example, candidates often receive more money when they are endorsed by media and prominent figures. That extra money, in turn, can buy more advertising. But endorsements also influence voters. So, some of the reason that a candidate who spends a lot of money on advertising gains votes wouldn't be caused by the ad spending at all but by this third factor of endorsements. Multivariate analysis allows us to control for the variance that is attributable to endorsements, allowing us to identify the unique variance that is attributable to ad spending.

Exactly how this control works varies based upon the chosen statistical approach. But nearly all multivariate statistics can be interpreted the same way. Initially, you have the full amount of measured variance present in the independent and dependent variables. When controlling for a third variable, the statistical procedure determines how much of the variance in one independent variable is predicted by the other independent variable. This explained variance is mathematically removed, and the variance that remains in the IV is tested to see what relationship it has with the DV. If the control variable is strongly related to the IV, there won't be much variance left in the IV to use in predicting the DV. If the specific variance controlled for in each is key to explaining why the IV and DV are related, the final statistic will be small. But if the remaining variance is key to why the IV and DV are related, the final statistic will be large.

Another way to understand this is to think about what the relationship between the IV and DV would look like if every case in the sample had the same level for the third variable.

Think again about the example of advertising spending and endorsements. Let's suppose that for every endorsement, a candidate can spend another $100,000. Further, suppose that for every endorsement, a candidate gains an extra 500 votes. Finally, suppose that the initial test of the relationship between spending and voting shows that for every $100,000 spent, a candidate gains 1,000 votes. Now consider two candidates, one of whom received three endorsements, spent $600,000, and received 10,000 votes, and another who received no endorsements, spent $100,000, and received 5,000 votes. Based on the relationship between endorsements and vote share, we can "adjust" the scores to reflect the influence of endorsements. Had the first candidate not received three endorsements, we would expect that she would have only received 8,500 votes. The remaining difference between votes is 2,500, and the spending difference is $500,000. So, after controlling for the effect of endorsements, we're left with an effect of spending equal to $100,000 per 500 votes. Basically, part of the apparent relationship between spending and votes is actually caused by the effect of endorsements. By considering what the data would look like if everyone had received no endorsements (or if everyone had received three endorsements) we can compute a truer measure of the effect of spending.

It's worth noting that this process works in reverse as well. In multivariate analyses, each IV is tested while controlling for all other IVs. Because of this, the relationship reported in the final analysis between endorsements and votes would control for the effect of spending. This can be problematic if we control for a mediating variable. For example, in this case, the effect of endorsements is twofold. Endorsements directly increase votes, but they also indirectly increase votes by allowing candidates to spend more money. Controlling for spending would show the direct variance explained, but it would omit the indirect influence. This is important to consider when developing analyses, and some types of regression analysis can help solve this problem.

Spuriousness

In the case of the relationship between endorsements, spending, and voting, the influence of endorsements on voting made the bivariate relationship between spending on ads and voting appear unreasonably large. In the end, it turned out that spending on ads did affect voting, but only about half as much as initially shown. Suppose, however, that we had found there was *no* effect of spending on voting once endorsements were accounted for. In this case, we would say that the relationship between spending and voting was *spurious*—that is, an apparent relationship found at the bivariate level was actually attributable to the influence of one or more third variables, and in reality, no true causal relationship exists between the two variables. (Note that when we mention a "causal" relationship here, it does not matter which is the cause and which is the effect; if

relationship
→ Unit 2

bivariate analysis
→ Unit 15

third variable
→ Unit 2

variable
→ Unit 2

theory
→ Unit 2

variance
→ Unit 14

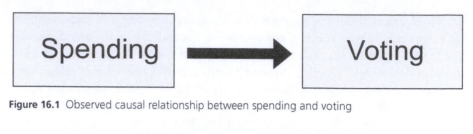

Figure 16.1 Observed causal relationship between spending and voting

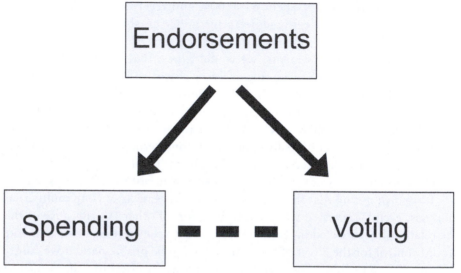

Figure 16.2 Changes in model with the inclusion of endorsements that reveals relationship to be spurious

the relationship is spurious, then neither would influence the other, and instead some third variable causes the variation in each.)

Consider the example of the relationship between the fear of crime and the amount of time a person watches television. According to cultivation theory, the more people watch TV, the more they should fear crime, because television shows a high level of violent crime. But an alternative explanation based upon a third variable is also possible. Perhaps people who are poor and live in bad neighborhoods tend to view more television because they lack other safe options for entertainment. These individuals fear crime because of their socioeconomic status, and they watch more television for the same reason. If income and related variables are controlled for, the remaining relationship between television viewing and fear of crime might no longer be significant. This would be an indication that the initial relationship was spurious. In fact, studies have shown that while a portion of fear of crime can be explained this way, there is plenty of remaining variance that is explained by television viewing. In that case, demonstrating that the relationship was *not* entirely spurious was important to adequately testing and supporting the theory.

Suppression

In contrast to spuriousness, suppression occurs in situations in which the initial bivariate test did not reveal a significant relationship, but after controlling for one or more third variables, a significant relationship emerged. The true relationship between the IV and DV was suppressed, or hidden, by offsetting influences from third variables. For example, consider the relationship between age, online political participation, and voting. In general, we might expect that people who participate online are more likely to vote. After all, if you are interested enough to sign petitions, e-mail political figures, or forward campaign ads, surely you would be interested enough to cast a ballot.

But now imagine that we conduct a study and find that there is actually very little relationship between online participation and voting. What would we make of this apparent nonrelationship? One explanation is that age is negatively related to online participation but positively related to voting. That is, older individuals tend to avoid active use of the Internet, including participatory actions, but they vote in significant numbers. If we only considered people between 18 and 35, we might find that they vote more when they participate online more. We might even find the same for people age 60 and over, but the rate of participation would be lower and the rate of voting higher. This is an example of suppression. If we controlled for age in our analyses, the relationship between participation and voting would be significant in those multivariate analyses.

bivariate analysis
→ Unit 15

relationship
→ Unit 2

third variable
→ Unit 2

variable
→ Unit 2

Interaction

In contrast to situations in which merely controlling a variable is necessary, such as spuriousness and suppression, testing an interaction requires identifying situations in which a third variable may moderate the effect of a relevant independent variable on a dependent variable. That is, the relationship between the IV and DV will not be constant but will vary based upon the level of the specified moderating variable. For example, we might expect that individuals who are interested in buying a new car will pay more attention to a car commercial and therefore remember more details from the ad, whereas those without such interest will retain little information and may not even remember the brand. In this case, number of times viewing the ad would be the IV, recalled information the DV, and interest in buying a car the moderating variable.

As noted, we cannot simply treat interest as an additional variable in multivariate analysis. This would control for the influence of interest on both variables, but it would not tell us whether the actual relationship between variables differs based on level of interest. Testing moderation requires constructing what is known as an *interaction term*, which tells the statistical software to evaluate for evidence of an interaction. This interaction term represents

variable
→ Unit 2

spuriousness
→ Unit 16

suppression
→ Unit 16

third variable
→ Unit 2

moderation
→ Unit 2

independent variable
→ Unit 2

dependent variable
→ Unit 2

an additional variable considered a predictor of the dependent variable, and when the appropriate statistical test is performed, we can evaluate the result to consider whether this interaction "variable" has a significant influence. If the interaction term is significantly related to the DV, that means we have evidence that moderation exists in the larger population. When this is the case, we want to be careful about how we interpret the effects of our other IVs that were thought to interact. We can no longer say that they have one broad effect. Rather, we must talk about their conditional effects, based upon the value of the moderating variable.

For example, if we found evidence that car interest moderated the effects of advertisements on knowledge, we would not say that advertisements caused knowledge. Instead, we would accurately state that advertisements increased knowledge only among those interested in buying a new car. Many different patterns of interaction exist, as we discussed when explaining the concept of moderation. Evaluating which is present in your data depends upon the specific test being used. However, the meaning of a significant interaction is always the same: you do have evidence of moderation.

Research in Depth: Alternatives to Null Hypothesis Testing

A growing number of statisticians and researchers are concerned that reliance on p values and the logic of null hypothesis testing is a flawed approach. For one thing, the logic of null hypothesis testing is complex and often confusing. Many researchers don't properly explain or interpret their findings. Proper training and references can help, but if there is a more intuitive approach that yields better results it would be helpful.

The question of better results is key. Some proposals for eliminating the use of null hypothesis testing don't offer a clear alternative, and they vary in terms of the problem they are trying to solve. For example, a major flaw with traditional p values is the excessive focus on statistical significance. The distinction between a p-value of .06 and .04 is arbitrary, and yet publication bias and other factors have elevated the latter in unfortunate ways. But one proposed solution to the excess of "just significant" results fueling the reproducibility crisis has been to set a more stringent p-value, such as .01 or .005, as significant. All this does is shift the problem without solving it, while increasing the likelihood of type II error.

One more viable alternative approach is to emphasize confidence intervals instead of p-values. A statistical result such as a regression coefficient or *t* test is a point estimate of the true value of the underlying relationship. As we learned in Unit 8, such estimates are best interpreted alongside intervals indicating the range of likely values for the population. If our coefficient is a statistic, the information we want is the parameter—the true linear relationship in the population. Providing confidence intervals better conveys the precision of our study. If the likely result for the population could be anything from strongly negative to strongly positive, clearly we have no good sense that a specific relationship exists. If our result shows a strongly positive relationship but the actual range is from nearly 0 to even more positive, we might have some confidence there is a relationship, but far less certainty about whether it is strong enough to be important. However, confidence intervals are still often interpreted in terms of whether they overlap with 0, falling back on the same logic of statistical significance. (Functionally, if *p* is less than .05 then in most cases that implies that a confidence interval for the statistic with a confidence level of 95 percent will not overlap with 0.)

Another more dramatic shift would be the use of Bayesian statistical reasoning. A full discussion of this approach is well beyond the scope of this book (see van de Schoot & Depaoli, 2014, for one reasonable overview aimed at a general audience). But the core logic involves considering a given study as additional evidence added to existing *prior* information. Bayesian reasoning considers how to gradually update our best estimate of relationships, and whether our current findings are unexpected given those priors. Konijn et al. (2015) argue for the use of Bayesian approaches as a way to consider the robustness of the claim that no relationship exists and reduce publication bias. At the same time, they acknowledge that if researchers become focused on Bayesian factors as evidence of "important" findings then the problem of *p*-hacking simply shifts to a new statistic. Ultimately, researchers need to understand that individual studies are just a single piece of evidence in a larger picture, and that the quality of the method and the appropriateness of the analyses are what matter—not the specific numbers obtained.

Konijn, E. A., van de Schoot, R., Winter, S. D., & Ferguson, C. J. (2015). Possible solution to publication bias through Bayesian statistics, including proper null hypothesis testing. *Communication Methods and Measures*, 9(4), 280–302. doi:10.1080/19312458.2015.1096332

van de Schoot, R., & Depaoli, S. (2014). Bayesian analyses: Where to start and what to report. *The European Health Psychologist*, 16(2), 75–84.

Analysis of Variance (ANOVA) With Multiple Independent Variables

Previously, we described a basic one-way analysis of variance, which allows us to test the relationship between a single, nominal independent variable and an interval- or ratio-level dependent variable. While this kind of analysis is both useful and common, ANOVA can be more powerful than that relatively simple technique. It is possible to consider multiple independent variables simultaneously. In such analyses, we refer to the test as an N-way ANOVA, where N is the number of independent variables considered. For instance, including three independent variables would be a three-way ANOVA, and including five independent variables would be a five-way ANOVA. Like a basic one-way ANOVA, each of these independent variables must be a nominal-level measure and can have any number of possible values. As with a one-way ANOVA, each group should have roughly equivalent variances, and the test is more robust when the group sizes are similar. Additional variations on ANOVA include ANCOVA (analysis of covariance), in which one or more *covariates*—variables measured at the interval or ratio level—are also accounted for in the test, and MANOVA (multivariate analysis of variance), in which the effects of various IVs on *multiple* dependent variables are considered simultaneously.

The basic interpretation of ANOVA results is the same whether a single IV or multiple IVs are included. The amount by which the total variance in the DV can be accounted for by the specific "group" into which the individual falls is considered and calculated as an F-statistic. For an ANOVA with multiple IVs, this calculation is carried out for each independent variable and, as with all multivariate statistics, controls for the variance accounted for by other IVs included in the test. If the F-statistic is large relative to the value that might be expected if the null hypothesis were correct, accounting for the number of groups being compared as well as the size of the sample, then the p-value will likely be small. A sufficiently small p-value is often considered evidence that a statistically significant relationship is present, although an exact measure of the estimated effect size and its likely range can also be computed (known as eta-squared).

In addition, all ANOVA models with multiple IVs default to testing the interaction of those variables. That is, the potential moderating influence of a given IV on the other IVs in the model is considered. So are any three-, four-, or even higher-way interactions, though interpreting these can be increasingly complex and deceptive. Just as in a standard one-way ANOVA, all ANOVA tests only indicate the overall effect of a given IV or interaction. To compare differences between two specific groups, further post hoc tests may be necessary.

To help understand the components of a more complex ANOVA test, consider a situation in which you want to determine the effects of political advertising on potential voters. You might want to evaluate whether a negative or a positive ad is more influential. This could easily be tested with an experimental design in which you randomly assign individuals to view either the positive or the negative ad, then measure their attitudes toward both candidates after exposure. Your initial results, from a one-way ANOVA or a simple t-test, might show a minimal difference between the ads. However, maybe you suspect that the effects of the ad depend upon individual political differences. Perhaps independents are turned off from politics altogether by a negative ad, feeling more negative about both candidates. If the ad is for a Democrat, members of that party might respond by lowering their liking of the opponent, while Republicans might lower their liking of the attacker, without opinions about their own candidates changing. The positive ad, on the other hand, might mobilize Democrats but have no effect on Republicans.

To test this, we would need to analyze multiple IVs. This two-way ANOVA test would, by default, include measures of the average effect of ad type and party membership, as well as an interaction term testing whether party membership moderates the influence of ad type. Given the one-way ANOVA results, we won't be surprised if the statistical test for the main effect of ad type is still not significant. The updated results will be somewhat different, as they will control for the effects of party identification, but assuming that we used random assignment, this should not be a major issue.

The more interesting test in this case would be the results for the interaction term. Our prediction was that the three political groups would respond differently and that their responses would further depend upon the type of ad viewed. If the F-statistic is large and the p-value small for the test of the interaction, we can conclude that for the population, there really is a moderated relationship. But we can't stop there. We would then have to look at the estimated marginal means for each group and see whether the differences match the expected pattern. We would also need to directly compare the different groups—for example, we would need to know whether, when we consider only independents, the negative ad produced more negative evaluations than the positive ad. This would be a post hoc comparison carried out between just those two groups. And, as with all post hoc comparisons, it would be most appropriate to adjust for the potential of increased type I error. (That is, we would want a more conservative test because there are six different groups to compare from the interaction, and with so many comparisons there's a greater chance of having a "large" result just by chance.)

ANCOVA

A more specific variation on a standard ANOVA design is an analysis of covariance, or ANCOVA. It shares the basic features of ANOVA, including F-statistics testing the influence of each nominal-level independent variable. By default, it also tests the interaction of those variables with one another. But ANCOVA differs from standard analysis of variance because of the inclusion of one or more

population
→ Unit 8

type I error
→ Unit 15

one-way ANOVA
→ Unit 15

F-statistic
→ Unit 15

435

covariates—interval- or ratio-level measures whose influence on the dependent variable is also measured and controlled. Including these variables serves two purposes. First, the analysis will report an *F*-statistic that measures the unique influence of each covariate on the dependent variable. While not as easy to interpret at the results from a regression analysis, this does offer a measure of the influence of an interval- or ratio-level IV on a similar DV while controlling for nominal-level measures. Second, the inclusion of the covariate(s) means those variables will be accounted for in measuring the influence of the nominal-level IVs on the DV.

Consider again the study of negative advertising. Suppose we discover that the negative advertising group was younger than the positive advertising group because our random assignment procedure did not work perfectly. We might worry that younger individuals are generally less likely to participate and more cynical about politicians. Thus, if we find a difference between the two ad conditions, it might be attributable to this confound. Including age as a covariate would control for any such influence, giving us more confidence in the final findings.

Another common example is situations in which the design of the study did not include random assignment but instead has a measured nominal-level IV. For example, we might classify family communication patterns, differentiating those families in which parents actively watch and discuss media with their children from more permissive households in which no discussion occurs and less permissive households in which parents simply block access to certain media content. These differences among families might help predict what lessons children learn from media, but the differences are not randomly assigned.

If we find that children in the less permissive households show more aggressive behaviors, it would be hard to know whether this is related to violent content being a kind of "forbidden fruit" that they seek out to defy their parents. It could be that less permissive households are different in some other way; maybe they are more likely to be households with lower incomes, and the stress of managing family finances might prevent parents from actively viewing media with their children. Income is also often related to aggressive behavior, so it could be that income and not viewing patterns really explains the relationship. This would, of course, be an example of a spurious relationship. By including income as a covariate in an ANCOVA and then evaluating the *F*-statistic for the main effect of family communication, we could test whether the relationship holds up against this alternative explanation.

MANOVA

Whereas the previous forms of analysis of variance focused on a single dependent variable, MANOVA, or multivariate analysis of variance, considers the relationship of the independent variables to more than one dependent variable. The other characteristics of the analysis are the same as previously discussed. The analysis can consider one or more nominal-level independent variables, as well as their interactions, and also one or more interval- or ratio-level covariates. All of these predict an interval- or ratio-level dependent variable. But the difference is that MANOVA is designed for situations in which several dependent variables are thought to measure related concepts, and the hypothesis is that the dependent variable should affect all of them in similar ways. MANOVA can be more sensitive to situations in which the independent variable exerts a small but consistent influence across several related measures that cannot, for whatever reason, be combined into an index. If the effects are consistent, MANOVA may more accurately detect them. But it is also more conservative in cases in which several measures of the dependent variable are possible. This helps discourage researchers from performing several different ANOVAs and then only focusing on the significant results. Just as with performing multiple post hoc tests, this can create a situation with an inflated likelihood of type I error. Thus the MANOVA serves as the omnibus test to establish whether such post hoc comparisons would even be warranted.

The MANOVA procedure provides an overall test for whether the "average" relationship between the IV and all of the dependent variables is significant, just as, in an ANOVA, the *F*-test gives an indication of whether the overall influence of the IV on the DV is significant without focusing on individual comparisons between single values for the IV. In fact, there are several different statistics used to measure this multivariate influence, the details of which are beyond the scope of this text but can be found in a statistics book. Each reflects the same basic principle and can be interpreted the same way. A significant multivariate test indicates that, on average, the IV (or interaction or covariate) in question has a relationship with the dependent variables that is strong enough to expect a relationship to exist in the population. This relationship may not be equally strong for all the dependent variables, but it is consistent enough to expect that the stronger findings are not attributable to chance. When a significant multivariate result is found, it then makes sense to proceed to evaluate the individual ANOVA results for each DV, as one might evaluate the individual post hoc comparisons based on a significant *F*.

While MANOVA can be a useful test, it is sometimes misunderstood or misused. Just because scholars have carried out an experiment with more than one DV, that does not mean that MANOVA is appropriate. MANOVA is based on the assumption that each DV is measuring a somewhat related construct. If a theory implies that multiple DVs should be correlated with one another and that they reflect either a shared concept or multiple concepts that are linked in some way, then MANOVA makes sense. But if scholars are testing multiple or even competing theories, based on which different DVs might be influenced, then MANOVA may not be appropriate. If there is no reason that the failure of the IV to be related to one DV would invalidate the logic of it being related to another, MANOVA is not an appropriate test. If you are worried about carrying out too many tests and inflating type I error, you can always use a Bonferroni correction on the *p*-values for all the individual ANOVA tests.

independent variable
→ Unit 2

nominal-level measure
→ Unit 5

interaction
→ Unit 16

interval-level measure
→ Unit 5

ratio-level measure
→ Unit 5

concept
→ Unit 5

index
→ Unit 6

type I error
→ Unit 15

one-way ANOVA
→ Unit 15

population
→ Unit 8

theory
→ Unit 2

Bonferroni correction
→ Unit 15

***p*-value**
→ Unit 15

***t*-test**
→ Unit 15

Suppose, for example, you want to study the effects of violent video games on players. You might hypothesize that playing a more violent game would increase aggression. There are several ways researchers measure aggression, including word-completion questions that measure aggressive cognition, physiological measures of arousal and affect, and behavioral measures of aggression. If a theory proposes that aggression in general should increase, then all of these should be affected by the more violent game. If we simply test each DV separately with a series of *t*-tests or ANOVAs, we might find that just one of them is influenced by the level of violence in the game. While this is interesting, there is a risk that this result is misleading. On the one hand, we might be ignoring results that show the other variables have a very similar pattern but are shy of traditional significance levels. On the other hand, we might be taking advantage of one fluke result when the other scores are all very different from what we predicted. By using a MANOVA, we could find patterns showing that the overall effect on all the measures of aggression are (or are not) significant, and we could be more confident in reporting our specific results.

Regression

Like ANOVA, regression is a flexible technique that allows for testing multiple independent variables simultaneously. In contrast to ANOVA, regression is primarily designed for testing the simultaneous influence of multiple interval- or ratio-level independent variables on a single interval- or ratio-level dependent variable. However, regression is a linear model, just like ANOVA, and the underlying math driving both statistical approaches is similar, as are the assumptions that must be met for the technique to be used appropriately. In all cases, these statistics measure the amount of variance in the dependent variable explained by the independent variable, controlling for the influence of all other independent variables. In regression, special steps must be taken to address interactions of nominal-level independent variables, but the influence of these can still be measured. Most of the time, though, the focus is simply on measuring the unique influence of each interval- or ratio-level independent variable. These are measured in terms of one of two *coefficients*, either unstandardized or standardized. Both reflect the linear influence of the IV on the DV. Additionally, regression provides measures of the overall effect size for one or more variables, captured by the R^2 statistic.

The basic logic of regression tests whether a line can be drawn that shows an increasing or decreasing relationship between an independent and dependent variable. For example, imagine the relationship between hours spent studying for an exam and your score on the exam. You might expect that the more hours you study, the better your score will be. If you were to plot every student's performance on a graph, the *x*-axis (horizontal) would show how many hours they studied, and as you moved to the right, time studying would increase. The *y*-axis (vertical) would show their scores, ranging from 0 to 100. If studying is linked to grades, you would expect that as you move to the right along the *x*-axis, the *y*-axis exam scores would increase. So, the average student who studied 0 hours might receive a score of 50, but the average student who studied 10 hours might receive a 90. Obviously, there would be some individual variation, but the pattern should be clear if there really is a relationship between these two variables. However, merely saying there is a clear pattern is not enough to specify the nature of that pattern. In regression, the analysis attempts to quantify the exact relationship between the IV and DV, as well as the precision of that relationship (that is, how sure we are that the relationship in our sample would be similar in the population).

To do this, regression draws upon a simple formula you may have learned in algebra. Specifically, this is the equation for a line: $Y = a + bX$, where Y is the DV, X is the IV, a is the point that the DV equals when the IV is 0 (the intercept), and b is the amount the DV increases for each 1-point increase in the IV (the slope). The key in regression is the value for b, the slope. The larger this value, the more the DV is expected to increase as the IV increases, showing a strong connection between the two. However, that strong connection is not necessarily meaningful. If there is a great deal of variation between values of the DV for a given value of the IV, then there is a lot of error in the prediction.

Suppose you are considering the connection between the age of a person, the number of Facebook friends that person has, and life satisfaction, rated on a 7-point scale. A few young people in the study with large numbers of friends (in the thousands) who also like their lives would be enough to draw a downward line, perhaps with a slope of –100 or more. But if there are also plenty of people who are young but have few friends, and some (though not as many) older individuals who have few friends, that line would be far away from many of the data points. Viewed as a scatter plot, these data would show a big cloud. If this were a correlation, the value of the correlation would be small because the dots are so scattered, even though the slope is sharply negative. Thus, when determining whether a regression result is significant, we don't just consider this *unstandardized* slope, or coefficient. We also take into account the *standard error* for this slope, defined in this case as a measure of how far the average individual value of the dependent variable is from the value predicted by the regression equation. When the standard error is large (equal to roughly half the value of the slope or more), then even though the slope is steep, we won't conclude that the result is significant. Our data may have been a fluke, given the apparently large range of values in the population, and we would fail to reject the null.

The intercept also has meaning in regression—it's an approximation of the value of the dependent variable when the independent variable equals 0. Most often, though, 0 is not a value contained within our data, and we try not to extrapolate

standardized coefficients
→ Unit 16

R^2
→ Unit 16

relationship
→ Unit 2

sample
→ Unit 8

population
→ Unit 8

prediction
→ Unit 2

correlation (Pearson's r)
→ Unit 15

range
→ Unit 14

MULTIVARIATE INFERENTIAL STATISTICS

from regression results to values that are not included in our study because we don't have firm data from which to make a prediction. Thus, most of the time, we focus on the value of the slope. In addition, regression results also report a *standardized* version of the coefficient, which can be more useful in communication research. This reflects the slope when the variables are converted to a standardized form, allowing comparisons between coefficients for different variables.

Finally, like any multivariate test, regression results account for the influence of other independent variables included in the analysis. Consider again our initial example, comparing exam scores to time spent studying. All else being equal, we would expect a positive relationship—the line should slope upward. But there are other factors that may be connected with both time studying and grades. Suppose a student missed several classes. That student might try to study more to make up for the absences, but he or she would still be expected to perform worse on the exam. A regression equation that includes both time studying and number of classes attended would thus provide a better estimate of the unique influence of each.

It is no longer possible to think about this more complex equation as a simple scatter plot, but the results provided will still include a value for *a* and a value of *b* for each independent variable. The value of *a* remains the intercept—the predicted exam score for a student who never missed class but also never studied. The coefficient, or slope, for each IV would represent our estimate of the increase (or decrease) in performance attributable each hour studying (or class missed), after adjusting for the connection between missing class and studying, if any. The standard error for each estimate would also be computed, and the analysis would determine whether the slope is sufficiently larger than this error to allow us to be confident that the finding applies to the population and reject the null.

Steps to Success: Assumptions of Statistical Tests

All statistical tests used to measure relationships are based upon specific requirements. These requirements are assumed to be met—if they are not, the software will often return a result, but that finding will be invalid. The following are some of the most common assumptions and the tests to which they apply.

1. *Normally distributed variables*: With few exceptions, tests that measure relationships between continuous variables assume that those variables follow a roughly normal distribution in the population.
   Tests: Both variables: correlation, ordinary least squares regression; dependent variable: *t*-test, ANOVA

2. *Equal variances*: When groups are compared, many tests assume that the variance for the dependent variable for each group is roughly equal.
    Tests: ANOVA

3. *Homoscedasticity*: When the IV is a continuous variable rather than a set of groups, the basic idea of equal variance still applies. The term to describe the idea that the variance in the DV at all levels of the IV should be roughly equal is *homoscedasticity*. By contrast, a relationship that does not meet this standard is *heteroscedastic*.

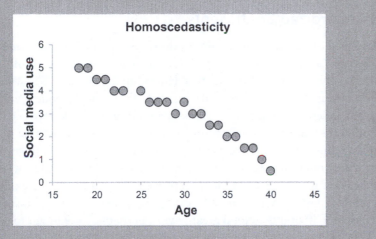

Figure 16.3 Scatter plot showing a homoscedastic relationship between age and social media use

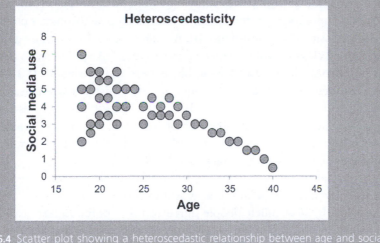

Figure 16.4 Scatter plot showing a heteroscedastic relationship between age and social media use

> *Tests*: Ordinary least squares regression
>
> 4. *Linearity*: For tests in which both the IV and DV are continuous (interval- or ratio-level measures), it's important to evaluate whether the relationship between the two is linear. That is, for all levels of the IV, an increase of a given size should result in a consistent increase in the DV.
> *Tests*: Correlation, regression

Unstandardized Coefficients

As described earlier, the simple value of the slope, b, represents the unstandardized coefficient in a regression equation. The coefficient will be positive if the relationship is positive and negative if is the relationship is negative. This value is useful when we want to make a numerical prediction about the dependent variable based upon our independent variable. Think again about the link between time studying and grades. Suppose your regression equation reported a value of a equal to 20 and a value for b of 5. We would predict that the average student who didn't study at all would earn a 20 on the exam. For each additional hour of studying, we would expect the student's grade to improve by 5 points. So, for example, a student who studied 10 hours might be expected to earn a 70 ([5 points × 10 hours] + 20 points = 70 points). Not a great payoff, perhaps, but enough to pass.

This same reasoning applies to regression analyses in which more than one IV is included. Suppose again that we ran our analysis of grades, this time including the number of classes missed. In our new result, the value of a would be 50. The value of b for hours studying would be 8 (because some of the effect was being suppressed by the negative relationship with missed class), and the value for missing class would be –10. A student who didn't study at all but also never missed class would be expected to earn a 50. A student who never missed class but also studied 5 hours would be expected to earn a 90 (50 + 8 × 5 – 10 × 0). A student who studied 10 hours but also missed three classes would be expected to earn a 100 (50 + 8 × 10 – 10 × 3). Of course, these are all just estimates. The larger the standard error for any of them, the more we would expect our prediction to deviate from the actual value—an idea reflected in the variance explained, which is measured by R^2.

Unstandardized coefficients are less useful when the units used to measure each variable don't have any real-world meaning. For example, suppose you are measuring how much people agree (on a 7-point Likert scale) with the statements "I enjoy playing video games" and "Some people deserve to be hit." Finding that a 1-point increase in the first predicted a .5-point increase in the second wouldn't tell us very much. Being a point higher on either scale is a fairly arbitrary increase, and the result would change if we simply used a different scale (switching, for example, from a 7-point scale to a 10-point scale for enjoyment of video games). In this situation, we might want to focus instead on the *standardized coefficient*. Similarly, we can't directly compare unstandardized coefficients to talk about how strong a relationship is. What if, in addition to measuring agreement on a 7-point scale, we also asked people how many video games they owned? Because people can own hundreds of games, we might find a small slope for that variable—owning one more game might only increase aggression by .1. But over the full range of the variable, this could add up to a big difference between those with few games and many, even though the actual number is smaller than the slope for the enjoyment scale. Thus, the size of the effect for game ownership might actually be larger, regardless of the size of the unstandardized coefficient.

Standardized Coefficients

In contrast to unstandardized coefficients, standardized regression coefficients try to place all variables in the model on a shared scale, so that their coefficients can be compared. Specifically, the standardized regression coefficient reflects the slope when both the independent variable and the dependent variable have been standardized (that is, centered so that the mean is 0 and the standard deviation is 1). As a result, the standardized coefficient will almost always range between −1 and 1, with values further from 0 representing stronger relationships. As with the unstandardized coefficient, the sign (negative or positive) reflects the direction of the relationship. Most computer software reports this standardized coefficient by default along with the unstandardized slope.

The advantages of reporting the standardized coefficient are essentially in direct contrast to those for the unstandardized coefficient. Because all variables are placed on the same scale, you can accurately state that a larger coefficient (ignoring the sign) indicates a stronger relationship within the sample. A coefficient of −.5, for example, would show a stronger relationship than one of .1. Consider again the example related to the connection between game ownership, enjoyment, and aggression. The unstandardized slope for number of games owned would probably be small, despite the importance of the variable. But the standardized coefficient might have been .4, while the standardized value for enjoyment might just have been .2. The relative importance is thus reflected more clearly. Because these values are estimates for the population based on a given sample, you must be careful in assuming that small differences between standardized coefficients show that one variable truly has a stronger relationship than another; the statistics for such comparisons are more complex and beyond the scope of this text. But even as a rough guide, standardized coefficients are very useful. However, because they don't correspond directly to the equation for the regression line, they cannot be used to make direct numerical predictions about the value of the DV for given values of the IVs.

unstandardized coefficients
→ Unit 16

regression
→ Unit 16

dependent variable
→ Unit 2

mean
→ Unit 14

standard deviation
→ Unit 14

range
→ Unit 14

relationship
→ Unit 2

variable
→ Unit 2

sample
→ Unit 8

population
→ Unit 8

R^2

While the coefficients in a regression equation are used to indicate the strength, direction, and, ultimately, statistical significance of a single independent variable's relationship with the dependent variable, they do not give a clear indication of how well the overall regression model predicts the DV. In some cases, though, we want to know that piece of information as well. The R^2 statistic provides a measure of the overall explanatory power of the model. Specifically, it measures the percentage of variance in the dependent variable explained by the combination of all independent variables. Remember that the goal of regression is to construct an equation in which the slope for each independent variable represents how much we predict that the DV will change for each one unit increase in the IV. If we imagine computing the predicted value of the DV for each individual in our data, based on their values for the IV, then we would be able to determine how much our predictions are wrong. That would represent the remaining variance left unexplained by the IVs. In contrast, we also know the *total* variance, as we can calculate that as a measure of dispersion. Suppose the total variance is 5, and the remaining unexplained variance is 2.5. Then our R^2 would be .5—we successfully explained half the variance. (The exact details of computing R^2 are slightly more complex than this, but it's a good way to understand what goes on.) In this way, R^2 serves as a measure of effect size, just as the square of Pearson's r provides such an indication for the single IV tested in that correlation.

Of course, the uses of R^2 are a bit more nuanced than a typical effect size measure. After all, the statistic describes the variance explained by all the independent variables in the model. Suppose you are studying the relationship between news viewing and interest in politics. You might measure several different types of news and include each measure as an independent variable predicting political interest in a single regression test. In this case, R^2 would give you a good indication of how much news use as a whole explained interest, while the individual coefficients would tell you whether specific kinds of news use had unique influences. But in this study, you might be worried about the effects of potential third variables. For example, older, better-educated, and wealthier individuals might all be more likely to use news and to be more interested in politics. You would probably want to include these as control variables in your model. Now, your regression coefficients would give an accurate indication of the unique effect of each type of news after accounting for those important demographic factors. But the R^2 statistic would inevitably be larger, as demographics account for some variance in political interest as well—that's why we included them as controls. The statistic is no longer pure measure of the effect size for news.

Because of this, some approaches to regression break the independent variables into blocks. Each block of variables is entered together, and the software reports the coefficients for all the variables when just that block is entered. Then the next block is entered, and the coefficients for all the variables in both blocks with all the variables in the model are presented. For example, we might want to first account for all the variance due to demographics—age, education, and income would be in our first block. Then, our second block would consist of all the news use variables. The computer would give two sets of coefficients for demographics. One would reflect the unique influence of each on political interest when the other demographics are controlled for and nothing else. The second would reflect the influence when both demographics and news use are accounted for. Because news use is our second block, this would only give one set of coefficients, which would reflect the effect of controlling for all the other variables in the model. There is no limit on the number of blocks we can have, but there are practical limits on how useful and easy to interpret the results become as more and more blocks are added.

Breaking the regression into blocks, which is called *hierarchical regression*, has an added benefit related to the R^2 statistic. The variance explained is calculated for each block. Thus, in the foregoing example, we would first find out how much variance was explained by all the demographics. Then, we would be given an *incremental R^2*, showing how much additional variance was accounted for by the addition of the news items. In this way, blocks can be used to better pinpoint the exact effect size of distinct sets of variables rather than just describing the model as a whole.

Logistic Regression

Ordinary least squares regression is a flexible tool used to test the simultaneous influence of many different independent variables on an interval- or ratio-level dependent variable. But often, we are interested in predicting how variables are related to a dichotomous dependent variable, which has only two possible values. For example, we might want to know whether someone did or did not vote, or whether they would or would not be willing to try our product. Fortunately, an alternative form of regression, known as logistic regression, is available for testing such relationships. The underlying mathematical details of this procedure are less important, but the basic logic parallels that of regression. Instead of predicting the exact value of the dependent variable (which would have to be either 0 or 1), logistic regression predicts a transformation of the dependent variable known as the *logit*. Because of this, the non-standardized regression coefficient does not have the same simple meaning of being a slope, but otherwise the approach mirrors ordinary regression. A significant coefficient (indicated by the size of the coefficient along with the standard error) indicates that we are confident that the link between the IV and DV is large enough not to be attributable to chance and that a similar pattern would hold in the population.

independent variable
→ Unit 2

interval-level measure
→ Unit 5

ratio-level measure
→ Unit 5

dependent variable
→ Unit 2

variable
→ Unit 2

relationship
→ Unit 2

standardized coefficients
→ Unit 16

For example, suppose you want to predict whether someone would be willing to endorse a message on a social networking site, such as by clicking a "like" or "+1" button. Ordinary regression would not be appropriate for such a test because the dependent variable is dichotomous. But logistic regression could be used. You might predict that evaluations of whether the content was enjoyable, credible, and interesting would all uniquely contribute to willingness to click the button. By running the analyses, you might find significant positive coefficients for enjoyment and interest but no unique effect of credibility. As with any regression analysis, this would show which variables have the clearest, most consistent relationship once you control for the influence of all other variables.

Odds Ratio

In ordinary least squares regression, we can evaluate the standardized coefficient to get a better sense of the relative influence of different independent variables by imposing a shared scale on those measures. Logistic regression does not produce a standardized coefficient. However, the analysis does produce an *odds ratio*, which can be used to compare the influence of different variables in a similar fashion and offers greater utility.

First, we must understand the idea of odds, which reflect the probability that something will occur divided by the probability it will not. For example, a fair coin has odds of 1 that it will come up heads. There is a .5 probability it will come up heads and a .5 probability it will come up tails. As .5/.5 = 1, the odds are 1, or perfectly even. When the odds are greater than 1, we are saying the event is more likely to occur than not occur. For example, the odds of seeing a presidential advertisement during an election are far greater than 1. If 95 percent of voters are exposed to at least one ad, the odds that any given voter will see an ad would be .95/.05, or 19. On the other hand, when the odds are less than 1, we are saying the event is less likely to occur than not occur. For example, the odds that a given individual will attend a political rally during an election are likely pretty small. If only 5 percent of people go to a rally, then the odds would be .05/.95, or about .053.

The odds ratio evaluates how these odds *change* as the value of a given independent variable changes. For example, while the average person might have small odds of going to a rally, someone who has volunteered for the campaign might be much more likely to go. If nonvolunteers have odds of .05 but volunteers have odds of .5 (still less than even, but considerably higher), the odds ratio would be 10—that is, the individual is 10 times more likely to go if they volunteered than if they didn't. The odds ratio thus represents the amount you have to multiply the first set of odds by to get the second set for each one-unit increase in the IV. Here, because the ratio is positive, it means that as the IV (volunteering) increases, the odds of the DV also increase. This is a positive relationship. On the other hand, consider the example of seeing an advertisement. Because ads tend to appear more on traditional media, we might expect that people who spend lots of time on social networking sites would be less likely to see an ad. Suppose that for someone who spent 1 hour on social networking sites, the odds of seeing an ad are 19, but for someone who spent 2 hours, they are 9.5. The odds ratio would be .5—if you multiply 19 by .5, you get 9.5. We would further expect that when the hours increased from 2 to 3, the odds would again drop—from 9.5 to 4.75 (9.5 × .5 = 4.75). This would be a negative relationship, as the odds ratio is less than 1. The odds ratio ranges from virtually 0 (for a very negative relationship) to essentially an infinitely high positive number (for a very positive relationship).

Steps to Success: Selecting the Appropriate Statistical Test

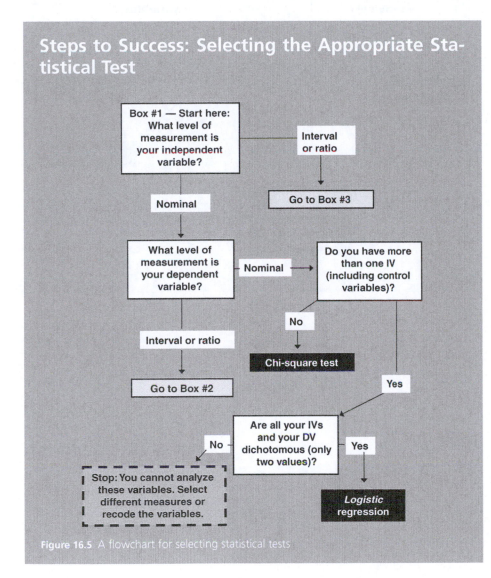

Figure 16.5 A flowchart for selecting statistical tests

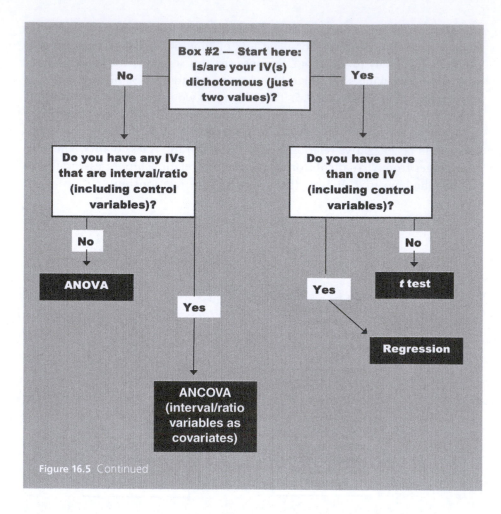

Figure 16.5 Continued

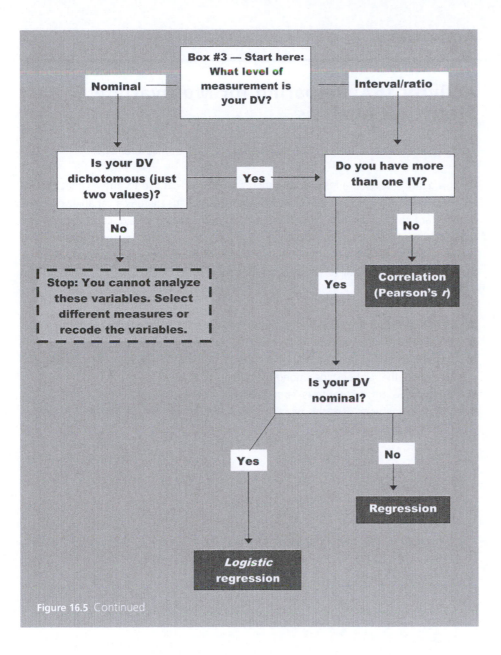

Figure 16.5 Continued

Activities

Activity 16A: Preparing for Multivariate Statistical Analysis

See terms: multivariate analysis; inferential statistics; level of measurement.

For this activity, develop a research question that you would like to answer that considers the relationship among three or more variables. Perhaps there is a variable you think is important to consider as a control variable, or perhaps you would like to explore the relationship between multiple independent variables and a single dependent variable. As you develop this research question, think about how you will measure the variables and the statistical tests that will be most appropriate for testing your relationship. Consider the following questions:

- Which of the variables will be the dependent variable? Independent? Control?
- What level of measurement do you expect your different variables to be?
- Based on these initial thoughts, what types of statistical analyses would you likely run to explore the relationships among the different variables?
- What makes this test (or tests) appropriate?
- What assumptions does this test have? How would you ensure that your data conform to those assumptions?

Activity 16B: Critically Assessing Statistical Analysis

See terms: statistical analysis; multivariate analysis; level of measurement.

For this activity, locate a research article that conducts some type of multivariate analysis. Start by describing the nature of the relationship (or relationships) and the test (or tests) that are used to assess the relationship. Use the following questions to guide your assessment:

- What particular tests are used in this research report?
- Identify each of the different types of variables (i.e., independent, dependent, and control). What is the level of measurement for each of those variables?
- Are these particular tests appropriate? Why or why not? Could the researchers have used different tests to test these relationships?
- How would you evaluate the quality as far as how the tests and their results are reported? Do the researchers clearly describe the results of their tests?
- Is there any information missing that would help your evaluation of the data and the results as described?
- Are the conclusions drawn from the data accurate based on the tests conducted?

451

Activity 16C: Multivariate Statistics in Survey Research

See terms: multivariate analysis; regression; inferential statistics.

For this activity, locate a research article that uses survey research as a methodology and some form of regression analysis as the analytical approach. Use the following questions to guide your analysis of the article:

■ What kind of regression was used for the primary analysis?
■ Was this type of analysis appropriate to the hypotheses or research questions asked?
■ What are the main findings based on the analysis?
■ What specific statistics do the authors discuss in their report? In what ways do they address statistical significance (or lack thereof)?

Activity 16D: Determining Appropriate Statistical Tests

See terms: chi-square; *t*-test; regression; correlation; ANOVA; logistic regression.

For the following research scenarios, determine the appropriate statistical test you would use to test the relationships described. In some cases, there may be multiple options that are appropriate. Therefore, be sure to indicate a clear rationale why you have selected the test you did. Finally, consider the assumptions of each test in making your decisions.

Research scenario	Appropriate test
You are interested in comparing test scores for the final exam in a research methods course for three different groups. Group 1 receives a weekly personal tutoring session beyond the regular course content. Group 2 receives enhanced course materials ahead of lecture. Group 3 receives both the weekly personal tutoring and the enhanced course materials.	
You work for a political campaign and are interested in testing the relationship between age and the amount of money donated to the candidate for whom you work.	
As part of your work for an advertising agency, you have been asked to explore the relationship between parenting and media preferences. In particular, the agency would like to know whether there are significant differences between people who are parents of kids under 18 and those who are not for their favorite social media platform.	
As part of your work for a nonprofit agency, you are interested in understanding whether the likeability of the agency's spokesperson is related to the amount of money donated by individuals. However, you expect that individual attitudes toward philanthropy and community volunteering also affect the amount of money donated. Your director has asked you to control for those two variables in assessing the relationship between spokesperson likeability and money donated.	
You are working with a client who is putting on a series of informational clinics on vaccine awareness. The client is interested in testing a series of ratio- and interval-level independent variables including income, education, interest in health, and skepticism toward science on whether or not people come to the informational clinic (a "yes" or "no" answer).	

Suggested Readings for Further Exploration of Unit 16 Topics

Examples

Eveland, W. P., Jr., Hayes, A. F., Shah, D. V., & Kwak, N. (2005). Understanding the relationship between communication and political knowledge: A model comparison approach using panel data. *Political Communication*, *22*(4), 423–446. doi:10.1080/10584 600500311345

Kahlor, L., & Eastin, M. S. (2011). Television's role in the culture of violence toward women: A study of television viewing and the cultivation of rape myth acceptance in the United States. *Journal of Broadcasting & Electronic Media*, *55*(2), 215–231. doi:10.1080/08838151. 2011.566085

Advanced Discussion

Hayes, A. F. (2009). Beyond Baron and Kenny: Statistical mediation analysis in the new millennium. *Communication Monographs*, *76*(4), 408–420. doi:10.1080/03637750903310360

Hayes, A. F., Glynn, C. J., & Huge, M. E. (2012). Cautions regarding the interpretation of regression coefficients and hypothesis tests in linear models with interactions. *Communication Methods and Measures*, *6*(1), 1–11. doi:10.1080/19312458.2012.651415

Hayes, A. F., & Matthes, J. (2009). Computational procedures for probing interactions in OLS and logistic regression: SPSS and SAS implementations. *Behavior Research Methods*, *41*(3), 924–936. doi:10.3758/BRM.41.3.924

Mundry, R., & Nunn, C. L. (2009). Stepwise model fitting and statistical inference: Turning noise into signal pollution. *The American Naturalist*, *173*(1), 119–123. doi:10.1086/593303

Preacher, K. J., & Hayes, A. F. (2008). Assessing mediation in communication research. In A. F. Hayes, M. D. Slater, & L. B. Snyder (Eds.), *The Sage sourcebook of advanced data analysis methods for communication research* (pp. 13–54). Thousand Oaks, CA: Sage Publications.

Index

Note: Page numbers in bold refer to the main entry for a listed term. Pages in italic indicate a boxed term.